$28.50

People
and Cultures
of Hawai'i

People and Cultures of Hawai'i

DISCARDED

The Evolution of Culture and Ethnicity

Edited by
JOHN F. MCDERMOTT
NALEEN NAUPAKA ANDRADE

UNIVERSITY OF HAWAI'I PRESS
Honolulu

16 15 14 13 12   6 5 4 3 2

Library of Congress Cataloging-in-Publication Data

People and cultures of Hawai'i : the evolution of culture and ethnicity /
edited by John F. McDermott and Naleen Naupaka Andrade.
    p. cm.
    Includes bibliographical references and index.
    ISBN-13: 978-0-8248-3580-4 (softcover : alk. paper)
    ISBN-10: 0-8248-3580-8 (softcover : alk. paper)
    1. Personality and culture—Hawaii.   2. Ethnology—Hawaii.
3. Cultural pluralism—Hawaii.   4. Cultural fusion—Hawaii.
I. McDermott, John F. II. Andrade, Naleen Naupaka.
    BF698.9.C8P46 2011
    155.8'209969—dc22
                        2010045094

University of Hawai'i Press books are printed on acid-free
paper and meet the guidelines for permanence and durability
of the Council on Library Resources.

Designed by Wanda China
Printed by Sheridan Books, Inc.

Dedicated to Terence A. Rogers, Ph.D., dean of the University of Hawai'i's new John A. Burns School of Medicine, who announced, "We are going to create a new middle class—of Hawaiian doctors."

Contents

Preface

John F. McDermott and Naleen Naupaka Andrade

This is the evolution of a book that describes the evolution of a society.

People and Cultures of Hawai'i: A Psychocultural Profile was published by the University of Hawai'i Press in 1980, and since then it has enjoyed modest but steady sales with serial reprinting. The readership grew well beyond the target audience of health professionals for whom it was written. In addition to a broad general bookstore purchase, the book was used in college social science courses both in Hawai'i and on the U.S. mainland. As *People and Cultures* became a standard reference in university and public libraries, the need for an updated revision was evident. The ethnic groups it described had matured, and new groups had appeared.

This new edition, *People and Cultures of Hawai'i: The Evolution of Culture and Ethnicity,* is built on the earlier 1980 volume but goes much further. It tells the story of what happened next. The book details not just the history of each of Hawai'i's different ethnic groups, but it goes on to examine the makeup of the unique ethnocultural identity of each and tells the story of how they live together to form America's most diverse multicultural society. The nature of that society is explored—a *group* identity that helped shape the *individual* identity of the forty-fourth president of the United States. Barack Obama grew up in Hawai'i.

Once again, the chapters are arranged in chronological order of the groups' arrivals in Hawai'i, with the insertion of three new ones into the continuum—the black American, Hispanic American, and Micronesian American chapters.

The editors begin and end the book with an introduction and conclusion that attempt to frame the chapter content into a common perspective, teasing out the threads that have allowed them all to come together to form our country's most diverse state.

The chapter authors and coauthors are a mix of old and new. Most of them, as in the first edition, share the ethnic background they describe. As a group, they span the generations and cultures, from the indigenous Hawaiians through the series of American and Asian inmigrations to more recent Pacific Islanders. Moreover, they represent a variety of professional disciplinary backgrounds, most being affiliated with the John A. Burns School of Medicine's Department of Psychiatry at the University of Hawai'i.

By the same token, the book's coeditors are a mix of old and new. Both are professors and present or past chairs of that same University of Hawai'i department. One is of indigenous Hawaiian and Portuguese descent from Hawai'i's Big Island and has lived there or on the island of O'ahu all her life. The other is a "naturalized haole" who settled in Hawai'i some forty years ago, coming from the University of Michigan to help build the new University of Hawai'i Medical School.

Finally, your editors express our gratitude to William Hamilton, director of the University of Hawai'i Press, who has served as editor for the publication of this volume. And once again, we offer a *mahalo nui loa* to our administrative assistant Gail Mastronardi for her seemingly effortless style in putting it all together with us.

Only you, the reader, can decide whether or not we have been successful.

The Editors

Introduction

John F. McDermott and Naleen Naupaka Andrade

Background

America is rapidly changing its color. Population projections tell us that by 2050, the white majority will be replaced by a plurality of minority groups: Hispanic, black, Asian, and white. Strategic models are needed to plan for this new pattern in the makeup of our country. Hawai'i serves as a cross-cultural laboratory offering one such model, the evolution of a multiracial society into a multicultural one, a model we call the "Hawaiian Stewpot."

How did it happen? This book tells the story.

To begin, the history of Hawai'i is very different from the rest of the United States.

In colonial America, the first European settlers dealt with the native population they encountered with confrontation and domination, as if the indigenous peoples, not they, were the intruders. Moreover, young America imported a black slave class for its labor, denying citizenship and social mobility to both native and imported groups.

These divisions became even more fixed as science began to define human nature by race—not just by physical characteristics like skin color and eyes, but intellectual and moral qualities as well. Social and scientific theory supported the religious belief that the races had been created separately by God, once and for all.

That belief was challenged by the publication of Charles Darwin's revolutionary *On the Origin of Species* in 1859. Variation had occurred by "chance," Darwin wrote. (The word "evolution" did not appear until much later.) But how could chance have produced the natural order, people wondered? So Darwin was dismissed, and the need to further classify the human race into subcategories continued. Studies of race as the most important factor marking the boundaries between people dominated scientific investigation. The fact that there was a hierarchy of civilizations was a given—racial types representing different stages of human development, with the white race at the top. This was the rationale used to justify slavery in America and colonialism throughout the world.

Meanwhile, other white Europeans had been allowed to immigrate to nineteenth-century America to settle its rapidly expanding borders. Soon it was feared that the uncontrolled influx of people from "inferior" cultures would lower the standard of American civilization. So strict immigration quotas were passed by Congress to control the numbers—quotas supported by conservatives and progressives alike.

To further protect its standard of civilization, a single model for becoming American evolved. It was called *assimilation*—an application of the "melting pot" theory. Assimilation involved renunciation of one's nationality and culture of origin, so that each successive immigrant group would become absorbed into the larger dominant group. This idea of substituting one culture for another is illustrated by a ceremony the automotive giant Henry Ford held for his immigrant employees. When they had finished their basic English language course, there was a graduation ceremony. Dressed in native costume, they were paraded off a mock gangplank onto a stage into a tunnel called the "Melting Pot." Soon they emerged at the other end as newly minted Americans, dressed in identical suits and waving little American flags.

Absurd as it seems today, the ceremony was symbolic of the desired process of simply exchanging one culture for another. It naively assumed that a change in language and dress would lead to a change in internal values and beliefs.

The assimilation philosophy of acculturation has persisted until today as the preferred model by which new minorities are incorporated into the majority culture. But it is rapidly changing to meet the realities of twenty-first-century America.

In Hawai'i, America's fiftieth state, however, this emerging plurality of minority groups is nothing new. Each arrived with its own ethnocultural identity, evolving and combining over time to form one multicultural society. Accommodation had replaced assimilation.

How did it happen?

The history of Hawai'i, especially its racial history, is very different from the rest of America. In early-nineteenth-century Hawai'i, the arriving white minority was received by the indigenous native population with their own cultural concepts of inclusiveness called aloha (love, affection, kindness, compassion), *lōkahi* (harmony, agreement, unity), and *'ohana* (extended family or clan). The newcomers were called haole (white person, American, Englishman, Caucasian; formerly it meant any foreigner, but since the first foreigners were white, it came to mean white).

The Hawaiian Islands occupy a crossroads in the Pacific, so soon after they were charted on the map, several nations, including America, Great Britain, France, and Russia, began to compete for favor. As time went on, American traders, merchants, missionaries, and whalers began to settle in Honolulu. There was room for all. The Hawaiian Kingdom was a tolerant society in which the laws held for native and haole alike. By mid-nineteenth century it had evolved into a constitutional monarchy—with a constitution that prohibited slavery: "Slavery shall under no circumstances whatever be tolerated in the Hawaiian Islands; whenever a slave shall enter Hawaiian territory, he shall be free."

Tragically, the indigenous Hawaiian population became devastated by foreign introduced diseases—from syphilis to smallpox. Deadly diseases and a series of sociopolitical events described in the chapters that follow swung the pendulum from Hawaiian to Euro-American as the dominant political group. Sometime later, Euro-Americans would overthrow the Hawaiian monarchy, and eventually Hawai'i would be annexed by the United States.

Nevertheless, there were several factors that kept Hawai'i from following in the racial path taken by the United States. The most obvious one was its history as an independent nation.

Another factor was its geography. Hawai'i is an island chain, farther from a major landmass than any other inhabited place in the world. Its strategic location in the mid-Pacific, halfway between North America and Asia, had been a factor in the downfall of the monarchy and annexation to the United States. But that same geography had advantages as well as disadvantages. An island environment limits the physical distance between groups and forces them to interact and adapt to one another. Biologists know that plants and animals living on isolated islands just behave differently. Biological survival encourages hybridization and mutation. Social survival encourages a similar process.

Kinship (who your ancestors were and what were the familial relationships—by blood or abiding friendship—that identified your origins), not race, was the organizing core around which Hawaiian society evolved. The Hawaiian Kingdom had set the tone as a tolerant and open society, consciously multiracial. There had been no quotas, no mandated separation of the races. Instead of racial polarization and antimiscegenation laws, there was intermingling from the beginning of contact. Without the hindrance of racial barriers, intermarriage, usually the last barrier to go, occurred early. The term "hapa haole" or "hapa" was coined to describe the offspring of this racial mixing. There was no stigma to the hapa racial heritage (which came to mean any mixture). It never had the negative connotation that half-breed or half-caste had in America. Nor were slang terms such as "banana" or "coconut" used to ridicule the marginal status of mixed race, as in the continental United States.

In such a favorable environment, the hapa population would steadily increase.

As early as 1853 there were almost a thousand individuals, or 1.3 percent of the total population, listed in the census as "Part Hawaiian," or hapa. By the end of the century, that number had grown to nearly ten thousand, or 6.4 percent (Lind 1955). It has steadily increased ever since, so that according to the Hawai'i State Department of Health, 60 percent of births are now recorded as "mixed race."

Hawaiian intermarriage had formed not just a new mixed racial class without stigma but a whole new social class as well. When the *ali'i*, or chief class, intermarried with the white traders and merchants, they created a new social class at the top, one reaching into the monarchy. Hawai'i's great Queen Emma, who personally started its private hospital system, was of mixed heritage. Robert Wilcox, the monarchist and Hawai'i's first elected delegate to the U.S. Congress, was hapa. Bernice Pauahi, heiress to the Kamehameha lands, married a white man—as did Hawai'i's last monarch, Queen Lili'uokalani herself, who would be overthrown by an oligarchy of white men. The colonial era would begin.

The overthrow of the monarchy represented a dramatic shift in the balance of political power. The Hawaiians had lost. The ordinary Hawaiian would be marginalized socioeconomically for generations. But racism was never institutionalized into apartheid. Kinship and its associated social class had trumped race. Some of Honolulu's most exclusive private clubs and cultural institutions had mixed membership from the beginning.

And the plantation era moved Hawai'i along the next step toward a multiracial society. While nineteenth-century America was experimenting with the quota system as a form of social racism, exactly the opposite was happening in Hawai'i. A series of new immigrant groups—mostly from Asia, some from Europe—were added to this already mixing society. A program of contract labor, originally initiated by the monarchy, was carried out by the planter society. First Chinese, then Japanese, Korean, Portuguese, and Filipino came in successive waves to work as field hands in the burgeoning sugarcane industry. They were given housing and a small paycheck. Life under contract was hard, often cruel. Nevertheless, when the contract was up, they could elect to stay. And most did stay, one immigrant group after another settling in town or on their own land to raise families. Japanese and Korean men had their picture brides from home; but the Chinese, and later the other groups, too, began to intermarry into the existing population.

The unintended but serendipitous consequence of this era of contract labor was further racial mixing and a rapidly changing society. The other consequence of intermarriage was the extension of kinship and ancestral ties, melding the ethnic groups. The number of interracial marriages, more than 10 percent in the 1912 census, rose steadily over the years (Lind 1955). In the most recent census, a fifth of Hawai'i's population claimed two or more races and a third of them three or more, a rate nine times that of the rest of the United States.

Assimilation of immigrants into Henry Ford's "Melting Pot" may have been the American dream, but there were just too many groups coexisting side by side to make it work in Hawai'i. Over time, there was no majority group. Everyone was part of a minority. And extensive networks of familial relationships—through intermarriage, hapa offspring, and abiding multiethnic friendships—became the social norm for Island society. The Hawai'i model was not a melting pot. It was more like a "Stew Pot," with various ingredients mixing together to create a common stock.

The Stew Pot model was an interactive one: accommodation over assimilation. Accommodation is a process described by anthropologists that occurs "when groups of different backgrounds engage each other, *leading to cultural and psychological changes in both parties, and the establishment of new relationships*" (Berry 2008; italics ours). These cultural and psychological changes and the establishment of new relationships comprise the story told in this book.

Meanwhile, across the Pacific in continental America, the long-standing rigid thinking about race was about to soften. Toward the end of the nineteenth century, a German scientist named Franz Boas (1968), working with Alaskan Inuit and Northwest Pacific Indians, proposed that the concept of *civilization* was not an absolute but a relative one. Instead of a hierarchy of civilizations, he argued for a spectrum, with similarities and differences among them. They were just different from each other, historically and culturally. In this way, Boas introduced the concept of diversity and cultural pluralism. This revolutionary thinking about racial groups intersected with Darwin's emerging concept of evolution, the adaptive plasticity of the individual. The notion of cultural evolution and diversity could now begin to catch on.

Eventually America would turn the page. Laws would be changed and institutionalized racism would become a thing of the past. Furthermore, science would recant on race. Increasingly, research on DNA has confirmed that the longstanding use of race as a biological and genetic marker was based on a false assumption. Its principal use today is in medical research and tracking the country's voting patterns.

But in Hawai'i, the use of race to define groups was already being replaced by the concept of *ethnicity*—a broader dimension of human nature that goes beyond ancestry, blood quantum, and physical differences. Ethnicity includes both the concept of kinship, or external relationships, and a concept of the inner self called *identity*—uniting the past with the present and the future. This shift was made possible because, in contrast to the melting pot dream of homogeneity, the Hawaiian Stew Pot accepted differences between the ethnic groups. It celebrated and strived to maintain the origins and enduring cultural traits of one's ancestors. Thus, in the stew, each ingredient contributes to the common stock, at the same time retaining its own essence—its own taste and flavor.

And with generational change, the Hawaiian spectrum would shift even further—from race to ethnicity to culture—as the principal identifying marker to distinguish and to connect one group with another in this emerging multicultural society.

Why did this occur?

In an ethnically pure culture such as traditional Japan, cultural transmission was a vertical process, moving down one generation to the next, with the goal of preserving a single ethnocultural tradition. But in a mixed society such as Hawai'i, this vertical transmission within the group was balanced with an ongoing horizontal interaction between groups, an overlapping of these ethnocultural identities through ongoing contact and ever-extending kinships. When you interact daily with people from another ethnic group, you inevitably learn their likes and dislikes, what makes them happy or sad—or angry. President Barack Obama put it another way when talking about his alma mater, Punahou School: "And if you're in a school that has Chinese kids, Filipino kids and Japanese kids and White kids, Samoan kids, by necessity, I think you're forced to learn to empathize with people who aren't like you" (Calmes 2009).

In addition to social interaction connecting the different groups with one another, another process—one of integration—occurs with intermarriage. And with increasing rates of intermarriage diluting the original biological blood ties in favor of kinship ties, skin color becomes less and less the most distinctive characteristic among its people. Indeed, as the emotional attachment to biologically determined skin color lessens, a new blended or hapa identity emerges, a correspondingly new culture becomes the most significant dimension among people.

Culture has more porous boundaries than race or ethnicity, boundaries that are easier to cross. Language is an example of this process. Pidgin developed as a common English dialect that crossed the language boundaries among the different races working the plantations. It allowed for essential communication. Today, when it is no longer essential, it has persisted as a shared cultural phenomenon among different ethnic groups. Food and local customs, originally ethnic, are now part of a common culture. Sashimi, *malasadas,* kimchi, *kalua* pig—the list of island dishes with different ethnic origins is today's multicultural menu. Hawai'i state holidays, Kamehameha Day and Kuhio Day, celebrate Hawaiian royalty but are observed by everyone. The original annual Japanese Boys' Day reflects a racial/ethnic tradition that could be shared, and it became Boys' and Girls' Day. First a racial/ethnic group observance, it is now celebrated as a wider community ritual—Children's Day.

This evolution from race to culture was made possible by the early tradition of multiracial tolerance and shared culture in the Hawaiian Kingdom: two cultures, Hawaiian and haole, living side by side, with kinship forming a bridge between them. They are not simply coexisting but interacting and producing what are called "psychological and cultural changes in each other" from the beginning of contact. Subsequently, the relatively rapid addition of a series of Asian as well as some European immigrants accelerated the shift from race to culture even further.

Finally, we must consider the role of socioeconomic class as a factor in this complex, changing cultural picture. Older stereotypes of the social structure of Hawaiian society die hard, such as Hawai'i as a haole-run corporate empire, Chinese dominating the professions and finance, and Japanese dominating the public educational system. Some have even proposed replacing this older stereotype with a newer one—a two-class socioeconomic scale. It would place three groups on top—Chinese, haoles, and Japanese—and the rest—Filipino, Hawaiian, Samoan, and other Pacific Islanders—at the bottom (Okamura 2008). But that, too, is an oversimplification, suggesting an unchanging society, and it is challenged by the detailed descriptions of the individual groups in the chapters of this book.

How is it challenged? Immigrant groups usually come from lower socioeconomic levels in their home country—that is, peasant farmers and working-class people. As soon as they realize that social mobility is possible in America, though, they search for the "success ladder." If, as most agree, that social class is determined by some combination of occupation, education, and income, they soon realize that the entry point to better occupation and income is education. Immigrant parents usually say they are working for a better life for their children and grandchildren. And that is true. Higher education becomes the goal for the second and third generations. Chinese, Japanese, Filipino, Vietnamese, and Korean immigrant groups are typical examples, rising by successive generations after coming to Hawai'i. And rapidly changing gender roles in these traditional cultures have only accelerated the process.

The Stew Pot model of Hawai'i's culture has been most visible in its politics. Ever since statehood, it has chosen from the stew's different ethnic groups to lead it. Consider the parade of the most recent governors of Hawai'i: first a local haole who grew up in Hawai'i, then a Japanese-American, next a Hawaiian, followed by a Filipino-American—and most recently, a middle-class Jewish haole who grew up on the mainland United States, moved to Maui, and became mayor of that county before her election as governor. Honolulu's most recent mayor is of Samoan/German ancestry.

The Chapters Themselves

In the earlier edition of *Peoples and Cultures of Hawai'i*, each chapter told the history of the immigration of a major ethnic group and developed a *psychocultural profile,* or a snapshot, of the "personality" of that group. But the picture has changed significantly. The original immigrant groups have matured and new ones have been added to the mix. This new edition of *People and Cultures of Hawai'i: The Evolution of Culture and Ethnicity* tracks the course of those changes. We attempt to construct a historical understanding of each group over time, as it evolved from race to ethnicity to culture as a product of this evolution.

The chapters in this book follow a common outline. They begin with an overview of the group—a summary from its arrival to the present. Gradually, the group develops its own unique ethnocultural identity, and this becomes the central organizing theme, the centerpiece of the chapter. Distinctive character traits such as temperament and emotional expression are explored—as well as ethnic stereotypes that may have been derived from them. Whether we like it or not, stereotypes are a reality and often reflect enduring traits that make this group stand out from the mainstream. Next, how the group's unique ethnocultural identity has become modified with time and generational change is discussed—which traits may have changed over the generations and which are more hardwired or enduring.

An important feature of each chapter is its focus on the group's family social structure, its generational and gender roles, its power distribution, and its central values and life goals. The ways it has been influenced over time by role changes, including intermarriage patterns, will be considered. You may even find the typical life cycle from childhood through old age described.

You will also find a description of the group's own internal social class structure, its social and political strategies, its occupational and educational patterns, and how education, especially higher education, may have influenced it—with the development of a professional and middle class.

Finally, each chapter will consider how that particular ethnic group has blended into Hawai'i's culturally sensitive society; that is, how it has overlapped with other groups, how values have been modified, and how new behavioral patterns have emerged over time. In some chapters you will find a unique dimension, a consideration of how the Native Hawaiian host culture has influenced the identity of the group to become more Hawaiian. It may show how the indigenous culture has served as a universal joint around which others have become integrated. Finally, at the end of each chapter you will find a list of suggested further reading, should you wish to explore an ethnic group further in more detail.

Some Suggestions for Reading This Book

How might you the reader best approach what the editors consider the central concept in the chapters of this book—the concept of ethnocultural identity making up the Hawaiian Stew Pot?

In reading each chapter, you will come to appreciate how the important values, beliefs, and behaviors that make up the group's core identity operate at different levels of awareness or consciousness. That means they may also operate at different levels of power and influence. So let's shift from the Stew Pot metaphor temporarily to more closely examine its individual ethnic groups. For a moment, try to imagine each group's ethnocultural identity as a metaphorical iceberg. Just like a real iceberg, less than 10 percent is visible above the waterline, the larger 90 percent mass lying beneath the surface, harder and harder to see as the depth increases.

What do we mean by different levels of ethnocultural visibility? Let's take an individual example. Religion is a very personal matter for most people, but its public expression can usually be seen easily above the surface as church affiliation (and even to some extent, its theological orientation). But the personal practices of one's religion, such as churchgoing and prayer habits, are not so visible. They are at or just below the surface. One's individual faith and spirituality are to be found at a much deeper level. They are not easily accessible to those outside the group and are less likely to change.

So you will easily see on the surface of a group's ethnocultural identity such things as folk practices, dance, festivals, and celebrations. But the ancient myths and legends from which they arise are at increasing depths below, harder and harder to see. Indeed, as the earlier example of Henry Ford's graduation ceremony for his immigrant workers illustrates, language and dress may be relatively easy to change, but deeper traditions affecting them as workers—attitudes toward authority, toward cooperation and competition—are much less easily changed.

Consider another human phenomenon: interpersonal relationships. Common patterns of social interaction, such as manners—courtesy in meeting and greeting others—may be apparent on the surface of the group's behavior, while much deeper and much more fixed are facial expression and eye contact or attitudes toward touching or being touched.

So here is the challenge. If you try to place core beliefs and values at different locations on an imaginary iceberg as you read about them, you will develop your own applied model for analyzing ethnocultural identity. Those values and behaviors above the waterline are more easily shared or changed, while those deeper down are more culturally fixed and enduring—what some refer to as hardwired.

Another task to keep in mind is just how those values, beliefs, and behaviors have influenced this group's move along the spectrum from race to ethnicity to culture to form the multiple ethnocultural identities in this Stew Pot society called Hawai'i. The process is not uniform. Some groups, like the Okinawans, have been more protective of early cultural traditions in order to differentiate themselves from others (in their case, the Japanese). They and the Samoans even have a special word in their language to describe their highly valued traditional culture. On the other hand, Hawai'i's own indigenous people, the *kānaka maoli* (whom we refer to as Hawaiians in this book), have temporarily *reversed* the process of moving from race to culture. The federal laws, as with other indigenous peoples in the United States, define Hawaiians' native land rights based on designated blood quantum or racial designation, which artificially places an intragroup wedge between who is a true Hawaiian. At the same time, contemporary Hawaiians, the majority of whom are hapa, are reclaiming their Hawaiian identity through their kinship ties and other cultural ways. They are reaching back into the deep past to retrieve ancient values in order to reinvigorate their contemporary ethnocultural identity. Emphasis on the *Hokule'a*—the Polynesian voyaging canoe used to recreate the original ocean exploration from ancient Polynesia to Hawai'i—is symbolic of that process. It represents personal and group characteristics from complex navigational skills to the sense of adventure and risk taking.

We hope you, the reader, will critically examine each chapter to trace the process by which that ethnic group may have moved along this continuum. We propose the spectrum from race to culture as a dynamic, moving process. How a specific group has moved from race—or biological ancestry—to ethnicity and a new sense of identity and then to a more permeable, socially determined boundary represented by culture is important to understand in this multicultural Stew Pot called Hawai'i. We believe what keeps the stew from overcooking and becoming a melting pot of homogenous soup is the Hawaiian concept of kinship that honors and sustains the enduring cultural traits of one's ancestral origins. With its overlapping and permeable ethnocultural boundaries, the Hawai'i model of today offers a direction for the rest of the United States.

Finally, however, we recognize the limitations of the approach we have taken in this book. There are other theoretical and strategic models beyond the one we have presented. The Stew Pot model may be unique, but it is not exhaustive. We believe that identity is a concept that is influenced by where one lives as well as one's ancestry. Others may disagree with this choice on our part.

We as the editors and authors in this book are a group of behavioral scientists approaching race, ethnicity, and culture from our own professional (and personal) perspective. There are other perspectives from other fields, such as education, sociology, archeology, humanities, and ethnic studies, to mention only a few.

There are also limitations to our attempt to recruit chapter authors from the ethnic groups they represent. The key is a balance of opinion with fact, of one's own internal or subjective perspective with an external or objective one, to combine breadth with depth. And while our chapter authors have strived to follow a common template or outline, you will find differences in methodology. Some authors have used individual informants in their research, others have gathered focus groups together, and others have chosen mainly to emphasize existing literature. In addition, there were limitations to the consistency of statistical data sets available across ethnic groups. Certain important data, such as on intermarriage, are not uniform across the groups over the same periods of time.

Nevertheless, we hope you, the reader, will find this book not simply the story of Hawai'i, but one that offers a way to read our own future as a country, that the emerging plurality of minority groups in the United States must do more than simply coexist to form a nation.

There is a corollary to diversity—called *connectedness*. That is our message.

Further Reading

Berry, J. W. 2008. "Globalization and Acculturation." *International Journal of Intercultural Relations* 32(4): 328–336.

Boas, Franz. [1921] 1968. "Ethnology of the Kwakiutl." In *Thirty-Fifth Annual Report of the Bureau of American Ethnology to the Secretary of the Smithsonian Institution, 1913–1914*. Washington, D.C.: Government Printing Office.

Calmes, Jackie. 2009. "On campus, Obama and memories." *New York Times*, January 3, A-11. http://www.nytimes.com/2009/01/03/us/politics/03Reunion.html.

Darwin, Charles. [1859] *On the Origin of Species by Means of Natural Selection, or the Preservation of Favoured Races in the Struggle for Life.* http:// www.talkorigins.org/faqs/origin.html.

Daws, Gavan. 1968. *Shoal of Time: A History of the Hawaiian Islands.* Honolulu: University of Hawai'i Press.

———. 2006. *Honolulu: The First Century.* Honolulu: Mutual Publishing.

Kamakau, S.M. 1992. *Ruling Chiefs of Hawai'i.* Revised ed. Honolulu: Kamehameha Schools Press.

Lind, Andrew W. 1955. *Hawaii's People.* Honolulu: University of Hawai'i Press.

Linnekin, Jocelyn, and Lin Poyer. 1990. *Cultural Identity and Ethnicity in the Pacific.* Honolulu: University of Hawai'i Press.

Okamura, Jonathan Y. 2008. *Ethnicity and Inequality in Hawai'i.* Philadelphia: Temple University Press.

Pukui, Mary Kawena, and Samuel H. Elbert. 1986. *Hawaiian Dictionary.* University of Hawai'i Press.

Stocking, George W. 1966. "Franz Boas and the Cultural Concept in Historical Perspective." *American Anthropologist* 68: 867–882. http:// www.hawaii-nation.org/constitution-1852.html.

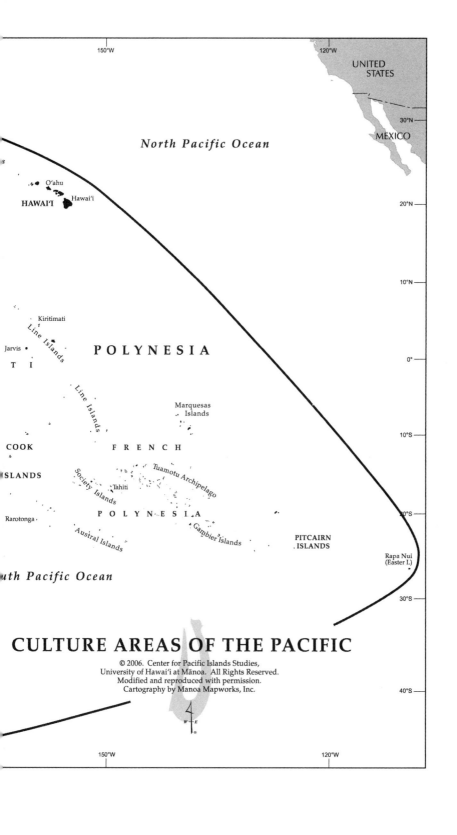

150°W   120°W

30°N

North Pacific Ocean   MEXICO

s

O'ahu
HAWAI'I   Hawai'i   20°N

10°N

· Kiritimati

Jarvis ·   *Line Islands*   P O L Y N E S I A

T   I   0°

Line Islands

Marquesas
· Islands

10°S

COOK   F R E N C H

SLANDS   *Society*   *Tuamotu Archipelago*
Islands   ·Tahiti

P O L Y N E S I A   30°S
Rarotonga ·
· Gambier Islands
Austral Islands   PITCAIRN
· ISLANDS

Rapa Nui
(Easter I.)

uth Pacific Ocean

30°S

CULTURE AREAS OF THE PACIFIC

40°S

W   E

150°W   120°W

Chronology

A.D. 300–1200	Migration of first Hawaiians from Tahiti and the Marquesas
1778	Arrival of Captain Cook in Hawai'i
1789	Individual Chinese begin arriving
1810	Hawaiian nation established by King Kamehameha I
1810	Individual blacks begin arriving
1820	Missionaries arrive from New England
1830s	Mexican vaqueros brought to Hawai'i by King Kamehameha III
1848	The Mahele land reform signed into law
1852	Chinese immigration begins
1878	Portuguese immigration begins
1885	Japanese immigration begins
1893	Hawaiian monarchy overthrown and Republic of Hawai'i begins
1898	Annexation of Hawai'i by the United States
1900	Okinawan immigration begins
1900	Puerto Rican immigration begins
1903	Korean immigration begins
1909	Filipino immigration begins
1924	Exclusion Act restricts immigration to the United States
1924–1936	Continued Japanese immigration to Hawai'i
1941–1945	World War II and martial law, with sharp rise in U.S. armed forces, white and black, many of whom return

1945	Samoan immigration begins
1954	Democratic Party revolution and end of haole oligarchy
1959	Hawai'i becomes the fiftieth state
1960s–1970s	Post–Korean War—second Korean immigration; Thai immigration begins
1970	Second Chinese immigration from Hong Kong/Taiwan
1970	Hawaiian land and native rights movement begins
1975	Vietnamese immigration begins
1978	Cambodian refugees arrive
1986	Marshallese and Chuukese immigration begins
1993–Present	Hawaiian sovereignty and self-determination movement

CHAPTER I

The Hawaiians

Naleen Naupaka Andrade and Cathy Kaheauʻilani Bell

It is axiomatic that the ideals and morals of tolerance, acceptance, diversity, and multiculturalism infusing Hawaiʻi society exist because of the *kānaka maoli* or Native Hawaiians. As Hawaiʻi's indigenous first nations people, their history and sociocultural development created the ethnocultural template influencing every subsequent group to the Islands.

How did this happen?

This chapter attempts to answer this question. It examines the long temporal sweep of history, interdigitated with the compelling immediacy of how individual Hawaiians (and non-Hawaiians) were and continue to be personally affected.

The Hawaiian ethnocultural template was formed by the twelfth century. It would be reshaped and redefined by intragroup and intergroup acculturative forces and events during the subsequent millennium. This ethnocultural evolution would at times be violent and destructive, and at other times restorative and creative—a spiraling, iterative progression of survival, rebuilding, and advancement. This template became the larger framework within which ethnocultural identity and identification for all peoples in Hawaiʻi would unfold.

From research in genetics, archeology, ethnography, linguistics, and anthropology, there is certainty that the ancestors of the Hawaiians came from Tahiti—or Kahiki—in the Society Islands and the Marquesas at around A.D. 300.[1] They sailed across immense ocean distances without navigational instruments, using the stars, winds, and currents and discovered a group of pristine tropical volcanic islands they named for their ancestral homeland—Hawaiki or Hawai'i.[2]

In subsequent centuries these Polynesian-Hawaiians sailed south to Tahiti and the Marquesas, then returned to Hawai'i—a distance of 5,000 miles—with family and others who served their personal, spiritual, military, and workforce needs. They brought domestic animals, plants needed for food, clothing, nets and rope, and other provisions needed for settlement.[3] These voyages selected for temperaments that were tolerant, resilient, and accepting of diversity and ambiguity. Together on their double-hulled canoes they became a family, or *'ohana*.[4] The values of aloha and *lōkahi* were reified out of necessity and natural selection. Practicing aloha nurtured a sense of security on the open ocean as crew members worked to meet each other's needs. They maintained their personal health and well-being, or *lōkahi,* by maintaining harmonious relationships in four domains: the individual, spiritual, social, and physical. The individual domain consisted of balancing one's body, mind, and spirit. The spiritual domain consisted of deities who guided and protected them: the major and minor gods, or *akua,* and personal family gods that were spiritual ancestors, called *'aumākua.* The social domain involved day-to-day interactions and relationships with others. The physical domain (the earth, nature) consisted of the physical manifestations or *kino lau* of the many *akua* and *'aumākua.* They believed the earth and nature possessed a spiritual life force or mana that came from the gods, and thus they were respected and could never be subdued. These first Polynesian-Hawaiians transferred their way of life from their canoes to their new homeland and developed a unique society and ethnocultural identity.

Creation Stories and Cultural Metaphors

Hawaiian ethnocultural identification begins with the spiritual.

While retaining elements of Polynesian theology, the early Hawaiians developed their own religion and cosmology.[5] The *mo'olelo* (stories or histories) of Papa (the earth mother), Wākea (the sky father), and their daughter Ho'ohokukalani (to create stars in the heavens) defined ethnocultural identification as a metaphysical genealogy.[6] These three creator gods were the mythic parents of the Islands (i.e., the land or *'āina*), the first taro or *kalo* plant from which the Hawaiian food staple poi (steamed mashed *kalo*) was made, and the first Hawaiian man or *kanaka* from whom all *kānaka maoli* descend. This *mo'olelo* explains why Hawaiians viewed the *ʻāina* as an older sibling—respected, cared for with prudent stewardship, and never owned.

The rootlets or *ʻoha* sprouting from the body of the first *kalo* plant were the subsequent generations of *kalo*. *ʻOha* is where the term *ʻohana* (family, kin group) derives. Hence, *ʻohana* metaphorically represents the generations of Hawaiians whose lineage and identity are continuous, back to the first ancestors.

Hawaiian identity and individualism was further defined through the *Kumulipo* (the source in the darkness), a creation chant organized into sixteen *wā* or periods of time, composed to honor an *aliʻi* child born in 1700.[7] In this later view, creation begins in the *lipo,* the deep darkness of the ocean floor slime. Within the *lipo,* the male and female elements of the universe combine to form the coral polyp, after which higher levels of flora and fauna follow in ascending order. Each life form originates in the sea and has its complement on land. The creation of men, women, and gods occurs midway, when day or *ao* replaces the time of night or *pō.* Genealogies of the child follow with the culmination of the chant being the naming of the child. The *Kumulipo* is an evolutionary model that declares the universe is ultimately sexual. The birth or creation of each child *is* its identity delineated by its genealogy back to the beginning of the universe.[8]

Precontact Hawaiian Society

The voyages south stopped by A.D. 1200. Several island chiefdoms developed by the end of the eleventh century. A highly stratified society was established consisting of a ruling class called *aliʻi,* a priestly and expert class (e.g., master craftsmen, healers, and professionals) called kahuna, and a commoner or planter class called *makaʻāinana.* There was also a class of outcasts called *kauwā* who were sometimes tattooed, used for human sacrifice to war *akua,* and restricted to living in designated settlements other classes could not enter.[9] The island rulers or *mōʻī* were *aliʻi* who ascended to power usually through warfare. A common language or ʻŌlelo Hawaiʻi was spoken, albeit with differences in phonetics and vernacular usage. Without writing, an oral tradition maintained the code of laws, genealogies, and *moʻolelo.*

MANA: THE PATHS OF KŪ AND LONO

The *kapu* system measured, protected, and managed mana. How much mana one possessed was determined by genealogy and actions.

Mana accumulated through actions came from two sources: Kū, *akua* of assertiveness, debate, aggression and war; and Lono, *akua* of peace, healing, fertility, sexuality, and sensuality. Mana, in essence, was the spiritual and cultural currency through which Hawaiians measured their wealth, well-being, and ability to rule.

THE *KAPU* SYSTEM AND ITS *'AIKAPU*

According to Kame'eleihiwa, the *kapu* regulated mana by separating the sacred, or *kapu,* from the common, or *noa* (being free from *kapu*).[10] This was achieved by the *'aikapu,* which protected the mana of men and the male *akua* from the defiling mana or *haumia* of women. Women could not eat *kino lau* (physical forms) of the male *akua* such as pig, coconut, and banana. For Hawaiians, what you eat—or *'ai*—is what you rule and control; therefore, food was *kapu*. Sex or *ai,* on the other hand, was *noa,* and hence sexuality—including bisexuality—was free of *kapu,* except where genealogical rank of *ali'i* progeny was essential. Strict codes for disposing of human waste, along with conservation *kapu,* preserved the land's fertility or mana. Fearful, fastidious adherence to these *kapu* ensured sanitation, prevented pollution of waterways, and sustained reforestation and conservation.

The *kapu* ensured leadership accountability via the practice of two cultural values: *mālama* (to care for, serve, and honor) and *pono* (to maintain balanced relationships that are moral, ethical, and just). To build and sustain mana, *ali'i* needed to *mālama* their gods, *'āina,* and people. After warfare ended, *ali'i* worked to *mālama* the *'āina* and those they had conquered, thereby balancing the paths of Kū and Lono and being *pono*. If this code was violated, *ali'i* were removed or killed.

SOCIOCULTURAL STRUCTURE AND ORDER

Hawaiian society was orderly, predominantly rural, and interdependent. Members of each class knew and conformed to their place, role, and purpose.[11] How was order maintained beyond the draconian enforcement of the *kapu?* Applying Merton's theory of social structure, function, and anomie, Hawaiian *culture goals* (i.e., established aspirations and measures of success) and *institutional means* (i.e., morals and ethics that regulate how one achieves culture goals) came from the *mō'i*.[12] According to Merton, when individuals can access the institutional means to achieve culture goals and ideally transcend class lines, social order results.

Mō'ī articulated the major culture goals their *kānaka* (men, humans, subjects) aspired toward. These were to work, or *ho'ohana*, to develop and sustain an environment that produced abundant food and other material resources from the land and sea; *mālama* those you lead and serve; achieve and maintain *lōkahi*; and heed the pleasures of the earth and each other through play, or *le'ale'a*.

Mō'ī and their *kāhuna nui*, or high priests, provided the institutional means through a system of reciprocal relationships between *akua, ali'i,* and *kānaka*. Kirch and Sahlins[13] posited two paradigms arising between A.D. 1400 and 1500 that defined this system of reciprocity: the first from the ancient Nanaulu chiefs of O'ahu and Kaua'i; the second from the younger, usurper Pili chiefs of Hawai'i Island and Maui.[14] In the first paradigm, firstborn sons of *ali'i* and *maka'āinana* became *hānai* (adopted children) to the *mō'ī*, who raised and trained them as his own sons. Thus, the *mō'ī* made his *kānaka* his kin and thereby gave them the means to transcend class lines. The alternative paradigm was of the "warrior-*mō'ī*" who conquered and then ruled the island and everyone on it. In contrast to Nanaulu chiefs, the Pili chiefs subjugated their *kānaka*. In the latter paradigm, transcending class lines was dependent on accumulated mana won through achievements, warfare, and being *pono*. Hawaiians thrived in both paradigms, but the tenets of the "warrior-*mō'ī*" prevailed and became the social order from the sixteenth century until the 1848 Mahele.

Thus, the Hawaiian ethnocultural template formed within a well-ordered social structure, driven by a culture of reciprocity between the physical and metaphysical elements of kinship and the *'ohana* bonded by aloha, *lōkahi*, and *le'ale'a*.

Postcontact Traditional Hawaiian Society

Hawaiian lives changed with sudden and lasting impact in 1778, when British explorer and navigator Captain James Cook and his crew arrived. It is a history marked by the irreplaceable loss of life: from a native war club that fatally struck Cook as he tried to kidnap the island *mō'ī* and the retaliatory destruction of Hawaiians from the weaponry on Cook's ships.[15]

Geographic isolation for almost a millennium meant Hawaiians had limited immunity to foreign diseases brought in on ships. After departing, the damage from Cook's crew (and seamen who arrived after them) continued through sexual transmission of venereal diseases to native women.[16] The nineteenth century brought more ships (as many as six hundred vessels annually by 1846) from Europe, North America, and Asia, along with diseases that decimated the population from an estimated 800,000 Hawaiians in 1778, to nearly 40,000 (Hawaiians and part-Hawaiians) in 1896.[17] Social scientists predicted—inaccurately it turns out—the extinction of Hawaiians by the end of the twentieth century. The 2000 U.S. Census counted about 240,000 Hawaiians in Hawai'i, of which nearly 10,000 are full-blooded natives. The rest are part-Hawaiian or hapa.[18]

KING KAMEHAMEHA

Among the *ali'i* who witnessed the power of British weaponry was Kamehameha, who began his twenty-eight-year quest to forge a nation in 1782. Combining Hawaiian and British military strategy and technology, he systematically brought the islands under his rule, creating the Hawaiian nation by 1810. Kamehameha recognized the mana of women and formalized political rule by *ali'i* women, notably his wife, Ka'ahumanu. He advanced the arts, as well as agriculture and aquaculture. An artistic representation of his reign was captured in the Kona Style of temple or *heiau* sculpture showing large heads with huge eyes that symbolized Kamehameha's noted intellectual prowess, called *'ike:* to observe, have insight, immediate comprehension, and vision. Before Kamehameha, knowledge or enlightment or *ao* were *na'auao* (knowledge from the gut), referring to the slow, methodical rumination of the intestines *(na'au)*.[19] Hawaiian ethnocultural identification would include these sociocultural changes.

HENRY OPŪKAHA'IA

Before peace and healing could exist, many Hawaiians became the collateral damage of Kamehameha's warriors. Among these survivors was a twelve-year-old boy named Henry Opūkaha'ia, who described the horror of seeing warriors slaughter his parents and infant brother.[20] Three years later, while being trained to succeed his uncle as *kahuna nui* at Hikiau Heiau, where Captain Cook was honored as Lono, he left Hawai'i on an American brig headed for New York. He eventually settled in New England, where he discovered Christianity and its promise of eternal life, or *ola hou*. Embracing this new religion, Opūkaha'ia sublimated his posttraumatic wounding and vowed to bring the gifts of *ola hou* and education to his countrymen. He died of typhus in 1818, his quest unfulfilled. Inspired by his story, members of the American Board of Commissioners for Foreign Missions sent the first company of Congregational missionaries to Hawai'i. They arrived in March 1820 and received the news that Kamehameha had died ten months prior.

SOCIOCULTURAL REVOLUTION: ENDING THE 'AIKAPU

During the investiture of Liholiho, Kamehameha's twenty-one-year-old son, Queen Ka'ahumanu recognized his succession as King Kamehameha II, then proclaimed, "But, we two shall share rule over the land."[21] Thereafter, women shared in governing the nation. Six months later, Ka'ahumanu and a group of ruling *ali'i* arranged a feast where men and women ate together, breaking the *'aikapu*. Liholiho joined them and defiled his mana. Perhaps in an effort to be *pono*, Liholiho, supported by Hewahewa the *kahuna nui*, decreed that the nation was free from the *'aikapu* and ended the *kapu* system.

Abolishing the *kapu* destabilized society. The state religion of the male *akua*—Kū, Lono, Kane, and Kanaloa—ended. *'Aumākua* worship continued within the *'ohana* and has remained a spiritual cornerstone for many Hawaiians into the twenty-first century. The lower classes were liberated. *Maka'āinana* entered the presence of *ali'i* without fear of punishment or death. They would rise as leaders alongside *ali'i*, as they mastered the *palapala* (reading and writing) at mission schools. *Kauwā*, who had been ostracized in discrete settlements, were now free to move and live among other Hawaiians, the stigma of their lineage eventually forgotten.[22] The protection of mana was now irrelevant; thus housekeeping and disposal of waste products became lax, sanitation was compromised, and increased disease spread, causing death rates to increase.

Within this environment of epidemics and death, *kahuna la'au lapa'au* (diagnostic and herbal healers) were powerless, yet they persevered, trying to understand and treat the new diseases.[23] As mission physicians gained influence, healers faded into the anonymity of their *'ohana*, entrusting their knowledge and skills to family members.

Without the *kapu*, there was no code of conduct to halt the avarice of nineteenth-century *ali'i* for wealth acquired through the sandalwood trade. They ordered *maka'āinana* to leave their farms to log sandalwood. Without *kapu* for conservation and replanting, they denuded rainforests. And their neglected farms reduced food production to the point of famine.[24]

Amid this sociocultural revolution, a new form of governance was needed, which neither Liholiho nor Ka'ahumanu and her *ali'i* oligarchy could immediately provide.[25]

THE MISSIONARIES

The New England missionaries brought knowledge and skills the *ali'i* oligarchy desired and needed to deal with the ever-increasing numbers of haoles who coveted their kingdom. Missionaries were educators who gave Hawaiians the *palapala* after translating 'Ōlelo Hawai'i into a written form. Ka'ahumanu established a system of mission schools led by *ali'i* teachers trained by missionaries to educate Hawaiians throughout the nation.[26] There was also an exclusive school for royalty, where missionaries taught future monarchs the principles of capitalism, fluency in English and European languages, and international diplomacy.

Most missionaries were between ages of twenty and thirty-five and had been raised in small Northeast American towns. Well educated and filled with Christian zeal and Calvinist austerity, they were determined to fulfill Opukaha'ia's vision by trying to remake Hawaiians in their image: devout Congregationalists, small farm owners, educated, industrious, nonviolent, and exercising New England temperance. Hawaiians who resisted were publicly shamed and punished via blue laws that, for example, sentenced them to build roads for fornicating out of wedlock.[27] More enlightened missionaries admired Hawaiian ways.[28] Some mission physicians combined *kahuna la'au lapa'au* healing with Western allopathy. Among them was Dr. Gerrit P. Judd, who defied entrenched haole opposition and opened the nation's first medical school in 1870. The first class of ten Hawaiian physicians graduated in 1872.[29] Judd's death that year closed the school.

Five years after their arrival, missionaries replaced the *kāhuna nui*. Congregationalism was the state religion. The paths to mana, once directed by Lono and Kū, gave way to Jesus Christ and *ola hou*. And the new *pono* Hawaiian leadership ideal was a faithful Christian—humble, nonviolent, industrious, and prudent.

Despite their good intentions, Christian ethics, and abhorrence toward slavery, missionaries possessed the racial and class attitudes of nineteenth-century Americans. They, like most of the affluent haole, *kama'aina*,[30] and upper-class Hawaiian families, separated their children from their lower-class native peers for schooling and social intercourse.[31] While the missionaries came from humble circumstances, their children would be educated with the privileged. Thus, mission descendants became part of Hawai'i's elite—landed, moneyed, and sometimes imperious. They would nevertheless maintain a deep sense of moral responsibility and aloha for Hawai'i.

The Hawaiian Monarchy

The monarchy spanned a century in which Hawai'i transitioned from provincial absolute rule to an internationally recognized constitutional monarchy. Six monarchs descended from the Kamehamehas; two from the Kalākauas. Each sovereign tried to be *pono* and effectively govern. Their greatest barrier was premature death. Except for Kamehameha I and Lili'uokalani, who died as elders, the monarchs' average life span was thirty-nine years. The *mo'olelo* of this era describe what Campbell called the "Cultural Hero."[32] They tell poignant stories of flawed, courageous men and women who moved beyond personal and historical limitations to inspire future generations.

ETHNOCULTURAL EFFECTS OF AN ANGLO-AMERICANIZED LAW

By 1830, Britain, America, and France began exerting their imperialistic might, ostensibly to protect their citizens residing in Hawai'i. It fell to King Kamehameha III, Kauikeaouli, to protect and move Hawai'i onto the international stage of nations. He did this by recruiting William Little Lee, a twenty-five-year-old Harvard-educated American haole attorney in 1846, to rewrite and transform Hawaiian law.[33] By 1850, Lee wrote a new criminal code based on Massachusetts law and a new Hawaiian Constitution in 1852.[34] At age thirty-one, he became the chief justice of the Hawaiian Supreme Court.

According to Merry, the rule of law penned and enforced by Lee and colleagues was biased toward the economics, civil rights, philosophy, and culture of nineteenth-century New England, America.[35] This meant the new system of laws was shaped by Anglo-American prejudice regarding the race and gender inferiority of women, Hawaiians, and plantation labor immigrants. Haole men bore what Rudyard Kipling called "The White Man's Burden" of colonizing and civilizing their inferiors, whom they reduced to stereotypes. Hawaiians were indolent, good-natured children without morals. Asians were untrustworthy and graspingly ambitious and needed to be kept in their place. Portuguese were white but not haole; tireless, loyal, and ignorant, they could rise from field laborer to *luna* (field supervisor), but no higher. And all women—brown, yellow, and white—served the needs of men. Although there were no segregation laws, these stereotypes underpinned a justice system that established an insidious institutional racism. It would impact the ethnocultural development of all ethnic groups from the mid-nineteenth century to the late twentieth century.

THE MAHELE

In 1848, Kauikeaouli signed the Mahele into law. It transformed the traditional land system into fee ownership with the aim to "create a body of landed commoners who would excel and prosper by means of small farms."[36] Less than 2 percent of Hawaiians received land awards of about three acres each. Rather than help Hawaiians, the Mahele permitted haoles to purchase large tracts of native land they developed into plantations. By 1882, landless Hawaiians made up 25 percent of the plantation workforce.[37] They could not, however, reconcile the incongruity that grueling, monotonous field labor produced wages inadequate to purchase enough food to feed their families. By 1930, only 1 percent of the plantation workforce was Hawaiian. Their rejection of plantations reinforced the stereotype of the lazy Hawaiian.[38] With profound regret, Kauikeaouli realized the Mahele had shattered the economy and social structures that had sustained order since the sixteenth century.

THE MOLOKAʻI LEPER COLONY: SAINT DAMIEN

In 1865, the Legislature passed and King Kamehameha V signed into law the Act to Prevent the Spread of Leprosy. It ordered lifetime quarantines of the infected to the Kalaupapa-Kalawao Peninsula, isolated by a natural barrier of towering cliffs, on the island of Molokaʻi. Men, women, and children were taken from their families and forced to live without organized health care until the Roman Catholic missionary Damien de Veuster arrived in 1873. He created an *ʻohana* from among the exiles. Where he could not bring a cure, the haole priest brought aloha. In 1889, he died a leper—poor, landless, but loved beyond measure. In 2009, he was canonized Saint Damien; his reliquary from Belgium was honored by thousands on its voyage home to Molokaʻi.

ALIʻI TRUST ORGANIZATIONS

The monarchs and their survivors gave—through four charitable trusts—their lands, wealth, and decree to restore and prepare their people for a future they could not imagine in their lifetimes. King Lunalilo established a home for elders. Princess Bernice Pauahi Bishop, great-granddaughter of Kamehameha I, established the Kamehameha Schools to educate Hawaiian children. Queen Emma endowed the Queen's Hospital to perpetuate the legacy of her husband, King Kamehameha IV, Alexander Liholiho, to restore the health of their people.

Lili'uokalani established the Queen Lili'uokalani Children's Center to advance the health and social well-being of orphaned children.

THE MERRIE MONARCH

King David Kalākaua was called the "Merrie Monarch" because he embraced the path of Lono.[39] While being worldly and educated in Euro-American ways, his ethnocultural identification was thoroughly Hawaiian. To the disapproval of missionaries, he called the kahuna masters to revive the Hawaiian culture and arts that had gone underground. At his coronation, the *Kumulipo* was chanted to assert his genealogical right to rule. He built the state-of-the-art 'Iolani Palace and brought European grandeur to the monarchy. His reign was a Hawaiian cultural renaissance whose aesthetic achievements are still celebrated during palace tours and the annual Merrie Monarch Hula Festival, a world-renowned event dedicated to the perpetuation of Hawaiian hula, arts, and culture.

ILLEGAL OVERTHROW OF THE KINGDOM

When Kalākaua died in 1891, his sister Lili'uokalani became queen. Answering her people's appeal, she introduced a new constitution that restored power to Hawaiians. In response, a haole oligarchy made up of mission sons and grandsons, sugar planters, and businessmen staged a coup and overthrew the kingdom on January 17, 1893, and established a provisional government.[40] They imprisoned the queen in 'Iolani Palace and ignored the recommendation of U.S. president Grover Cleveland that they return sovereignty to her. In violation of international law, they proclaimed themselves the Republic of Hawai'i.

American Colonization

By the end of the nineteenth century, American colonization prevailed.[41] Hawai'i society was divided into two major classes: an upper class of elite, professional *kama'āina,* haole, *ali'i,* and mission families; and a lower working class of rural farmers, called *kua'āina,* and blue collar skilled and unskilled laborers. There was also a small emerging lower middle class of Hawaiians, Asians, and Portuguese made up of clergy, schoolteachers, scholars, politicians, jurists, storekeepers, and tradesmen.

AMERICAN ANNEXATION

The leaders of the Republic of Hawai'i imposed American ways on the native population with the aim to annex Hawai'i to the United

States. In 1896, Act 57, Section 50 was passed into law, prohibiting 'Ōlelo Hawai'i in schools. Hawaiians remained loyal to Lili'uokalani and their nation. Within a three-week period in 1897, a petition signed by more than 50 percent of the Hawaiian population stopped annexa-tion.[42] In 1898, however, the Spanish-American War made the Islands strategically valuable, and Hawai'i became a U.S. territory. Statehood followed sixty-one years later.

HAWAIIAN HOMES COMMISSION ACT

In 1919, Congress passed the Hawaiian Homes Commission Act (HHCA) and set aside about 200,000 acres of land for homestead set-tlement. As described by Kauanui,[43] the HHCA was not restitution for lands Hawaiians had lost in the Mahele. It was a land welfare system to rehabilitate landless Hawaiians. The HHCA enforced a 50 percent or more blood quantum as the criterion for lessees and their successors (in 1995, Congress lowered the required blood quantum for successors to 25 percent native blood quantum). Prior to the HHCA, Hawaiian identity was based on kinship, social class, genealogical ties—by birth or *hānai*—birthplace, ability, achievement, and mana.[44] After 1919, the law defined a Hawaiian by blood quantum or race. Thereafter, part-Hawaiians who lacked or appeared to lack the 50 percent blood quan-tum would have to defend their Hawaiianess.

Class, Race, Kinship, and Ethnocultural Boundaries

How Hawaiians perceived, defined, and navigated through the boundaries of class, race, kinship, ethnicity, and culture determined the functions and structure of Hawai'i's multicultural society. Three intergroup coping strategies—intermarriage, food, and ethnocultural humor—emerged out of Hawaiian ethnocultural identification to sub-due blatant racist cruelty and segregation common to Euro-American civilization. Through these intergroup strategies, Hawaiians and immi-grants navigated the boundaries between them.

SOCIAL CLASS AND RACE

While there was resonance between Hawaiian and haole under-standings of class hierarchy, there was none with regard to race. Several events indicate that racism based on skin color and physical features was not part of Hawaiian society. Captain Cook's deification as Lono was not due to his white skin but to cultural *mo'olelo* his ships' arrival fulfilled.[45] In chanting the *Kumulipo* to honor him, Cook was recognized as Hawaiian. In the end, Cook was killed not because he was haole but because he failed to be *pono*. King Kamehameha I accorded his haole British advisors, Young and Davis, *ali'i* status with the same authority, privileges of land, and marriage into his *'ohana* as Hawaiian *ali'i*. Crown Prince Alexander Liholiho's June 1850 journal entry described being nearly thrown out of his train car in Washington, D.C., by a conductor who thought he was Negro (see chapter 10, "The Blacks").[46] As Kamehameha IV, he maintained the prohibition of slavery and racism. The absence of apartheid encouraged black immigration from America and the Cape Verde Islands during the nineteenth-century whaling boom. Blacks were accepted, married Hawaiians, and melded completely into Hawaiian society. Their descendants would be identified as ethnocultural Hawaiians tied to the kinship of their *'ohana*.[47]

KINSHIP AND INTERMARRIAGE

Kinship ties formed from early and frequent intermarriage enervated any attempt to legislate racial segregation. While Hawaiians loathed haole rule and feared the growing numbers of Asians, they did not take these beliefs to the marriage bed because sex, or *ai*, was *noa*.[48] Nineteenth-century marriages between Hawaiian women and haole, Chinese, and Japanese (and in the twentieth century, Portuguese and Filipino) men were due to the inclusivity of Hawaiian culture and the shortage of haole and Asian women.[49] Interracial marriage was and remains a nonideological social institution driven by aloha, not race ideology.

FOOD REMAINS SACRED

Food *('ai)* retained a special sociocultural function. It was and is the most common means of crossing the boundaries of ethnicity and culture. Hawaiians and immigrants socialized and learned about each other when they prepared and ate ethnic foods together during family, work, and religious and cultural gatherings. In contemporary Hawai'i, food has a culturally ritualized significance. Food gifts for friends, colleagues, and family during visits is cultural protocol among all ethnic groups.

ETHNOCULTURAL HUMOR

On plantations, ethnocultural humor served as a coping strategy through which natives and immigrants dealt with social tensions between each other. Plantation wits transformed nineteenth-century stereotypes into jokes that playfully mocked *every* ethnic group, including the elite haole. It would develop into a comedic art form that remains part of Island culture (see chapter 4, "The Portuguese").

WORLD WAR II AND MARTIAL LAW

The bombing of Pearl Harbor moved Hawai'i into World War II and martial law rule from 1941 to 1944.[50] The U.S. military introduced an overt racism directed toward blacks[51] and Asians.[52] The intergroup coping strategies were assaulted by white racism enforced by military power. Two anti-racism movements led by groups of multiethnic Hawai'i leaders were established (see chapter 10, "The Blacks," and chapter 5, "The Japanese"). Among these leaders was John "Jack" Anthony Burns, a haole police captain who saw, resisted, and worked to stop the military injustices against Asians. After the war, returning Japanese and Okinawan veterans joined Burns to build a coalition between labor unions and the Hawai'i Democratic Party to overthrow the haole oligarchy.

DEMOCRATIC PARTY RULE

The GI Bill of Rights gave veterans (most were Japanese and Okinawan) the means to attain college educations and professional degrees. In 1948, they began working with Burns and executed the 1954 Democratic Party Revolution, ending haole oligarchy rule.[53] Burns and colleagues had a strategy and vision to create a multicultural society framed by the tenets of the Aloha Spirit and American statehood. The Aloha Spirit became the cultural metaphor for contemporary Hawai'i.

Among the minority of Hawaiians in the revolution was William Shaw Richardson, a Hawaiian-Chinese-haole attorney who chaired the Democratic Party (1956–1962). In 1962, he became chief justice of the Hawai'i Supreme Court and began a systematic reform of Hawai'i jurisprudence that neutralized the nineteenth-century legacy of William Little Lee. The Richardson Court reinstituted traditional Hawaiian law and cultural practices and recognized and upheld indigenous land, water, and ocean rights.[54]

ETHNOCULTURAL EFFECTS OF TOURISM

Tourism was the Democrats' fiscal brainchild, replacing large-scale agriculture as the top economic driver. It lured visitors seeking respite in the "Land of Aloha," an idyllic island paradise immersed in sensual pleasures.[55]

Tourism generates thousands of jobs and revenues that sustain the education, housing, social welfare, and health of nearly every Hawai'i resident. Environmentally, however, it exposes pristine rainforests to thousands of visitors. Ethically, it exploits the Hawaiian and immigrant cultures. Spiritually, it opens sacred sites that risk being desecrated. Given these opposing forces, the question must be asked: Is there a utility and justification for tourism beyond material sustenance?

Three major festivals originated from tourism: May Day is Lei Day, the Aloha Festival, and the Merrie Monarch Hula Festival. Although spawned by commercial strivings, these festivals are among the most effective civic forums through which people learn and experience multiculturalism and diversity. They perpetuate and evolve Hawaiian (and immigrant) ethnocultural identification.

As tourism grew, so did the value of Hawaiian culture, because keeping Hawai'i Hawaiian met visitors' expectations. The 1986 Aloha Spirit Law (Hawaii Revised Statutes, Chapter 5, Section 7.5) outlined the cultural and spiritual meaning and practice of aloha. It recognized that the Aloha Spirit was a gift from Hawai'i's indigenous people and charged civic leaders and citizens to practice aloha. Tourism, therefore, was a serendipitous vehicle advancing Hawaiians and their culture.

Ethnocultural Identity

Mary Kawena Pukui remains the most influential scholar on Hawaiian ethnocultural development. The *hiapo* (firstborn) and only child of a Hawaiian mother and New England haole father, she was *hānai* to her maternal grandparents. She belonged to the sacred Kanaka'ole *'ohana* of Ka'ū on Hawai'i Island, whose ancestral lineage went back to Pele, the female *akua* of volcanoes. Fluent in 'Ōlelo Hawai'i and English, her *kūpuna* taught and trained her to be a guardian of Hawaiian culture and traditions. Her work built a literary trove on Hawaiian language, geography, customs, and traditions. The information in this section draws from her work, as well as that of contemporary scholars (see Further Readings and Notes).

THE *AHUPUA'A-'OHANA* SOCIOECONOMIC SYSTEM

Ali'i settled with their *'ohana* and followers on wedges of land running from the mountains to the sea called *ahupua'a*. Within an *ahupua'a*, several *'ohana* households, or *kauhale*, lived. Ideally, an *ahupua'a* provided the resources needed to feed, clothe, shelter, and transport its members. Thus, the *ahupua'a-'ohana* system was the basic socioeconomic unit in Hawaiian society. It was, in essence, a metaphorical voyaging canoe situated on land.

Temperaments that had been selected for during ancient ocean voyages continued on land, as did the values of aloha and *lōkahi*. Hawaiians were hardworking and task (not time) oriented. Open, generous, patient, and fun loving, they maintained a dynamic balance between work, love, and play. Men cooked. They also planted, harvested, and gathered. They alone handled the foods *kapu* to the male *akua*. Women made cloth or *kapa* because it was sacred to Hina, the major female *akua*. Except for the feeble, the very young, or the *kapu* restricted, everyone in the *'ohana* worked to plant, harvest, gather, and build.

Amid their daily labors, the *'ohana* celebrated beauty and aloha through the making and giving of leis. Each flower, fern, leaf, seed, or feather used in lei making had meaning. Some were sacred *kino lau* restricted to designated spiritual religious uses, others signified new beginnings and endings, and most symbolized celebrations of aloha between the giver and recipient.[56]

THE HAWAIIAN FAMILY SYSTEM

The *'ohana* remains the major developmental influence upon Hawaiians from infancy to old age. From the youngest to the oldest, the generations include the following: *mo'opuna* or *keiki* (infants and children or grandchildren, commonly up to the age of 10), *'ōpio* (youths, usually ages 10–24), *mākua* (parent generation, usually ages 24–54), and *kūpuna* (elders or grandparents, usually ages 55 and older). The Hawaiian language had no words for uncle, aunt, or cousin. Every member of an *'ohana* who was within the *makua* generation was your father, or *makuakane*, and mother, or *makuahine*. Members within a generation were siblings rather than cousins.

Elements of this traditional family system remain within contemporary Hawai'i. Families using 'Ōlelo Hawai'i use the traditional generational titles. Other Hawaiian and non-Hawaiian families transformed the terms into a Hawaiian-Pidgin vernacular mix. *Mo'opuna, keiki,* and *'ōpio,* as well as members within the same generational peer group, are referred to as "Bruddah" or "Brother" and "Sistah," "Sister," "Sis," or "Tita." *Mākua* are called "Aunty," "Uncle," "Mama," or "Papa." And *kūpuna* are referred to as "Grandpa," "Grandma," or "Tūtū," as well as "Papa" and "Mama." These terms convey respect and/or kinship through blood and aloha.

INDIVIDUAL DEVELOPMENT

The age, gender, and ordinal ranking (except for the *hiapo*) were not as important as the social role played by persons within the *'ohana*. *Mo'opuna* (literally "the generational wellspring") and *kūpuna* (literally "the backbone of the wellspring") were cherished because they represented, respectively, the perpetuation and generativity of the *'ohana*. *Kūpuna* were the keepers of the traditions, ancestral knowledge, and culture. *Mākua* supported and protected children and elders. They also trained *'ōpio* to acquire and master life skills needed to be a productive *makua*. As a general rule, *'ōpio* were given increasing levels of responsibilities based on their interests and capabilities. *'Ōpio* developed within the organizing structure of their *'ohana*. They discovered—and their elders observed and affirmed—their interests and talents that were then sharpened under the complementary supervision and mentoring of *mākua* and *kūpuna*.[57]

HĀNAI

A form of adoption called *hānai* developed out of the cultural practice of aloha and was common among members of an *'ohana*. Traditionally, *hānai* most often occurred when the firstborn *(hiapo)* was raised by grandparents to perpetuate cultural knowledge, genealogy, and family *mo'olelo*. Children were also *hānai* to *mākua* who could not bear children.

As immigrant populations grew, *hānai* expanded to include nonnatives. Pukui's eldest daughter, an orphaned Japanese child, was *hānai*.[58] These *hānai* and their descendants were inseparable from the kinship of their *'ohana*. From a Hawaiian ethnocultural perspective, a nonnative *hānai* raised from childhood is Hawaiian. From the perspective of U.S. law, however, race, not culture, determines a person's identity and ethnic classification. Therefore, a nonnative *hānai* is not Hawaiian. Given this race-based definition of Hawaiiness, nonnative *hānai* cannot serve as their parents' successor to HHCA lands. Moreover, if they became beneficiaries of Hawaiian endowments (e.g., admission to Kamehameha Schools), they increase the risk for nonnatives, who are not ethnoculturally Hawaiian, to access and exhaust entitlements dedicated to Hawaiian restoration and well-being.[59]

IMPACT OF POSTCONTACT SOCIETY

The *ahupua'a-'ohana* system could not survive the tumultuous events of the nineteenth century. Epidemics left massive disability, death, and devastation in their wake. The Mahele was the coup de grace severing the relationship between *ahupua'a* and *'ohana*.

Hawaiians began moving to plantations, towns, and cities looking for work. Employment consisted primarily of skilled and unskilled laborers, policemen, firemen, correctional officers, stevedores, harbor pilots, tug boat captains, and entertainers. The traditional *'ohana* fractured as *mākua* left their *kūpuna* and commonly their youngest children.[60] Away from their *ahupua'a*, families in urban settings became more nuclear and centripetal. Earning money to feed, clothe, and house the *'ohana* became paramount and superseded individual aspirations. Without *kūpuna*, roles and responsibilities of *'ohana* members began to blur as the demands of company shift work left older children in charge of running the household. *'Ōpio* were expected to take on the responsibilities of *mākua* without direct supervision and mentoring by their elders. When the integrity of roles (e.g., *'ōpio* carrying the burdens of *mākua*) was compromised, the *'ohana* could not thrive.

In the city, time was measured by the clock and Sunday Sabbath. Protestant and later Catholic churches and Mormon wards were important social gathering places. At home and at sacred sites, many families continued their reverence to *'aumākua*. Sunday worship and family centered religious-spiritual practices helped to maintain a thriving *'ohana* in urban sites.

MODIFYING THE CULTURAL CONCEPT AND PRACTICE OF *'OHANA*

Families could not reconstruct the *ahupua'a-'ohana* system in the city. Yet it was inconceivable for them to sever the bond to their ancestral *'āina*. They adapted by transforming the cultural meaning of *'ohana* from a noun and place (i.e., a family on their ancestral *'āina*) to a noun and process. Forming a syncretistic fusion of their Christian and Hawaiian beliefs, they created a virtual link to their ancestors, *ahupua'a*, and culture. In the city, *'ohana* became a three-step ritual practiced by household members.[61] *'Ohana* was led by the family's spiritual leader or *haku* and began in the early evening with a family prayer circle. After the opening prayer, each participant recited their biblical memory-verse. These memory-verses were given to each member by the *haku*, kept throughout life, and provided an internalized spiritual yardstick and guide for one's conduct. During the second step of *'ohana*, members exchanged thoughts and feelings around topics chosen and facilitated by the *haku*. Commonly, participants shared challenges and/or achievements they experienced and asked for forgiveness for hurtful actions.

Members then considered what was shared and offered ways they could help address the challenge, celebrate the achievement, and/or *hala,* or forgive and redeem one another. On other evenings, this second step was used to recite the family *moʻolelo,* the family oral histories going back six or more generations. The third and final step of *ʻohana* was a closing prayer.

In this way, *ʻohana* continued to serve as the fundamental social and economic unit in urban settings. The definition of *ʻohana* was expanded to mean a group of people united by a common history, purpose, or goal without the requisite ancestral ties to the *ahupuaʻa.* *ʻOhana* in this new cultural context extended the definition of kinship to include unrelated Hawaiians and non-Hawaiians united by their shared interests, organizational affiliation, and dedication to aloha and *mālama* Hawaiʻi (e.g., Protect Kahoʻolawe ʻOhana, described later).

Education

Hawaiians quickly learned the *palapala* (literacy). Before the 1896 ban on Hawaiian language, Hawaiʻi was a predominantly literate nation. For the majority of Hawaiians, who entered the workforce to support their *ʻohana,* education beyond high school was improbable. At the Kamehameha Schools, led by trustees who were members of the haole oligarchy, children were taught vocational as opposed to pre-college curricula. Financial aid and affirmative action programs from 1970 onward significantly increased Hawaiian college enrollment and graduation.

The Contemporary Hawaiian Family

Contemporary families in rural areas usually function as close-knit, self-reliant households that maintain the values, functions, and structure of the traditional *ʻohana.* They tend to live on or close to their ancestral *ahupuaʻa,* even if they cannot purchase the land in fee. In addition to day jobs, rural *ʻohana* sustain their large extended families by farming, fishing, hunting, and gathering from the ocean and rainforests. Hawaiian yards typically have an abundance of fruit trees, a shaded area for the family to gather, and patches of flowering plants and ferns to make leis.

The sociocultural integrity of urban families separated from their ancestral lands relies heavily on their ability to maintain their religious affiliation and/or spirituality to their *'aumākua*. They make do within their suburban homes, apartments, and churches. They access the *'āina* and sea via public access trails, beach parks, and city gardens—and, for those who can afford it, visits to their rural *'ohana*. Families among the working poor who lack access to farms or the ocean to supplement their family's sustenance suffer the most.

During special family gatherings, Hawaiian homes (rural and urban) fill with an explosion of activities: cleaning; food preparation; music, singing, and hula dancing; gathering (or in the city, purchasing) flowers, ferns, and ti leaves; lei making; and talking story. To untrained observers, the activities seem chaotic, yet each person knows their tasks, each intuitively complements the other—the many hands working together, or *laulima*, pulling together, or *alu like*, in a singular focus to complete their tasks while having fun. Hawaiians believe work, especially arduous work, should be infused with joy and playfulness, or *le'ale'a*, which then assures the work is completed and celebrated with aloha. At the hub of this cacophony is the designated family organizer (a *kupuna, makua,* or *hiapo*) quietly guiding, directing, and encouraging each member of their *'ohana*. To the trained eye, an *'ohana* that behaves thus is one that continues the ethnocultural elements—values, temperament, and practices—of the metaphorical voyaging canoe with its navigator and crew.

Who and What Is a Hawaiian?

According to the 2000 U.S. population census, there are about 400,000 Hawaiians in the United States, of which 64 percent live in Hawai'i. Most are part-Hawaiian, thereby making race or blood quantum an inadequate measure of Hawaiian identity. Removing race as a measure of identity begs the question: Who and what is a Hawaiian? To address this query, let us examine the impact of history on Hawaiian society and apply Merton's theory of social structure and anomie.

By fate, serendipity, and design, the 1819 *'aikapu* revolution cleared a path for haoles to increasingly introduce, influence, and impose upon Hawaiians a new government, religion, education, law system, and economy, along with the concept of race. The 1848 Mahele dismantled the *ahupua'a–'ohana* socioeconomic unit and the social order that had served Hawaiians for almost a millennium.

At the turn of the nineteenth century, most Hawaiians had little faith in America and the colonizing society thrust upon them. Outraged by the humiliation of their queen, they felt impotent against American annexation and imperialism and filled with righteous anger and bitterness—or worse, with resignation and submission. They mourned the loss of their kingdom and the passing of their *ali'i nui* from whom their mana, morals, and ethnocultural identification flowed.

By 1898, Hawaiians had lost their traditional culture goals and institutional means. Without these two social elements, Merton predicted that individuals who were unable to retain a success-aspiration mechanism would not conform to the dominant social order. And hence, Hawaiians without their traditional culture goals and institutional means developed behavioral responses that form the following five social patterns that persist today:

Assimilation: The smallest group threw aside their Hawaiian identification and totally assimilated to American ways. They would either reject their Hawaiianess or cynically reduce it to a checked box on a survey for entitlements their children and grandchildren might access.

Colonial Mimicry: Many Hawaiians who belonged to or had married into the upper class elite used colonial mimicry to survive. They ostensibly embraced the values and culture of their colonizers, while suppressing and repressing their ambivalence toward abandoning their native identity.[62] Many of their descendants would seize and regain their Hawaiian identity as a result of the Hawaiian Sovereignty and Self-Determination Movement.

Orthogonal Biculturalism: Many part-Hawaiians learned to "frameshift" or change the expressions of their native and immigrant identities to adapt to the context, situationally defining themselves as Hawaiian, American, and/or immigrant (i.e., haole, Asian, or Portuguese). These sociocultural chameleons would survive and thrive into the twenty-first century.

Hawaiian Anomie: Many Hawaiians could not retain the success-aspiration mechanism. They retreated. They would define themselves by their centuries-long grievances, becoming bitter, alienated, cynical and/or apathetic. Entangled in a past writhing with pathological grief, anxiety, and distrust, they could not imagine a future filled with safety and promise. They and their descendants became strangers in their homeland. Vulnerable to alcohol and drug addictions, some perverted the mana-building paths of Lono and Kū into hedonistic and antisocial pursuits, existing in a sociocultural netherworld. Sadly, significant numbers of their *mo'opuna,* especially young men, would choose suicide.[63]

Sublimation–Cultural Synthesis: The final social pattern was sublimation. Inspired by the monarchy's cultural heroes, this group sublimated the rage and trauma of their wounding and transformed their historical grievances into a noble purpose and vision. They raised children and grandchildren educated and fluent in the Hawaiian and American worlds. Through their descendants, they would assert their first nations status, calling themselves Native Hawaiians, and finally, *kānaka maoli.*

A New Ethnocultural Identity

ENDURING HARDWIRED SOCIOCULTURAL FACTORS

The new Hawaiian ethnocultural identity emerged in the late twentieth century, reconstructed from enduring sociocultural factors that were hardwired into the ethnocultural template that existed from A.D. 1100 to 2010.[64] These factors include the following: (a) the values and practice of aloha, *le'ale'a, lōkahi, mālama,* and *pono;* (b) a thriving *'ohana* whose *kūpuna* and *mākua* support the development of children and youth; (c) spirituality via organized religion and/or *'aumākua* worship; (d) access to the land and sea; (e) basic proficiency in 'Ōlelo Hawai'i; and (f) familiarity with historical-cultural *mo'olelo.* These factors endured because all of Hawai'i's people came to understand, embrace, and perpetuate their humanistic beauty, utility, and transcendent power or mana.

The following events are historical milestones that have determined and continue to determine the development of the new Hawaiian ethnocultural identity. Together they form the interconnected facets of a progressive wave of continuity and iterative change.

A HAWAIIAN PROFESSIONAL MIDDLE CLASS

Creating a cadre of Hawaiian professionals was needed to bring about transformational change. It took visionary native and nonnative leaders who successfully carried out a decades-long feat of social engineering. They used government civil rights (affirmative action) and health care legislation to replicate for Hawaiians what the GI Bill of Rights had done for veterans. Hawaiians began their ascent to sociopolitical power in 1970 and established a professional middle class by 1993.

Affirmative action programs, and later the Native Hawaiian Health Scholars Program (a competitive federal scholarship program) at the University of Hawai'i (UH), recruited Hawaiians (and other minorities) and employed learning models that retained Hawaiian and Asian traditions while students were immersed in the predominantly Euro-American world of academia. This model yielded impressive results. The UH School of Medicine's Imi Ho'ola (Seeking to Heal) Program increased the percentage of Hawaiian medical students from about 2 percent when it began in 1974 to 18 percent in 2010. To date, nearly three hundred Hawaiians have become physicians; the majority are Imi Ho'ola graduates. Minority support programs within UH's Schools of Social Work, Nursing, and Law also significantly increased the numbers of Hawaiian social workers, nurses, and lawyers.

In 1984, a cadre of Hawaiian and non-Hawaiian educators began a movement to teach 'Ōlelo Hawai'i. They established Pūnana Leo (Nest of Voices), a preschool modeled after the nineteenth-century Hawaiian language schools. It became an iconic catalyst inspiring a statewide Hawaiian immersion school system from preschool through the twelfth grade. UH campuses on Hawai'i Island and O'ahu established schools for Hawaiian academic studies that substantially increased scholarly publications.[65] There is a cable TV station teaching 'Ōlelo Hawai'i and Hawaiian language radio. After over a century of government suppression, 'Ōlelo Hawai'i is restored to Hawaiians and Hawai'i and is again a core part of Hawaiian identification.

Like the Asian veterans before them, these Hawaiian professionals became the arbiters and leaders of sociocultural and political change. Among them, the state's first Hawaiian governor; the director of the State Department of Health; judges on the family, district, and circuit courts; a chancellor, a dean, several center directors and department chairs, and numerous faculty on the ten UH campuses; and trustee leaders, including four board chairs of the *ali'i* charitable trust organizations.

HAWAIIAN HEALTH AND TRADITIONAL HEALING

In 1985, a consortium of researchers published the landmark *E Ola Mau Native Hawaiian Health Needs Study Report*.[66] *E Ola Mau* and subsequent studies showed that Hawaiians have a life span nearly seven years shorter than other Hawai'i ethnic groups. They have higher rates of cardiovascular disease, cancer mortality, diabetes mellitus, and chronic pulmonary disease. And they also have higher rates of alcoholism and drug addictions (especially methamphetamine addiction), child abuse and neglect, suicide (particularly among young men), anxiety disorders, and incarceration among adults and youth.[67] *E Ola*

Mau recommended using cultural interventions and traditional healing to augment extant treatments. A resurgence of traditional healing
followed: herbal healing, or *la'au lapa'au*, massage, or *lomilomi*, and
ho'oponopono (to restore balance and make right), an intervention for
conflict resolution. In 1988, the U.S. Native Hawaiian Health Care
Act became law and provided for Hawaiian healers to practice within
Hawaiian health centers.

HAWAIIAN RIGHTS, *HOKULE'A*, SOVEREIGNTY, AND SELF-DETERMINATION

Described by Trask and Milner, the Hawaiian movement for native
rights began in 1970 at Kalama Valley after farmers fought eviction
from land they leased from Kamehameha Schools.[68] The movement
was and continues to be characterized by its tenacious, nonviolent, and
progressively effective protests conducted by natives and immigrants.

Protect Kaho'olawe 'Ohana. Described by McGregor, the 1976
Kaho'olawe protest strived to stop the U.S. military from using the island
for bombing practice.[69] It was led by a multiethnic, politically bipartisan
group of men, women, and youth called the Protect Kaho'olawe 'Ohana
(PKO). PKO inspired the public to practice *aloha 'āina* and *mālama
'āina*. PKO *kūpuna* and experts shared Kaho'olawe's *mo'olelo*, revealing
its spiritual and cultural significance to ocean voyaging canoes and their
navigators. After a fourteen-year struggle, in which two PKO Hawaiian
leaders died trying to access the island, the bombing stopped. Working
with the military, PKO restored Kaho'olawe as a *wahi pana* (sacred, legendary place) for Hawaiians and all the people of Hawai'i.

Hokule'a: The Hawaiian Voyaging Canoe. Coincidentally in 1976,
the Polynesian Voyaging Society launched the *Hokule'a*, a sixty-foot
double-hulled canoe modeled and built to replicate the vessels that had
carried the first Polynesians to Hawai'i. Led by Micronesian master
navigator Mau Piailug, Hawaiians sailed without instruments, employ-
ing the navigational skills akin to those of their fourth-century ancestors and made landfall in Kahiki. Pialug trained Nainoa Thompson, a
Hawaiian-French-Chinese-Tahitian, to master the astronomical charts
of the ancient way finders.[70] Thompson became a master navigator after
he led several crews of native and nonnative men and women across the
Pacific and back to Hawai'i. *Hokule'a* affirmed ancestral *mo'olelo*, and it
validated for people in Hawai'i and the world the capability and worth of
Hawaiian (and Micronesian) navigation.

Native Hawaiian Sovereignty and Self-Determination Movement.

During the 1980s, native and nonnative lawyers researched and proved the illegality of the 1893 overthrow of the Hawaiian Kingdom. These findings formed the basis for the Hawaiian Sovereignty and Self-Determination Movement. This movement was formally recognized in January 1993 during the one-hundred-year observance of the over-throw and was marked by three significant events: an apology from the United Church of Christ, 18th Synod, for the role their Congregational missionaries had played in the overthrow; U.S. Public Law 103–150 read by President Bill Clinton "to offer an apology to Native Hawaiians on behalf of the United States for the overthrow of the Kingdom of Hawai'i";[71] and a march to 'Iolani Palace of an estimated 15,000 Hawaiians and non-Hawaiians in support of Hawaiian sovereignty and self-determination.

Described comprehensively by MacKenzie, models of sovereignty include the following: (1) the Office of Hawaiian Affairs, a quasi-independent state organization established during the 1978 State Constitutional Convention; (2) Ka Lāhui Hawai'i, a grassroots organization modeled after Native American tribes and nations with a nation-within-a-nation structure; and (3) the self-proclaimed Independent Nation of Hawai'i, which advocates total independence.[72] Hawaiians disagree on which model should prevail, but they unite on four principles: (1) formal U.S. recognition that Hawaiians are the indigenous, first nations people of Hawai'i; (2) self-determination of Hawaiian ethnocultural identity, traditions, language, and practices; (3) restitution for the loss of lands, language, education, livelihoods, and health stemming from wrongs intentionally or unintentionally perpetrated by America; and (4) restoration of a native land base formed by HHCA and ceded (Hawaiian Crown and government) lands. Most people predict that this movement will be the vehicle through which the new Hawaiian ethnocultural identity will continue to evolve.

Summary and Conclusions

Hawaiians occupy every social class: the destitute, working poor, middle-class tradespeople and professionals, and elite upper class. Too many still make up the destitute and working poor. However, a growing professional middle class of scholars and leaders dedicated to the advancement of their people now exists. Legislation supporting Hawaiian rights, along with collaborative strategic efforts by the *ali'i* charitable trusts to restore and advance Hawaiian well-being, are progressing steadily.

The factual events of history indicate that race and racism were never part of Hawai'i's indigenous society. Assessed within the contextual review and wisdom of history, the race-based blood quantum definition of Hawaiian identity does not meet the test of ethnocultural validity. It is a continuation of nineteenth-century American colonization.

The ideal Hawaiian ethnocultural identity is composed of the following criteria: first, indigeneity and an enduring bond to the *'āina;* second, kinship to each other—by blood and aloha—organized within the structure and function of a thriving *'ohana;* third, accountability of leaders (and those they lead) to a code of conduct that follows the precepts of *mālama* and *pono;* fourth, progressing daily to achieve and sustain *lōkahi* and basic proficiency in 'Ōlelo Hawai'i; and finally, living aloha.

Inclusivity encompassed in the value and practice of aloha is the gift from the Hawaiians. Through it, America's fiftieth state has been able to achieve a level of multiculturalism that continues to evolve. The Hawaiian way of life—immersed in its roiling history of trauma, loss, grief, and renewal—contrasts the fluid strength of ethnocultural diversity against the flawed rigidity of racism. The Aloha Spirit is more than a revenue generating sound bite for tourism. It is the living essence or spirituality of mana—free from the rigidity of religion and dogma.

Further Reading

Bushnell, O. A. *The Gifts of Civilization: Germs and Genocide in Hawai'i.* Honolulu: University of Hawai'i Press, 1963.

Fuchs, L. *Hawaii Pono: An Ethnic and Political History.* Honolulu: Bess Press, 1961.

Kamakau, S. M. *Ruling Chiefs of Hawaii,* rev. ed. Honolulu: Kamehameha Schools Press, 1992.

Kame'eleihiwa, L. *Native Lands and Foreign Desires.* Honolulu: Bishop Museum Press, 1992.

Kauanui, J. K. *Hawaiian Blood: Colonialism and the Politics of Sovereignty and Indigeneity.* Durham, NC: Duke University Press, 2008.

Kirch, P. V., and M. Sahlins. *Anahulu: The Anthropology of History in the Kingdom of Hawaii.* Vol. 1: *Historical Ethnography.* Chicago: University of Chicago Press, 1992.

Kuykendall, R. S. *The Hawaiian Kingdom.* Vols. 1, 2, and 3. Honolulu: University of Hawai'i Press, 1967.

Lili'uokalani. *Hawaii's Story by Hawaii's Queen.* Honolulu: Mutual Publishing, 1990.

Malo, D. *Hawaiian Antiquities.* Trans. N. B. Emerson. Honolulu: Bishop Museum Press, 1951.

Merry, S. E. *Colonizing Hawai'i: The Cultural Power of Law.* Princeton, NJ: Princeton University Press, 2000.

Osorio, J. K. K. *Dismembering Lāhui: A History of the Hawaiian Nation to 1887.* Honolulu: University of Hawai'i Press, 2002.

Pukui, M. K., E. W. Haertig, C. Lee, and J. F. McDermott. *Nana I Ke Kumu.* Vols. 1 and 2. Honolulu: Lili'uokalani Trust, 1972.

Notes

Authors' note: Benjamin B. C. Young, M.D., emeritus dean of students, University of Hawai'i at Mānoa School of Medicine, contributed ideas and writing to this chapter. As the founding director of the Medical School's Imi Ho'ola Program, he developed the curricula that produced three generations of Hawaiian physicians. He also served as crew physician on the maiden voyage of the vessel *Hokule'a* from Tahiti to Hawai'i.

1. J. K. Lum, O. Rickards, C. Ching, and R. L. Cann, "Polynesian mitochondrial DNAs reveal three deep maternal lineage clusters," *Human Biology* 66(4) (1994): 567–590; J. K. Lum, J. K. McIntyre, D. L. Greger, K. W. Huffman, and M. G. Vilar, "Recent Southeast Asian domestication and Lapita dispersal of sacred male pseudohermaphroditic 'tuskers' and hairless pigs of Vanuatu," *Proceedings from the National Academy of Sciences* 103(46) (November 14, 2006): 17,190–17,195 (retrieved from www.pnas. org/cgi/dol/so.1073/pnas.0608220103; P. V. Kirch, *Feathered Gods and Fishhooks,* Honolulu, HI: University of Hawai'i Press, 1985: 58–66.

2. Kirch 1985: 1.

3. Kirch 1985.

4. N. Thompson, "E ho'i mau: Honoring the past, caring for the present, journeying to the future," *Hulili: Multidisciplinary Research on Hawaiian Well-Being,* 4(1) (2007): 9–34.

5. V. Valeri, *Kingship and Sacrifice,* Chicago: University of Chicago Press, 1985: 3–36.

6. The various *mo'olelo* of Papa, Wākea, and Ho'okulani include L. Kame'eleihiwa, *Native Lands and Foreign Desires,* Honolulu: Bishop Museum, 1992: 23–25; A. Fornander, *Fornander Collection of Hawaiian Antiquities and Folk-lore,* vol. 1 (1919): 186 and vol. 4: 2–16, Honolulu: Bishop Museum Press; and M. Beckwith, *Hawaiian Mythology,* Honolulu: University of Hawai'i Press, 1970: 293–306.

7. The name of the child was Kalani-nui-'ī-a-mamao, also called Lonoikamakahiki. Captain Cook was believed to be Lonoikamakahiki returning from Kahiki during the Makahiki season. J. Charlot, *Chanting the Universe,* Hong Kong: Emphasis International, 1983; Queen Lili'uokalani [1897], *An*

Account of the Creation of the World According to Hawaiian Tradition: The Kumulipo, Honolulu: Pueo Press, 1978.

8. R. K. Johnson, *Kumulipo: The Hawaiian Hymn of Creation*, vol. 1, Honolulu: Topgallant Publishing Company, 1981.

9. *Kauwā* were descendants of Kekeu, the child Papa gave birth to after mating with her husband Wākea's male companion or 'aikane. This liaison occurred after Wākea left Papa. *Kauwā*, therefore, were *ali'i* whose social roles were based on class, not race. D. Malo, *Hawaiian Antiquities*, 2nd ed., Honolulu: Bernice P. Bishop Museum, 1997; D. Malo, *Ka Mo'olelo Hawai'i—Hawaiian Traditions*, Translated by M. N. Chun. Honolulu: First People's Productions, 2006: 55–58; S. M. Kamakau, *Ruling Chiefs of Hawai'i*, rev. ed., Honolulu: Kamehameha Schools Press, 1992.

10. L. Kame'eleihiwa, *Native Lands and Foreign Desires*, Honolulu: Bishop Museum, 1992.

11. B. C. Young, "The Hawaiians," in *Peoples and Cultures of Hawai'i: A Psychosocial Profile*, edited by J. F. McDermott, W. S. Tseng, and T. W. Maretzki, Honolulu: University of Hawai'i Press, 1980: 5–24.

12. R. K. Merton, "Social structure and anomie," *American Sociological Review* 3(5) (October 1938): 672–682. Retrieved from http://www.jstor.org/stable/2084686.

13. P. V. Kirch and M. Sahlins, *Anahulu: The Anthropology of History in the Kingdom of Hawaii*, vol. 1: *Historical Ethnography*, Chicago: University of Chicago Press, 1992: 21–27.

14. Ma'ilikūkahi, *mō'i* of O'ahu, is the founder of the first paradigm. The alternative paradigm was established by Kāka'alaneo, *mō'i* of Māui (Kirch and Sahlins 1992). Several generations later, Umi-a-liloa—who was half *ali'i* and half *maka'āinana*—used the second paradigm to become a great *mō'i* despite being a commoner. Umi-a-liloa's leadership model became part of the Hawaiian ethnocultural identification (Kame'eleihiwa 1992: 53–54.)

15. Kamakau 1992: 103.

16. O. A. Bushnell, *The Gifts of Civilization*, Honolulu: University of Hawai'i Press, 1993: 230–231.

17. R. C. Schmitt, *Demographic Statistics of Hawai'i*, Honolulu: University of Hawai'i Press, 1968: 10, 74; L. H. Fuchs, *Hawaii Pono: An Ethnic and Political History*, Honolulu: Bess Press, 1961: 18; D. E. Stannard, *Before the Horror*, Honolulu: University of Hawai'i Press, 1989.

18. U.S. Census, "The Native Hawaiian and Other Pacific Islander Population: 2000," *Census 2000 Brief*, retrieved from www.census.gov/prod/2001pubs/c2kbr01–14.pdf, 2001.

19. Charlot 1983: 121.

20. E. Dwight, *Memoirs of Henry Obbokiah, a Native of Owyhee, and a Member of the Foreign Mission School; Who died at Cornwall, Connecticut*

February 17, 1818, Honolulu: Woman's Board of Missions for the Pacific Islands, 1968.

21. Kamakau 1992: 220.

22. Kepelino, *Kepelino's Traditions of Hawai'i*, Honolulu: Bishop Museum, 2007: 142.

23. Bushnell 1993.

24. E. S. C. Handy and M. K. Pukui, *The Polynesian Family System in Ka'u, Hawai'i*, Tokyo and Rutland, VT: Charles E. Tuttle, 1976: 234–235.

25. Liholiho died of measles in 1824 and was succeeded by his twelve-year-old brother Kauikeaouli. Ka'ahumanu as regent or *kuhina nui* ruled until Kauikeaouli came of age.

26. Kirch and Sahlins 1992, vol. 1: 91.

27. T. A. Barrot, *Unless Haste Is Made*, Kailua, HI: Press Pacifica, 1978.

28. N. B. Emerson, *Unwritten Literature of Hawai'i*, Washington, D.C.: Smithsonian Institute, Bureau of American Ethnology, 1909: 261

29. Bushnell 1993: 117–119.

30. *Kama'āina* (children born of the land) were members of an elite haole subgroup possessing Hawaiian *ali'i* and haole ancestry (see chapter 2, "The Euro-Americans").

31. Fuchs 1961: 31, 43–49.

32. J. Campbell, *The Hero with a Thousand Faces*, 2nd ed., New York: Princeton University Press, New Jersey and Bollingen Foundation, Inc., 1972: 18–20.

33. S. E. Merry, *Colonizing Hawai'i: The Cultural Power of Law*, Princeton, NJ: Princeton University Press, 2000.

34. J. K. Osorio, *Dismembering Lāhui: A History of the Hawaiian Nation to 1887*, Honolulu: University of Hawai'i Press, 2002: 85–91.

35. Merry 2000: 1–32.

36. Kame'eleihiwa 1992: 295–306.

37. Fuchs 1961: 70.

38. The *Honolulu Star-Bulletin* quoted John H. Wise on April 12, 1921: "I am anxious not to...give the highly cultivated cane lands to Hawaiians...they will fail for sure....As the governor told you long ago, we believe the temptation for them to sit on the lanai [veranda] and watch some Japanese do the work would be too great. The only way for rehabilitation to benefit the Hawaiian is through his own efforts—hard, honest work."

39. Kame'eleihiwa 1992: 313–314.

40. Queen Lili'uokalani, *Hawaii's Story by Hawaii's Queen*, Honolulu: Mutual Publishing, 1990.

41. Fuchs 1961: 3–85; H. K. Trask, *From a Native Daughter*, Monroe, ME: Common Courage Press, 1993; Merry 2000; J. K. Kauanui, *Hawaiian Blood*, Durham, NC: Duke University Press, 2008.

42. N. K. Silva, *Aloha Betrayed: Native Hawaiian Resistance to American Colonialism*, Durham, NC: Duke University Press, 2004.

43. Kauanui 2008.

44. B. C. Ledward, "On being Hawaiian enough: Contesting American racialization with Native hybridity," *Hulili: Multidisciplinary Research on Hawaiian Well-Being*, 4(1) (2007): 107–143; J. P. 'Ī'ī, *Fragments of Hawaiian History*, Honolulu: Bishop Museum Press, 1995; S. M. Kamakau, *Ka Po'e Kahiko: The People of Old*, Honolulu: Bishop Museum Press, 1992; Malo 1997.

45. Kamakau 1992: 96–99; Malo 1997: 145.

46. J. Adler, ed., *The Journal of Prince Alexander Liholiho*, Honolulu: University of Hawai'i Press, 1967: 108.

47. E. C. Nordyke, "Blacks in Hawaii," *Hawaiian Journal of History* 22 (1988): 241–255.

48. Ibid. Fuchs, L.H. (1961) pp.83–85.

49. Merry 2000: 202–203.

50. T. W. Maretzki and J. F. McDermott, "The Caucasians," in *Peoples and Cultures of Hawaii: A Psychosocial Profile*, ed. J. F. McDermott, W. S. Tseng, and T. W. Maretzki, Honolulu: University of Hawai'i Press, 1980: 25–52.

51. A. S. Broussard, "The Honolulu NAACP and Race Relations in Hawai'i," *Hawaiian Journal of History* 39 (2005): 115–133.

52. Fuchs 1961: 299–307.

53. Ibid.: 308–322.

54. M. K. MacKenzie, editor. *Native Hawaiian Rights Handbook*. Honolulu, HI: Native Hawaiian Legal Corporation (distributed by University of Hawai'i Press), 1991.

55. H. K. Trask, *From a Native Daughter: Colonialism and Sovereignty in Hawai'i*, rev. ed., Honolulu: University of Hawai'i Press, 1999.

56. M. A. McDonald, *Ka Lei: The Leis of Hawai'i*, Honolulu: Topgallant Publishing Co., 1978.

57. I. Else, N. Andrade, and L. Nahulu, "Suicide and suicide-related behaviors among indigenous Pacific Islanders in the United States," *Death Studies* 31 (2007): 479–501.

58. M. K. Pukui, *Olelo No'eau: Hawaiian Proverbs and Poetical Sayings*, Honolulu: Bishop Museum Press, 1987: xi–xix.

59. B. Suyama "Judge rules Non-Hawaiian student can attend Kamehameha," retrieved from KITV.com: *TheHawaiichannel.com*, August 20, 21, 2003.

60. Fuchs 1961: 70; A. W. Lind, *An Island Community: Ecological Succession in Hawaii*, Chicago: University of Chicago Press, 1938: 322–324.

61. This use of 'ohana has also been called 'ohana pule (family prayer), but in cultural practice Hawaiian families called it 'ohana.

62. Merry 2000: 12–13.

63. Else et al. 2007.

64. S. M. Kanaʻiaupuni, "Identity and diversity in contemporary Hawaiian families: *Hoʻi hou i ka iwi kuamoʻo*," *Hulili: Multidisciplinary Research on Hawaiian Well-Being* 1(1) (2004): 53–71; B. D. Debaryshe, S. Yuen, N. K. Nakamura, and I. Rodriguez Stern, "The roles of family obligation and parenting practices," *Explaining the Well-Being of Native Hawaiian Adolescents Living in Poverty* 3(1) (2006): 103–125.

65. Ka Haka 'Ula O Keʻelikōlani College of Hawaiian Language at UH Hilo in 1997 and Hawaiʻinuiākea, School of Hawaiian Knowledge at UH Manoa in 2007 were established.

66. Alu Like: *E Ola Mau Native Hawaiian Health Needs Study Report*, Honolulu, 1985.

67. R. K. Blaisdell, "Historical and cultural aspects of Native Hawaiian health," *Social Process in Hawaiʻi* 32 (1989): 1–21; M. A. Look, *A Mortality Study of the Hawaiian People*, Honolulu: Research and Statistics Office, State Department of Health Publication R&S Report, 38, 1982; K. L. Braun, M. A. Look, and J. U. Tsark, "High mortality rates in Native Hawaiians," *Hawaii Medical Journal* 54 (September 1995): 723–729; N. Andrade, E. S. Hishinuma, J. F. McDermott, R. C. Johnson, D. A. Goebert, et al., "The National Center on Indigenous Hawaiian Behavioral Health study of prevalence of psychiatric disorders in Native Hawaiian adolescents," *Journal of the American Academy of Child and Adolescent Psychiatry* 45 (2006): 26–36; I. Else, R.N., "The breakdown of the *kapu* system and its effect on Native Hawaiian health and diet," *Hulili: Multidisciplinary Research on Hawaiian Wellbeing*, 1(1) (2004): 241–255; Else et al. 2007.

68. H. K. Trask, "The birth of the modern Hawaiian movement: Kalama Valley, Oʻahu," *Hawaiian Journal of History* 21 (1987): 126–153; N. Milner, "Home, homelessness, and homeland in the Kalama Valley: Reimagining a Hawaiian nation through a property dispute," *Hawaiian Journal of History* 40 (2006):149–176.

69. McGregor, D. P. *Nā Kuaʻāina: Living Hawaiian Culture*. Honolulu: University of Hawaiʻi Press, 2007, pp. 249–285.

70. Thompson 2007.

71. U.S. Congress, *100th Anniversary of the Overthrow of the Hawaiian Kingdom*, Public Law 103–150, 103rd Congress, 1st session, 107 State 1510, S.J. Resolution 19, November 23, 1993.

72. MacKenzie 1991, chapter 4, "Self-Determination and Self-Governance": 77–104.

CHAPTER 2

The Euro-Americans

Kathryn Braun and Deborah Goebert

In this chapter, we examine Euro-Americans or Caucasians in Hawai'i, those individuals who can trace their ancestry to white Europeans, commonly known in the State of Hawai'i as haoles ("haole" has been pluralized in this text as "haoles" in keeping with English-language conventions; in the Hawaiian language, however, the plural of *haole* would be *hāole*). We begin with an exploration of the term "haole," followed by a brief history of haoles in Hawai'i. We then present some of the values common to white culture that influence haole behavior and are reflected in U.S. social policies. We then provide a demographic and mental health profile of haoles in Hawai'i and review some of the haole subgroups in the state. We conclude with the notion that the definition of "local" is changing and now can encompass those haoles who are aware of, understand, and appreciate all the peoples and cultures of Hawai'i.

What Is a Haole?

In Hawai'i, people often refer to each other by their ethnicity.[1] Although European-Americans represent scores of different cultural groups, they are seen in Hawai'i as a single ethnic group. For Hawai'i residents of white European descent, the term "European-American" is rarely used, nor is the term "white" (although this is the preferred term used in U.S. government reports). In Hawai'i, the term "Caucasian" is commonly used. However, "haole" has become a term that is closely linked with the history and challenges of the Islands, and henceforth it will be our term of reference in this chapter.

The word "haole" is not commonly found in the Hawaiian literature, but when used it appears to denote "foreign" or "strange"—for example, *'āina* haole (foreign land). Pukui and Elbert note that the term "haole" was used historically in reference to any foreigner (non-Hawaiian) in Hawai'i.[2] Although debatable because it is unsupported by the Hawaiian language, a folk etymology exists that has joined two words together to form the word *hā'ole*, literally meaning "without breath." In Hawaiian culture, a full greeting would include an oral exchange of genealogies, a *honi* (the touching of noses and/or foreheads), and the exchange of *hā* (breath or life).[3] When Captain Cook arrived, he stood silent. Thus he was seen as *'ole* (without) *hā*. Reed provides a contemporary definition of "haole" as a Hawaiian word used to designate "Caucasian."[4] Initially, haoles came from capitalist-industrial societies, and their European rules of commerce, governance, religion, education, and communication became dominant. In this context, immigrants from other societies (e.g., China, Japan, and the Philippines) were simply thought of as non-haole.[5] Trask defines "haole" as "white foreigner," indicating that the term has both racial and class connotations.[6]

Although haoles are thought of as an undifferentiated group in Hawai'i, there are some exceptions. For example, people of Portuguese descent in Hawai'i were exempted from the haole category because of their unique position as middle managers and *paniolo* (cowboys) in the plantation social structure under the white plantation bosses.[7] Other Caucasian groups that maintained a unique culture were Greeks, German-Americans on Maui, and those defined by the Jewish religion. References are made to haole subgroups, including the mainland haole (living on or coming from the continental United States), the local haole, the *kama'āina* (native born) haole, and the hapa haole.

Today, the dominant culture is difficult to determine in Hawai'i and depends on the situation and power relationships. Reed suggests that the dominant culture is somewhere along the continuum of "mainland" to "local." "Mainland" refers to the dominant American culture of predominantly European values and styles of interaction found in the continental United States.[8] "Local" refers to the common identity of people in Hawai'i that share lifestyle, behavior, values, and norms that developed from plantation culture characterized by waves of immigrants and shaped by labeling, categorization, and social evaluation.[9]

A Brief History of Haoles in Hawai'i

The first haoles in Hawai'i were explorers. In 1778, Captain James Cook became the first European to document the islands by name, which he spelled Owyhee, and publish their geographical coordinates. He renamed the archipelago the Sandwich Isles, after the Fourth Earl of Sandwich, one of his patrons.[10] Once charted, sailors and whalers visited Hawai'i to restock and establish trade. These visitors introduced a number of Western diseases to which the indigenous Hawaiians had no immunity, and the native population declined precipitously.[11]

Although Christian missionaries began arriving early after "discovery," the first wave of haole immigration is marked by the arrival of the Boston missionaries in 1820.[12] Hawaiian rulers allowed the missionaries to preach and came to rely on them for advice. The missionaries learned the Hawaiian language, then developed the Hawaiian alphabet and used it to translate the Bible into Hawaiian. They also established schools, attended by children of missionary families and *ali'i* (ruling-class Hawaiian families).

Despite protests from some *ali'i* factions, the missionaries integrated into Hawaiian society, while encouraging Hawaiian chiefs to emulate the European lifestyle. Assisted by various haole advisors, Kamehameha III issued a declaration of rights in 1839 and established a constitutional monarchy in 1840. There was pressure to change rules about land as well. Traditionally, all land belonged to the Hawaiian king, who could grant others the right to use it temporarily. The Mahele (land division) was enacted in 1848, which divided the land between the king, his chiefs, and the new government and cleared the way for foreigners to own land in Hawai'i.[13] The Mahele was proposed as a mechanism by which *maka'āinana* (commoners, or people who attend the land) could secure their own land. However, few *maka'āinana* were able to purchase land, and some chiefs lost land when they did not comply with the foreign system of land registration. Concurrently, children of missionary families married into *ali'i* families, giving them access to land, as well as power, in Hawai'i. This shift in power is summarized by two well-known, if apocryphal, sayings: "The [haole] missionaries came to Hawai'i to do good, and they did very well" and "When the [haole] missionaries came, they had the Bible and we had the land...now we have the Bible and they have the land." Nevertheless, intermarriage was a natural development and resulted from the inclusiveness of Hawaiians and the *ali'i* desire, which began with Kamehameha I, to reward haoles that had served them well.

In the following decades, commercial ties between Hawai'i and the United States increased. Haole-owned business enterprises continued to expand, especially into sugarcane and pineapple plantations, with Caucasians in ownership, supervisory, and management roles. Plantation managers imported laborers and, by the early twentieth century, more than 270,000 workers had arrived from China, Japan, Korea, the Philippines, and other countries. Eventually, five major corporations grew out of plantation companies: Castle & Cooke, Alexander & Baldwin, C. Brewer & Company, Amfac (initially Hackfeld & Company), and Theo H. Davies & Company. They became known as the Big Five and wielded considerable economic and political power.[14] During this time in Hawai'i, kama'āina culture evolved, referring to haoles born and raised in Hawai'i who reflected upper-middle-class, New England values and promoted colonialism.

The involvement of the U.S. military in Hawai'i dates back to 1826, when the USS Dolphin was sent to investigate and recover debts owed to American merchants by the ali'i.[15] In 1893, U.S. naval forces were positioned in front of Hawaiian government buildings and 'Iolani Palace in what President Grover Cleveland described as "an act of war, committed with the participation of a diplomatic representative of the United States and without authority of Congress," to support a group of haole missionary descendants and business and plantation owners who executed the illegal overthrow of Queen Lili'uokalani and the Hawaiian monarchy, leading to the annexation of the kingdom to the United States in 1898.[16] More members of the U.S. military arrived after annexation. The majority of servicemen were single Caucasians from working-class families, while the officers were from prominent U.S. families.

In September 1931, Hawai'i received national attention when Thalia Massie, white wife of a U.S. Navy officer, accused five "local" plantation workers of rape.[17] This is the first documented use of the term local to collectively categorize people from Hawai'i, encompassing two Hawaiians, two Japanese, and a Chinese-Hawaiian born and raised in the Islands. The evidence against the five men was not substantiated, and the jury could not reach a verdict. However, Mrs. Massie's husband and mother and two sailors took matters into their own hands, severely beating one of the accused and shooting and killing another, Joseph Kahahawai. This resulted in a second trial in which the white perpe-

trators were convicted. Outraged by the court's punishment, the territory's white leaders and the U.S. Congress signed a letter threatening
to impose martial law over the territory, and they pressured Governor
Lawrence M. Judd to reduce the sentences to an hour each. The case
illustrates how whites were culturally segregated from other groups
in Hawai'i and distinguished them as not only a privileged class but a
group that could get away with murder. The case also catalyzed a change
in the way locals and Caucasians in Hawai'i began to look at race privilege.[18] Indeed, it helped mobilize public opinion to move Hawai'i from
territorial status to the legal protections offered by statehood.[19]

By the 1940s, Caucasians represented 25 percent of the territory's
population. World War II marked a change in perception about the military across the United States and in Hawai'i, with increased support
for American values. World War II also brought a shift toward racial
equality and justice, as local nonhaole men who had enlisted to fight
in this war returned to pursue postsecondary education and professional careers. Some joined political movements against colonialism
and in support of civil rights.[20] Caucasian labor leaders—such as Jack
Hall, Robert McElrath, Dave Thompson, and the California-based head
of the International Longshore and Warehouse Union (ILWU) Harry
Bridges—came to Hawai'i to help develop the first multiethnic labor
union for plantation and dock workers. They represented some of the
first haoles to side with laborers against the Big Five, and many of them
married local women. The 79-day sugar strike of 1946 that shut down
thirty-three or thirty-four plantations and the 171-day dock strike of
1949 further broke down divisions among nonhaole ethnic groups and
forced haole management to humanize worker wages and benefits.[21]
Another haole, John A. Burns, helped build coalitions with organized
labor and Asian-Americans to strengthen the Democratic Party and
lobby for statehood.[22] Burns mobilized a force of men and women from
Hawaii's multicultural society, using principles from American law to
create an even playing field for all. He would become the state's first
elected governor.

Hawai'i became the fiftieth U.S. state in 1959. Statehood attracted
majority support among all ethnic groups. Today, however, several
Hawaiian organizations criticize the legitimacy of the vote.[23] With
statehood, increasing numbers of Caucasians migrated to the Islands,
known as malihini (newcomers or transplants). Many were attracted to
the Islands by their beauty and temperate climate. Others came for new
professional opportunities that accompanied statehood, including the

expansion of federal and state government. Commercial air travel eased the strain of relocating to an island 2,500 miles from the continental United States. Like other migrants, these haoles missed home and family, but those who established local ties and social contacts integrated into the local communities.

Beginning in the 1960s, Caucasian surfers, hippies, and others seeking an alternative lifestyle began relocating in Hawai'i. By the 1980s, young adults outnumbered professional Caucasians moving from the continental United States, and the percentage of Hawai'i residents born outside of the state increased from 31 percent in 1970 to 41 percent in 1990.[24] Many haoles in this wave of immigration questioned traditional European-American values, supported the Hawaiian renaissance, and helped expand an acceptance of lifestyles and ecological consciousness in Hawai'i.

On the other hand, newcomers seeking alternative lifestyles had a tremendous impact on social systems, as they tapped into legal, welfare, health, and psychiatric services. An illustration of this extreme is Taylor Camp, established in 1969 when Howard Taylor, brother of actress Elizabeth Taylor, bailed out thirteen hippie vagrants and invited them to camp on his oceanfront land in Hā'ena, Kaua'i.[25] This "pot-friendly, clothing optional, tree-house village" became home to a diverse group of people, from California surfers to Vietnam veterans who had undergone intense psychological suffering. The inhabitants were bonded by a desire to live their version of a hassle-free life, hoping to be transformed and healed by their experiences together as a community. However, local residents claimed that the lack of sanitation polluted surrounding waters, resulting in the disappearance of mullet and other fish. The camp was condemned and burned down by the state in 1977. The legacy of this movement is evident today, especially in rural areas where the hippie communes were located, through organic farming that perpetuates the value of caring for the earth.

In the last couple decades, increasing numbers of Caucasians born in Hawai'i have relocated to the continental United States in search of education, employment, and affordable housing. From 1995 to 2000, domestic in-migration to Hawai'i was 108 per 1,000 residents while domestic out-migration and was 173 per 1,000 residents, with the highest percentages moving to and from California, Texas, and Washington.[26] The *Hawai'i Data Book* figures show a gradual rise in the average age of Hawai'i's citizens, in part due to the fact that young people of all ethnicities are leaving Hawai'i.[27]

Ethnocultural Identity

In the continental United States, many white Americans do not see their own culture and do not describe their identity in ethnic terms.[28] Understandably, people do not need to define or question their culture until they encounter a contrasting culture.[29] Although the United States is far from homogenous, in the past its social policies and behavioral norms have been set, for the most part, by the dominant culture of white people from Europe who came to the new world in search of personal freedom.[30]

In this section, we attempt to articulate some of the values and beliefs of European-American culture, which we believe underlie social policies in Hawai'i as a U.S. state.[31] Cultural values can be defined as universal statements about what we find attractive and correct, and they reflect relational style, person-nature relationships, beliefs about human nature, and time orientation.[32] Explorations of the values and beliefs associated with European-Americans can be found in literature on cross-cultural communication, intercultural understanding, and cross-cultural counseling.[33]

Findings from the literature were supplemented by interviews of Hawai'i-based informants with expertise on European-American and/or haole culture.

INDEPENDENCE AND AUTONOMY

Traditionally referred to as "rugged individualists," European-Americans tend to see the individual as the primary unit of society with responsibility for him/herself. There is an expectation that people shape their own destiny and solve their own problems. Personal achievement and success are believed to stem from character and hard work, less so than from the environment or the socioeconomic system.[34]

European-Americans value independence and autonomy, and U.S. culture promotes and rewards behaviors that reflect individual control and responsibility. These values underlie the U.S. Declaration of Independence, the Bill of Rights, and a number of health-related policies. For example, physicians and researchers must seek permission directly from an individual for his/her participation in medical care and research, and the individual is expected to make these decisions for him/herself after considering the risks and benefits.[35] Individual adults must sign their own contracts and consent forms, or they must have completed legal documents that authorize others to sign for them. Even in regard to decisions about starting, continuing, or withdrawing life-sustaining care, expectations outlined in an individual's advance directive (even if it was executed decades in the past) legally trump treatment preferences of family members and care providers.[36]

In Hawai'i, some physicians recognize cultural differences in decision-making preferences and adjust their approach accordingly. Findings from a study at the Rehabilitation Hospital of the Pacific suggested the doctors would give medical news directly to elderly Caucasian patients, but may ask Asian, Filipino, or Pacific Islander families who in the health care team should talk to them about the elder's care status and future care plans.[37] Other investigators also have found that Asians and Hispanics are more likely to prefer family-centered decision making than European-Americans.[38]

An individualistic orientation supports and rewards ambition, competition, freedom of action, and self-expression. Emphasis on individual achievement begins in childhood. Caucasian students are often encouraged to "speak up" and "stand out." Hawai'i teachers have described Caucasian girls as "perky" and boys as "assertive" and think both are likely to go to college.[39] This tendency to promote oneself in school contrasts with the Japanese saying, "The nail that sticks up gets hammered down" (discouraging the emphasis of the individual over group harmony) and with the Hawaiian way of learning that emphasized watching, listening, trying, and then teaching.[40] These values, when exaggerated, become stereotypes. Thus, haoles may sometimes be seen by non-Caucasians as loud, arrogant, and self-centered. An individualistic orientation also supports the individual accumulation of personal wealth without real obligation for sharing it beyond the nuclear family. Ironically, perhaps, it is American foreign aid and individual philanthropy that lead the world.[41]

WORK, ACTIVITY, AND ACTION

European-American culture places great value in action and activity, as opposed to passivity and contemplation. Many Americans feel there is always something they can "do" about a situation. The value of hard work is often referred to as the "Protestant work ethic."[42] Because Americans are expected to work and to value work, U.S. unemployment and social assistance benefits are time-limited and require recipients to show proof that they are in search of employment.

The belief that hard work begets success is the foundation of the American dream—that is, that any child born in America can grow up to be president, regardless of parentage and social status, or that an immigrant who arrives in the United States with nothing can become a millionaire through hard work and perseverance. This orientation contrasts with societies that tend to sort people into categories at birth (e.g., India, through its caste system) or during adolescence based on academic performance (e.g., France, where only students passing the *baccalauréat* examination can attend university).[43]

Many European-Americans have great faith in science and scientific reasoning. The culture admires logic, linear thinking, and cause and effect.[44] Medical professionals assess patients to identify their constellation of symptoms and then match it against criteria outlined for each known disease, and these criteria are objective, measurable, and tangible.[45] This contrasts with cultures that may attribute some (but of course not all) illnesses to being out of balance internally (e.g., Chinese, Korean) or with God, nature, spirits, or other people (e.g., Filipino, Hawaiian, Samoan).[46] The individualist and scientific perspective has also supported the view of the planet as something to be mastered, though this has given way today to the modern environmental movement,[47] and in Hawai'i, the idea that humans must live in harmony with God and nature, as suggested in the Hawai'i state motto, *Ua mau ke ea o ka 'āina i ka pono* ("The life of the land is perpetuated in righteousness").[48]

NUCLEAR FAMILIES

It is in the European-American tradition to choose one's own friends and to marry whomever one pleases. Despite the recent expansion of relational options through same-sex unions, divorce/remarriage, childlessness, surrogacy, and adoption, many European-Americans still tend to restrict their definition of family to nuclear and blood-related family. Parents are responsible for their children, and other adults are reluctant (or reminded not) to butt in. This is in contrast to societies in which social norms dictate that children show respect to older adults regardless of their relationship to the child. It is a Hawaiian "kinship" custom that any older adult may be introduced to a child as "auntie" or "uncle," signifying to the child that the adult is a friend of the family and someone to whom they should show respect. This free use of the terms *auntie* and *uncle*, however, may cause confusion among young people who relocate to Hawai'i from the continental United States, where the terms *aunt* and *uncle* are reserved for one's parents' siblings.[49]

Compared to other ethnic groups, European-Americans tend to

score lower on measures of familism, the name given to the particular importance placed on close family relationships. In fact, European-
Americans may appear detached from their extended families. This
contrasts with most locals in Hawai'i whose families have lived in the
Islands for generations and who know their first, second, third, and
fourth cousins. Also serving to extend local families are the Hawaiian
practice of *hānai* (informal adoption of children into another family)
and the labeling of close friends and neighbors as "calabash cousins."[50]

The European-American value of the primacy of the nuclear family also is supported by U.S. health care policies. For example, Social
Security was developed to support retirees so that their adult children
would be free to work and to relocate for work. Medicare and Medicaid,
insurance programs that pay for acute and long-term care, help keep
young and middle-aged adults in the workforce, rather than home caring for parents and grandparents.

The stereotyped notion that European-Americans do not care for
their parents and grandparents is widespread in Asia. This perception
may stem from their views that haoles do not observe a long period
of mourning for deceased parents and grandparents (in contrast to the
Asian cultural observance of forty-nine days), and that European-Americans appear willing to have parents cared for by strangers in nursing
homes. Although family members meet the bulk of long-term care
needs of older Americans, caregiving for some European-Americans
may become burdensome because it hinders their ability to work.[51]

EGALITARIAN RELATIONSHIPS

European-Americans prefer relationships to be informal and egalitarian as opposed to formal and hierarchical, or they feel that hierarchy
should be based on achievement rather than on birthright, birth order,
or gender.[52] They are quick to call people by their first names, rather
than using titles or honorifics, in contrast with many Asian cultures.[53]
Japanese, for example, offers various honorifics that can be used to
denote respect, including *sensei* (added to the last names of teachers,
doctors, politicians, and other authority figures) and *sama* (used when
addressing people of higher in rank than oneself). American English
does not offer different forms for the word "you" in addressing people
of higher or lower status or of a different generation, in contrast to many
European languages.[54] Confucian-based cultures have rules about family hierarchy as well, with authority seated with the oldest male and
oldest sons responsible to care for parents and the family ancestors.

In Hawai'i, it's not uncommon to hear Japanese, Chinese, and Korean women say that they would rather marry a haole than a firstborn son of Japanese, Chinese, or Korean ancestry, because of potentially greater leeway in defining family relationships.

Although the founders of the United States spoke to equality in their documents and speeches, this equality was conceptualized initially for Euro-Caucasian, Christian, male landowners. Consequently, European culture has long been patriarchal, and male preference is often still evident.[55] Workforce studies show that men, on average, earn more than women in similar occupations, and women are still underrepresented in seniormost jobs. Similarly, European-Americans are more likely to hold leadership roles than other ethnic groups in most settings. Yet most European-Americans hold equality in relationships as the ideal and feel that they should approach everyone in the same manner—directly and with good eye contact and a firm handshake.

European-Americans today may be seen as a homogenous group. But, European-Americans are born of individuals from diverse regions of Europe, and these regions have different cultures and a long history of interallegiances and disagreements. Documentation of discrimination among European-American subgroups extends across the twentieth century. In the 1940s, it was not unusual for a son to be disowned by his German Lutheran family for marrying an Irish Catholic, and vice versa. Some white European immigrants to the United States—notably Jews, Germans, Poles, and Irish—have changed their names to mask their ancestry and thus reduce their exposure to intra-Caucasian prejudice.[56] But today, more and more white European-Americans tend to be unprejudiced toward groups that are different, and are becoming "colorblind."[57]

As individualists, European-Americans typically believe that each individual's opinion is weighted equally. Every American can vote, and the simple majority rules. Someone wins, and someone loses. This is in contrast to societies that use consensual decision making in order to preserve group harmony, like Japan, where leaders try to facilitate listening and compromise until a solution is reached that all can live with.[58] Several European countries require the formation of coalition governments, comprised of members of opposing parties, when an election does not lead to a clear victory for one side.[59]

TIME AND SPACE

In line with industrialization and notions of control, Caucasian-dominated U.S. society has become very time oriented.[60] Appointments are scheduled and individuals are expected to be on time. In contrast, many agricultural societies work according to timelines set by nature and weather.[61] Some new immigrants to Hawai'i are unaccustomed to the rigors of Western time constraints and may frustrate health workers by coming late to appointments. While European-Americans are watching the clock, there are many opportunities to disconnect from the environment.[62] Temperatures are controlled, and stores carry produce that is out of season. Although the ability to delay gratification is admired, in actuality there are few requirements to do so, as everything is at our fingertips. Thus, patience, which is seen as a virtue in many cultures, may seem less so in white, European-American culture.[63]

Demographic and Health Characteristics of Haoles in Hawai'i

DEMOGRAPHICS

According to the 2007 U.S. Census estimates, there were 1,283,388 people living in Hawai'i.[64] Of those people, one in four (almost 25 percent) were non-Hispanic Caucasians. Overall, the Caucasian population has declined as a proportion of the total population since 1990, from outmigration as noted above and from the addition of "mixed ethnicity" as a reporting category in 1996. More than 18 percent of the population identified themselves as belonging to two or more races, compared to 1.5 percent of the entire U.S. population. In Hawai'i, 15 percent of residents reported being part-Caucasian. Many factors have contributed to the high rates of interethnic marriage in Hawai'i, including the lack of an ethnic majority in the state and a lack of stigma.[65] About half of all marriages in Hawai'i are interethnic.[66]

Per the 2000 census, Hawai'i has the largest percentage of its population in the military among the states. The military-connected population in Hawai'i totals 217,030 (17 percent of the state's total population). This includes active duty, reserve, National Guard, and retired military personnel and their dependents. In 2006, Hawai'i ranked fourteenth in the nation for the number of active-duty army recruits per thousand youth ages fifteen through twenty-four, and Honolulu was ranked twenty-second out of the top hundred U.S. counties for the number of active-duty army recruits.[67] It is estimated that 60–70 percent of the military-related population in Hawai'i is Caucasian, with a higher percentage among the officer ranks.

HEALTH AND SOCIOECONOMIC STATUS

Caucasians are used as the reference population in the United States against which other ethnicities are compared because, for the most part, health and longevity indicators are best for the Caucasian group. However, this is not the case in Hawai'i. Based on life tables from 2000, Chinese, Japanese, Koreans, and Filipinos in Hawai'i all boast longer life expectancies than Caucasians, by 7.1 years, 3.8 years, 2.4 years, and 1.9 years respectively.[68] The Chinese and Japanese groups also have lower birthrates in Hawai'i than Caucasians.

U.S. Census data from 2000, reported by racial (rather than ethnic) categories, suggest that whites in Hawai'i have lower median household incomes and lower rates of home ownership (48 percent vs. 70 percent) than Asians in Hawai'i.[69] This is surprising, given that 71 percent of Caucasians in Hawai'i report some postsecondary education, versus only 53 percent of Asians. Behavioral health data from 2008 suggest that significantly more Caucasians than Japanese are obese (21 percent vs. 16 percent), are limited by health problems (22 percent vs. 14 percent), complain of poor mental health (34 percent vs. 25 percent), do not have health insurance (7 percent vs. 3 percent), and cannot see a doctor because of cost (7 percent vs. 3 percent).[70]

Caucasians make up large numbers of homeless and people on welfare in Hawai'i.[71] Although homelessness is not a new problem, the rising number of homeless people—estimated to have increased approximately 39 percent in Hawai'i from 1999 to 2009—is noteworthy. Of the thirteen thousand people who were homeless in Hawai'i in 2004, 35 percent were Hawaiian/part-Hawaiian, 29 percent were Caucasian, 11 percent were other Pacific Islanders, and 26 percent were of other or unknown ethnicities. Caucasians appear be overrepresented in the sex trade.[72] The "average" street prostitute is Caucasian, born in Hawai'i, high school educated, about 29 years old, and either male or female.[73]

MENTAL HEALTH

Common mental health problems associated with European-Americans are depression, substance abuse, and eating disorders. Depression is a common side effect of a perfectionist, high-expectation view of oneself. If Caucasians are rewarded for being busy and successful, they can easily be disappointed if they fail to meet expectations (whether explicit or internal). A study of 2006 depression and anxiety suggests that whites have a significantly higher lifetime prevalence of anxiety than Japanese and are more likely than Hawaiian, Chinese, Filipino, or

Japanese in Hawai'i to report having had depression sometime in their lives.[74] Interestingly, Caucasians do not have the highest prevalence of current depression, suggesting that they may seek out mental health services when depression occurs. Leach suggests tapping into Judeo-Christian beliefs in the afterlife when treating depressed elderly of European descent by asking, "What happens to you after you've died?" and "What are your family's views?"[75]

Studies have shown that a greater proportion of Caucasians drink alcohol and consume larger quantities of alcohol than Asians living in the same community.[76] Wood reported that Caucasians were most likely to be the heavy users of drugs, and they had the lowest proportion of nonusers.[77] Alcohol and drug use patterns can be influenced by social and cultural factors such as ethnic group norms and attitudes regarding substance use and the extent of their acculturation into American society. For example, a group's norms refer to how one should behave in relation to alcohol—such as beliefs about how much drinking is appropriate for a parent in the presence of small children, for a man at a bar with friends, or for someone at a party at another person's home.[78]

In Hawai'i, eating disorders and disordered-eating attitudes are highest in haole women and lowest in haole men compared to other ethnic-gender groups.[79] Furthermore, haole women were more likely than other women to eat in response to anger and anxiety. The prevalence of eating disorders has increased in the military, where results from fitness and weight tests are considered in promotion decisions.

Per a 2004 report, Caucasians had the highest overall rates of suicide among the state's major ethnic groups: 63 per 100,000, compared to 60 per 100,000 among Native Hawaiians and 49 per 100,000 among Japanese.[80] Rates of suicide among Caucasians increase steadily across the age range, from 44 per 100,000 in the 20–34 age group to 101 per 100,000 in the 65+ age group. Older suicide victims are more likely to have had a history of mental illness, particularly mood disorders. They also are coping with losses associated with aging, such as reduced financial resources, widowhood, and poor health and the depression triggered by these losses. European-American men may view suicide as an act of independence and courage in the face of adversity.[81]

Haole Subgroups Today

HAOLE NEWCOMERS

To newcomers, Hawai'i may be their first exposure to a community in which people from so many different cultures live, work, and create families together. Newcomers may have problems understanding pidgin (Hawai'i creole) or may cause others to raise eyebrows when they try to speak it. Common pidgin words learned early upon arrival include *howzit* (hello, how are you), *k-den* (all right), *try wait* (one moment, don't rush), *bumbye* (later), and *get 'em* (I have it covered, it's under control). Astute haoles also will pick up and use a few key words from the Hawaiian language, such as *mahalo* (thanks), *'ono* (delicious), *akamai* (clever), and *pau* (finished) and learn to give directions using *mauka* (toward the mountains) and *makai* (toward the sea).[82]

When you get invited to dinner, it is likely that your host's extended family will be there too, and that you will be asked or expected to bring food and beverages to contribute to the dinner.[83] Many individuals are of mixed ethnicity, especially Native Hawaiians, and newcomers may be shocked to hear people being teased with "that's so haole of you" or "you act so *pake* (Chinese)" or to hear locals attributing certain behaviors to their "Hawaiian side" versus their "Japanese side." Within Hawai'i, rituals from various cultures are observed by many, and it is quite acceptable for haoles to celebrate Girls' Day (from Japanese culture), Makahiki (a harvest celebration, from Hawaiian culture), and Chinese New Year, in addition to holidays such as Thanksgiving and Independence Day from American culture.

Haole newcomers in Hawai'i may perceive a loss of centrality and status, as they are now members of a group (Caucasian) that does not comprise the majority of the population. Some may feel confused because they do not understand local pidgin and local culture. Haole newcomers that migrate by themselves, perhaps for school or with the military, or who come only with nuclear family, may feel isolated. Raised to be self-reliant, they may not establish good support networks, which could lead to further isolation. Some may become disheartened after hearing stories about "kill haole day" or being addressed by the moniker "haole" preceded by "damn" or worse.[84] Others may claim "rock fever," a sense of confinement on a small island and in a multicultural community in which everyone seems to know everyone.[85]

On the continental United States, one can find many neighborhoods and schools that are predominantly white, and within these communities, whites are not that aware of their own culture.[86] When haoles come to Hawai'i, they are exposed to other ways of thinking and seeing, and they may begin to view themselves in relationship to other, different cultures. Whereas they may have been rewarded for asserting their individuality and expressing their opinions in continental communities, they may be stereotyped as aggressive, opinionated, atten-tion-seeking, and power-hungry in local communities. Frank DeLima, a local comedian whose humor pokes fun at each of Hawaii's ethnic groups (see chapter 4, "The Portuguese"), mocks haoles this way: "They talk too fast and laugh too loud. They embarrass you when you're in a crowd."[87] Haoles in Hawai'i who have difficulty adjusting to the local low-key lifestyle may choose to return to the continental United States.

KAMA'ĀINA TODAY

Kama'āina literally translates as child *(kama)* of the land *('āina)* and refers to those born and raised in Hawai'i or native to a particular place in the Islands.[88] The first white *kama'āina* were primarily descen-dants of the early haole families that brought New England missionary values to Hawai'i.[89] Prominent *kama'āina* families advised the Hawai-ian kings, influenced Island politics, acquired land, and established businesses. Although this group supported colonialist views, many *kama'āina* families had close associations by marriage with Hawaiian families and played a significant role in preserving Hawaiian tradi-tions and artifacts.[90] The Daughters of Hawai'i was founded in 1903 by daughters of the early missionaries to perpetuate the memory and spirit of old Hawai'i and to preserve the Hawaiian language.[91] Today they maintain and operate the Queen Emma Summer Palace and Hulihe'e Palace.

To older generations in Hawai'i, the *kama'āina* names still evoke a sense of elitism, akin to the Kennedy and Rockefeller clans, but also a sense of altruism. For example, families such as the Castles, Athertons, and Wilcoxes accumulated substantial wealth and eventually estab-lished several of the earliest charitable foundations to support public education in Hawai'i. Although some *kama'āina* still hold political and economic power, the high status of *kama'āina* changed after World War II.[92] The GI Bill of Rights (officially titled Servicemen's Readjust-ment Act of 1944) leveled the playing field by providing college or voca-tional education for returning World War II veterans of all ethnicities, enabling them to complete college and become leaders in Hawai'i (a good example of this is Senator Daniel Inouye). However, the change was not immediate. It wasn't until the mid-twentieth century that all country and city clubs were admitting Asians.[93]

The word *kama'āina* still serves to describe haoles who have lived in the Islands for generations and for the most part is viewed as a pres-tigious title, especially to newcomers, or malihini. Newcomers may believe that they can achieve *kama'āina* status, until they learn the history of the title and realize that they will never meet the strict criteria. Today, not all *kama'āina* represent the political and economic elite, and the term has evolved to include haoles who have a meaningful connection to Hawai'i as an ancestral home.

GROWING UP HAOLE IN HAWAI'I

In his play "Haole Boy" and its sequel, "Haole Boy 2—Haole-er Than Thou," actor Mark Pinkosh (a.k.a. Haole Boy and high school classmate of second author) relates his experiences as a boy raised outside of Hawai'i in a predominantly haole neighborhood who moves with his family to Hawai'i.[94] His first exposure to racial prejudice as a newly arrived third-grader was when a Japanese girl ran up to him, called him a "f***ing haole," spat at him, and ran away. Pinkosh tells of the many times that he was judged solely by his skin color, although sometimes he was able to use this to his advantage. Importantly, the experience of being haole in Hawai'i was only a small part of his story. While Pinkosh was able to compartmentalize his haole experiences, others he went to school with were not as successful. In seeking to belong, they would take on a bully role, displaying strong feelings of hatred for all groups. On "kill haole day," a day that entailed picking on and, in some schools, beating up haoles, these bully haoles joined in the fray.

HAPA HAOLE TODAY

The term *hapa haole* is used today to designate someone who is part-Caucasian and part-Asian and/or Pacific Islander. Root suggests that the adoption of a mixed-race reference group is an indication of a healthy mixed-race identity.[95] Linnekin contends that hapa haoles are more readily accepted in Hawai'i because they are family or close friends and because they fulfill the Hawaiian expectations of those relationships.[96]

MILITARY TODAY

The military and its leadership in Hawai'i remain predominantly haole. Given the large number of military in Hawai'i and its significant contributions to the state's economy, it is important to examine how the military is evolving. Dunivan describes the paradigm shift between two cultural models, the traditional military and the evolving military.[97] The traditional military model was characterized by social conservatism; masculine white, heterosexual, Christian values and norms; and exclusionary laws and practices. They lived in enclaves with their own schools, stores, and medical services and socialized in clubs based on rank (e.g., the officer's club vs. the noncommissioned officer's club). Military families were expected to be supportive and do nothing to embarrass dad and reduce his chances for promotion.

Membership in the military still comes with uniforms, identification cards, short haircuts, salutes, and military-specific acronyms and phrases. However, the military is evolving into a socially heterogeneous force, with increasing numbers and proportions of minorities and women in uniform. Several branches of the military now have "all-rank" clubs, which can be frequented by members regardless of rank. Since the 1960s, the military has supplemented the incomes of some members so they can live off base, and most military children attend public schools (which are infused with federal dollars to defray costs). Many bases operate family support centers and counseling services to help families, especially those with parents deployed to war zones.

With so many military in Hawai'i, several subgroups exist, including residents that have joined the military or the reserves, military newcomers, and military retirees. Each has a different perspective, experience, and culture. Residents that have joined the military and are stationed in the Islands or those in the reserves struggle to balance their military and family obligations. Upon arrival, many receive materials touting Hawai'i as paradise.[98] They have experiences similar to other haole newcomers; however, they do not have the option to relocate. Confrontations between the military and local populations are not common, but when they occur they are highly publicized. These may be fueled by a resentment fostered by the military's occupation of land in Hawai'i, including Makua Valley on O'ahu and the sixty-year use of the island of Kaho'olawe for bombing practice.[99]

A New Ethnocultural Identity: The Local Haole

Contemporary culture in Hawai'i is rooted in the blending of diverse cultures. For generations, this was an inadvertent outcome brought on by European-American colonialism and Hawaiian cultural acceptance. Over the years, immigrants integrated into the labor force with indigenous Hawaiians and began to reposition Eurocentric culture away from the center. A local culture emerged that is different from

U.S. mainland culture and continues to evolve as new cultural groups integrate into the mix.

In Hawai'i, the definition of "local" has changed over the years, and today fewer people contend that haoles can never be locals. Localness is determined less by the way an individual looks and more by the embodiment of local style (the understanding and expression of cultural values) and how he/she is connected. In Hawai'i, the latter is often done by asking the question, "What school you went?" Referring to high school, this question is used to distinguish those who grew up in Hawai'i from those who did not.[100] *Akamai* (astute) haoles that did not attend high school in the Islands know to establish connections in new groups by identifying local friends that they may have in common. Haoles that can function well socially within the local culture usually are accepted.

Reed illustrates this with an example of a local second-generation Filipino teacher working on the island of Kaua'i. He quotes this teacher as saying, "There are 'haoles' and there are 'haole haoles.' I got good haole friends, but you don't wanna be around a haole haole."[101] A distinction is made between *haole* as a neutral racial designation and *haole* as a derogatory term. In another vignette, Reed quotes another interviewee, Dora, who begins her discussion by expressing shame at having a haole boyfriend but describes this one as different. "He was Local haole and he understood my language and my history and my home. He was in some ways more 'Local' than I'll ever be. He attended a public high school, and later Windward Community College, the University of Hawai'i and Kapi'olani Community College. He was an artist who could express Hawai'i in more creative ways than I could ever do. He was an avid surfer, hiker and free diver."[102] She is able to draw on a wider definition of local identity by explaining how her boyfriend is connected to Hawai'i. It is indicative of local Hawai'i culture that such explanations are acceptable.

The term "local haole" suggests that, even though a person is white, he/she is aware of, understands, and appreciates Hawai'i. For example, he/she enjoys local foods, honors local customs, has befriended local people, and appreciates the ocean and the land. In a study by Engel, 128 University of Hawai'i students were surveyed on what being local means to them.[103] Nearly all students mentioned some kind of cultural criteria, while only about half mentioned being born or raised in Hawai'i. As one respondent described it, "Being Local is more than just being born and raised in Hawai'i, more than just knowing all the cool

Local spots, or knowing how to speak pidgin; it is claiming a responsibility to/for this place—to the land and *all* of its peoples."[104] Although the definition implies that there are no racial and ethnic boundaries to localism, one student suggested that it is easiest to consider Hawaiians local, then Asians, and then whites.

Clearly, being local is more than being born and raised in Hawai'i. It no longer just represents the working class. At the heart of local identity are values such as prioritizing and respecting family and knowing and respecting the diverse cultures that make up Hawai'i.[105] It is living together harmoniously and welcoming others to the Islands.

Summary and Conclusion

In this chapter, we examined the history and ethnocultural evolution of European-Americans or haoles in Hawai'i, beginning with the evolution of the term *haole*. This was followed with a demographic and health profile of haoles in Hawai'i and a review of some of the haole subgroups in the state.

Haoles are one of the largest ethnocultural groups in Hawai'i, with increasing numbers of hapa haoles. However, they do not represent the dominant culture. Haole newcomers to Hawai'i often are seeking a pluralistic community that goes beyond tolerance to acceptance. A growing number of haoles are born and raised in the Islands without traditional *kama'aina* ties. The Hawaiian ethnocultural values that once permitted the first haoles to impose their New England values upon the people of Hawai'i are now leading to their integration into local culture. The definition of local is changing, and an opening for haoles has been made. It now includes all those who are aware of, understand, and appreciate all the peoples and cultures of Hawai'i.

Further Reading

Benham, M. K. P. *Culture and Educational Policy in Hawai'i: The Silencing of Native Voices*. Mahwah, NJ: L. Erlbaum Associates, 1998.
Edles, L. K. "Rethinking 'race,' 'ethnicity' and 'culture': Is Hawai'i the 'model minority' state?" *Ethnic and Racial Studies* 27 (2004): 37–68.
Giordano, J., and M. McGoldrick. "European families: An overview." In *Ethnicity and Family Therapy*, 2nd ed., ed. Monica McGoldrick, Joe Giordano, and John K. Pearce. New York: Guilford Press, 1996: 427–441.
Katz, J. H. "The sociopolitical nature of counseling." *Counseling Psychologist*

13 (1985): 615–624. http://tep.uoregon.edu/workshops/teachdiversity/ beingwhite/whiteculture.html.

Myers, C. A., D. C. M. Meehan, and C. Negy. "Caucasian Americans: The Forging of an Identity and Culture." In *Cross-Cultural Psychotherapy: Toward a Critical Understanding of Diverse Clients*, ed. C. Negy. Reno, NV: Bent Tree Press, 2004: 187–204.

Reed, G. G. "Fastening and unfastening identities: Negotiating identity in Hawai'i." *Discourse: Studies in the Cultural Politics of Education* 22 (2001): 327–339.

Smith, P. B., and M. H. Bond. *Social Psychology Across Cultures: Analysis and Perspectives*. London: Allyn & Bacon, 1994.

Sue, D. W. "Whiteness and ethnocentric monoculturalism: Making the 'invisible' visible." *American Psychologist* 59 (2004): 761–769.

Warren, A. "The haoles." In *Cross-Cultural Caring: A Handbook for Health Care Professionals in Hawai'i*, ed. N. Palafox and A. Warren. Honolulu: John A. Burns School of Medicine, 1980: 51–60.

Notes

1. G. G. Reed, "Fastening and unfastening identities: Negotiating identity in Hawai'i," *Discourse: Studies in the Cultural Politics of Education* 22 (2001): 327–339.

2. M. K. Pukui and S. H. Elbert, *Hawaiian Dictionary*, Honolulu: University of Hawai'i Press, 1986. Hawaiian Dictionaries Online, http://www .wehewehe.org/, retrieved May 26, 2009.

3. Ibid.

4. Reed 2001.

5. L. K. Edles, "Rethinking 'race,' 'ethnicity' and 'culture': Is Hawai'i the 'model minority' state?" *Ethnic and Racial Studies* 27 (2004): 37–68.

6. H. K. Trask, "Settlers of color and immigrant hegemony: 'Locals' in Hawai'i," *Amerasia Journal* 26 (2000): 1–24.

7. J. A. Gerschwender, R. Carroll-Seguin, and H. Brill, "The Portuguese and haoles of Hawai'i: Implications for the origin of ethnicity," *American Sociological Review* 53 (1988): 515–527.

8. Pukui and Elbert 1986.

9. J. Okamura, "Aloha kakaka me ke aloha 'aina: Local culture and society in Hawai'i," *Impulse* (spring 1981): 54–56; J. Okamura, "Why there are no Asian Americans in Hawai'i: The continuing significance of Local identity," *Social Process in Hawai'i* 35 (1994): 161–178.

10. M. Haas, "A brief history," in *Multicultural Hawai'i: The fabric of a multiethnic society*, ed. M. Haas, New York: Garland, 1998: 23–52.

11. D. Stannard, *Before the Horror: The Population of Hawai'i on the Eve of Western Contact*, Honolulu: University of Hawai'i Social Science Research

Institute, 1989; H. K. Trask, *From a Native Daughter: Colonialism and Sovereignty in Hawai'i*, Monroe, ME: Common Courage Press, 1993.

12. R. S. Kuykendall, *The Hawaiian Kingdom [Vol. 1] 1778–1854: Foundation and Transformation*, Honolulu: University of Hawai'i Press, 1938.

13. Ibid.

14. G. Cooper and G. Daws, *Land and Power in Hawai'i*, Honolulu: Benchmark Books, 1985.

15. B. Ireland, *Sugar-Coated Fortress: Representations of the U.S. Military in Hawai'i*, retrieved March 6, 2009, from Dissertations & Theses: Full Text Database, 2004.

16. U.S. Public Law 103-150, "Joint Resolution: To acknowledge the 100th anniversary of the January 17, 1893 overthrow of the Kingdom of Hawai'i, and to offer an apology to Native Hawaiians on behalf of the United States for the overthrow of the Kingdom of Hawai'i," http://frwebgate.access.gpo.gov/cgi-bin/getdoc.cgi?dbname=103_cong_bills&docid=f:sj19enr.txt.pdf, retrieved September 28, 2010.

17. J. F. McDermott, W. S. Tseng, and T. W. Maretzki, *People and Cultures of Hawai'i*, Honolulu: University of Hawai'i Press, 1980.

18. Ibid.

19. Stannard, D., *Honor Killing*, New York: Penguin Books, 2005: 401–423.

20. University of Hawai'i: West O'ahu Center for Labor Education & Research, "Hawai'i labor history," http://clear.uhwo.hawaii.edu/, retrieved May 26, 2009.

21. Ibid.

22. Cooper and Daws 1985.

23. Trask 1993.

24. L. Leong, "Hawai'i's brain drain," Special Edition, starbulletin.com (March 24, 1999), http://archives.starbulletin.com/specials/braindrain.html, retrieved April 4, 2009.

25. "Taylor Camp: Living the '60s Dream," (film) R. Stone, director, http://www.taylorcampkauai.com/, retrieved May 26, 2009.

26. State of Hawai'i, Office of State Planning, "Hawai'i in-migration and out-migration 1995–2000" (2000), http://state.hi.us/dbedt/gis/maps/migration_1995-2000.pdf, retrieved April 4, 2009.

27. State of Hawai'i, Office of Business, Economic Development, and Tourism, *State of Hawai'i Data Book* (2000–2008), http://hawaii.gov/dbedt/info/economic/databook/, Retrieved April 4, 2009.

28. J. H. Katz, "The sociopolitical nature of counseling," *Counseling Psychologist* 13 (1985):615–624, http://tep.uoregon.edu/workshops/teachdiversity/beingwhite/whiteculture.html; C. A. Myers, D. C. M. Meehan, and C. Negy, "Caucasian Americans: The forging of an identity and culture," in *Cross-Cultural Psychotherapy: Toward a Critical Understanding*

of Diverse Clients, ed. Charles Negy, Reno, NV: Bent Tree Press, 2004: 187–204; E. C. Stewart, *American Cultural Patterns: A Cross-Cultural Perspective*, Pittsburgh: Regional Council for International Education, University of Pittsburgh, 1972; J. Giordano and M. McGoldrick, "European families: An overview," in *Ethnicity and Family Therapy*, 2nd ed., ed. Monica McGoldrick, Joe Giordano, and John K. Pearce, New York: Guilford Press, 1996: 427–441; P. B. Smith and M. H. Bond, *Social Psychology Across Cultures: Analysis and Perspectives*, London: Allyn & Bacon, 1994; D. Sue and S. Sue, *Counseling the Culturally Different: Theory and Practice*, New York: John Wiley, 1990.

29. Stewart 1972.

30. Giordano and McGoldrick 1996.

31. M. K. P. Benham, *Culture and Educational Policy in Hawai'i: The Silencing of Native Voices*, Mahwah, NJ: L. Erlbaum Associates, 1998.

32. Smith and Bond 1994.

33. Katz 1985; Myers et al. 2004; Stewart 1972; Giordano and McGoldrick 1996; Smith and Bond 1994; Sue and Sue 1990; Benham 1998; A. Warren, *Cross-Cultural Caring: A Handbook for Health Care Professionals in Hawai'i*, Honolulu: John A. Burns School of Medicine, 1980.

34. Katz 1985; Myers et al. 2004; Stewart 1972; Giordano and McGoldrick 1996; Smith and Bond 1994; Sue and Sue 1990.

35. Department of Health, Education, and Welfare, "Belmont report: Ethical principles and guidelines for the protection of human subjects of research," Washington, D.C.: DHEW Publication No. (OS) 78–0012, 1978.

36. U.S. Patient Self-Determination Act, http://www.dgcenter.org/acp/pdf/psda.pdf, retrieved May 26, 2009.

37. K. L. Braun, N. Mokuau, and J. Tsark, "Cultural themes in health, illness, and rehabilitation among Native Hawaiians," *Topics in Geriatric Rehabilitation*, 12(3) (1997): 19–37.

38. J. Kwak and W. E. Haley, "Current research findings on end-of-life decision-making among racially or ethnically diverse groups," *Gerontologist* 45 (2005): 634–641.

39. C. K. Alameda, "Hawaiian elementary school students' ratings of perceived academic ability of Hawaiian, Japanese, and white American children: A formulation from the racial identity perspective," Ph.D. dissertation, University of Nebraska–Lincoln, 1999, retrieved May 21, 2009, from Dissertations & Theses: Full Text Database.

40. Benham 1998; Warren 1980; M. K. Pukui, E. W. Haertig, and C. A. Lee, *Nana i ke Kumu: Look to the Source*, Honolulu: Queen Liliuokalani Children's Center, 1979.

41. Katz 1985; Myers et al. 2004; Stewart 1972; Giordano and McGoldrick 1996; Smith and Bond 1994; Sue and Sue 1990.

42. Ibid.

43. Stewart 1972.

44. Katz 1985; Myers et al. 2004; Stewart 1972; Giordano and McGoldrick 1996; Smith and Bond 1994; Sue and Sue 1990.

45. Warren 1980.

46. Ibid.

47. Katz 1985; Myers et al. 2004; Stewart 1972; Giordano and McGoldrick 1996; Smith and Bond 1994; Sue and Sue 1990.

48. Trask 1993; Pukui et al. 1979.

49. Warren 1980.

50. Warren 1980; Pukui et al 1979.

51. R. John, C. H. Hennessy, T. B. Dyeson, and M. D. Garrett, "Toward the conceptualization and measurement of caregiver burden among Pueblo Indian family caregivers," *Gerontologist* 41(2) (2001):210–219.

52. Katz 1985; Myers et al. 2004; Stewart 1972; Giordano and McGoldrick 1996; Smith and Bond 1994; Sue and Sue 1990.

53. Stewart 1972.

54. Ibid.

55. Myers et al. 2004; Giordano and McGoldrick 1996.

56. Ibid.

57. D. W. Sue, "Whiteness and ethnocentric monoculturalism: Making the 'invisible' visible," *American Psychologist* 59 (2004): 761–769.

58. Stewart 1972.

59. Ibid.

60. Katz 1985.

61. Stewart 1972.

62. Trask 1993; Katz 1985.

63. Katz 1985; Myers et al. 2004; Stewart 1972; Giordano and McGoldrick 1996; Smith and Bond 1994; Sue and Sue 1990.

64. U.S. Census Bureau, "State and County QuickFacts: Data derived from Population Estimates, Census of Population and Housing, Small Area Income and Poverty Estimates, State and County Housing Unit Estimates, County Business Patterns, Nonemployer Statistics, Economic Census, Survey of Business Owners, Building Permits, Consolidated Federal Funds," report last revised February 20, 2009.

65. X. Fu, "An interracial study of marital disruption in Hawai'i: 1983 to 1996," *Journal of Divorce and Remarriage* 32 (2000): 73–92; T. Labov and J. A. Jacobs, "Intermarriage in Hawai'i 1950–1983," *Journal of Marriage and the Family* 48(1) (1986): 79–88.

66. U.S. Census Bureau 2009.

67. Active-duty Army recruits: Top 100 counties, FY 2008. http://www.nationalpriorities.org/militaryrecruiting2008/countyrank2008, retrieved April 4, 2009.

68. C. B. Park, K. L. Braun, B. Horiuchi, C. Tottori, and A. Onaka, "Lon-

gevity disparities in multiethnic Hawai'i: An analysis of 2000 life tables," *Public Health Reports* 124 (2009): 579–584.

69. U.S. Census Bureau, "Census 2000 summary file 3–sample data," http://factfinder.census.gov, retrieved May 12, 2008.

70. Hawai'i Department of Health, Behavioral Risk Factor Surveillance System, http://hawaii.gov/health/statistics/, retrieved May 26, 2009.

71. Aloha United Way, *Quality of Life in Hawai'i Annual Report* (2005), http://hawaii2050.org/images/uploads/AUW.QualityofLifeRpt.2005.pdf, retrieved February 9, 2009.

72. Department of the Attorney General, State of Hawai'i, *Crime in Hawai'i*, Honolulu: Crime Prevention Division, 1993.

73. G.J.Knowles, "Heroin, crack, and AIDS: Examining social change within Honolulu, Hawai'i's street sex trade," *Crime, Law and Social Change* 30 (1999): 379–397.

74. C.Sungkun, F.R.Salvail, P.L.Gross, A.Crisanti, D.Gundaya, and J.M.Smith, *Depression and Anxiety among Adults in Hawai'i* (2006), http://hawaii.gov/health/statistics/brfss/reports/nri_samhsa_poster_hi.pdf, retrieved May 26, 2009.

75. M.M.Leach, *Cultural Diversity and Suicide: Ethnic, Religious, Gender, and Sexual Orientation Perspectives*, Philadelphia: Haworth Press, 2006.

76. P.Akutsu, S.Sue, N.Zane, and C.Nakamura, "Ethnic differences in alcohol consumption among Asians and Caucasians in the United States: An investigation of cultural and physiological factors," *Journal for the Study of Alcohol* 50 (1989): 261–267; R.C.Johnson, C.T.Nagoshi, F.M.Ahern, J.R.Wilson, and S.H.L.Yuen, "Cultural factors as explanations for ethnic group differences in alcohol use in Hawai'i," *Journal on Psychoactive Drugs* 19 (1987): 67–75; D.W.Wood (2009), "State of Hawai'i 2004 substance abuse treatment needs assessment," http://hawaii.gov/health/substance-abuse/prevention-treatment/survey/2004needsassessment.pdf, retrieved March 28, 2010.

77. Wood 2009.

78. R.Caetano and C.L.Clark, "Trends in situational norms and attitudes toward drinking among whites, blacks, and Hispanics: 1984–1995," *Drug and Alcohol Dependence* 54 (1999): 45–56.

79. J.L.Edman and A.Yates, "A cross-cultural study of disordered eating attitudes among Filipino and Caucasian Americans," *Eating Disorders* 13(3) (2005): 279–289.

80. Hawai'i Department of Health, "Profile: Suicide," http://hawaii.gov/health/healthy-lifestyles/injury-prevention/injuryinfo/suicide.pdf, retrieved May 26, 2009.

81. R.K.Unger, *Handbook of the Psychology of Women and Gender*, Hoboken, NJ: John Wiley and Sons, 2004.

82. Pukui and Elbert 1986.

83. Warren 1980.

84. Warren 1980; B. J. Cayetano, *Ben: A Memoir, from Street Kid to Governor,* Honolulu: Watermark Publishing, 2009; Reed 2001: 327–339.

85. Warren 1980.

86. Sue 2004.

87. F. DeLima and J. Hopkins, *The Da Lima Code: Formerly Frank DeLima's Joke Book: A Parody,* Honolulu: Bess Press, 2006: 118, 103.

88. Pukui and Elbert 1986.

89. Benham 1998.

90. H. Wood, *The Kama'āina Anti-Conquest in Displacing Natives: The Rhetorical Production of Hawai'i,* Lanham, MD: Rowman & Littlefield, 1999: 37–52.

91. Daughters of Hawai'i Web site, http://www.daughtersofhawaii .com, retrieved June 13, 2009.

92. McDermott et al. 1980.

93. T. Coffman, "Hiram, Henry and the peaceable weaving of Hawai'i," *Honolulu Star-Bulletin,* Sunday, November 14, 2004.

94. J. Berger (2002), Pinkosh reprises one-man play exploring bias against whites, http://archives.starbulletin.com/2002/02/02/features/ story2.html, retrieved April 26, 2009.

95. M. P. P. Root, *The Multiracial Experience: Racial Borders as the New Frontier,* Thousand Oaks, CA: Sage Publications, 1996.

96. J. S. Linnekin, "Defining tradition: Variations on the Hawaiian identity," *American Ethnologist* 10 (1983): 241–252.

97. K. O. Dunivan, *Military Culture: A Paradigm Shift?* Air War College Maxwell Paper No. 10 Maxwell, AL: Air University Press, 1997.

98. United States Military Guides in Hawai'i, http://www .yourmilitaryinhawaii.com/, retrieved May 26, 2009.

99. Trask 1993.

100. D. Y. H. Lum, *Local Genealogy: "What School You Went?": Stories from a Pidgin Culture,* unpublished dissertation, University of Hawai'i at Mānoa, Honolulu, 1997.

101. Reed 2001: 337.

102. Ibid.: 338.

103. J. W. Engel, "Male/female role values: A comparison of Caucasian and Japanese American college students," paper presented at the Annual Meeting of the National Council on Family Relations, Dallas, November 1985.

104. Ibid.: 57.

105. Edles 2004.

CHAPTER 3

The Chinese

Victor Yee and Kwong-Yen Lum

The history of Chinese immigration to Hawai'i is unique in the history of Chinese moving to the West, inasmuch as those who came to Hawai'i were not immigrating to the United States of America but to the Kingdom of Hawai'i, with its ethnic mix of peoples quite different from those of the Western states, which had seen a large influx of Chinese men by mid-nineteenth century. Immigrating to Hawai'i, a society fundamentally less hostile to them, enabled the Chinese to adapt more easily than their mainland U.S. counterparts to the host culture. The ethos of Hawai'i gave the descendants of the early Chinese who settled in the Islands an easier time adapting and assimilating to the cultural norms of Hawai'i.

Chinese Migration to Hawai'i

In 1989, Hawai'i commemorated the two hundredth anniversary of Chinese on its shores. Prior to 1852, when contract labor brought increasing numbers of Chinese to Hawai'i, most Chinese came as merchants, businessmen, technicians, and skilled craftsmen. By the mid-nineteenth century, sugar became a crop that was grown profitably in the Islands, and the sugar plantations needed field workers, since the indigenous Hawaiians did not take easily to the rigidness of work on the plantations. The sugar planters began recruiting labor from Asia, principally Chinese from South China, most of whom signed five-year contracts to work in the fields.

South China, especially the province of Guangdong, boasts historically of having China's highest population density, with its concomitant pressure on land, intensive cultivation, and diminishing resources. By the late eighteenth century, world economic and demographic changes and trends intensified the abject conditions of life in China at the same time that economic opportunities elsewhere became appealing. The traditional Confucian food and commodities economy was rapidly being overwhelmed by population pressures. By the end of the eighteenth century, the Chinese population had increased at a rate far in excess of fertile arable land, making the marginal living (in good years) in such places as the Pearl River Delta difficult.

Guangzhou (Canton) and its environs constituted the earliest part of China to have come into contact with seaborne foreign influence, boasting a foreign resident population of over 100,000 in the eighth and ninth centuries. In the nineteenth century, almost as a matter of course, this became the major area from which Chinese emigrated to the New World, looking for places to make a better living. Many went to the U.S. mainland, which was called the Golden Mountain (Gum Saan), and in the mid-nineteenth century, many came to Hawai'i, calling it the Sandalwood Fragrance Hills (Tanxiangshan). Although those who came were often called "coolies" (the Indian word *coolie* also happens to be a homophone of the Chinese words for "bitter labor"), they were basically peasants who were generally skilled in agricultural work. Almost all came as sojourners abroad (*huaqiao*, Chinese expatriots), expecting to return to China after accumulating some money, but for many, their Hawaiian experience turned them into settlers (*huayi*, domiciled persons of Chinese ancestry).

Between 1852 and 1876, some 1,800 Chinese came on labor contract; 12,000 came between 1877 and 1884, and 25,000 Chinese were in Hawai'i between 1886 and 1896. First coming as single men on five-year contracts, they came to answer an economic need, but social conditions on and off the plantations turned them into a social problem. The *Pacific Commercial Advertiser,* a contemporary newspaper, contained frequent stories of cheap Chinese labor as a threat, remarking on their social in-assimilability. Anti-Chinese feelings mounted, on the West Coast as well as in Hawai'i, reaching a height in the 1870s culminating in the Chinese Exclusion Act of 1882 by the US Congress.[1]

The Kingdom of Hawai'i acted somewhat differently in the 1880s, restricting immigration to 2,400 Chinese men a year, and it did not restrict the immigration of Chinese women. According to Takaki, "Between 1852 and 1887, 26,000 Chinese arrived in the islands, and 10,000 or 38% went back.... Married Chinese women increased from 559 in 1890 to 1555 in 1910 and 3112 in 1930. By then 39% of the Chinese population was female. Many Chinese men married Hawaiian women."

When Hawai'i became a territory of the United States in 1900 (annexation having occurred in 1898), U.S. laws prevailed, and it was not until 1943 that the Chinese Exclusion Act was lifted and not until then that non-American born Chinese could be naturalized.

Following World War II, with different immigration laws prevailing in the United States, a different wave of Chinese came to Hawai'i— not directly from mainland China, where movement was restricted due to Communism, but largely from Taiwan, Hong Kong, and Vietnam. This wave doubled the population of ethnic Chinese from its pre–World War II size of approximately 30,000 to almost 60,000 today. This second group of Chinese continues to arrive today and includes Chinese from a variety of educational and economic backgrounds. This group includes the wealthy who escaped mainland China to Hong Kong and then immigrated to Hawai'i; Chinese from Taiwan and Hong Kong, including many university professors and educators; and those who have come to Hawai'i to work as waiters and cooks and look for a better life. Many of them are ethnic Chinese immigrants from Vietnam who were refugees of the Vietnam War.

A comparison of telephone directories of the 1960s and current ones reveals more different renderings of surnames, with more and more in the Pinyin (PY) romanization, indicating increasing migration from mainland China or Taiwan, and therefore more Mandarin speakers. The First Chinese Church in Honolulu, after having services in Cantonese since its inception, has had services only in Mandarin (and English) for at least the past ten years, reflecting the recent influx of the non-Cantonese Chinese. English has to be the common language among all these different language groups. This last immigration pattern is a trend that occurred after the normalization of relations between the United States and China in 1978.

CURRENT SITUATION

The 2000 census lists 56,600 Chinese in Hawai'i (5 percent), or 170,635 (14 percent) if part-Chinese are counted, out of a total population of 1,211,537. Among Asian groups in Hawai'i, this ranks the Chinese behind the Japanese and Filipinos in numbers, but larger than the Korean and the Vietnamese groups.

EARLY SETTLERS

The early Chinese immigrants came largely from a farming tradition in the Pearl River Delta. Having an agrarian orientation in a land that is 60 percent mountainous accustomed the Chinese to full use of human labor, a high density of human contact, and intense judgment of utility in human terms. In Hawai'i, while the agricultural experience stood the Chinese in good stead in sugarcane production, working conditions on the plantations were deplorable, and many Chinese left plantation work and either returned to China or ended up settling and raising their families in Hawai'i. Those who left the plantations started small farms of their own or opened small businesses of various kinds. Of the 15,000 Chinese contract laborers brought to Hawai'i, two-thirds had left the plantations to work on their own.[2] Chinese interest in business, which had never achieved doctrinal approbation in traditional Chinese society—although it had always played an important role— came to the fore. In China, orthodox Confucianism assigned a disdain for being profit minded rather than virtue minded, but there was no such restraint in the Hawaiian setting, and many of the early Chinese settlers were able to thrive as small businessmen.

The Chinese became known in Hawai'i by their nickname of *pake*, believed to be the warped homophone of the Cantonese *bāk-yeh* (literally, father's elder brother). When shouted at by immigration officials and plantation bosses for their names, the Cantonese would shout back "*bāk-yeh*" (your elderly uncle). That there was diversity and cleavage among the Chinese carried over from old divisions in China can also be seen in the terms "Punti" (PY: "Bendi") and "Hakka" (PY: "Kejia"): The former was what the Fragrant Hills people called themselves and the latter was what they called the people from East River (to the east of the Pearl River), not unlike what *kama'āina* and malihini connote. While in China during the eighteenth and nineteenth centuries there was open, often armed conflict between the Hakka and Punti, differences were milder in Hawai'i and have lessened to the point where some Chinese-Americans do not know if they are Punti or Hakka.

One of the key differences in the Chinese experience in Hawai'i compared to that of those who settled on the mainland United States was that the Chinese were not geographically restricted as to where they might own land. Although there were covenants regarding certain areas, land was unrestricted and most residential areas were open to Chinese. Although there was and still is a Chinatown in Honolulu, where many early settlers lived after leaving the plantations, other Chinese lived in different parts of Honolulu. The Chinese in Hawai'i were never restricted economically or socially in their Chinatown, as were many of their compatriots who had settled in the mainland United States.

Traditional Chinese Culture

In belief, the Chinese held onto Confucian concepts of interpersonal values that treasure the five cardinal relations of ruler and rule, father and son, husband and wife, brother and brother, friend and friend. Two other relations—that between strangers (adhering in political and social relationships) and human relationship with things (science and technology)—are lacking in this view. Long centuries of Confucian primacy have accustomed the Chinese to value the human-to-human position in life much more than the human-to-thing proposition. The latter adjudges human effort in utilitarian terms of making things work and making things useful to human needs. This latter view characterizes the modern business ethic of the capitalist West, which values bottom-line considerations much more than interpersonal feelings and views. Family regard still appears to be the yeast of Chinese economic enterprises among Chinese communities. This familism is rooted in ancestor worship, a religious form going back to times before Confucius. The respect for elders or parents (filial piety) structures the Confucian society and often leaves little debate in issues and matters of the family. Whether this family- and human-centered view explains and/or promotes Chinese business acumen or inhibits it is still a much-debated topic.

The two-thousand-year evolution of the Confucian Chinese state (ending in 1912) produced a historical stratification of society. Confucian insistence on the primacy of agriculture and agroeconomy, with its concomitant disdain for merchantry and the profit motive, produced a five-tier valuation of social scale. This scale places the scholar *(shi)* at the top, followed by the peasant *(nong)*, laborer *(gong)*, merchant *(shang)*, and soldier *(bing)*. Not to be viewed as classes or castes, these tiers of society were not hermetically sealed, yet they announce Chinese social values. The great divide was education; all strove to advance through the levels of the civil service examination in hopes of achieving fame and fortune. Chinese culture heroes were the successful scholars for whom literature and drama have sung praise. Rising from one level to that of the scholar is the ultimate approbation.

The content of the examination system was Confucian history, arts, and letters, and when it was abolished in 1905 during the course of revolution and reform, this Confucian humanistic universe fractured. But the cultural habit of viewing education as the great divide remained, if not even stronger among Chinese at home and abroad. The thousands who went abroad to study, a phenomenon not seen among Japanese and Korean youth, attests to this compelling force of education. But education for modern Chinese at home and abroad no longer serves the Confucian universe of the Chinese humanities. Yet the premier status of the scholar has never changed, even though the other levels might shift as local and temporal exigencies beckon.

Ethnocultural Identity

The long-standing Chinese civilization, with its rich cultural traditions, no doubt influenced the characteristics of the Chinese in Hawai'i. Characteristics of the individual, the family unit, and social relationships have a common core, but yet they are modified by the culture of Hawai'i.

INDIVIDUAL TEMPERAMENT

Francis Hsu, an anthropologist who has studied Chinese in China, Hawai'i, and the continental United States, describes the Chinese as "situation-centered." Situation-centered persons are those who seek to find satisfactory adjustments to relationships. They will attempt to fit in and harmonize with what exists. This is contrasted to the "individual-centered person," who will attempt to bend the external world to their satisfaction.[3] Situational adaptation generally has led to successful adaptation in Hawai'i, primarily evidenced by educational attainment and success in business and family.[4]

While many ethnicities may have an emotionally dominated temperament, the Confucian social structure has influenced a goal-oriented, studious temperament. Like the Chinese in China and on the mainland United States, attaining educational goals remains a major goal of Chinese families in Hawai'i. Education also influences the way Chinese children are brought up. Much emphasis on the seriousness of education tends to create more parental discipline in general. Respecting your parents and elders tends to result in less rebellion among young Chinese, less crime, and more obedience to parental restrictions.[5]

Education also acts as an economic springboard for many Chinese in Hawai'i, leading to greater professionalization. Real estate was an early interest for the Chinese, as the Chinese culture in China was agrarian in nature and emphasized the value of property in bringing prestige to its owner. Additionally, the Chinese are interested in saving, investing, and the prestige of elders giving to other family members.[6] These conservative values have led to the word *pake* meaning not only "Chinese" in Hawai'i but also "frugal."

GENERATIONAL DIFFERENCES

The Chinese had been in the Islands since the latter part of the eighteenth century, and there were already a number of generations of Chinese in Hawai'i by the mid-1800s. The pre–World War II Chinese in Hawai'i could be grouped into three distinct generations based on whether they were from China or born in Hawai'i.

When the first Chinese immigrated to Hawai'i, the Caucasians and Hawaiians were the established groups. The Chinese worked with these groups, first on the plantations and then as merchants. Many did not speak English and socially remained among themselves. Most of this first generation had expected to return to China once they had fulfilled their contracts. Because of the lack of Chinese women, Chinese men, in adapting to the situation, often took Hawaiian wives. The 2000 census shows the extent of this intermarriage: Only 33 percent of Chinese are of pure Chinese ethnicity. This first generation adapted, did not return to China, and became integrated into the culture of Hawai'i.

The second generation of Chinese comprised those born in the Islands to the first settlers. The core cultural values of education and business led this generation to adapt to the host cultures by identifying with or emulating the Caucasian culture, with its drive for education and material success. Most second-generation Chinese (those born just before or in the early decades of the twentieth century) learned to speak standard English and generally finished high school. Although many continued to work in businesses started by their fathers, many of this second generation entered the professions of teaching, medicine, dentistry, and law. Part of the reason for striving to get into one of the professions is that the major businesses were controlled by Caucasians, and many of the second-generation Chinese who worked in these enterprises did not feel that they could penetrate into the executive levels.

A handful of second-generation Chinese in Hawai'i rose to fame in business and politics. Chinn Ho and Hiram Fong both graduated from

McKinley High School in 1924. Ho illuminated Hawai'i and the Pacific with his financial vision and genius until his death in 1987, and his name was used for a Chinese detective in the television series *Hawai'i Five-0*. Hiram Fong became the first U.S. senator of Asian decent.

The third and subsequent generation of Chinese born in Hawai'i has generally assimilated itself into the host culture. Most cannot speak any Chinese dialect. However, the core characteristics of Chinese culture remain imbued in this generation: education, business, family. Continuing the pattern of successful situational adaptation, they have identified themselves as Americans and have striven for equal treatment. With the economic rise of China, Chinese in Hawai'i also seek business affiliations with their ancestral home—continuing to adapt to situations, even if they lead to a full circle back to China—not necessarily driven by cultural affinity, but much more so because they lead to successful economic adaptation.

MARRIAGE, FAMILY, AND CHILD REARING

The concept of marriage for life persists among Chinese in Hawai'i. The 2000 census indicates that the divorce rate among ethnic Chinese, 7.5 percent, is among the lowest of any ethnic group, second only to the Filipino rate of 5.9 percent. The general reasons for divorce among Americans—economic difficulties, adultery, incompatibility, and religion—seem to be more tolerated in Chinese marriages because of shame and the lingering Confucian imperative of the importance of family. Shame is externally (situationally) motivated by what others (such as your family) think of you, while guilt is thought to be more internally motivated.

Old China was a patriarchal society, with men working in the society at large wielding economic power and women ruling the family on a day-to-day basis. This division of power still exists strongly among Chinese, even among the more assimilated. Chinese mothers tend to be overprotective and dominant in the upbringing of children, so that the mother-child bond tends to be stronger than the father-child bond. This matriarchal family orientation and child bond may also lead to less adolescent rebelliousness and less delinquency.

Historically, the Chinese family, both in China and after immigration to Hawai'i, lived with more than one married couple and more than two generations under the same roof. The exposure and early training of children regarding how to act with respect and care for the elderly has led to interesting psychological developments among the Chinese.

In Western nuclear families, the primary relationship for children is with parents, which leads to a child having an internalized perception of his father or mother and an individualized sense of self. An important stage of development is called separation-individuation, in which a child generally becomes individual-centered. In a Chinese family, disciplinary power is more diffused, including not only parents but grandparents and perhaps in-laws. The Chinese child, in learning how to deal with various kinship relationships, learns to become situation-centered.[7] For example, a Chinese child may be taught by his mother not only to say "thank you" for a small gift from his or her grandparents but to *say it nicely*. This shade of gray teaches a behavioral difference in connoting respect for the relationship with a grandparent that is greater than what might be received from an older sibling or parent. The child learns grades of relations that could not be conveyed in a nuclear family.

FAMILY STRUCTURE, POWER STRUCTURE, GENERATIONAL AND
GENDER ROLES

The family structure of the first Chinese families, as noted, was traditionally patriarchal, with the men working outside of the home and the wives generally taking care of the family. In rural areas, wives would also have engaged in agricultural work. In traditional China, females were treated as lesser than males because they could not carry the family name nor be of much economic value to a family.[8] In Hawai'i, by the second generation many daughters had been educated through high school and went into clerical work. A good number went to normal school—a predecessor of teachers college at the university level—and became elementary schoolteachers. Many went into nursing as a profession. The economic as well as educational balances of power shifted toward the modern American model so that the family became less patriarchal, and the power structure became more evenly divided between the husbands and wives. By the third generation, there is no discernable difference in power sharing in Chinese families from the modal American model. Situational adaptation can change traditional family values for Chinese in Hawai'i, as the working woman has become valued over the traditional role.

Chinese family values and goals in Hawai'i include striving for economic well-being, perhaps reflecting some survivalist origins necessary in the world's most populous country. Esteem of the community at large, and especially the Chinese community, is also of importance. In traditional China, civil service exams could elevate a family's esteem and offer individuals a privileged lifestyle. Chinese families in Hawai'i will sacrifice much to see their children in private schools if they deem them better than the public schools, or they will move to neighborhoods to ensure that their children can attend better public schools. Education is seen and sought after as a means of achieving economic and social success.

Although the focus of Chinese families has traditionally been on family and education, among second-generation Chinese there began to develop more awareness of the needs of the larger community and more participation in community efforts to work with the less fortunate. By the third and fourth generations, the awareness of needing be part of the social structure of the community appears no different from the community as a whole.

EDUCATIONAL AND OCCUPATIONAL PATTERNS

The fundamental place education has for Chinese in Hawai'i has been discussed regarding its importance to culture, the individual, and the family. Chinese in Hawai'i have influenced the development of higher education in the state. Higher education in Hawai'i has in turn educated many Chinese outside the United States, incorporated Chinese studies, and allowed for the upward mobility of Chinese in Hawai'i. William Kwai Fong Yap, an assistant cashier at the Bank of Hawai'i, successfully lobbied early in the twentieth century to have what was then the College of Agriculture and Mechanic Arts of the Territory of Hawai'i, which began classes in September 1908, incorporated as the University of Hawai'i. When the university's College of Arts and Sciences officially began offering classes on July 1, 1920, Chinese history and language courses were in the curriculum.

Chinese studies, along with the study of other parts of Asia, also thrived, especially after World War II. With statehood and the formation of the East-West Center, the impetus became even greater. However, while students from other Asian countries flocked to the East-West Center, the Communist revolution in China and the ensuing Cultural Revolution precluded mainland Chinese youth from attending the East-West Center and University of Hawai'i classrooms throughout the 1960s and 1970s. Chinese students from Taiwan, Hong Kong, and Singapore took up the slack, however. President Nixon's trip to China in 1971 began contacts with the mainland, which grew after the formal resumption of relations in 1978.

Professor Daniel W. Y. Kwok was involved in the revival of interest in China-Hawai'i relations both academically and publicly. First was the forging of a curriculum of Chinese studies at the university in consonance with the historical significance of China studies and the contemporary international significance of U.S.–China relations. These efforts culminated in the establishment of the university's Center for Chinese Studies in 1987. The decade of the 1980s saw close to four hundred students from China on the University of Hawai'i campus engaged in graduate studies in the humanities, social sciences, and physical sciences. The Tiananmen Square episode of 1989 halted this two-way exchange for a few years, with a return to exchange in earnest in the early twenty-first century. Census 2000 figures of Chinese gaining permanent resident status in the last two decades indicate this immigration pattern: There were 27,027 foreign-born Chinese in Hawai'i out of the 56,600 pure ethnic Chinese in Hawai'i.

The 2000 census also indicates that 27.1 percent of Chinese have a bachelor's degree or greater, higher than other ethnic groups in Hawai'i except for the Japanese, with 30 percent. The number of physicians, dentists, lawyers, and teachers is disproportionate to their numbers in the larger community. Because of the strong nineteenth-century Caucasian oligarchy, it was difficult for the early Chinese to engage in the larger business community, so many opened small businesses, some of which have grown quite large over the years. Partially because of their affinity for owning land, a number of Hawai'i Chinese became quite wealthy over the years by buying land that was not considered very valuable at the time but that, over time, became some of the most valuable property in the world.

After World War II, a number of Chinese enterprises entered the larger community and became major forces in the economic life of Hawai'i. For example, Finance Factors, a diverse financial services company, was started and is still owned by a group of Chinese. Aloha Airlines, a major interisland and Pacific carrier, was started by a Chinese businessman after World War II because, as he related, he wanted to show that Chinese could do more than run laundries and restaurants (unfortunately, after a successful fifty-year run, Aloha Airlines succumbed to the 2009 economic recession).

The current economic structure of Hawai'i has changed considerably since the beginning of the twentieth century. Many of the dominant companies in the first part of the last century are now owned by national conglomerates. Hawai'i's Chinese are now welcomed on the boards of major economic and charitable institutions.

In language and dress, the Chinese are no different from those in the larger community of Hawai'i. Very few assimilated Chinese can speak Chinese. With China's recent rise in economic power, Mandarin has become an important world language, and along with the rest of Americans, a number of young Chinese in Hawai'i have signed up for courses in that language. Of course, the post–World War II immigrants still retain their Chinese language.

Food remains an important cultural tie among the Chinese of any generation. In fact, food is something of a Chinese obsession. Every family celebration is celebrated with food being served: a christening, birthday, wedding, a postfuneral gathering, or a simple get-together. It is quite common to have banquets of two or three hundred (usually Chinese food and held at a Chinese restaurant, but often Western food served in a hotel banquet room) consisting of one's extended family, friends, and business associates for an occasion as simple as a birthday. Among the more affluent, guest lists of a thousand or two thousand are not unusual.

The Chinese family style of eating, where dishes are placed in the center for all to share, is the standard for the potluck local way of eating and bonding. The Chinese and Hawaiians both share a cultural liveliness involved with sharing foods, eating together, bonding, and celebrations. This has become part of the Hawai'i lifestyle.

Because the Chinese were among the first groups to immigrate, and because they have such a passion for food, Chinese food has blended into the general culture of Hawai'i. A long-standing Hawaiian favorite among all segments of the population is the *manapua*. It is a white bun steamed with delectable pork inside. The term *manapua* comes from *mea ono pu'a'a*, meaning "little delicious pork things," which was a sign found on a Chinese food stand selling what in Chinese is called the *chashaobao* (*ts'a-siu-bao* in Cantonese). For many years, this *manapua* was large in size and the meat within was roasted with red dye. To new Chinese arrivals at the beginning of statehood, this was not the same item they were used to in Hong Kong, where Cantonese cuisine has a comfortably secure reputation. Hawai'i has since seen the arrival of the smaller *chashaobao*, with dark brown and not red barbecued pork. *Manapua* is currently available in establishments as ubiquitous as 7-Eleven and lunch wagons and is seen as a basic food of Hawai'i. A second favorite local dish is the braised pork rump or shoulder, affectionately called the *kauyuk* (Cantonese for the mandarin *kourou*). Again the older version is dyed red to suit Hawaiian Chinese taste, whereas the new arrivals stay attached to the dark brown version simmered long over a gentle fire.

TRADITIONS, CUSTOMS, AND FOLK BELIEFS, LEGENDS, AND MYTHS

There are several forms of folk beliefs and mores still prevalent among the Chinese in Hawai'i. That of geomancy—feng shui, literally "wind-water"—is of truly ancient origin. Feng shui is a system of positioning objects correctly in keeping with the principles of yang (the male force) and yin (the female principle), which need to be in balance in order to have good outcomes in life. This often translates into positioning a house correctly or buying a house with the right feng shui and placing furniture facing in the "right" direction. Practices such as not situating the front door in front of a perpendicular roadway, of not having the front door face north, or not bestriding some subterranean veins of qi (energy-impulse) are some features of this art. The practice has its own professionalism and is therefore a business.

A custom among Chinese is the social, familial, and generational practice of giving *lycee* (PY: *lishi*)—money in red wrappers with fortuitous wording. Such occasions are especially happy occasions for the young of one's own family and sometimes of others for birthdays and New Year's. This practice is also the traditional way of the Chinese to give gratuity, as in "tipping" the lion dancers that appear at large group functions. At these functions, another Chinese custom is that of setting off firecrackers to drive away evil spirits. This Chinese practice, banned in Hong Kong (but not Macau), is a topic debated yearly in Honolulu in great earnestness, as its cultural importance (not only for the Chinese but for large segments of the population) clashes with health and environmental concerns. Firecrackers are universal in Hawai'i during the Western New Year and are primarily celebrated in Chinatown during the Chinese New Year. Chinese New Year is also celebrated by eating special foods such as *jai*, composed largely of dried vegetables, symbolic of cleaning one's system for the coming year.

Regardless of religion, whether Christian or Buddhist, some families still practice ancestor worship, or *pai shan* (literally "worship the mountain," because graves tended to be on hillsides on nonarable land). Families bring food to the graves of family members who have passed away. Sometimes the food is taken back and eaten by the family after the ritual, and sometimes it is left for the grave keepers to enjoy later in the day.

The Chinese in Hawai'i observe some traditional festivals and have created others not found in China. The Luna New Year, the fifteenth of the first lunar moon (the Lantern Festival); Qingming (the third lunar month, usually calibrated to around April 5), for grave visitation and sweeping; and the Mid-Autumn Festival, with its full moon signifying family reunion, are the most commonly shared and observed. But the Narcissus Queen event, like its beauty contest counterparts, is strictly an overseas Chinatown invention, coming as it did from commercial requirements of colorful pulchritudinous confirmations of wealth and charm. It is a very successful "do" and ends in the queen and her court touring Chinese towns and cities with officers of *huiguans* (Chinese societies or associations of the towns) trailing along or in the lead.

RELIGIOUS, MORAL, AND SPIRITUAL BELIEFS

As Confucianism is more social ethic than religion, the Chinese of Hawai'i follow different persuasions. There are Chinese Christian churches of various denominations, and there are Buddhist temples and Daoist practicing priests officiating at funerals, births, and weddings. Of the non-Christians, the general religious outlook of the Chinese identifying with Buddhism, Daoism, and Confucianism actually exhibits what in mainland China is called the "three-teachings-in-one" attitude. There is no doctrinal intransigence between them; rather, there is an appreciation of the strengths in each. Confucian teaching supports success of a moral life, Buddhism offers nirvana in the afterlife, and Daoism offers expiation of sin and guilt as well as communion with nature. To characterize, one can easily wear a Confucian robe, don a Daoist cap, and stride about in Buddhist sandals, sartorially unified and contingencies guaranteed.

Many Chinese are Christians, both Protestant and Catholic. In some part, this is because Christian missionaries had been in China during the nineteenth century, and a number of Chinese who immigrated to the Hawaiian Islands were already converts. Perhaps a more important factor is the intense proselytizing of the American missionaries throughout the Islands during the nineteenth century, as well as the strong Catholic school system that developed, which attracted many Chinese in search of a better education than was felt to be afforded by the public school system. Ever adaptable, the Chinese have adopted religions that lead to success.[9] Christianity must be considered one of the forces pushing Chinese of Hawai'i toward assimilation.

SOCIOECONOMIC AND POLITICAL PATTERNS

Assimilated Chinese tend to mingle easily with other ethnic groups, although this is largely a post–World War II behavioral pattern. Hiram Fong Jr., a third-generation Chinese whose father was the U.S. senator, said, "I have always felt myself Hawaiian first, American second, and Chinese third." Prior to World War II, Chinese generally formed social networks only among themselves. When the Chinese first came to Hawai'i, clan and village associations formed and persisted through the early parts of the twentieth century. These associations not only formed a safety net for recent immigrants but also served in helping one move up the socioeconomic ladder.

As the children of these earlier Chinese immigrants became more adapted to their environment, these clan and village associations were no longer needed for their original purposes, and they now play a much less significant role in the Chinese community. However, yearly banquets are still held among some of these associations.

Social network patterns now tend to occur, as in most American communities, among high school friends and fellow workers. However, extended family contacts remain a source of relationships, and nuclear family relationships remain strong. In Hawai'i, more than in most communities, those born here tend to stay here—hence the continued strength of family relationships. But as economic and occupational opportunities are often greater on the mainland United States, more and more young, educated Chinese have developed careers away from Hawai'i.

Politically, the Chinese do not form a bloc. Whether a Chinese is a Republican or a Democrat is probably due more to socioeconomic status than belonging to a particular ethnic group. While there are quite a few legislators of Japanese ancestry, there are relatively few Chinese legislators.

Chinese traditionally tend to organize in families and do not share the loyalty to the emperor that the Japanese historically shared. So while the Japanese company's sense of mission and organization and lifetime employment may be a model taught in business schools, and the individual "captain of industry" may be the American model, the traditional roots of the family business persist among Hawai'i's Chinese. Quite a number of large businesses run by Chinese are still family centered. Recently, however, this has changed, as recent generations have risen to become CEO/owners of the largest corporations in Hawai'i.

Health problems among the Chinese do not differ significantly from the norm, but with some exceptions. There is a higher incidence of nasopharyngeal cancer (NPC) among Chinese from South China. There may be genetic factors involved, but research has shown that some Chinese populations in the United States have a decreased incidence of NPC, decreasing by successive generations living outside of South China, indicating that environmental and dietary elements may be playing an important role in the development of this disease.[10] Occasionally, thalassemia (a form of anemia found primarily in countries closer to the equator) can be found among Chinese in Hawaiʻi. The disease can vary from severe to mild. The active form of the disease is infrequent among Chinese in Hawaiʻi.

Mental health problems do not deviate much from the norm, except that alcoholism is less among Chinese than in the community as a whole. The reasons for this may be cultural as well as genetic. Culturally, Chinese traditionally drink as part of toasts to others, and one who drinks independently may be seen as rude. With assimilation, these traditions have changed, but a good proportion of Chinese in Hawaiʻi are from abroad, have descended from the post–World War II immigrants, or associate with traditional Chinese—leading to less change in this area.

A genetic component due to a variant of the enzyme aldehyde dehydrogenase, which is involved in the metabolism of alcohol, may also lead to the "flushing effect" that afflicts about 50 percent of Asians. Flushing or blushing is associated with reddening (caused by dilation of capillaries) of the face, neck, shoulder, and in some cases the entire body after consumption of alcohol. These symptoms are generally unpleasant. Because alcohol is not fully broken down, a residue similar to formaldehyde is left.

Among traditional Chinese, it was considered a blow to a family's esteem and close to a moral blot to have a member who needed psychiatric or psychological care, but in recent years Chinese will seek mental health help as easily as members of any other group in the community. Families who have been in Hawaiʻi for generations frequent Western-trained physicians. However, more recent immigrants and those who favor alternative medicine may seek out herbalists and other folk healers.

Acupuncture, an ancient Chinese treatment based on a theory of meridians of force in the body, has achieved some respectability in the

West, similar to interest in other alternative medicines. Acupuncture, like feng shui, has Daoist roots and works to balance the yin and the yang of the body and clear the meridians of blockages that may inhibit the qi energy. Of course, this Chinese paradigm differs from the scientific paradigm, which is founded on what can be observed through the X-ray, laboratory, and the human body. Similarly, with herbology—another aspect of Chinese medicine in which herbs and foods are also conceptualized not by vitamins and minerals but on the yin and yang of "cool and hot"—many have found results (from experience, empirical trials, or the placebo effect) by using Chinese medicine.

As in China, the pragmatic Chinese in Hawai'i blend both Eastern and Western medicine, finding cures and symptomatic relief in each.

Influence of the Native Hawaiian Host Culture

The Hawaiian openness to other ethnic groups has had a profound effect on the Chinese-Americans of the third generation. The high percentage of out-marriages, the tolerance of people who are not Chinese, and the weakening of the Chinese societies all attest to the separation from old Chinese customs. However, filial piety remains fairly strong. The Chinese have always thought of themselves as a superior people (as do many other groups), being from and isolating themselves in the "Middle Kingdom" (the Chinese written characters loosely translate to this). Living in Hawai'i, the Chinese have developed a better sense of parity among groups.

The father of one of this chapter's authors grew up in a neighborhood consisting largely of Hawaiians and a smaller percentage of Chinese, but he never expressed feeling unaccepted by the Hawaiians. Although his friends were all Chinese, there was no feeling of animosity from the Hawaiians. This tolerance of other groups on the part of the Hawaiians was genuine, and it permeated the culture of the Chinese in Hawai'i.

As noted, Honolulu has a "Chinatown" that originally consisted of Chinese-owned businesses and markets as well as living quarters. The Chinese areas were not segregated and confined to Chinatown, but rather Chinese lived in diverse areas and their children attended public schools that afforded them interaction with other ethnic groups. In many ways, this integration gave younger generations a less intense feeling about being Chinese than those in the continental United States and gave Hawai'i-born Chinese a sense of being part of the larger culture of Hawai'i. Young Chinese learned to play the ukulele and steel guitar, dance the hula, and sing Hawaiian songs. These activities are engaged in by the young of every ethnic group, and they play a significant role in the generally relaxed, joyous nature of the young in Hawai'i. Younger Chinese in Hawai'i may be considered more relaxed and mellow when compared to younger Chinese in the United States or abroad. As for stereotypes, it is interesting to note that the stories of the evil Fu Manchu came out of the American mainland, while the benign but wise Charlie Chan came out of Hawai'i.

Changing Group Adaptive Strategies and Life Goals across Time

We have noted that most of the Chinese who came to Hawai'i in the nineteenth century planned to go back to China after saving money from their work on the plantations. Many did return to China but married and developed families in the Islands, either with wives from China or with Hawaiian wives. Interesting among some second-generation Chinese men who had obtained American university educations are those who opted to return to "save" China.

"Save China" was a clarion call by Sun Yat-sen (the father of the Chinese revolution, who completed his high school education at 'Iolani, a private Episcopal-sponsored Honolulu school) in his revolutionary efforts, and it became the motto for generations of Chinese efforts toward the motherland: money, service, education, journalism, and so on. The first revolutionary society he founded was in Hawai'i (1895). China of the nineteenth century was shamed by the opium wars and the treaties of extraterritoriality imposed by the Western powers on her coastal cities. Japan had industrialized in less than a century and had defeated a European power in its war with Russia, and China was governed by a feckless empress dowager who let the country slide further backward.

Of those Chinese-Americans who did go back in the early part of the twentieth century, most returned to Hawai'i after the Communist takeover in 1948.

The Chinese-Hawaiianization of Names

The mutual influences of Chinese and Hawaiian cultures can nowhere be more clearly seen than in Chinese surnames that appear Hawaiian. Local practices at the entry ports, on the plantations, and in schools caused a number of Chinese surnames to have become given names and given names to become surnames. First of all, Chinese habits of listing surnames first often lost them in front of immigration officials and school registrars who turned them into given names. Second, on plantations the Chinese workers were identified by their given names, sometimes with an "a" added. Thus was created a whole class of surnames with the ubiquitous "a" and "ah" added to given names, and in some cases the "a" appears at the end.

"A" and "ah" in these Hawaiian-sounding names came from the Cantonese habit of using it to indicate the diminutive function, somewhat like the "ie" in Annie and Jimmie or the "y" in Sonny in English. Among family members and friends, such usage was common. Thus a given name like Fook Sing would become Asing, and Ling Fook would become Afook. Some a-preceding names come from family relationships, like Apo from grandmother, Ako from elder brother, and Ai or Ah Nee from number two. When the "a" is added at the end, it indicates intimate attention getting. Thus Akan becomes Akana, Awan becomes Awana, Ahin becomes Ahina. A study by Irma Soong of the Hawai'i Chinese History Center of 1988 lists eighty-nine such Hawaiian-sounding Chinese names.

In the matter of names, the telephone directory of various years and decades will also indicate the Chinese community's Hawaiian realities. The romanizations of Chinese names follow several bewildering systems: personal choice according to dialect phonetics, Wade-Giles (WG), and pinyin, as well as corruptions and confusions of all of the above. When people from mainland China who are Mandarin speakers get listed in the directory, the older Mr. Cheong (Cantonese) becomes the new Mr. Zhang (PY) and Mr. Chang (WG), and the former Ms. Chow (Cantonese) becomes Ms. Zhou (PY) and Ms. Chou (WG). Many Wongs are also accompanied by many Wangs. The surname Kwok (Cantonese) is also Guo (PY), Kuo (WG), Quo (personal), or Gwek (Fujian); but its older Hawaiian original is Kwock, with the added "c." Such is the diversity of Hawaiian influences on names.

Biopsychosocial Factors: Enduring Characteristics

The story of the Chinese in Hawai'i is more one of hard work and education than of preexisting genetics or wealth brought from China. The cultural memes (a unit of human cultural evolution analogous to the gene) of Hawai'i Chinese can be attributed to cultural learning.[11] Even the thought that Asians are genetically more suited than other groups for mathematics is probably more based on environmental factors than any innate superiority due to genetic influence.

Malcolm Gladwell's recent bestseller, *Outliers: The Story of Success*, describes Chinese facility with numbers as due to the Chinese language and numbering system.[12] Chinese number words are brief, consisting of one syllable, allowing one to memorize and mentally manipulate numbers, making early learning and later computation easier. Chinese numbers are always named with the tens first and the unit number second; for example, "19" would be one ten and nine versus "nineteen" in English. This also allows for easier mental manipulation of numbers (i.e., adding and subtracting in your head). Instead of having difficulties with math, many Chinese begin to enjoy the ease of this system.

Gladwell also cites a Chinese peasant proverb: "No one who can rise before dawn three hundred sixty days a year fails to make his family rich." The Chinese agrarian society was built on the cultivation of rice in land that is 60 percent mountainous. The small rice paddy, about the size of a hotel room, requires the attention, knowledge, and labor to assure that the exact level of water covers the plant. Generations of live-or-die exactitude may have led to the inculcation of a cultural belief that hard work will lead to survival—and perhaps a future advantage.

Although the civil service examination focused on the humanities, modern Chinese in America are seen as excelling in mathematics and the sciences. For foreign-born Chinese, the language of the numbering system may have an advantage, as well as the close relationship between mathematics and science. A difficulty for those studying away from China is that the language of the humanities means education in one's second language. The language of mathematics and science offers a level playing field. Any genetic or hardwired skill in these areas has not been identified.

Family Cohesion: An Enduring Characteristic

Family cohesion has been the basis of social strength among the Chinese in Hawai'i. Determining whether this cohesion will continue to play a major role or whether atomization of the extended family will lead to nuclear families is in question. Certainly as the generations have established themselves in Hawai'i, the extended family has generally become the nuclear family. Will the Chinese adolescents' decreased rebelliousness change over time? Will the American ideal of self-realization overtake what heretofore has been general submissiveness to parental wishes be checked by increasing individuation during adolescence? Earlier we discussed the westernization of the traditional role of women, leading to more working women and greater equality. Adolescents may not rebel because there is much shame involved with misbehavior, from both family and culture. Divorce may not reach the same prevalence among Chinese as with other ethnicities for the same reasons. While Chinese in Hawai'i may have less rebellious youth and a lower divorce rate because of shame, they view the progress of women as a value, similar to Western society.

Summary and Conclusions

Despite the challenges of westernization, Chinese brought up in Hawai'i retain a bright future based on an understanding of their long history of civilization in China and recent history in Hawai'i. Challenged by population pressures and lack of arable land, Chinese who immigrated to Hawai'i thrived economically in a society unfettered by the Confucian disdain for being profit minded rather than virtue minded. The early plantation Chinese who came to Hawai'i arrived without women, yet these Chinese men were able to intermarry with Hawaiian women, and this intermarriage and integration with other ethnicities in Hawai'i has continued. Chinese "religions" of Confucianism, Buddhism, and Daoism traditionally coexisted, and the Chinese in Hawai'i easily accommodated the Christian religion as well. Accommodation—adaptation or being "situation-centered" in anthropologist Francis Hsu's terminology—is a hallmark of being Chinese. Hard work, perhaps developed in some ways from the difficulties of cultivating rice as well as population pressures, remains a value for Hawai'i's Chinese. The focus on education, historically beginning in China with the Confucian civil service exam, has persevered in the culture of the Chinese in Hawai'i.

Two differences are noticeable among the Chinese in Hawai'i as compared to those in other parts of the world. First, the relaxed nature of the Chinese in Hawai'i is a reflection of the generally more relaxed atmosphere in Hawai'i compared to the mainland United States. Second, they do not have the often defensive characteristic of other Chinese who grew up as minorities among majorities. Being fully accepted members of their community has nurtured the self-esteem of Chinese in Hawai'i; they are proud of who they are.

Relatively small (14 percent) in number compared to the population as a whole and mostly mixed with other ethnicities, Chinese in Hawai'i are known by the food enjoyed in Chinatown and other neighborhoods, in studies presented at the University of Hawai'i, and in various businesses and professions. If the Chinese are a happy chapter in Hawai'i's history, how important is it how much "Chinese" is in Hawai'i or how much Hawai'i is in the Chinese? In Hawai'i, the potluck family-style meal is influenced both by the Chinese and all the other ethnicities that make up the culture of the Hawai'i 'ohana.

Further Reading

Chan, S., and H. M. Lai. *Chinese American Transnationalism.* Philadelphia: Temple University Press, 2006.
Finding Sandalwood Mountain. A DVD film by A2Media, Honolulu, 2008.
Fuchs, L. H. "Success, pake style." In *Hawai'i Pono: A Social History.* New York: Harcourt, Brace and World, 1961.
Gladwell, M. *Outliers: The Story of Success.* New York: Little, Brown and Company, 2009.
Glick, C. E. *Sojourners and Settlers.* Honolulu: University of Hawai'i Press, 1980.
Hsu, F. L. K. "The Chinese of Hawai'i: Their role in American culture." *Transactions of the New York Academy of Sciences* 13 (1951): 243–250.
Kinkead, G. *Chinatown: A Portrait of a Closed Society.* New York: HarperCollins Publishers, 1992.
Lum, K. Y., and W. F. Char. "Chinese adaptation in Hawai'i: Some examples." In *Chinese Culture and Mental Health,* ed. W. S. Tseng and D. Y. H. Wu. New York: Academic Press, 1985: 215–226.
Pan, L., ed. *Encyclopedia of the Chinese Overseas.* Cambridge, MA: Harvard University Press, 1999.
Takaki, R. T., ed. *From Different Shores: Perspectives on Race and Ethnicity in America.* Oxford: Oxford University Press, 1987.
———. *Strangers from a Different Shore.* New York: Back Bay Books, Little Brown and Company, 1998.
Tobin, J. J., D. Y. H. Wu, and D. H. Davidson. *Preschool in Three Cultures: Japan, China and the United States.* New Haven, CT: Yale University Press, 1989.

Notes

Authors' note: Daniel W. Y. Kwok, Ph.D., emeritus professor of history, University of Hawai'i at Mānoa, contributed both ideas and writing to this chapter.

1. R. Takaki, *Strangers from a Different Shore*, New York: Back Bay Books, Little Brown and Company, 1998.

2. Ibid.

3. F. L. K. Hsu, "The Chinese of Hawaii: Their role in American culture," *Transactions of the New York Academy of Sciences* 13(6) (1951): 243–250.

4. K. Y. Lum and W. F. Char, "Chinese adaptation in Hawaii: Some examples," in *Chinese Culture and Mental Health*, ed. W. S. Tseng and D. Y. H. Wu, New York: Academic Press, 1985: 215–226; L. H. Fuchs, "Success, *pake* style," in *Hawaii Pono: A Social History*, by L. H. Fuchs, New York: Harcourt, Brace and World, 1961: 86–105.

5. Interagency Council on Intermediate Sanctions, www.hawaii.gov/ icis, March 2007.

6. Fuchs 1961.

7. F. L. K. Hsu, "Suppression versus repression: A limited psychological interpretation of four cultures," *Psychiatry* 12 (1949): 223–242.

8. C. Loo and P. Ong, "Slaying demons with a sewing needle: Feminist issues for Chinatown's women," in *From Different Shores*, ed. R. T. Takaki, New York: Oxford Press, 1987: 186–191.

9. Hsu 1951.

10. P. Buell, "The effect of migration on the risk of nasopharygeal cancer among Chinese," *Cancer Research* 4 (May 1, 1974): 1189–1191.

11. R. Dawkins, *The Selfish Gene*, New York: Oxford University Press, 1976.

12. M. Gladwell, *Outliers: The Story of Success*, New York: Little, Brown and Company, 2009.

CHAPTER 4

The Portuguese

Naleen Naupaka Andrade and Stephanie T. Nishimura

Portuguese from the Atlantic islands of Madeira and the Azores were the largest group of Europeans to immigrate to Hawaiʻi during the sugar plantation era. Between 1878 and 1913, approximately 25,000 Portuguese men, women, and children came as plantation contract laborers to work on the islands of Oʻahu, Kauaʻi, Māui, and Hawaiʻi Island (also called the Big Island).

Before 1905, most of these immigrants had been born into the peasantry within Portugal's absolute monarchy. Locally, they were governed by hereditary landowners who controlled island commerce through the commodities produced on their lands. Major exports included oranges, lemons, and wheat from the Azores and sugar, bananas, and wine from Madeira.[1] The Crown conscripted their sons to fight a civil war on the mainland, as well as conflicts in Portugal's African colonies. At the end of the civil war in 1882, Portugal became a constitutional monarchy where every citizen was equal, at least on paper. In reality, the landlords continued to control the livelihoods of the former peasants, who remained their land tenants and sharecroppers. Born into a kind of hereditary servitude, these former peasants were the labor force for their islands' primary agricultural industry.

Beginning in 1850, a fungus began killing the grape vines in Madeira, nearly destroying its wine production.[2] In 1877 another blight hit, this time in the Azores, devastating the citrus groves.[3] The fungus and blight crippled the agricultural industry, destabilized the economy, and in turn threatened the livelihoods of laborers and the towns' tradesmen and merchants.

The convergence of these political, social, agricultural, and economic events created the desperate necessity for Azoreans and Madeirans in the late nineteenth century to look for opportunities beyond their homeland. Many went to Brazil and North America. The rest looked to Hawai'i.

Among the Hawai'i immigrants were tenant farmers and sharecroppers, ranchmen, dairymen, fishermen, stonemasons, engineers, and skilled tradesmen who brought their intact, multigenerational extended families. Grandparents, parents, aunts, uncles, godparents, children, godchildren, and cousins were the members of the family, or *la familia*—the fundamental sociocultural unit of the Portuguese.[4] They spoke Portuguese and knew little to no English—and no Hawaiian. Mostly poor, courageous, intelligent, yet uneducated and hence illiterate, they agreed to plantation labor contracts they could not read and thus often misunderstood. Leaving their homeland, the men hoped and the women prayed for a new and better life. Their aspirations were modest—earn enough money to feed, clothe, and house their families; save a portion of their earnings to purchase land and build a home; and provide their children with enough schooling to learn to read and write and do numbers. With their contracts in hand, they crossed the world's two largest oceans to start a new life in Terra Nova, the "New Land"— their name for Hawai'i.[5]

Portuguese Immigrants before 1878: The Brava Sailors

There were approximately four hundred Portuguese in the Hawaiian Kingdom when the first shipload of Portuguese immigrants arrived in 1878. Most of them had been sailors who left whaling ships and settled in Hawai'i during the early to mid-nineteenth century.[6] They came from seaports that provisioned whaling ships with men and supplies: the Azores, Madeira, and the Cape Verde Islands (a Portuguese colony off the North African coast). The men from the Cape Verde island of Brava were known as "Black Portuguese" because of their mixed-race Portuguese-African heritage.[7] Unlike America, where pure and mixed-blood Africans had been sold into slavery before the Civil War, Hawai'i was ruled by indigenous brown-skinned monarchs who prohibited slavery. In Hawai'i, being of mixed-race or hapa held little to no stigma. To live within a nation where slavery did not exist and mixed-race Africans were equal to everyone else had to be appealing to the swarthy Brava Portuguese. A slow, steady stream of Brava sailors left their ships, married Hawaiian women, and melded into the indigenous host culture—their Portuguese surnames the only link to their European heritage.[8]

Model Hawaiian-American Citizens—White but Not Haole

Also among the four hundred immigrants who arrived prior to 1878 were those who maintained their ties to the homeland and assisted their fellow Portuguese in Hawai'i through the Santo Antonio Benevolent Society that they established in 1877. Later, the Lusitana (in 1882) and the San Martino (in 1903) Benevolent Societies were founded. Funded by membership dues and donations from Portuguese throughout Hawai'i, these societies provided financial assistance to the indigent and orphans, sick benefits to workmen who were convalescing from injuries or illness, death benefits to widows, and pensions to invalids. In 1909 they were disbursing nearly $1 million annually to Portuguese beneficiaries.

Three decades after their arrival, both Hawai'i and the Portuguese group had changed. Queen Lili'uokalani had been overthrown in 1893 and the Hawaiian Kingdom dissolved. Annexation to the United States followed in 1898, and Hawai'i became a U.S. territory. During this same period, the Portuguese community thrived. The first-generation Portuguese, who stayed on the plantation after their contracts ended, had steadily risen up the ranks to be field supervisors, or *luna*. Many more saved significant portions of their earnings and left the plantations when their contracts ended to lease and purchase land in rural communities, establishing their own farms, ranches, and dairies; some became commercial fishermen; and others moved to the city and towns, becoming skilled laborers, or they opened bakeries and shops to ply their trades.

Members of the 1.5 generation (i.e., those who immigrated as infants and children) and the second and third generations were becoming more territorial Americans than Portuguese. Compulsory education for children dramatically raised literacy rates. Small but steadily growing numbers of these children pursued higher education, returning to serve as educators, clergy, physicians, attorneys, and businessmen, while a few in the mid-twentieth century entered plantation management.

In 1909 there were 22,294 Portuguese (12 percent of the population) in Hawai'i, of which 1,239 were registered voters (nearly equal to the number of American voters then in Hawai'i). Government property records show that 1,531 Portuguese had recorded $2.5 million of real estate and personal property. Deposits from all territorial banks show that 16 percent of depositors were Portuguese and that they owned 18 percent of the total deposits.[9] In a span of thirty-one years, the former impoverished peasants were emerging as part of a new lower middle class of tradesmen—an economically self-sufficient ethnic group that took care of the most vulnerable among them.

Only one stigma haunted them. Despite being white, Portuguese were never considered part of Hawai'i's haole ethnic group. Even among other white European immigrant plantation workers such as the Germans (who came in 1881 and 1897) and Norwegians (in 1881), who were subsumed into the haole ethnic group, Portuguese remained distinct.[10]

After 1905, Portuguese from mainland Portugal began arriving along with the Azoreans and Madeirans.[11] More of the Portuguese who immigrated during this time period were urban merchants and tradesmen with some education, as well as teachers, physicians, lawyers, and academics. Hundreds came and left within a few years (over 2,000 from 1904 to 1908; and 2,600 from 1911 to 1914) to move on to California with its promise of better jobs and wages, without the provincial stigma of being plantation workers.[12] Many of these later immigrants considered Hawai'i's Portuguese community a colony of Portugal.[13] Ethnocentric cultural ties were strengthened through initiatives such as the founding of La Patria, the Portuguese language school. They advocated for equality between Portuguese and haoles and demanded better wages and upward mobility in the sugar companies.[14]

The 1940 census removed the separate nationality or ethnic classification of Portuguese (the haole classification was also removed). Portuguese were henceforth reclassified, along with haole, as Caucasian.[15] The lack of specific census data on Portuguese subsequently hindered epidemiological studies of ethnic, cultural, and socioeconomic factors associated with disparities of health, educational achievement, and social welfare for this distinct Hawai'i ethnic group. Despite these hindrances, data from the 1990 American Community Survey indicated there are approximately 900,000 individuals of "Portuguese ancestry" currently residing in the United States, with equal numbers of men and women.[16] The 2000 U.S. Census information shows that there were 1,177,112 individuals of Portuguese ancestry, of which 48,527 live in Hawai'i, making it the state with the sixth-largest Portuguese population.[17]

Today, 131 years and six generations later, Portuguese make up approximately 4 percent of Hawai'i's 1.2 million population (2000 U.S. Census). While their numbers as an ethnic group are low relative to Hawai'i's other ethnic groups, the ethnocultural influence of Portuguese is distinct, touching multiple dimensions of everyday life in Hawai'i—its foods, language, music, dance, industry, politics, arts, and ethnic humor.

Ethnocultural Identity

A NEW PLANTATION SOCIAL CLASS

By the mid-nineteenth century, sugar was the economic hub of Hawaiian society, built on the backs of ever-increasing numbers of Asian contract laborers. Haole plantation landowners governed this society. Below them, the day-to-day running of their sugar companies was led by managers—usually ambitious haole men who began as field supervisors or *luna,* who over a ten- to twenty-year period rose to the ultimate position of manager. As managerial positions became filled with the sons of owners and managers, the need arose for a new working class of white supervisors to direct the Asian workforce *without* following the usual managerial leadership track. The starting job for this new *luna* class would be at the bottom, as field hands or *hana hoe* men. Over the span of ten to twenty years, they could rise through the rank and file, up to the imposed glass ceiling, where they became *luna* without further advancement. To become this perpetual man-in-the-middle supervisor, these new *luna* would have to possess a particular set of qualities and temperament. They had to be honest, reliable, extraordinarily hardworking, loyal, and uncomplaining. They had to lack the ambition and/or ability to enter management. In this way these new *luna* would maintain order in the social hierarchy of plantation life— separating the elite haole and *kama'āina* at the top from the ambitious Asians who needed to stay at the bottom.[18]

Looking to America and Europe for the right people to form this *luna* class, the plantation owners found the perfect group among the Portuguese. Dr. William Hillebrand, a botanist and former physician to Hawai'i's royal families, was appointed by King Kalākaua to serve as commissioner of immigration.[19] As commissioner, he negotiated the immigration of foreign laborers for the sugar plantations.[20] At the time, Hillebrand was living in Madeira studying flora and possibly taking advantage of the climate that was thought to be healing for those with tuberculosis.[21] He espoused the virtues of the Portuguese, stating that Hawai'i "could not possibly get a more desirable class of immigrants...(and) they are inured to your climate."[22] In 1877, Hillebrand negotiated a labor agreement between Portugal and the Hawaiian Kingdom. The contracts required that Portuguese begin their work on the plantations as field laborers (regardless of their trade or skill), with a monthly wage of $10.00 for men and $6.00 for women, which was more than other Hawai'i field laborers; over time these wages increased up to $24.00 for common or unskilled labor.[23] A year later, on September 30, 1878, the ship *Priscilla* landed in Honolulu Harbor with 120 Portuguese men, women, and children.

THE HOMELAND: THE AZORES AND MADEIRA

What made the Portuguese the right fit for this new *luna* class? Portuguese ethnocultural identification and the forces that shaped it are central to answering this question. The evolution of the ethnocultural identity of Hawai'i's Portuguese immigrants began in 1419, when Madeira and the Azores were discovered by the Portuguese explorer Prince Henry the Navigator. Madeira (meaning "wood"—named for its woodland forests) is approximately six hundred miles southwest of Lisbon, Portugal. The Azores (meaning "hawk"—named for its large population of hawks) are located approximately a thousand miles west of Portugal. The subtropical climate and fertile soil are ideal for agriculture.

Originally uninhabited, the islands were settled beginning in 1432 as possessions of Portugal under the control and direction of Prince Henry. To encourage settlement, Prince Henry established the Donatario system of hereditary landownership.[24] Most Donatario were absent landlords who granted land to trusted men, called Capitão or Captains. Capitão developed the lands according to what the soils, terrain, and climate supported. The first Donatario and Capitão were from Portugal and Flanders and brought the workforce of peasants and skilled laborers to the islands. Over the subsequent centuries, these Portuguese and Flemish groups would intermarry and their cultures seamlessly accommodated.

In 1750, the Colonia Contract system of landownership and land use was established in the islands, replacing the Donatario system. The key difference between the Donatario and Colonia systems was a written contract, as opposed to a royal edict, that gave landlords hereditary title to the land.

Under the Donatario and subsequent Colonia Contract systems, the islands were quickly developed into vineyards and plantations, towns and churches were built, and an island aristocracy supported by the peasantry and tradesmen grew. The harbors of these islands would become the last landfall for provisioning ships sailing from Europe and Africa on to the Caribbean, South America, and around the Horn to the Pacific.

Unlike other Western European nations that were entering the Industrial Revolution in the late eighteenth century, Portugal and its Atlantic islands were underdeveloped in terms of scientific and industrial advances. This meant that life for the Azorean and Madeiran working class was harsh far into the early twentieth century. Their life consisted largely of subsistence farming and fishing, grueling work for meager wages with little hope to own land, landlord fees to pay for using the community ovens, or *forno*, to bake bread, and no public schools. While there were hospitals and capable physicians, they were expensive. Most used folk healers called *curadeiras* (female healers) and *curandors* (male healers) for their ailments and injuries. With barely enough to feed their own families, extending hospitality to strangers was rare. Frugality was central to a family's ability to feed and clothe themselves and to save a coin for the Church.

The Roman Catholic Church was the spiritual wellspring for the poor (as well as the wealthy). Religious faith and prayer comprised the peasant's central coping strategy for dealing with the unending strife and to ward off the curses, the evil eye, and bad omens cast by the sorcerers or witches called *feitiçieras*. Even the poorest homes had a family altar, called *presepios* or *lapinha*, on which they displayed the nativity scene made up of dolls, candles, pieces of glass, pebbles, and plants with offerings of flowers, food, and gifts for the baby Jesus. Answered prayers from royals that resulted in miracles were memorialized through festivals, or *festas*. *Festas* served a larger secular purpose beyond religious piety and spiritual renewal. During *festas*, work ceased and music was played by troubadours who sang their soulful, improvised songs, or *fado*—songs of fate extemporaneously describing life lessons, beauty, and romance. Young men played their guitars and traditional instruments to attract and court their future wives. Families and dancing troupes walked to neighboring villages to share food, sing, and dance the *chamarita*—a kind of square dance with rhythmic movements that embodies the Iberian Peninsula, Mediterranean, and African musical influences. Thus, *festas* were community rituals that reaffirmed and strengthened their solidarity or ethnic identification as Portuguese.

Portuguese landlords had almost total power over the lives of the peasants and working classes on these relatively isolated islands. Any material assets these peasant and working-class families accumulated could be unilaterally taken away by their landlords; thus they remained quietly self-reliant within their homes and obedient to their landlords. Survival and success in such an insular and authoritarian system favored temperaments that were pragmatic, long-suffering, tolerant, perfectionistic, loyal, and good-natured. Humor and teasing, rather than outright anger and aggression, were used to cope with the unfairness of an unjust landlord or the frustrating reality that, with rare exceptions, your lot in life at birth was your fate.

Portuguese humor among the working classes was manifested in the peculiar tradition of nicknames, or *alcunhas,* that stayed with a person for life, often becoming their actual names and thereby passed on for generations. *Alcunhas* playfully mocked different kinds of characteristics or situations about a person. These included describing a physical peculiarity such as O Beiça (Thick Lips), a mannerism such as A Maria Bufa (Windy Mary), an occupation such as Rosa das Vacas (Rose of the Cows), a birthplace such as A Maria do Canto (Mary of the Corner), or of incongruous utterances such as O Chove Neve (It's Raining Snow).[25]

Azorean and Madeiran immigrants thrived within a craftsmen's culture—where the work of one's hands honored and celebrated their ability to create beauty within and between the grueling daily toil of peasant life. They planted extraordinarily vibrant flower and herb gardens filled with profusions of marigolds, roses, scented heath, bougainvillea, basil, and lavender that thrived in the Atlantic subtropical climate. Men built handsome furniture, cabinetry, and stringed instruments. Women created elegant needlepoint embroidery and crocheted fine laced doilies and spreads to bring an unexpected refinement to the pedestrian instruments of daily living—covering kitchen tables, chairs, beds, nightstands, and toilets.

There was one certainty for these Portuguese families: The social order of their lives did not change. From the mid-fifteenth century through the mid-nineteenth century, a period of over three hundred years, the Donatario and Colonia Contract systems determined and influenced nearly every aspect of daily living—local governance, taxation, the court system, land use, economic development, social welfare, health care, and education—for the people of Madeira and the Azores. These systems shaped the knowledge of farming and land development for Hawai'i's Portuguese immigrants, especially those who came before

1905. Even more important, the Donatario and Colonia systems developed the ethnocultural template that determined the internal characteristics, qualities, perceptions, and behavior patterns commonly seen among the members of this ethnic group. This ethnocultural template determined the nature of the relationships that Portuguese immigrants would have with each other, their plantation bosses, the field laborers they supervised, and the other ethnic groups they would meet in Terra Nova.

The Portuguese *Luna:* Plantation Stereotype, Scapegoat, and Symbol

Given the ethnocultural evolution in their Portuguese homeland, the first generation of immigrants related to the sugar plantation owners and managers as they had their Azorean and Madeiran landlords. In doing so, they exactly met the qualifications for the new *luna:* white men (and women) accustomed to hard work, compliant, and perfectionistic. They were loyal to their bosses, followed Christian morals, albeit with papist rituals, and accepted their place in Hawai'i's plantation society. As *luna* they were unrelenting taskmasters who drove the laborers they supervised hard, whether Asian, Hawaiian, or Portuguese.

Plantation managers had power similar to fifteenth-century Portuguese landlords and governed nearly every aspect of daily plantation life. Some managers—particularly those closely affiliated with missionary families—were progressive and fair. Other managers were dictatorial and ruthless—building jails and using whips to punish and correct nonconforming laborers, especially the Asians.[26] An important day-to-day role of the Portuguese *luna* was to serve as buffers between the Asians and haoles. How these *luna* supervised their labor crews was shaped by the character and temperament of the plantation managers and haole overseers who directed them. Within this context, the stifled rage of Asians against their haole bosses was displaced to their Portuguese man-in-the-middle supervisors. This harsh work environment spawned the stereotype of the sadistic, whip-wielding Portuguese *luna,* who in reality was an exaggeration and symbolic representation of the unfairness, racism, and brutal conditions of plantation life. It was historical irony that the Portuguese, who had lived for centuries oppressed by the wealthy and powerful in their homeland, became the proverbial scapegoat and thus labeled the "dumb Pawdagee" who kept a fragile peace on the plantations between haoles and Asians.

Terra Nova—The "New Land" of Hawai'i

The first impressions of the Hawaiian Kingdom that nineteenth-century Portuguese immigrants shared as their ships sailed along the coastline heading for landfall was how uncannily similar Hawai'i was—in climate, terrain, and flora—to their Atlantic homeland. The differences of color and customs began to appear after they landed. At the harbors, they could not understand nor speak the languages being used. The mix of skin colors, facial features, nationalities, and races was unlike anything they had seen. Whites like themselves were called haole and spoke English. Brown-skinned *kānaka* with big, round, dark eyes, broad smiles, and easy liquid movements spoke Hawaiian and were members of the native race whose monarchs ruled the kingdom. Yellow-skinned Orientals or coolies, who avoided eye contact, moved in quick, purposeful motions and spoke their own indecipherable languages. This mix of people communicated and worked together by speaking Pidgin, a language created on the plantations that combined English and Hawaiian with words from each of the Asian ethnic groups.

The Portuguese were transported to their plantations and put to work immediately; they quickly learned Pidgin. Soon Portuguese words were added to the Pidgin vernacular. Portuguese in Pidgin became the Hawaiianized Pokoki, the anglicized Pawdagee, or the Asian diminutive Pocho. Plantation life was similar to what they had known in Portugal, with several significant differences: Wives and children could also work for wages that helped contribute to the family savings; it was the law that their children attend school; they could bake bread in community *furno* free of charge; and they could plan for a future beyond the plantation.

THE PORTUGUESE INDIVIDUAL AND FAMILY

Plantation life for the first, 1.5, and second generations of Portuguese, who lived in camps segregated by race, was a continuation of life in their homeland villages. They followed the ethnocultural template of their parents and grandparents in temperament, humor, work ethic, gender roles, language, religion, and home life. Families were large, multigenerational, and close-knit. As they moved off the plantations, they settled in the higher elevations that have temperatures similar to their homeland.

Individualism and competition among Portuguese within the workplace was expressed through the culture of craftsmanship, such as developing special harvesting equipment on the plantation, designing a custom guitar, or leatherwork. Outside the workplace, individualism and competition were expressed in their attire, singing, dancing, flower gardens, and homemaking skills such as cooking, baking, and crocheting.

Individual development among Portuguese is inseparable from *la familia* because it is within the family that children learn (a) their expected roles, (b) to develop core relationships that influence their future relationships, and (c) how to relate to the physical and spiritual world. It is also within the family that these immigrant children taught their parents what they learned in school: speaking, reading, and writing in English.

In the workplace, Portuguese men were subservient to their plantation bosses, but at home they ruled. Their household was their domain and everything (and everyone) within it belonged to them and was their responsibility. Portuguese fathers were usually strict and not given to verbally expressing their affections for their children and wives directly. Instead, they showed their affections through the craftsmen's culture by doing creative projects that brought joy. With their children watching and participating, they built toys, musical instruments, or vehicular inventions (e.g., wagons, kites, guitars) that delighted and taught practical skills. To show their devotion to their wives, they turned over their wages on payday, went to mass each Sunday, serenaded and danced with them on special occasions, made significant financial decisions jointly, and worked on home improvements and yardwork that met their wives' expectations.

Portuguese women were the queens of their households—their activities in the home aimed to serve their husbands, honor their parents, and raise upstanding children who looked out for each other. Free to express their feelings for their children, Portuguese mothers (and grandmothers) showered their children with verbal and physical expressions of their affections, praises, dislikes, criticisms, and discipline. Portuguese mothers and daughters developed close relationships as they worked together to complete the household chores: cooking, baking, cleaning, caring for babies and young children, sewing, crocheting, gardening, and so on. Throughout the day—every day—they shared their thoughts, feelings, and hopes, and sought mutual advice from each other about events in their lives. These mother-daughter relationships endured even after daughters married and were raising families of their own.

Within their homes, Portuguese fathers, grandfathers, eldest sons, and sons who brought home a wage were served first and given the best foods at every meal. After their workday was done, fathers and sons returned home to tend livestock and complete outdoor chores. After dinner they might play their guitars, sing *fados*, and drink beer or wine. Their laundry, work lunches, and housekeeping were done by the women and girls of the house. Unmarried sons, like their fathers, gave their wages to their mothers, out of which they received an allowance. With these earnings, wives and mothers paid for the family expenses— usually setting a portion of the wages for the bank savings deposit. The household expenses and savings were reviewed regularly by the head of the household, and any withdrawals had to be done with his consent. Grandparents had special places in their sons' or daughters' home, but it was the male head of the household or breadwinner—not the family patriarch—who had the final say in major decisions.

Portuguese family size through the mid-twentieth century was large, averaging four children per family, with ranges from one to fifteen children per family. Children's roles and relationships were shaped by predetermined gender roles and their ordinal birth ranking. Sons, particularly firstborn sons, had authority over and responsibility for their younger siblings. As young men, they had some authority over their mothers, superseded only by the authority of their fathers. Ideally, sons would follow in the footsteps of their fathers—not rising higher than their fathers, but rather to succeed in their vocations and professions in order to affirm and enhance their father's esteem and bring pride to the family name. Daughters were born to serve their fathers, mothers, grandparents, and older brothers and care for their younger siblings—in that order. Girls often pursued higher education by becoming nuns or going into professions such as secretarial work, teaching, nursing, and social work. If a girl was found to be gifted as a healer, she was trained—often by a family or community elder—to become a *curadeira*. Despite the hierarchical pecking order and sibling rivalries in these large families, when a family member was threatened by anyone outside the family, an instantaneous familial reflex was triggered, differences set aside, and siblings united in a singular focus of defense and support.

Marriage among the first and 1.5 generation of immigrants was predominantly kept within the Portuguese group. Unlike the old country, where courtships were long and revolved around village *festas*, Hawai'i plantation life required shorter courtships in which young men (and widowers) would see a woman—often a girl of fifteen or sixteen—

while visiting friends at another camp. He would tell his mother (or in the case of a widower, make a query to the girl's parents) of his intentions. Shortly thereafter, mothers would arrange for the man to speak to the woman's father. If the father approved of the suitor, he formally introduced his daughter to the suitor and asked if she approved of the match. If she agreed, the couple received her parents' blessing, were married by the priest, and set up a home of their own.

SOCIOCULTURAL RELATIONSHIPS AND NETWORKS

Indigenous Portuguese culture began with the Lusitania warrior tribes of the Iberian Peninsula that were eventually conquered by the Romans in the fifth century A.D. Later, the cultures of the African and Indian Portuguese colonies were integrated. Hence, Iberian, Mediterranean, North Africa, and Indian cultural influences have created the fusion of Portuguese culture expressed in native dress, foods infused with spices and olive oil, soulful folk songs, and folk dancing. While their native dress changed to Hawai'i or American attire, Portuguese continue to wear vibrant colors with crocheted lace, sequins, and embroidered vests and shawls.

In Hawai'i, the Roman Catholic Church continued to be the central religious and spiritual orientation and social gathering place for Portuguese, even with marriage to non-Catholics. The Church, bishop, and parish priest continued to govern the major rites of passage within the Portuguese family—marriage, conception of children, baptism, confirmation, communion, confession, penance, death, burial, and the afterlife. Prayers said by women, girls, and young boys to God, the Holy Virgin, Jesus, the Holy Ghost, and the appropriate Catholic saints continued to be the first response to all problems and challenges, while the men and older boys stood stoic and penitent. The family high altars, or *lapinhas,* adorned with the nativity scene were displayed during the designated holy days.

Festas celebrating traditional holy days—such as Boas Festas (Christmas), Easter, and other Portugal observances such as the Feast of the Holy Ghost—continued to be celebrated in Hawai'i. These *festas* brought Portuguese together and were the forum through which their culture was perpetuated and showcased. Religious spiritual beliefs and reaffirmation of the royal miracles within the homeland were interwoven with the preparation—and selling for Church fund-raising—of traditional foods and crafts, traditional dance and music, and storytelling of the homeland and coming to Terra Nova.

With later generations, Portuguese foods moved out of the Church and into the larger community. Notable examples are the baking of Portuguese sweetbread, or *pão duce*, during Boas Festas; and the Portuguese Catholic religious observance of Shrove or Fat Tuesday, the day before Lent, in which all the fat, sugar, and leaven of the household are used up to make Portuguese holeless donuts or *malasadas*. As immigrants left the plantations, Portuguese bakeries opened and began selling these goods to the larger communities. Portuguese ranches and farms prepared and sold *linguiça* (Portuguese sausages). Other traditional dishes that became a part of the contemporary local culture of Hawai'i include *vinha d'alhos* (hunks of pork or beef marinated in vinegar, garlic, and spices and then roasted with potatoes), *hulihuli* chicken (chicken dry-rubbed with spices and barbequed on a turning spit or *hulihuli*, the Hawaiian verb for "turning over"), pickled *bacãlao* (dried salted cod) with sweet onions, and an island version of the original *caldo verde*, or Portuguese bean soup.[27]

Education and intellectual pursuits were new to the majority of the early immigrants, and thus individualism and competition in education were neither common nor encouraged. The combination of (a) having Portuguese as their primary language, (b) high illiteracy rates, and (c) being stuck in the middle between the haole plantation management (with their imposed glass ceiling) and their fellow laborers (who were predominantly Asian, ambitious, and their designated "inferiors") created daunting obstacles for Portuguese immigrants to educationally advance. In 1920, the Portuguese were the only group that petitioned against the plan to establish English Standard Schools, which required that children pass a *written* English language test to be admitted. The petitioners desired "that the sole consideration, aside from ordinary scholastic requirements for the grade, be the *quality of the applicant's oral English.*"[28] Most Portuguese children were unable to pass the written exam and were sent to non-English standard schools. These obstacles greatly diminished the foresight of Portuguese parents to see education as a means of social advancement for their children. As soon as the compulsory age for schooling was reached, most ended the formal education of their children, who were expected to work to help support the family.

The free plantation health care significantly reduced the need for *curadeira*, and by the mid- to late twentieth century these healers were largely replaced by allopathic physicians. As Portuguese moved off the plantations and had to pay for their medical care, many used *curadeira* for traditional vacuum cup treatments to ease breathing, muscle aches, and inflammation, and massages with poultices to help with a specific affliction of infancy called *bucho virado,* or "turned stomach."[29] *Curadeira* were respected community elders who often taught non-Portuguese wives of Portuguese men how to bake in the *furno* and prepare Portuguese dishes.

A New Ethnocultural Identity

From the moment of their arrival, the process of cultural accommodation began between the Portuguese and indigenous Hawaiian cultures. Hawaiian cultural values such as aloha, *lōkahi,* and *'ohana* were central to building an Island society that was motivated and renewed by its ability to interact with and discover the dimensions of resonance—in physical appearance, language, food, work, play, aesthetics, emotional attachments, beliefs, and behaviors—between and among different people. The ethnocultural evolution between the two groups resonated in several areas: the centrality of the extended family and communal support for members within their ethnic group; dedication to spiritual-religious pursuits; an oral—as opposed to written—tradition of storytelling and songs to record life events; reverence for the land and farming, as well as love for the sea and fishing; and a passion for music, song, and dance.

DESIGNING THE UKULELE: A PORTUGUESE HAWAIIAN FUSION

Making music was the first and perhaps most powerful resonance between indigenous Hawaiians and Portuguese. The traditional four-stringed *machete* (also called the *braguinha*) and the five-stringed *rajao* made their notable appearance on the vessel *Ravenscrag,* which arrived in Honolulu Harbor on August 23, 1879, with 419 Portuguese from Madeira. Three cabinetmakers and village *festa* musicians onboard— Augusto Dias, Manuel Nunes, and José do Espírito Santo—sang and played their instruments that looked like miniature guitars.[30] These men would transform the *rajao* into the taro patch fiddle and the *machete* into the ukulele—the iconic musical instrument of Hawai'i. King Kalākaua popularized the ukulele when he had Dias make him one, which he played to songs and hula he composed. Kalākaua, a patron of Dias, had Dias play at his social gatherings.[31] Dias introduced the Portuguese tradition of the traveling troubadour, moving through the king's garden parties or luaus with his small band of musicians and hula dancers.

Today's singing troupe of musicians and hula dancers strolling through a luau continues this Portuguese tradition, whose origins came from the eighteenth- and nineteenth-century tradition of traveling between villages to celebrate *festas* with music, dance, and food. What had begun as a Portuguese instrument had been redesigned and embraced as an indigenous Hawaiian musical instrument. The ukulele would artistically enhance and extend the development of Hawaiian dance into the hula *'auana* (informal hula without ceremony or offering). Out of this dance form, the hula-hula girls wearing ti-leaf skirts and flower leis were spawned—Hawai'i's international symbols of aloha and paradise.

INTRAGROUP RELATIONSHIPS AND AN EVOLVING SOCIAL STRUCTURE

Formal education was not an ethnocultural bridge for Portuguese in Hawai'i. While other immigrant groups in Hawai'i rose in social status through education, Portuguese in Hawai'i rose in social standing by being frugal, building up substantial bank savings, buying land, and developing productive farms, dairies, ranches, and other commercial businesses in construction, retail, and craftsmanship. Despite their relatively low levels of higher education, Portuguese were active civic leaders—first through their benevolent societies and the Church, then through civic organizations such as the YMCA, unions, and political parties. Portuguese were active voters who became high-ranking members in the Hawai'i Republican and Democratic parties, as well as elected politicians. From 1909 to the present day, there have been over two hundred county council members and territorial and state legislators of Portuguese ancestry, among whom were three Senate presidents, four speakers of the House, four mayors, and two lieutenant governors.

Race was another dimension of resonance for Portuguese, who felt a kinship to their fellow whites or haoles. In the early twentieth century, Portuguese advancement in social status was predominantly driven by an assimilation model, with immigrants trying to become haole and/ or American. Those who achieved this sociocultural goal did so at the cost of their ethnocultural identity—that is, they stopped being Português—possessing and living the culture of their ancestral homeland. Rather than build and modify their ethnocultural template through an evolutionary process, they threw it out and replaced it with their perception of what was the haole or American ethnocultural identity. Some anglicized their names: Jaõa Diniz became John Dennis, Antonio De Andrade became Antone Andrade, and Maria Perreira became Mary

Perry. Others left the Roman Catholic Church and became Anglicans or Protestants. Many, mostly women, married haoles or Americans. In tactically redrawing the racial boundaries that allowed them to cross over into the haole American world, assimilated Portuguese gave up their ability to navigate the ethnic and cultural boundaries that made them Português.

A ROLE MODEL FOR A NEW PORTUGUESE ETHNOCULTURAL IDENTITY

Dr. John M. Felix was the third generation of Madeiran immigrants and the first Hawai'i-born Portuguese physician.[32] He was a trailblazer whose life story elevated him to mythic status and created a catalytic ripple within the ethnocultural evolution of Portuguese in Hawai'i. John Felix was delivered anoxic and unresponsive by his maternal grandmother, Josephine Rodriquez Branco, a midwife—trained on the job, delivering Portuguese babies within the immigration station at Honolulu Harbor. Josephine had come from Madeira at age thirteen and put to work (with no time for school) on the Maui plantations. After stabilizing her daughter, Josephine resuscitated her grandson. And he, inspired partly by Josephine, became a physician.

Felix developed a thriving medical practice made up of Portuguese families, along with patients of all colors and ages. He served as president of the Hawai'i Medical Society. A devout Catholic, he served his Church and worked to advance education as a regent at Hawai'i's Catholic-run Chaminade University. At age forty-three, Felix was awarded a papal knighthood by Pope John XXIII, a crowning achievement for a remarkable servant leader who had risen to the pinnacle of Hawai'i and American society while remaining within his ethnocultural core Português, and something more—he possessed the deep resonance and fluency with indigenous Hawaiian and American cultural values. This was a new ethnocultural identification model, as the haole assimilation model waned, replaced by Portuguese ethnic pride, acculturation, and accommodation into a new multiculturalism.

INTERGROUP RELATIONSHIPS AND THE NEW HAPA ETHNOCULTURAL IDENTITY

Intermarriage. Like every other ethnic group that came to Hawai'i, intermarriage occurred early for Portuguese. By the second and third generations, intermarriage markedly increased, with more Portuguese females than males married outside of their ethnic group. Between

1930 and 1934, close to half of Portuguese brides married non-Portuguese, while just over one-fourth of the Portuguese grooms married non-Portuguese; in total, over a third of the Portuguese married individuals outside their ethnic group.[33]

Intermarriage would continue to increase rapidly. In 1938, the Hawai'i Board of Health vital statistics show that half of Portuguese brides married, by a 2-to-1 ratio, grooms who identified themselves as "American"—usually white or haole. Portuguese grooms continued to prefer marrying within their group, choosing Portuguese brides most of the time. However, by 1938 out-marriage had increased to a 2-to-1 ratio. These Portuguese grooms married women who identified themselves as Hawaiian and part-Hawaiian.

By 1941, Portuguese had the highest out-marriage rates of any ethnic group in Hawai'i—a trend that would continue through the rest of the twentieth century. This intermarriage trend, seen within the context of the U.S. Census, which lacked the ethnic designation of Portuguese or part-Portuguese, suggests that the population of Portuguese in Hawai'i may be significantly underestimated.

Today's fourth-, fifth-, and sixth-generation hapa Portuguese arguably possess the most integrated ethnocultural identities in Hawai'i. This Portuguese hapa group seamlessly integrates the cultures of the ethnic groups from whom they descend.

Ethnic Humor. The peculiar tradition of Portuguese humor expressed through nicknames or *alcunhas* was applied to the different ethnic groups on the plantations. Hence, peculiar physical traits, cultural practices and ways of thinking, communication and behaviors associated with Hawaiians, haoles, Chinese, Japanese, Filipinos, and Portuguese (and still later, Samoans) were identified and playfully mocked. Like *alcunhas,* these ethnic peculiarities were passed on for generations through the comedic Pidgin art form of the Pawdagee joke. These ethnic peculiarities included the dumb Pawdagee; the haole surrogate, whose problem-solving logic is limited to his personal and provincial reference point; the big-bodied, strong Hawaiian who made up the majority of the police and firemen; the frugal Chinese or *pake* businessman whose singular focus was on making money; or the Filipino whose food delicacies included eating dog and goat.

Superficially, these ethnic peculiarities were stereotypes; however, in the insular plantation environment, teeming with diversity and the potential for violence between the race-based hierarchy, the Pawdagee joke was more than that. It provided the haole bosses at the top, the

Asian and Hawaiian *hana hoe* men at the bottom, and the Portuguese *luna* in the middle the framework and means to share each other's ethnocultural peculiarities and laugh about them *together without fear of retaliation*. The Portuguese *luna*, being the proverbial man in the middle, got it from both sides via the dumb Pawdagee stereotype jokes that served the respective needs of the managers and the *hana hoe* men. A dumb Pawdagee could not ascend to manager, and he would never be as smart or ambitious as the Asians, nor as big and strong as the Hawaiians. This form of ethnic humor forged intergroup relationships between the Portuguese *luna*, the Chinese, Japanese, Filipino, and Hawaiian *hana hoe* men, and even the haole managers, who all used the Pawdagee joke to mute the tensions between them. Portuguese *luna* tolerated being the butt of the joke for their bosses and subordinates—perhaps because this fulfilled their role as the buffer between the *hana hoe* men and haoles and because they knew firsthand from their Azorean and Madeiran landlords the need for the oppressed to use humor to vent anger.

In present-day Hawai'i, comedian Frank Wilcox Napuakekaulike DeLima, a Hawaiian, Portuguese, Chinese, hapa haole, has perfected the Pawdagee joke. One of DeLima's favorite jokes echoes back to plantation life:

> Three men are stuck on the 17th floor of a burning building: a Chinese, a Filipino and a Pawdagee. A fire truck races to the scene. All the firemen are big Hawaiians. When they step off the truck, the truck goes up 3 feet. They pull out a big net. And, the Chinese on the 17th floor yells, "Halp! Halp!" The Hawaiian firemen yell, "Come on Pake, jump!" He jumps and before he hits the net the Hawaiians pull the net away. SPLAT! And the Hawaiians say, "That's what you get for changing the prices every 2 minutes!" The Filipino is next.... He jumps and again the Hawaiians pull the net away. SPLAT! And the Hawaiians say, "That's what you get for eating (the dog) Spot!" The Pawdagee guy yells, "Halp! I scared!" And the Hawaiians yell back, "Come on, Pawdagee jump!" The Pawdagee yells down, "No way! I saw what you did to the uddah two guys. No way you goin' pull the net away from me. Put the net down on the ground!"[34]

DeLima's comedy, which grew out of plantation life, is a form of sophisticated play in the twenty-first century that serves the purpose of negotiating diversity, cultural differences, and socioeconomic power differentials.

Biopsychosocial Factors: Enduring Ethnocultural Traits

The ethnocultural development of Portuguese in Hawai'i moved in three alternative paths, each influenced by the environment within which these immigrants found themselves when they arrived in Hawai'i. Environmental factors that influenced which path was taken included sociocultural, economic, political, and geographic dimensions. The mixed-race Portuguese-African Brava sailors took the first path. They unshackled themselves from Portuguese colonization in exchange for their emancipation within the indigenous Hawaiian monarchy, where institutional racism did not exist. Many married Hawaiians and assimilated into the indigenous host culture. By the twentieth century, their children and grandchildren would identify themselves as Hawaiian.

Some Portuguese plantation immigrants from the second and third generations followed the second path. They threw out the visible characteristics of their ethnocultural template (e.g., Portuguese language and Catholicism) created in Portugal's oppressive landlord system and chose to assimilate into the American haole ethnic group, replacing Catholicism with Protestant beliefs.

Most Portuguese plantation immigrants chose the third path and kept their ethnocultural template that had been developed over three centuries in their homeland. They accepted the fate they had been brought or born into in Terra Nova, which contained a promise of prosperity and multiculturalism unimaginable in Portugal. With each passing generation, they and their descendants learned to build the ethnocultural bridges—through acculturation, accommodation, intermarriage, and humor—that would reshape their ethnocultural template. The modified template would produce a new ethnocultural identity that retained the enduring values of Português while fluidly integrating the indigenous Hawaiian, Asian, and American cultures in their environment.

No matter the path taken in their ethnocultural evolution, several values, behaviors, and beliefs have endured among Hawai'i's Portuguese and can be organized into four overarching themes: work ethic, artistry and aesthetics, communication modes to establish and sustain relationships, and ethics and morals. A description of the four overarching themes by biopsychosocial factors is provided in Table 4.1. Of the sixteen factors listed in the table, five are malleable and modifiable over time. Eleven are enduring ethnocultural factors that originated in Portugal and persisted after nearly five centuries among Portuguese immigrants in Hawai'i and the continental United States.

While Roman Catholicism is still the predominant religion of Portuguese, it is the affiliation to a religious community of faith and, in the case of Hawai'i, a personal commitment to practice indigenous spiritual beliefs that guide and sustain one's relationship to others, as well as to the land and sea. Geography and socioeconomic opportunities appear to be significant influences that support the enduring factors and modify the malleable factors. In looking at the top six states that have large Portuguese communities, virtually all of them are geographically near the ocean (e.g., Hawai'i, the West Coast, the East Coast, and the Gulf of Mexico) or a relatively short distance from the ocean in rural areas used for pastureland and farming.

Socioeconomic opportunities, particularly within communities that did not stigmatize Portuguese as illiterate and therefore intellectually challenged, enhanced the social and educational advancement of Portuguese. Higher socioeconomic status influenced all five of the malleable factors through the mediating factor of higher education (e.g., high school or college). Educated Portuguese became less provincial in their lifestyle, are more likely to sketch and paint to express themselves, are drawn to urban settings, are more likely to vote and become civic leaders, and do not need to rely on the Pawdagee joke or ethnic humor to create an ethnocultural bridge with their colleagues and peers. Finally, all of the enduring factors have the common threads of keeping orderly control in one's surroundings and sustaining meaningful relationships—with the boss, the family, people you must communicate with, and with the Divine—that keep one safe, nurtured, playful, and thriving. Not surprisingly, those factors that endured found powerful ethnocultural resonance in the indigenous Hawaiian host culture.

Summary and Conclusions

The ethnocultural development of Portuguese in Hawai'i represents a unique opportunity to examine how members of the nineteenth-century's "superior" white race evolved outside their European homeland. If the nineteenth-century theory of white superiority and advanced civilizations was sound, the Portuguese immigrants—like

Table 4.1. Enduring (hardwired) and malleable ethnocultural factors

	OVERARCHING THEMES			
	WORK ETHIC	ARTISTRY & AESTHETICS	COMMUNICATION MODES	ETHICS & MORALS
BIOPYCHOSOCIAL FACTORS	An indefatigable capacity to work (hardwired)	The culture of craftsmanship— to value the utility, versatility, and beauty of what one creates with your own hands out of the mundane. (hardwired)	The need to use storytell- ing—rather than trenchant parsi- mony—to relate everyday events. (hardwired)	The dedication and devotion to the safety, nurturance, integrity and well-being of the family. (hardwired)
	Perfectionism (hardwired)	The apprecia- tion of nature's beauty in flowers and planted gardens. (hardwired)	The prepara- tion of food as the penultimate act of giving. (hardwired)	The need to possess an abid- ing spiritual- religious faith in a Divinity that guides your life and the life of those you love and care about by the answering of your prayers. (hardwired)
	Loyalty and respect for authority figures (hardwired)	Telling a story by creating sketches and paintings. (malleable)	Using music, songs, and dance to communicate feelings and intentions that cannot otherwise be expressed. (hardwired)	Reverence for the land and sea. (hardwired)
	Provincial introspection of actions done by others that affect your well-being. (malleable)	Preference for the pastoral. (malleable)	*Alcunhas*—the Pawdagee joke or ethnic humor. (malleable)	Civic virtue and civic duty. (malleable)

other European working-class whites—should have easily risen to the social pinnacle of haole superiority in Hawai'i. This did not happen. Instead, they were unique in taking three different paths: assimilation to Hawaiians, assimilation to haoles, and acculturation and accommodation to all Hawai'i ethnic groups. While the intra- and intergroup dynamics of ethnocultural identification for each of these subgroups differed and resulted in a new ethnocultural identity, all three groups held fast to the deeper and more enduring cultural factors (shown in Table 4.1) that had been shaped in their homeland, then reinforced and modified by Hawai'i's indigenous population.

In 1978, the Portuguese celebrated the centennial of the Portuguese immigrants who arrived on the *Priscilla* in September 1878. Events during that centennial year catalyzed a critical examination of written and oral histories, an assessment of the Portuguese contributions to Hawai'i, and a resurgence of ethnic pride. To mark this historic event, centennial planners did what their ancestors would have done—they created the *festa*. Currently, the annual Portuguese Festa is open to the public and celebrates the oral and written history, genealogical research, music, dance, arts, crafts, and foods of Portuguese in Hawai'i. About two thousand people attend, and many attendees come seeking leads to determine who their forefathers were. Some are the descendants of second- and third-generation Portuguese who assimilated to become haole. Others are sixth- and seventh-generation grandchildren of Brava Portuguese who have discovered that their ancestor was a Portuguese sailor. Through the Portuguese Genealogical Society's database, as well as talk story sessions with Portuguese elders and historians, these seekers of identification and identity are trying to comprehend how the boundaries of race, ethnicity, and culture have reduced or enhanced their ethnocultural inheritance.

Further Reading

Basto, A. P. "Voyage of the *S. Miguel* Portuguese sailing vessel." *Hawaiian Journal of History* 21 (1987): 77–97.

Correa, G., and E. C. Knowlton. "Portuguese in Hawai'i." *Social Process in Hawai'i* 29 (1982): 70–77.

Estep, G. A. *Social Placement of the Portuguese in Hawai'i as Indicated by Factors in Assimilation.* San Francisco: R. and E. Research Associates, 1974 (originally an MA thesis, University of Southern California, 1941).

Ethnic Research and Resource Center. *The Portuguese in Hawai'i: A Resource Guide.* Honolulu, 1973.

Felix, J. H., and P. F. Senecal. *The Portuguese in Hawai'i: The Centennial Edition*, Honolulu: Felix and Senecal, 1978.

Kuykendall, R. S. *The Hawaiian Kingdom, Volume 3, 1874–1893: The Kalakaua Dynasty*. Honolulu: University of Hawai'i Press, 1967.

Marques, A. J. 1911. "The Portuguese in Hawai'i." In *Thrum's Hawaiian Annual and Standard Guide* 13 (1911): 43–53, Honolulu: Honolulu Star-Bulletin Printing Co.

Nordyke, E. C. "Blacks in Hawai'i." *Hawaiian Journal of History* 22 (1988): 243.

Santos, R. L. *Azoreans to California: A History of Migration and Settlement*. Denair, CA: Alley-Cass Publications, 1995.

Walker, W. F. *The Azores or Western Islands: A Political, Commercial and Geographical Account*. London: Trubner and Co., 1886. Retrieved on June 10, 2009, from http://www.archive.org/details/azoresorwesternioowalk.

Notes

1. W. F. Walker, *The Azores or Western Islands: A Political, Commercial and Geographical Account*, London: Trubner and Co., 1886, retrieved from http://www.archive.org/dtails/azoresorwesternioowalk; B. Camara, "The Portuguese civil code and the *colonia* tenancy contract in Madeira (1867–1967)," *Continuity and Change* 21(2) (2006): 213–233.

2. Camara 2006.

3. Walker 1886.

4. J. H. Felix and P. F. Senecal, *The Portuguese in Hawaii*, Honolulu: Felix and Senecal, 1978: xviii.

5. Ibid. Henry, John and Peter F. Felix Senecal (1978)

6. E. C. Knowlton, "Portuguese in Hawaii," paper presented at the Thirteenth University of Kentucky Foreign Language Conference, Lexington, KY, 1960.

7. E. C. Nordyke, "Blacks in Hawaii," *Hawaiian Journal of History* 22 (1988): 243; G. E. Brooks, "Cabo Verde: Gulag of the South Atlantic: Racism, fishing prohibitions, and famines," *History in Africa* 33 (2006): 101–135.

8. R. S. Kuykendall, *The Hawaiian Kingdom, Vol. 3, 1874–1893: The Kalakaua Dynasty*, Honolulu: University of Hawai'i Press, 1967.

9. A. J. Marques, "The Portuguese in Hawaii," in *Thrum's Hawaiian Annual*, Honolulu: Star-Bulletin Printing Co., 1911: 43–53.

10. J. A. Geschwender, R. Carroll-Seguin, and H. Brill, "The Portuguese and haoles of Hawaii: Implications for the origin of ethnicity," *American Sociological Review* 53 (1988): 515–527.

11. Felix and Senecal 1978, Compilation of Harbor Master's Record from State of Hawaii Archives: 28–30.

12. Marques 1911.

13. A. P. Basto, "Voyage of the *S. Miguel* Portuguese sailing vessel," *Hawaiian Journal of History* 21 (1987): 77–97.

14. E. C. Knowlton, "Portuguese language resources for Hawaiian history," in *Hawaiian Historical Society Annual Report* (17th ed.), Honolulu: Honolulu Advertiser Publishing Co., 1961: 24–37; J. F. Freitas, *Portuguese Hawaiian Memories,* Honolulu: Portuguese Genealogical Society of Hawaii and Hawaii Council on Portuguese Heritage, 1930: 146.

15. G. A. Estep, *Social Placement of the Portuguese in Hawaii as Indicated by Factors in Assimilation,* San Francisco: R. & E. Research Associates, 1974 (originally an MA thesis, University of Southern California, 1941).

16. U.S. Census, "USA Portuguese Census 2000," retrieved via the Internet on January 28, 2009: http://www.census.gov/population/socdemo/ancestry/Portuguese.txt.

17. U.S. Census, "The American Community Survey," retrieved via the Internet on January 28, 2009: http://www.crgate.com/scensus.htm.

18. L. H. Fuchs, *Hawaii Pono: An Ethnic and Political History,* Honolulu: Bess Press, 1961.

19. F. W. Clarke, "Biographical memoir of William Francis Hillebrand, 1853–1925," *National Academy of Sciences* 12 (1925): 41–70, retrieved from http://books.nap.edu/html/biomems/whillebrand.pdf.

20. D. E. Kelley, "Historical collections of the Hawaiian Islands: King Kamehameha IV," December 9, 2000, http://www.genrecords.net/emailregistry/vols/00026.html#0006374.

21. Ethnic Research and Resource Center, *The Portuguese in Hawaii: A Resource Guide,* Honolulu, 1973; Walker 1886. William Hillebrand came to Hawaiʻi because the climate was thought to be healing for his pulmonary tuberculosis, which he contracted in Germany after his medical studies were completed. He lived in the Hawaiian Kingdom for twenty years. During his time in Hawaiʻi, he founded the Hawaiʻi Medical Society, was the first chief of physicians at the Queen's Hospital, and served as the physician to King Kamehameha IV, Queen Emma, and the royals. As Hawaiʻi's commissioner of immigration, he also negotiated the Chinese labor contracts of 1877.

22. Kuykendall 1967.

23. Ethnic Research and Resource Center 1973: 12.

24. Walker 1886: 32–35; C. O. Sauer, *Northern Mists,* Berkeley, CA: University of California Press, 1968: 12–29.

25. E. T. Cabral, "The romance of Rosa Das Vacas," in *The Portuguese in Hawaii,* Honolulu: Felix and Senecal, 1978.

26. Fuchs 1961: 61–65.

27. J. Peralto, *Traditional No Longer: How Hawaii Changed Portuguese Cuisine,* McMinnville, OR: n.p., 2007.

28. J. R. Hughes, "The demise of the English Standard School System in Hawai'i," *Hawaiian Journal of History* 27 (1993): 65–89.

29. E. W. Carvalho, "The Portuguese," in *Peoples and Cultures of Hawaii: A Psychosocial Profile*, ed. J. F. McDermott, W. S. Tseng, and T. W. Maretzki, Honolulu: University of Hawai'i Press, 1980: 100–110.

30. J. King and J. Tranquada, "A new history of the origins and development of the ukulele, 1838–1915," *Hawaiian Journal of History* 37 (2003): 1–32.

31. E. Cabral, "Grandpa was a troubadour," in *The Portuguese in Hawaii*, Honolulu: Felix and Senecal, 1978: 143–148.

32. L. Fruto, "Portuguese pioneer knows many faces," *Honolulu Star-Bulletin* article of October 5, 1966, reprinted in *The Portuguese in Hawaii*, Honolulu: Felix and Senecal, 1978: 79–80.

33. Estep 1941: 43.

34. D. Hall, "An interview with Frank DeLima," 2004, retrieved from http://www.forbisthemighty.com/acidlogic/frankdelima.htm, downloaded on March 29, 2009.

CHAPTER 5

The Japanese

Courtenay Matsu, Junji Takeshita, Satoru Izutsu, and Earl Hishinuma

The largest number of Japanese came to Hawai'i from Japan as contract laborers, beginning in 1885 during the reign of King David Kalākaua. In the main, these laborers were farmers who were assigned to various plantations in the Hawaiian Islands. Large numbers came from the Fukuoka, Kumamoto, Hiroshima, and Okinawa prefectures. Few arrived from the urban areas. By 1920 the Japanese constituted 42.7 percent of the population, and there was growing concern that the Japanese in Hawai'i would maintain loyalty toward Japan.[1] Individuals born in Japan who immigrated to Hawai'i were considered the first generation (or Issei). Subsequent generations included the Nisei (second generation), Sansei (third generation), Yonsei (fourth generation), and Gosei (fifth generation). Over the years, prefecture identification would be perpetuated, mostly by Nisei and some Sansei, with the formation of Kenjin Kai (prefecture organizations) such as the Kansai, Fukuoka, and Hiroshima Clubs. These organizations continue to provide social and cultural identity, although the Yonsei and Gosei groups have become less interested and involved in such structures today.

The popular aim for the contract laborer was to return to Japan economically triumphant. Some returned to Japan, dejected that their dreams were not realized. Their goal was thwarted by the harsh realities of plantation life of dirt, grime, long hours, meager wages, and often brutal rules of the plantation managers. Understandably, few saw a future as a plantation worker, and there was the growing belief that education was key to success. A survey of boys at McKinley High School in 1922 showed that only 0.5 percent hoped to be laborers, the majority

wanting to be professionals or skilled workers.[2] The successive generation of Japanese fulfilled these dreams.

The majority of the immigrant men were uneducated and not the
eldest of the family, and thus they would not inherit the family's land in
Japan. Despite these issues, individuals were committed to perpetuate
the family name. In America lay the opportunity to advance, gain wealth,
and create a better life. There was a sprinkling of Buddhist priests who
served as Japanese language schoolteachers, physicians, and businessmen. Japanese physicians were not welcomed in the established health
facilities in Honolulu, and Kuakini Hospital was built especially for the
treatment of Japanese contact laborers. Emperor Meiji donated funds
toward the building of this first Japanese hospital.

Immigrants frequently believed that things Japanese, such as the
educational system, were superior to those found in Hawai'i. Children
were sent to live with relatives in Japan and enrolled in schools there
so that parents in Hawai'i could concentrate on working. Some grew
up bitter and resentful that they were abandoned in this manner. With
the advent of World War II, these Nisei were stranded in Japan. A few
returned after the war as Kibei (a returnee to a place of origin) and found
the United States to be a foreign environment. They were no longer
native English speakers. They were foreigners in the land of their birth.

World War II (1941–1945) changed the core of being Japanese
in Hawai'i. This event influenced the entire makeup of the meaning
of being Japanese. In the beginning there was the complete blackout
of Japanese language, festivals, and artifacts. Language schools were
closed. Buddhist temples were minimized. Advisory groups consisting
of Nisei were formed to work with the military and police to maintain
positive relations with the Japanese communities. Japanese teahouses
in Honolulu, which were replicas of geisha houses in Japan, such as
Mochizuki, Kanraku, Nuuanu Onsen, and Natsunoya, experienced difficult financial times. Suspicious Japanese aliens were rounded up,
interrogated, and sent to holding camps on Sand Island and Honou-
liuli on O'ahu and Kalāheo on Kaua'i. The most "dangerous" two thousand men were sent in batches to internment camps on the mainland
United States. Some were joined by their families at a later date. During
World War II, more than 100,000 Japanese immigrants and Japanese-
Americans, mainly from the West Coast, were essentially imprisoned
and lost their homes and businesses, although the Japanese in Hawai'i
were mostly spared this humiliation.[3]

In 1943, in the midst of World War II, 10,000 or more men of

Japanese ancestry, predominantly from Hawai'i, volunteered to form the now legendary 100th Infantry Battalion and 442nd Regimental Combat Team. Ironically, many men in the military had families who were incarcerated in internment camps and identified as dangerous enemy aliens. Their goal in enlisting was to demonstrate loyalty and commitment to the United States. This was the first time that many had left Hawai'i for the continental United States. There was often tension between the Japanese-Americans from Hawai'i and those on the U.S. mainland. Interestingly, in spite of others questioning their loyalty to the United States and the internment of their families, these units became the most decorated military units of their size in the history of the nation.[4] Their battle cry was, in Pidgin, "Go for Broke!" ("Charge, with all your might!"). An interesting sidebar is that the last cry before imminent death for the Nisei soldier is said to have been *"Okā-san!"* ("Mother!"), the identical cry of the Japanese kamikaze (divine wind) pilots as they plunged their planes into enemy targets.

The GI Bill of Rights for veterans of World War II made higher education beyond high school possible for many of Japanese ancestry who otherwise could not afford such goals. A college-educated Japanese-American was rare in Hawai'i prior to this period, as every able body in the family was used to support the financial viability of the family. Many graduated from professional schools on the mainland, primarily in law. Nisei and Sansei lawyers of the Democratic Party, such as Sparky Matsunaga, Daniel Inouye, and George Ariyoshi, with the alliance of the local haole John A. Burns as a leader, would forever change the political and economic face of Hawai'i. In education, Fujio Matsuda and Richard Kosaki, as president and acting chancellor, respectively, rose to the highest levels at the University of Hawai'i. In a similar vein, the labor unions were significant forces in bringing equity into Hawai'i's workforce. This shift dramatically changed the modern history of Hawai'i.

Overall, the Japanese-American population in Hawai'i has decreased since 1980 in terms of its percentage of the Hawai'i population. According to the U.S. Census, there were approximately 240,000 (25 percent) in 1980, 248,000 (22 percent) in 1990, and 202,000 (17 percent) in 2000 in Hawai'i. One contributing factor is that the Nisei, who acted as a bridge between the Issei and Sansei, are slowly dying, and by 2030 they will have essentially disappeared. Other factors include the cessation of significant Japanese immigration to Hawai'i for decades, fewer children for Japanese-American families in Hawai'i, and interracial and interethnic marriages.

However, a new Japanese group in Hawai'i is composed of the relatively educated, young and middle-aged business professionals who recently moved to Hawai'i from Japan. They seem insular and in some ways may experience difficulty in being accepted by the local Japanese-Americans. There may be a perception by these new immigrants that, although Japanese-Americans in Hawai'i may be economically comfortable, they are poor culturally when it comes to things that are Japanese.

In a span of over 125 years, individuals with Japanese ancestry who live in Hawai'i have taken their place primarily in the American middle class socially, economically, educationally, and politically. Some may describe this as melding into the "melting pot" of Hawai'i's various ethnic groups. However, a "melting pot" connotes everyone becoming one substance, which would not be accurate. A better description is one that acknowledges the uniqueness of each individual's ethnocultural identity that is embedded within the multicultural social environment that is Hawai'i.

Ethnocultural Identity

The ethnocultural identity for Japanese-Americans in Hawai'i (JAHs) was relatively homogenous, characterized by a strong affiliation with the Japanese home culture, especially for the Issei and Nisei.

INTRAGROUP RELATIONSHIPS

Intragroup relationships supported the traditional values, beliefs, and behaviors of JAHs that served as the foundation of their success, at least in terms of fitting into the "American dream" (e.g., higher education attainment, higher income levels, more white-collar occupations). In addition, there were traditional Japanese values that were consistent with Western or American concepts, including being competitive, being achievement oriented, and striving to be "Number One" (i.e., *ichiban*). This sense of high achievement extended to the family, the community, and even the larger society.

INTERGROUP RELATIONS

Despite the relatively homogenous cultural experience of JAHs, there were circumstances that fostered intergroup relationships. For example, because the men came to Hawai'i alone without siblings or close relatives, the Nisei did not experience relationships with biological

grandparents, uncles, aunts, and cousins. Instead, children often identified a neighbor woman as "aunty" and her husband as "uncle." Their
children became "cousins." These "relatives" may not have been ethnically Japanese. To this day, children in Hawai'i frequently generically
call endearing adults, related or otherwise, "aunty" or "uncle."

Race and ethnicity, however, were at the forefront of thinking for
the Issei and Nisei. These generations may have more likely referred
to a man of, say, Filipino ancestry as "the Filipino man" or the woman
of Hawaiian ancestry as "the Hawaiian lady" or "the wahine." In fact, a
common question in the discussion of an individual concerned the ethnicity of the person. This was not uncommon for the Japanese as well
as other groups in Hawai'i. Differences in ethnicity and race were readily acknowledged, perhaps because most ethnic groups were minorities
themselves.

RELATIONSHIP WITH OKINAWANS

The Okinawans (Uchinanchus) came to Hawai'i during the same
period as the Japanese (Naichis) from mainland Japan. At that time,
they were identified by the labor contractors as Japanese rather than as
a separate group, despite the Okinawans having a separate language,
as well as distinctly different food, culture, and religion (see chapter
6, "The Okinawans"). The difference in languages made interethnic
communication challenging for this immigrant group identified as
Japanese. Although they were categorized similarly by outsiders, both
the Uchinanchu and the Naichi generally disdained intermarriages
between the two groups. This outlook may have had historical origins,
as the Kingdom of Ryukyus (Okinawa) had become a colony of Japan,
which may have conveyed prejudices and practices toward the "conquered." It is speculated that the attitudes of the Issei may be remnants
of this relationship, fanned by cultural practices and a language foreign
to the Japanese.

In Hawai'i, especially after World War II, significant leaders such
as Robert Oshiro, a lawyer, and Albert Miyasato, an educator, rose from
the Okinawan group. Oshiro was the strategist behind the winning
campaigns of the first Democrat to be elected governor and the first
Japanese-American and Hawaiian governors.[5] Miyasato was a public
schoolteacher, principal, and deputy superintendent of the Department of Education before becoming an aide to Governor George Ariyoshi in 1976, specializing in building relationships between Japan and
Hawai'i.[6]

INTERRACIAL AND INTERETHNIC MARRIAGES

Despite the fact that few women accompanied the waves of immigrant men, marriages generally still involved a Japanese man and woman. Within one to three years of the men's arrival, they were matched with women, usually from the same village or a nearby village in Japan, by exchanging photos arranged by matchmakers. This began the flow of picture brides to Hawai'i. The picture brides worked alongside their husbands. These strong and determined women recounted incidents of giving birth in the cane fields at the end of the rows they were weeding. Fellow workers helped with the birth process because there were few trained midwives, let alone physicians.

However, subsequently during World War II, "whiteness" was emulated primarily in the managerial, business, and military worlds. World War II introduced other classes of those with European ancestry, such as laborers from California—former Okies who migrated largely from Oklahoma to California due to the parched Midwest farmlands caused by drought—and less-educated military personnel. As eligible Japanese men were off to war, Japanese women built relationships with military men stationed in Hawai'i, sometimes risking being viewed derogatorily by their own ethnic group members.

The undertone to issues of interracial and interethnic interactions was traditional ethnic pride and, to some degree, the belief in the superiority of Japan and of its people (i.e., ethnocentrism). Being hapa—that is, being of both European ancestry (typically from an American serviceman) and of another heritage such as Japanese—entailed negative connotations.

VALUES, CUSTOMS, AND BELIEFS

Many traditional values, customs, and beliefs were exhibited that made earlier generations of JAHs relatively homogenous—almost a monolithic social family or society. One of the most common and overarching values was that of collectivism. This concept included putting the group's interest first before oneself, sacrificing for the betterment of the group, being loyal to the group, not making waves, blending in, and being a cooperative and contributing member. The "group" could have referred to the nuclear family, extended family, coworkers, community, and even the nation.

On a more individualized basis, the Issei were historically viewed as having characteristics of cleanliness, orderliness, and stoicism, which were adaptive characteristics to the harsh immigrant life. Despite hardships, however, the Issei prospered, pooled together resources, and achieved success. A concrete example of enduring ethnocultural group values is *tanomoshi*, a rotating credit association adapted in Japan during the thirteenth century from China and later brought to Hawai'i.[7] Unable to get loans from banks, the Issei contributed money monthly to a pot from which each contributor could bid once per year to obtain the month's total.

Many Nisei and Sansei maintained these characteristics, including the JAH women who rose in administrative support staff positions. They were organized and made work easy for their bosses, such as the presidents of banks and large companies who were typically European Americans. There were few complaints, despite adversity and individual sacrifice. The perceived stereotype of the JAH male was the samurai (warrior) who said little and whose emotions were difficult to read, much like the stoic cowboy of the American frontier. These features were nonetheless very adaptive for success in Hawai'i's culture and contributed to the JAHs' sociopolitical success story in Hawai'i.

FAMILY

Traditionally, JAH families involved the father, who was the breadwinner and decision maker, and the mother, who was a homemaker and parent to their children and provided emotional support—roles that were common for the rest of the U.S. population as well in the 1950s and 1960s.[8] The wife's role was to care for the children and ensure the smooth running of the home, whereas the husband's role in these areas was quite minor. Historically, JAH women took on the surname of the husband, similar to other cultures. An exception to this was the family with only daughters. In these families, often the husband of the eldest daughter could take the family's surname to perpetuate the family name.

In the past, marriages were commonly arranged as in *miai* (arranged marriage meetings) or picture-bride agreements. The process of *miai* arose from traditional samurai culture in which marriages allowed for unions between families to ensure military alliance and support. In Hawai'i, this custom of arranged marriage allowed for a *nakodo*—a family member or friend who was a matchmaker—in Japan to find suitable wives for the Japanese laborers in Hawai'i. The picture-bride arrangement seems to have had its origins with the immigration of the Japanese. Using a matchmaker who did not know the candidates, brides from Japan were selected mainly by photographs. Despite this, divorce was uncommon, partially to avoid shame to the family or to lose face, but also because of the public commitment made between couples with so many individuals involved in these marriage arrangements. Domestic violence was not uncommon, particularly in picture-bride arrangements in which women had limited resources of support in Hawai'i. When marital discord or abuse occurred, this was often endured or kept between the husband and wife to reconcile. In this regard, a woman named Yeiko Mizobe So was instrumental in providing shelter and support to abused picture brides in Hawai'i from 1895 to 1905.[9]

Traditional JAH family structure favored the eldest child, particularly if the eldest was a son. For bath time, the father of the family bathed first, then the eldest son, followed by the other sons and then the daughters. The mother bathed last and cleaned the bathtub. The eldest were given first choice in nearly everything, even including inheritance.

Historically, elderly were cared for in the home rather than in nursing homes, with the daughter or daughter-in-law (wife of eldest son) being primarily responsible. As a result, homes were largely multigenerational. Families consisting of grandparents, parents, and three to five children were common. Boys were favored, as they could work and contribute to the family's finances, whereas girls left the home to join their husband's family.

LANGUAGE

A classic and concrete example of JAH cultural change involves language. The Issei spoke Japanese fluently (with dialects of their prefectures) and spoke minimal English. They attempted to speak a kind of broken English or Japanese, which was composed of both elementary school level English and Japanese that was understood by other ethnic groups. The Nisei—sons and daughters of the first-generation Issei—typically spoke pidgin Japanese to their parents and Pidgin English to others. The Sansei—grandsons and granddaughters of the first-generation Issei—spoke less Japanese, unless their grandparents lived with them, and considerably more Pidgin English, with perhaps even standard English on a day-to-day basis when required.

EDUCATION

For many Nisei and Sansei, traditional Japanese schools essentially functioned as after-school care for a generation of JAHs, as their mothers were in the workforce and had work obligations until the late afternoon. During Japanese school, children met other JAHs, learned about cultural issues, sang Japanese songs, wrote Japanese calligraphy, and learned some Japanese words without many attaining fluency. The structure of the Japanese schools brought some semblance of life in Japan, as the day began with greetings to the teacher and classmates (*"sensei konnichiwa, minna-san konnichiwa"*), and permission to enter the room was asked if one was late (*"sensei osokunarimashita haitemo iidesuka"*).[10] Saturday-morning classes were devoted to developing ethical and moral values necessary in living, as success was felt to be dependent on effort and character rather than inborn ability.[11]

There were examples that illustrated the influence of the non-Asian oligarchy. Common knowledge at the time was the often forgotten part played in Hawai'i's educational history by the English Standard Schools. A system existed that separated those of European decent (with a few mixed Hawaiians) from Asian children who attended the large public schools.[12] On Kaua'i, Makaweli Annex, Grades 1–8, though supported by the territorial government, was kept separate from the public schools and was primarily for children of plantation managers who were predominantly of European ancestry. Examples of English Standard Schools on O'ahu were Kapālama, Ali'iolani, Lincoln, Thomas Jefferson, Stevenson, and Roosevelt Schools.[13] Similar schools were also present on the islands of Maui, Hawai'i, and Kaua'i. Though separation was based upon the use of correct English, ethnic minorities most often did not meet this standard. This seemingly unintentional segregation of the school system occurred from 1920 to 1947, essentially ending shortly after the end of World War II.[14] For the majority of JAHs who gave up the notion of returning to Japan, emphasis was placed on the children's education, at least to complete high school. For most, college was not economically attainable. In many families, the eldest sons or daughters would enter the workforce as teenagers to support a younger sibling to complete his or her education. It was taken for granted that the educated sibling would, in turn, contribute to their nieces' and nephews' educational goals.

SOCIOECONOMIC STATUS AND POLITICS

The Issei were primarily plantation workers earning a low wage, and they had minimal sociopolitical power. Plantation-union struggles and oppression and financial ties due to common prefectures in Japan *(kenjinkai)* were major issues. However, after World War II and due to opportunities such as the GI Bill, the Nisei dramatically advanced the JAHs' status to the middle class in nearly a single generation. Robert Katayama, a recipient of the GI Bill who earned a law degree from Yale University, put it succinctly: "We understood that education was our ticket to making it in life...and it was available to us through the GI Bill."[15]

HEALTH AND MENTAL HEALTH

For traditional JAHs and many other Asian cultures, alternative forms of treatment for health ailments were common, especially by the Issei. For example, traditional Japanese practices, such as *yaito* (moxibustion) or *kampo* (herbs), were used. Moxibustion refers to the practice of using moxa or mugwort herb to stimulate acupuncture sites. Moxa is frequently burned directly on the skin. *Kampo* is the Japanese adaptation of traditional Chinese herbal medicine.

For traditional JAHs and many other Asian cultures, mental illness carried a strong negative stigma that could bring shame upon the family, and some of these sentiments still remain, including for depression and help-seeking behaviors.[16] Mental illness was hidden or somatized, because physical ailments were more acceptable.

SENSE OF "HOME"

The concept of "home" is complex. The Issei, who were relatively recently displaced from Japan, knew of really just one homeland, that of Japan, and had no choice but to become acclimated to a new one, that of Hawai'i. The Nisei, on the other hand, were born and raised in Hawai'i. With the advent of World War II, the Nisei were to some degree cut off from Japan for a period and thus were more likely to view Hawai'i as home, despite being only one generation removed and being in the Hawaiian host culture.

New Ethnocultural Identity

What is the new or contemporary ethnocultural identity of JAHs? Although remnants of traditional values remain as strong foundations for many, the main theme for contemporary ethnocultural identity of JAHs is in how much more heterogeneous and diverse are the mixtures of the values, beliefs, and behaviors. Although patterns are no doubt discernable through careful and systematic study, the argument could be made that each JAH's ethnocultural identity is composed of a unique combination of values, beliefs, practices, and behaviors—much more so compared to previous generations. Much *less* common now is someone who is raised in an intact family, speaks fluent Japanese, is a high achiever in academics, marries another JAH, has children, has different expectations for the firstborn son, practices an Eastern religion, stays in Hawai'i, and takes care of his or her aging parents.

When examining each JAH, there is perhaps no one universal factor that has singularly shaped that JAH's ethnocultural identity. Changes in the types of norms are likely due to a combination of forces and influenced by the diverse ethnic cultures of Hawai'i. These cultures include the host Hawaiian culture, other Asian and Pacific Islander cultures, and Western or Americanized culture. They blend to create the so-called local Hawai'i culture. Other factors more external to the local culture that affect change include the media, technology, and globalization.

HAWAIIAN HOST CULTURE

Many of the core values, beliefs, and behaviors of the host Hawaiian culture are fundamentally in concert with and reinforce the foundations of traditional Japanese culture and thus JAHs. These include the importance of ancestry, family, interdependence, collectivism, social groups, respect of elders, sanctity of the homeland, and preservation of culture. The Hawaiian Renaissance that started in the 1970s created a cultural environment whereby Hawaiians could be proud of their own heritage. This also includes JAHs of mixed Hawaiian ancestry who identify themselves as being "Hawaiian," although only having a small percentage of Hawaiian blood.

There has also been a healthy exchange of beliefs and customs between the Hawaiian and JAH cultures, resulting in a connection with the local culture in Hawai'i. For example, JAHs are learning more about Hawaiian beliefs and customs (e.g., hula) and certainly enjoying other aspects of the Hawaiian culture, including Hawaiian foods (e.g., *laulau, kalua* pig, and poi). Further, the common values of the sanctity of the homeland, preservation of culture, and respect for self-determination (i.e., internment of Japanese immigrants and Japanese-Americans during World War II) have also initiated respected JAH leaders to support self-determination and sovereignty for Hawaiians (i.e., the Akaka bill).[17]

Overall, in contrast to a loss or blending of more traditional JAH values, contemporary JAHs' ethnocultural identities incorporate a mixture of local culture and other ethnic identities that form a culture-spirituality that may not be as grounded in the realities of the past. Instead, they may be based on a unique set of experiences and perceptions that define the contemporary JAHs' self-concept and self-identity in present-day Hawai'i. This self-identity has evolved greatly from the Issei, who struggled to make ends meet as plantation workers earning $1 per day, to contemporary JAHs, who enjoy a much higher standard of living and where the media, technology, and globalization play a much greater role in the development of their self-identity.

INTERGROUP RELATIONSHIPS

The local culture in Hawai'i is the outcome of an amalgamation of different ethnic traditions and cultures, each interjecting itself at different points in time and at different locations during this history of Hawai'i's evolution. In this context of race and ethnic similarities and differences, more so at present, contemporary JAHs may see people as people first rather than the ethnic groups being represented (e.g., the man who happens to be Filipino, rather than the "Filipino man"). Yet, as in the past, differences in race and ethnicity are readily recognized, spoken about, and integrated into the local culture.

INTERRACIAL AND INTERETHNIC GROUP MARRIAGES

One explicit example of how intergroup interactions have changed the face of JAHs involves interracial and interethnic marriages, which by definition impact the ethnocultural identities of JAHs. Ethnocentrism fell by the wayside to more Americanized concepts of equality of the races and the disdain for presupposing superiority or inferiority in one race or ethnic group compared to another.

Through the generations, interethnic marriages have become more accepted as compared to the original arranged marriages that typically involved couples of full Japanese ancestry. Based on 1989–1996 Hawai'i data, intermarriages between Japanese and Chinese and Japanese and Korean couples are more common than by chance, and every Japanese-American ethnic combination is represented among the other ethnic groups (i.e., African-Americans, Caucasians, Filipinos, indigenous Hawaiians, Samoans, Vietnamese).[18] In fact, Nisei already have bicultural values, and there appears to be growing acceptance of individuals of mixed ethnicities from a societal standpoint.[19] Today, "hapa" is not considered derogatory. In fact, it is sometimes seen as favorably fitting the Hollywood images of attractiveness.

Another example of change involves the Cherry Blossom Festi-val.[20] Since 1953, the Cherry Blossom Festival has been the "Miss America" for the JAHs, with its culmination the election of a queen. Given the changes in ethnic demographics (i.e., fewer full-blooded JAHs), the current requirements for a queen are such that candidates no longer have to be of full Japanese ancestry and no longer have to have a Japanese surname (unlike the Narcissus Queen for the Chinese, which requires a Chinese surname). Therefore, potential contestants are often of mixed ethnicity. Nonetheless, the focus of this celebration is learning about Japan, spreading goodwill, and perpetuating Japanese culture in Hawai'i. Indeed, many local Japanese in Hawai'i frequently travel to Japan despite the lack of knowledge of the Japanese language.

In cases of interracial and interethnic marriages, there is a blending of beliefs and values, and the children may not identify with just one or the other race or ethnicity but with a relatively unique mixture of races or ethnicities. The latter may be determined by who primarily raises the children and imparts his or her values to the children, including extended family members (e.g., grandparents, aunties, uncles, neighbors).

RELATIONSHIP WITH OKINAWANS

In the last thirty years, there has been a renaissance and recognition of Okinawan ethnicity and culture. In the past, children from a union between Okinawan and Japanese were popularly identified as Japanese. Today, however, it is common to hear, "I am half Okinawan and half Japanese." There is pride in Okinawan foods, dance, language, martial arts, and music. There is intragroup support for Uchinanchus in businesses, such as restaurants and food catering.

VALUES, CUSTOMS, AND BELIEFS

Although an underlying foundation remains, many traditional values, customs, and beliefs have been shed, or at least their original meanings have been lost. Younger JAHs' context of Japanese culture may be influenced more from the media and technology (e.g., music, Internet, movies, anime, and TV shows).

Some traditional personality characteristics may remain. For example, characteristics of *enryo* continue, whereby individuals may not want to take the last piece of food on a tray at a party. Young JAH students are torn between the demands of the group versus speaking up. At the University of Hawai'i's John A. Burns School of Medicine, medical education in the preclinical years is modeled on Problem Based Learning (PBL), which emphasizes group learning and active participation rather than the traditional lecture base. There are instances where JAH students in the classroom setting are criticized for reticence and are asked to speak up rather than participate by quiet observation and going with the flow. The male JAHs may be particularly quiet in this setting. Problems may not be addressed with assertiveness or aggressiveness. Rather than speaking up or making waves, JAH students may quietly complain—or worse, act in a passive-aggressive (resistant) manner.

Some traditional Japanese activities remain popular or have even experienced a resurgence of interest, such as the martial arts (judo, aikido, and kendo), drum *(taiko)*, flower arrangement (ikebana), and dance *(odori)*. In Hawai'i, judo has become an interscholastic high school sport, and in 2005, according to the Judo Black Belt Association of Hawai'i, it was one of the only states to have it. Conversely, an Internet search for *taiko* groups in North America (www.taiko.com/taiko_resource/groups .html) yielded over 160 organizations throughout the country.

Interestingly, some customs, such as floating lit candles in a river or canal to honor the dead *(toro nagashi)*, are practiced in Japan mainly in rural regions, so that Japanese tourists, typically from urban areas, often view JAHs with fascination. These types of customs in Hawai'i were learned from a grandparent's generation, perhaps Nisei, but without knowledge of the background or reasons for the ritual. An example of this is the cleaning of one's house prior to the start of the New Year. Other customs, such as making paper (origami) cranes, have been altered. In Hawai'i, 1,001 paper cranes are created for wedding celebrations, whereas in Japan, 1,000 cranes are sometimes created during times of illness.

Overall, however, it appears that for many contemporary JAHs, although interdependence remains valued, so is the more Western or Americanized concept of person-centered individualism. The current group of younger JAHs may share characteristics more similar to the so-called Generations X and Y. For example, an individual with high aspirations should not be held back by the family or group. Win-win scenarios are sought in which both the individual and group can attain their goals without being at the expense of the other. Blind loyalty is more likely to be frowned upon. The traditional Japanese value of *giri*, or obligation, may be less observed.

Activities such as pounding rice *(mochi)* on New Year's Day and celebrating different birthday ages (*yakudoshi* [41], *kanreki* [61], and *beiju*

[88]) are still practiced by some JAHs but much less so than in previous generations. Similarly, holidays celebrated in Japan, such as Girls' Day (March 3) and Boys' Day (May 5), are still celebrated, although much less than before. In modern Japan, both of these holidays are now subsumed under Children's Day, a national holiday, which is celebrated on May 5.[21]

In recent years, Buddhist services have been no longer only in Japanese but have adapted to include English. Increasingly more JAHs attend Christian services. Traditional customs, such as ancestor worship *(hotokesama)* and visiting the graves *(ohakamairi)*, have largely been lost by the younger JAH generations. Traditional kimonos are no longer worn, with the exception of perhaps the younger children in a family portrait for Children's Day. Even in those instances, JAH families no longer own kimonos and need to rent one at the photo studio.

Other customs such as the tea ceremony *(chanoyu)*, flower arrangement (ikebana), and miniature tree (bonsai) creation are often favored by both JAHs and non–JAH groups. Obon season is marked by *bon* dances at various Buddhist temples or community centers throughout the summer months. These gatherings have become popular, with a festival-like atmosphere, and they attract all ethnic groups to partake in the foods as well as participate in the dancing. Many customs practiced by the Japanese, such as *omiyage* (gift-giving from trips) and removal of footwear before entering a house, have become commonplace and incorporated by most ethnic groups of Hawai'i.

Japanese food is more mainstream in American culture and is no longer viewed as foreign even on the continental United States. Sushi, sake, and teriyaki are commonplace. *Izakaya* (a Japanese-style pub that serves small portions of home-style cooking) was featured as a current food obsession replacing tapa bars in the March 2010 *Sunset* magazine. While the mainland United States embraced Japanese foods, Japanese food in Hawai'i has adapted and often includes items from other cultures, resulting in the popular "mixed plate," which epitomizes the blending of cultures.

FAMILY

Overall, the roles of different family members have changed considerably for JAHs. Partially due to the Americanized role of women to have careers, as well as due to the cost of living in Hawai'i, one is more likely to find both parents working and sharing the responsibility of child care. Despite the traditional male-dominated family structure, one can readily find matriarchal JAH families. The wife may outwardly show deference toward the husband, but in reality the wife may control the family and doles out money to the husband for his "allowance." In addition, contemporary JAH women are more likely than before to keep their maiden name or utilize a hyphenated surname.

Divorce is now common among all ethnicities, including JAHs, and there is much less of a stigma associated with divorce. In Hawai'i, the divorce-to-marriage ratio for within JAH couples is lower than for Filipinos, Koreans, Vietnamese, and African-Americans but higher than for Caucasians, Hawaiians, Chinese, and Samoans.[22]

With the American principle of equality, the eldest child, especially the eldest son, typically no longer holds a favored status as compared to the other siblings. In addition, this power structure has changed in many families, as the oldest son may have moved to the continental United States or may not be as financially successful as a younger sibling.

As with other ethnic groups, JAH parents and families struggle to balance providing a better and higher standard of living to their children with not spoiling them. These issues are, of course, not unique to the JAHs and indeed are common to all of the middle-class groups.

Gender roles for the care for elderly JAHs are more complicated than in the past. One person being primarily responsible for the care of an elderly JAH is less likely because of the decreased number of children, the need for two wage earners in families, and the increase in the life span of the elderly JAHs. Women still tend to be responsible for care for the elderly, although this too is changing. In Hawai'i, the cost of elder care is significantly higher than on the continental United States, and nursing homes are much fewer in number. Despite a preference for nursing home placement, due to financial limitations the elderly are often cared for at home. Therefore, a common scenario is dividing the care for the aged among different family members of the nuclear and extended families. Because property is the main asset in Hawai'i, on rare occasions there can be bitter disputes regarding inheritance of the family home and how tangible assets are divided. Who cares for the elderly on a day-to-day basis can influence such disputes. These are issues not exclusive to the JAHs.

LANGUAGE

There may be a small proportion of JAHs who are actively going back to their Japanese cultural roots in pockets of resurgence by learning the standard Japanese language and culture in Hawai'i via formal schooling (e.g., high school and college Japanese language courses) and even visiting or living in Japan.

In general, however, knowledge of the Japanese language is fading. The Yonsei and beyond tend to know little Japanese and understand and speak either Pidgin English or perhaps even only standard English, especially in certain demographic circles. When the Japanese language is learned, typically through high schools and colleges, the language is closer to standard Japanese.

EDUCATION

Japanese language schools have dwindled in number today, although there are now new schools for Japanese nationals to maintain their competitiveness with the Japanese educational system. The Japanese nationals, however, are very distinct from the JAHs. The Japanese nationals are typically wealthy transient Hawai'i residents, relatively small in number, residing in Hawai'i for business or even an extended vacation, quite unlike the rural Issei who came for plantation work.

Compulsory English education remains a cornerstone of importance for JAH families. Many strive to send their children to private schools, shuttle their children for additional tutoring and extracurricular activities, and then favor universities on the continental United States over any of the local universities or colleges. Families may save for college, sacrificing other financial goals, including retirement, with the implicit expectation that the child will later help the family, although uncertainty exists on exactly what form any such future assistance might take.

Of course, there are JAH families with less tangible Western successes, including having sons or daughters who dropped out of high school or were involved with crime or substance use. More so for contemporary JAHs, the shame is reflected on the individual who dropped out, committed the crime, or used drugs instead of on the family, thus supporting the more American concept of individualism and individual responsibility.

SOCIOECONOMIC STATUS AND POLITICS

Previous political legacies of "Americanism" of the 100th and 442nd are gradually becoming history for contemporary JAHs, although there are now cars with license plates featuring "Sons and Daughters of the 100th/442nd." Socioeconomic and political issues are less likely than before to be tied to JAHs as a block. Now, firmly entrenched as middle class in Hawai'i, JAHs are generally less concerned about the ethnic background of politicians and are more concerned about the political agenda of candidates.

Professional jobs are generally preferred, consistent with the model-minority striving for Anglo-Saxon ideals. During the young JAH's adult life, home ownership is typically a goal, with adult children living with their parents until there is enough saved for a down payment, loan, or gift to help with the purchase. Other JAHs live in multigenerational houses or additions as part of the main house. The high cost of living and the "paradise tax," which results in lower salaries, cause financial strain for many families. This goal of upward mobility is not different from many other ethnic groups in Hawai'i. As with every new generation, there appears to be greater emphasis on materialism and advanced technology.

HEALTH AND MENTAL HEALTH

Although alternative forms of treatment are utilized by JAHs, and some might argue that there has been resurgence in areas such as acupuncture, which is covered by some health insurance policies, the more ancient practices are less known, accessible, and used when compared to utilization by Issei.

The increase in intergroup interactions and relationships and of the media and technology in general has likely played a double-edged-sword role regarding the stigma of mental illness and seeking effective treatments. Approximately half of all individuals will have a mental disorder in their lifetime.[23] In previous generations, the stigma of mental illness and disability may have engendered guilt and shame (e.g., being "crazy," "mental," "insane") that prevented individuals and families from seeking help and/or professional assistance.

Contemporary JAHs are likely exposed to more conflicting information regarding the stigma of mental illness. For example, on the one hand, Western or Americanized views of mental health take on a much more objective or neutral stance (i.e., mental illness is like any other health problem that should be diagnosed and treated), and there is greater awareness of and education regarding diagnostic and treatment alternatives for mental health–related issues. On the other hand, individuals who are not well informed, as well as the media portrayal of the mentally ill as unpredictable or dangerous, reinforce the more traditional notions of the mentally ill.

Anecdotally, in contrast to JAHs with physical illnesses, JAHs with a psychiatric illness may go untreated for many years or may refuse to accept treatment despite clear benefits over the risks. As an example, the use of antidepressants in Hawai'i is much less than in the continental United States, which may reflect vastly lower rates of depression— or more likely, lower rates of treatment.[24] JAHs may present with an advanced form of mental illness, such as schizophrenia, due to unwillingness to get treatment. Nonetheless, there are growing numbers of JAHs in the mental health field and there is much less stigma for these JAHs who are working with psychiatric patients.

SENSE OF "HOME"

Despite their beginnings as immigrants, many contemporary JAHs identify Hawai'i as home. There is no doubt that some JAHs can feel claustrophobic living "on a rock" in the middle of the Pacific (having to take a 2,500-mile plane ride to anywhere else on the Pacific Rim). For many JAHs, however, there is a strong sense of not seeing themselves living anywhere else in the world and feeling great appreciation and gratitude in not only becoming part of the local culture that permeates welcome and aloha but also contributing to the rich amalgamation of the local culture.

One could speculate that the generations beyond the Gosei may identify themselves as being Hawaiian—not in the blood-quantum sense but in the sense of a group of individuals with a rich, mixed heritage in arguably the most beautiful place in the world located at the crossroads between North America and Asia.

Enduring Factors

BIOLOGICAL CHARACTERISTICS

One of the most important physical or health outcomes is life expectancy. Although there are many factors that determine one's life expectancy, including environmental influences, Asian-Americans who live in Hawai'i, including JAHs in particular, tend to have longer life expectancies than the other ethnic groups in Hawai'i.[25] This finding is consistent with the notion that Asians have biological attributes that contribute to the longevity.

On the one hand, JAHs have shorter life expectancies than Japanese in Japan, and on the other hand, they have longer life expectancies than Japanese-Americans who live on the continental United States. Collectively, these findings suggest an interplay between heredity-biology and the environment (e.g., diet, lifestyle, life stressors).

PSYCHOLOGICAL CHARACTERISTICS

Despite the dispersion of Japanese-Americans throughout the United States and the changes through intermarriages, pride in being Japanese remains. An interesting question is: What does it mean to be Japanese? The answers will vary depending upon factors such as generation and locale. Members of the older generation may find themselves referring back to their roots, to their grandparents' or parents' stories and traditions. As their parents or grandparents may have been the first generation (Issei) to immigrate to Hawai'i, their traditions may be more similar to those of native Japan. The younger generation may similarly look into family traditions and customs; however, these may have been diluted through assimilation or acculturation or evolved to incorporate the host culture, becoming a hybrid of sorts. In a similar manner, locale is influential. For example, Japanese in Hawai'i are different from Japanese on the continental United States. There is a gradual shift from Hawai'i to the western states and to the eastern states. As one moves farther east, there is more prominence of the stereotypical American lifestyle and less of the Japanese culture seen in Hawai'i. Nevertheless, regardless of dilution or hybridization, there is pride in being Japanese.

Reticence has also continued through the migrations and through time. It is an understated presence to avoid upstaging others. It is also a communication style in which little is exchanged to avoid revealing too much. It is relatively rare to see a Japanese individual who is flamboyant, brash, and loud. Interestingly, in Western society reticence is the polar opposite of valued upfront communication and interaction patterns. The Japanese may have needed to adapt to this, in school, work, and community activities with a conscious decision to speak up and voice one's opinions, which may have been uncomfortable initially and is even still.

The value of *shikata-ga nai,* or "acceptance with resignation," has changed overall; however, at distinct periods it seems to have played a supportive role. This value was essential in helping Japanese-Americans to endure challenging situations, such as being immigrants, the harsh working conditions of the plantations, and, on the continental United States, being minorities. Over time, attitudes have shifted. Individuals have become more active in pursuing outcomes that reflect their beliefs. This is evident in the rise of the JAHs in arenas of higher administration. Perhaps individuals who were chosen or who chose to pursue an adventure in Hawai'i and leave their homeland were selected for their ability to sacrifice, their persistence, and their strength. They believed in making something better for themselves.

SOCIOCULTURAL CHARACTERISTICS

Despite their migration and the influence of Western cultures, within the Japanese there seems to be some degree of a persistence of gender-role stereotypes. In Japan, women are usually housewives, tending to the care of the children, husband, and the household. To outsiders, the head of the household may be presented as the husband and it may seem to be a patriarchal hierarchy, but behind closed doors, it may be matriarchal. During the plantation period in Hawaiʻi, women worked alongside their husbands and continued to have the responsibilities of caring for the children and husband as well as the household. Regardless of whether the woman is working or not, these roles appear to persist even today. Perhaps some Japanese cultural values are deeply ingrained and support the perpetuation of the gender-role stereotypes. In addition, however, even American culture may subtly give the message that the woman is supposed to care for the children. *Sekinin* (responsibility, taking care of oneself and others, fulfilling obligations) describes the characteristics of the matriarch.[26]

With migration, there has also been a modification of behaviors. For example, a once exclusive and family-centric focus has become more inclusive. The initial Japanese immigrants arrived without extended family members. In this new environment, they formed new "families" of unrelated individuals, although frequently with the same Japanese ethnicity. With time and with each move across the United States, these families have expanded to include individuals of other ethnicities. Despite families more likely being of mixed ethnicity as compared to the past, some Japanese values still appear to persist to some degree, such as *chugi,* or "loyalty," to the family and its members.

Summary and Conclusion

Since their immigration in 1885, the Japanese-Americans in Hawaiʻi, as a group, seem to have attained the "American Dream." Although ghosts of the hierarchy of the plantations in Hawaiʻi, the internment of Japanese-Americans, and the defeat of Japan during World War II may still color the view of Japanese-Americans in Hawaiʻi and elsewhere, they have generally thrived. As a group, they have been able to overcome adversities and hardships to create opportunities for their children to advance and have better, more comfortable lives. In areas such as education, business, medicine, law, and politics, they are well represented and have achieved notable success in Hawai'i. The Japanese adapted well to Western culture and expectations despite divergent and seemingly contradictory values, such as group collectivism versus individualism. Perhaps the values of achievement and hard work, similar to those of Protestants, were more influential in their pursuit of their dreams.

Group collectivism may have been a protective factor during the beginning stages of the Japanese migration to Hawai'i by providing solidarity, strength, and support. Interestingly, as they became more successful in various arenas, the close-knit group became less interdependent. Group collectivism changed. With acculturation, the Japanese moved toward individualism. As a group, the Japanese have become less homogeneous. Differences are not shameful but are embraced and celebrated more than in the past.

With these changes, one may question whether there is identity diffusion of the Japanese. Rather than identity diffusion, one should consider an evolution of a new hybrid identity that incorporates local and other ethnic cultures of Hawai'i. It is a bidirectional or multidirectional integration of cultures. What is considered local in Hawai'i may have its roots in the Japanese culture or language (e.g., removing one's shoes at the entrance of a home prior to entering is a custom of Hawai'i). The opposite is also true, in that what may be considered Japanese is actually a variation of the original Hawaiian host culture. This mixture of cultures is not without its challenges, as some values are polar opposites. Yet, as the people of Hawai'i have shown, there is strength in diversity and unity regardless of differences.

Further Reading

Hazama, D., and J. O. Komeiji. *The Japanese in Hawai'i: Okage sama de.* Honolulu: Bess Press, 2008.

Kotani, R. *The Japanese in Hawai'i: A Century of Struggle.* Honolulu: Hawai'i Hochi, 1985.

Nordyke, E. C. *The Peopling of Hawai'i*, 2nd ed. Honolulu: University of Hawai'i Press, 1989.

Ogawa, D. M. *Jan Ken Po: The World of Hawai'i's Japanese-Americans.* Honolulu: Japanese-American Research Council, Honolulu Japanese Chamber of Commerce, 1973.

————. *Kodomo no Tame ni, for the Sake of the Children: The Japanese-American Experience in Hawai'i*. Honolulu: University of Hawai'i Press, 1978.

Okamura, J.Y., guest ed. "The Japanese-American contemporary experience in Hawai'i." *Social Process in Hawai'i* 41 (2002): 1–172.

Rogers, T.A., and S.Izutsu. "The Japanese." In *People and Cultures of Hawai'i: A Psychocultural Profile*, ed. J.F.McDermott, W.S.Tseng, and T.W.Maretzki. Honolulu: University of Hawai'i Press, 1980: 73–99.

Takaki, R. *Strangers from a Different Shore*. Boston: Little, Brown and Company, 1989.

Tamura, E.H. *Americanization, Acculturation, and Ethnic Identity: The Nisei Generation in Hawai'i*. Chicago: University of Illinois Press, 1994.

Yamamoto, G.K. "The Japanese." *Ethnic Sources in Hawai'i, Social Process in Hawai'i* 29 (1996): 46–54.

Notes

1. G.Y.Okihiro, *Cane Fires: The Anti-Japanese Movement in Hawai'i, 1865–1945*, Philadelphia: Temple University Press, 1992.

2. R.Takaki, *Strangers from a Different Shore*, Boston: Little, Brown and Company, 1989.

3. D.Ige, C.Fukunaga, W.Kaneko, K.Nakasone, R.Okata, S.Saiki, and T.Tsukiyama, "AJAs support the Akaka bill," *Honolulu Advertiser*, June 8, 2006: A17.

4. E.H.Tamura, *Americanization, Acculturation, and Ethnic Identity: The Nisei Generation in Hawai'i*, Chicago: University of Illinois Press, 1994.

5. M.Adamski, "Dem's visionary dies: The political strategist helped Govs. Burns, Ariyoshi and Waihee," *Honolulu Star-Bulletin*, February 14, 2008, retrieved from http://archives.starbulletin.com/2008/02/14/news/story10.html.

6. R.Ohira, "Former educator was ex-governor's 'right arm' in Japan," *Honolulu Advertiser*, March 2, 2006: B2.

7. R.Takaki, *From Different Shores: Perspectives on Race and Ethnicity in America*, New York: Oxford University Press, 1994.

8. J.Ching, J.McDermott, C.Fukunaga, E.Yanagida, E.Mann, and J.Waldron, "Perceptions of family values and roles among Japanese-Americans: Clinical considerations," *American Journal of Orthopsychiatry* 65 (1995): 216–224.

9. Z.Serrano, "She was their light: Yeiko Mizobe So's shelters protected hundreds of abused picture brides in Hawai'i," *Honolulu Advertiser*, April 5, 2009: D1 & D4.

10. J.Tobin, D.Wu, and D.Davidson, *Preschool in Three Cultures: Japan, China and the United States*, New Haven, CT: Yale University Press, 1989.

11. Ibid.

12. Okihiro 1992.

13. Ibid.

14. N. Meller, "Hawai'i's English Standard Schools," Legislative Reference Bureau Report No. 3 (Request No. 273), Honolulu, 1948; R. K. Steuber, "Hawai'i: A case study in development education, 1778–1960," Ph.D. diss., University of Wisconsin, 1964 (Ann Arbor, MI: University Microfilms).

15. M. Tsai, "Hawai'i's Nisei vets were crucial in achieving statehood for Isles: Japanese-Americans' heroism in WWII eased congressional suspicions," *Honolulu Advertiser*, April 20, 2009: A1–A2.

16. S. Hirai, "Attitudes toward depression, anti-depressants and seeking professional psychological help among Japanese, Japanese-American and American students: A cross-cultural analysis," Unpublished dissertation, University of Hawai'i at Mānoa, Honolulu, 2005; L. S. Ma, "The study of attitudes toward mental illness in Hawai'i among local students," Unpublished M.A. thesis, University of Hawai'i at Mānoa, Honolulu, 2002.

17. Ige et al. 2006.

18. S. Y. C. Wong, "Exogamous and homogamous patterns of marriage and divorce among nine racial/ethnic groups in Hawai'i: 1989–1996," Unpublished dissertation, University of Hawai'i at Mānoa, Honolulu, May 2001.

19. S. Izutsu, E. Yanagida, L. Matsukawa, and J. Takeshita, "Nisei Japanese-American cultural identification," Unpublished report, University of Hawai'i at Mānoa, Honolulu, 1999.

20. C. R. Yano, *Crowning the Nice Girl: Gender, Ethnicity, and Culture in Hawai'i's Cherry Blossom Festival*, Honolulu: University of Hawai'i Press, 2006.

21. *Marukai Newsletter*, "Celebrating Boy's Day," *Marukai Wholesale Mart Newsletter*, April 14, 2009: 1.

22. Wong 2001.

23. R. C. Kessler, P. Berglund, O. Demler, R. Jin, K. R. Merikangas, and E. E. Walters, "Lifetime prevalence and age-of-onset distributions of DSM-IV disorders in the National Comorbidity Survey Replication," *Archives of General Psychiatry* 62 (2005): 593–602.

24. J. Takeshita, K. Masaki, I. Ahmed, D. J. Foley, Y. Q. Li, R. Chen, D. Fujii, G. W. Ross, H. Petrovitch, and L. White, "Are depressive symptoms a risk factor for mortality in elderly Japanese-American men? The Honolulu-Asia aging study," *American Journal of Psychiatry* 159 (2002): 1127–1132.

25. C. B. Park, K. L. Braun, B. Y. Horiuchi, C. Tottori, and A. T. Onaka, "Longevity disparities in multiethnic Hawai'i: An analysis of 2000 life tables," *Public Health Records* 124(4) (2009): 579–584.

26. R. Fujita, M. Fujita, K. Omiya, G. Omiya, E. N. Hasegawa, et al., *Kachikan (Values)*, Honolulu: Japanese Cultural Center of Hawai'i, 2001.

CHAPTER 6

The Okinawans

*Ryokichi Higashionna, Gilbert Ikehara, and
Leslie Matsukawa*

Yuimaru: A community spirit of working *together.*
Ichariba chode: Once we have met, we are brothers and sisters.

Today it is estimated that there are over 50,000 people who can
trace their roots to Okinawa. Though the evolution of the Okinawan
people of Hawai'i has occurred, there is evidence of the persistence of
possibly hardwired biological characteristics, traits, and behaviors that
have been retained, leading to hardiness and a resilience of body, mind,
and spirit. Okinawans are known for their longevity and good health
into their old age. *Yuimaru,* a spirit of working together for the benefit
of all, and *ichariba chode,* seeing everyone as brothers and sisters, are
two of the persisting values that are very similar to Hawaiian values that
opened doors for the Okinawans settling in the Islands and hold them
in good stead today.

The Old Country

To better understand the social and cultural behavior and adaptation of the Okinawans in Hawai'i, a brief discussion about Okinawa
itself is needed. The Ryukyu Islands lie south of Kyushu, Japan, and
stretch in a southwesterly direction from Kyushu to Taiwan. Of the
160 islands, 40 are inhabited. Okinawa is the major island, with other
groups including Ōsumi, Tokara, and Amami to the north and Miyako
and Yaeyama to the south. The fauna and flora of this subtropical zone

are very similar to that in Hawai'i. Hibiscus, bougainvillea, ginger, papaya, pineapple, sugarcane, and banana thrive in Okinawa.

The average temperature in winter is about 60 degrees Fahrenheit and about 85 degrees in summer. In summer, the predominant wind direction is from the south. This south wind brings moisture-laden warm air, creating an unbearable atmosphere and making clothing stick to the body like wet rags, even in the shade. In the summer and fall months, typhoons from the South Pacific destroy homes and farm crops, but these storms bring much-needed rain, which restores the watersheds. The strong winds uproot vegetation and any loose material not anchored to the ground, ravaging acres of farm crops painstakingly raised on the limited arable land. The coral islands have limited land area suitable for agriculture. The northern portion of Okinawa is mountainous, and only strips of land along the seacoast can be farmed. The southern half of the island is fairly flat and is most suitable for farming. Historically, a few times each year, the people suffered from famine following devastating typhoons. They were able to survive these hardships by helping and encouraging each other.

Anthropologists and archeologists believe that the people of Okinawa and southern Japan are from the same racial background. It is thought that people from Southeast Asia and southern China rode the summer current that sweeps from the equator northward along the east coast of China and Taiwan to settle in Okinawa and Kyushu. As there appear to be some genetic links between the people of Taiwan and eastern China and the Polynesians, *ichariba chode* could be quite literally true for the Okinawans and the Hawaiians.[1]

The culture of Okinawa was predominantly shaped by geography, interaction with its neighbors, and the arrival of European merchants in the nineteenth century.[2] In the fourteenth century, when the islands were unified and a profitable maritime commerce began, the port of Naha became a center of trade for goods produced in Japan, China, Korea, and Southeast Asia. These goods included Chinese finery and herbs, Japanese swords and textiles, and spices, artifacts, and sugar from Southeast Asia. Okinawa imported ideas and products and transformed them to suit their needs. Chinese writing, martial arts, and musical instruments such as the samisen were imported from China, along with the sweet potato and sugarcane. Pottery was introduced from Korea and China. Okinawan dance movements were influenced by the dance of Southeast Asian countries.

The culture of the people of Okinawa, with its strong influences from China, Korea, and Southeast Asia, was very distinct from that of Japan. The Okinawans had their own king and government. Their language is also distinct. The people of the Ryukyu Islands look different than people from Japan proper, being shorter, darker in skin, hairier, and more often with double epicanthic folds in their eyelids. They were known for their easygoing and fun-loving temperament coupled with cooperative diligence in work. Okinawans traditionally have lived extremely long lives, and their good health into old age has been studied scientifically.[3]

The freedom and prosperity enjoyed by the people of the Okinawan Kingdom were dashed when the Satsuma samurais from southern Kyushu invaded the kingdom, subjugated its people in 1606, and took the king as a prisoner to Kagoshima in 1609. Okinawa experienced harsh rules and taxation imposed by the aggressive Satsuma warrior clan from Japan. This occupation continued until the Tokugawa government was replaced and Okinawa became a Japanese prefecture in 1879, eight years after the Meiji government was established in Japan.[4]

The arrival of Western merchants affected maritime trade. The Okinawan overseas trade, at its highest point in the fourteenth century, began to wane when the Spanish and Portuguese arrived in the region. European products were traded for goods made in Asia. About this time the Japanese merchants also entered the maritime markets. It is said that the Western sailors who came upon Okinawa on their way to Japan in the early 1800s were surprised to meet gentle and peace-loving people who carried no weapons.[5] The people were kind, hospitable, and had an intense dislike of violence and crime. The people of Okinawa had adapted to conditions that were beyond their control and learned to accept and live with distressing situations such as natural disasters and subjugation by Satsuma samurais. Everyone, regardless of social status, pitched in to do the work of farming, fishing, and raising pigs. They survived hardships by working together. The harsh living conditions in Okinawa requiring mutual dependence and assistance resulted in the emergence of a horizontal society. By contrast, the Japanese social structure is hierarchical, that of a vertical society, created by the samurai to rule the populace.

Yuimaru, the community spirit of working together, resulted in farmers all helping each other to harvest sugarcane, rice, sweet potatoes, and other crops requiring many hands. They worked on one farm, then moved on to the next until every cane stalk or grain of rice was harvested. This community-based mutual aid concept spread to other activities such as rebuilding homes destroyed by typhoons, cleaning streets and public areas, and keeping the village safe from unsavory activities. Everyone acted as the community's eyes and ears. The Okinawans brought the value of *yuimaru* with them to Hawai'i.

Immigration

They sailed from the "Land of the Immortals" to the "Islands of Aloha." Contract laborers from Okinawa first came to Hawai'i in 1900, fifteen years after the first contract laborers arrived from Japan. Kyuzo Toyama, known as the Father of Immigration, saw the need for young people to leave Okinawa to earn a better life.[6] It was the custom for the eldest son to inherit the farm, leaving the other siblings to fend for themselves. Toyama made numerous requests to the Meiji government to allow Okinawans to emigrate before approval was finally given. Twenty-five thousand people emigrated from Okinawa to Hawai'i between 1900 and 1924.[7] These men, women, and children hoped to find a better life than they would have in Okinawa with its few natural resources, typhoons, famine, and overpopulation. Some left Okinawa to escape conscription into the Japanese army, which was fighting the Russo-Japanese War of 1904–1905. For some of the more adventurous young men, going to Hawai'i was exciting, inviting, and the "in" thing to do.

Many of the Okinawan Issei (first-generation arrivals) had planned to come to Hawai'i, work for a few years, and then go back to Okinawa with their riches. They sent money home, which helped the Okinawan economy. However, conditions in Okinawa deteriorated, with a postwar depression following the Russo-Japanese War and World War I, and people were starving. Compared to immigrants from other parts of Japan, more Okinawans brought wives or sent for their wives and children. The presence of their wives and children made it easier for them to adapt to Hawai'i, so many of them ended up staying. Others stayed because as their family size increased, with the Okinawan Issei women having the highest fertility rate of all the Japanese, the return to Okinawa became an unattainable dream.[8] About half of the Okinawan immigrants either returned to Okinawa or moved to the mainland United States in search of better opportunities.

On the plantations, people worked ten-hour days under the blazing sun and were subject to brutal whippings by the *luna*. Uchinanchu, as they called themselves, were looked down upon by the Naichi (Japanese from other prefectures) and were assigned the harder jobs. Part of the discrimination stemmed from the fact that many of the Okinawans spoke only the Okinawan dialect, foreign to the Japanese, and they could not communicate with the Japanese laborers who had arrived fifteen years earlier and had an advantage in the plantation camps. The Okinawan culture, as noted, was distinct from the Japanese culture, and such common Okinawan practices as the raising of pigs and slaughter of animals was foreign and abhorrent to the immigrants from Japan proper. Thus there was often tension between the Uchinanchu and the Naichi.

In the early years, wages were extremely low and living conditions were quite poor. In 1909, the pay was $18/month, which consisted of twenty-six workdays.[9] Workers rarely could make the $18, as poor sanitation, bad water, and squalid living conditions led to illness and sick days for which they would not get paid. Since the income from plantation work was not enough to feed and educate their children, many of the men and their wives and children worked in side businesses such as raising pineapple and sugarcane and selling it to the plantation, doing laundry for the single men, mending clothes, making and selling tofu, and running the community bathhouse.

Most of the Okinawans came as laborers, but many left the plantations as soon as they could to open businesses such as stores, barbershops, bakeries, and auto-repair shops in the towns of Hilo, Waipahu, Wahiawā, and Honolulu.[10] Okinawans are noted for owning successful family-run businesses, for which they were well prepared, with all the side businesses manned by the wives and children of the laborers in the plantation camps. Some of these ventures became Hawai'i household names, such as the general merchandise Arakawa Stores, Aloha Tofu, and several well-known restaurants.

The banks were reluctant to lend start-up money to fund some of these business ventures, as the aspiring entrepreneurs had minimal assets for collateral. The custom of *moai*, another example of community spirit at work, is a means of raising a substantial amount of money from friends and relatives to pay for business start-ups or unexpected expenses. *Moai* usually has a life of twelve months with twelve participants. It could have a different time span with a corresponding number of participants. At the start of *moai*, the participants decide on the monthly dollar amount, such as ten or one hundred or another sum. The participants bid for the use of the money collected for a given month. The person who bids the highest will receive the money collected for that month. In the subsequent months, that person will continue to pay the set monthly sum plus the bid amount for the remainder of the *moai* life. The monthly meeting will continue until the last person receives his or her share. In this example, the *moai* ends after twelve months. Obviously, the person who waits until the last month will receive the largest amount of bid monies. Doing *moai* requires much trust among the participants, as a dishonest person could abscond town after collecting the monthly sum.

Ethnocultural Identity

THE INDIVIDUAL

Certain character traits and behaviors helped the Okinawans to settle into their new homes in Hawai'i. *Tege,* meaning easygoing, is an adjective describing the Uchinanchu personality. Translated it means "almost acceptable" or "it will do for now." The people of the Ryukyus operate on "Okinawan Time," which means doing things on one's own terms rather than someone else's terms and schedules. It is an amazing lack of time-urgency, a sense of "What is the hurry? We have tomorrow." The predominant mood and emotional range of Okinawans can be described as happy and easygoing, enjoying and sharing good food, drink, and company.

"*Iji nu njira tihiki, ti nu njira iji hiki*": "When you are roused to anger, put back your fists. When your fists are clenched to strike, keep down your wrath."[11] In the old country, having been subjugated for so many years by Satsuma, the trait of acceptance and bearing of anger without resorting to violence was cultivated to preserve one's sanity. Since no one was allowed to carry swords, karate was taught for self-defense, not for killing or maiming anyone. Karate means "empty hands." The philosophy of acceptance and bearing of anger helped the Okinawans tolerate the abusive treatment by the *luna* and the discrimination by the Naichi on the plantations.

THE FAMILY

Gender Roles: The Okinawan Woman. "*Yinago ya nu kajitui*": "A wife is the helmsman of the house."[12] Women held important roles in the spiritual life of the family. They served as the protector and conveyed *shiji*, thought to be power and strength from a supernatural source, to their male kinsmen.[13] A sister could provide this power to her brother, a wife to her husband. They were the guardians of the spiritual strength of the family. The woman would intervene and ask for help from the deities when someone took ill. They would call upon their ancestors to help restore health to a sick family member.

Though religions such as Shintoism, Buddhism, Taoism, and Christianity have been introduced into Okinawa over the centuries, the indigenous religious practices continue to be popular. In the villages of Okinawa, gods of nature are thought to reside in shrines located in wooded areas. The *noro*, a woman priestess, is the religious leader of the village who presides over religious services and festivities at these shrines. Only women could serve the gods. They were able to commune with the gods and ancestors and pray for the welfare of all.[14] The *noro*, originally appointed by the king's court starting in the fifteenth century, would pass down the position in the family to a female relative. Rural areas in Okinawa continue to uphold this tradition.

The *yuta* is a shaman who is able to read the future and guides people in taking proper actions. This is similar to the Western seer or spiritual reader. The Okinawans consult the *yuta* for many things, including business ventures, wedding dates, the best time to build a home, and so on. These seers are usually women. Even today, the *yutas* continue to be popular in Okinawa, and there are a few practitioners in Hawai'i.

The head of worship at home is the oldest woman in the family. She informs the family members of upcoming religious observances and prepares food and offerings for the ancestral *butsudan,* or altar, located in the home. Ancestor worship was introduced from China and continues to flourish in Okinawa.

The Okinawan woman has been described as hardworking, resourceful, and business-minded. The women ran side businesses with the help of the children. They made and sold tofu, raised chickens and sold the eggs, raised pigs, and sold vegetables and fruits from their garden to supplement the family income. Character traits of the women were patience, endurance, and strength.[15] They married earlier and bore more children that the Japanese women from other prefectures, with a mean of six children for the Okinawa-born Issei compared to five children for Japan-born Issei.[16] Married Okinawan women in the plantation days came to Hawai'i with tattoos on the backs of their hands. During the Satsuma occupation of Okinawa, young women tattooed their fingers to repel the samurai, who considered the markings distasteful. In Hawai'i, the Japanese from other prefectures considered tattoos to be a sign of low class or of a criminal element. This made many of the Okinawan women ashamed, so they often hid their hands from people.

The Okinawan Man. According to Kyuzo Toyama, the leader of the forty immigrants from Okinawa who arrived in Hawai'i in March 1903, the men were considered to be "physically fit and have a reputation as the best immigrant workers from Japan."[17] They were strong and had an excellent work ethic. They cooperated well and helped each other. They were compassionate and kind and nonviolent. This made the whippings by the *luna* even more disturbing to the Okinawan men, who were used to a more horizontal system where everyone pitched in to help. They did know how to defend themselves, practicing karate, a form of self-defense. Stories from Okinawan immigrants tell of the use of martial arts. One story is told of a *luna* who whipped a contract worker for something he did not do. The worker took the *luna* head on and subdued the much larger man with a karate throw. On another occasion, a fight broke out between an Okinawan laborer and a laborer from another country. After putting in a full day's work, it was common practice to do overtime work to earn additional income cutting cane into a couple of foot-length seed pieces. Apparently the cuttings were stolen, leading to the altercation. The Okinawan was attacked with a cane knife, but because he was an expert in karate, he disarmed the attacker and threw him to the ground. In both cases, the Okinawans could have killed their attackers, but it was and still is against the teachings of karate to maim or kill a person unless one's life is in danger.

Although the living and working conditions on the plantation were not what they had bargained for, they were able to endure the harsh environment because of their experience with great hardships created by typhoons, famines, and harsh treatment of the Satsuma in Okinawa. They lived by the proverb *"Nan kuru nai sa"*: "Don't worry, it'll work out."[18]

Children. Children were expected to help with the family work. They were taught the value of hard work and making an honest living by example and started their contribution to the family welfare early on. A Nisei Okinawan woman in her eighties recalled how their family ran the camp *furo*, the community bathhouse. Starting in grade school, she and her three sisters would cut the firewood used to heat the bathwater. The older sisters would be on either side of a two-man saw, and she and her other sister would grip either side of the log to be cut. She and the other gripper would get distracted watching their friends playing marbles and having fun. They would distractedly loosen their grip on the log and the saw would stick, resulting in a knock on the head by the older sisters. They would also collect leftover food and kitchen scraps from houses in their plantation camp to make food for the pigs they raised. Because of embarrassment, they would pull the wagon full of slop with their heads completely down, trying to hide their faces from children who taunted them. The Naichi thought of the Uchinanchu as being dirty and below them, due in part to their raising pigs and eating pork. In Japan, raising and slaughtering animals was left to the *eta* class, considered untouchable. The Naichi did not eat meat until the Meiji era, whereas in Okinawa, pork dishes were common. An insult hurled at the Okinawans was *"Okinawa ken ken, buta kau kau,"* which means, "Okinawans eat pig slop." The Okinawan children would then yell back, *"Naichi Naichi, chi ga nai,"* meaning, "Naichi has no blood."[19]

Elders. Elders are revered in a culture that has ancestor worship as one of the basics of its spiritual life. According to the Okinawan Centenarian Study, the character traits most notable in elderly Okinawans are low tension and a lack of time-urgency.[20] They have great self-confidence and determination. The term *gajuh* means "self-willed character" and describes an unwillingness to yield or give up.[21] Mrs. Kamada Nakazato, a 102-year-old Okinawan woman, was asked about how she lived such a long and healthy life. She responded, "Eat your vegetables, have a positive outlook, be kind to people and smile."[22]

FAMILY AND COMMUNITY VALUES AND GOALS

The Okinawans were able to integrate so well into the Hawaiian Islands because they shared the same values as many Island people. *Yuimaru* is quite similar to the Hawaiian value of *laulima*—to join hands to help. In the Okinawan family, just as in the Hawaiian family, the cooperation of every member was valued and expected in order to survive. The value of hard work was impressed upon the children by having them work side by side with their parents. One Okinawan family in Ewa Camp had seven girls and two boys working together cleaning and running the camp bathhouse, collecting food scraps from neighbors to feed their pigs, and delivering tofu made by their mother. Having learned how to run side businesses, many of the Nisei and Sansei (second- and third-generation people) went on to open successful Hawai'i restaurants, such as the Zippy's chain and Tamashiro Market.

Makutu (doing the right thing) is similar to the Hawaiian value *pono*. A seventy-eight-year-old Uchinanchu Nisei man recalled learning about *makutu* by watching his father, who was a camp policeman in Ewa Plantation. People would come to his father when they were upset with each other, with family problems, or problems with a neighbor or at work. He sat everyone around the table in the kitchen, and they would all have a chance to talk and tell their side of the fight. Everybody had their say, similar to the Hawaiian practice of *ho'oponopono* (see chapter 1, "The Hawaiians"). Then his father would stress to them the importance of being honest and doing the right thing by each other. Both sides usually left satisfied.

Education was valued highly by the Okinawans. One Okinawan Issei put it this way to his children: "I don't mind emptying my pockets to fill your heads." They felt that education was a treasure that couldn't be lost or stolen. One Issei woman told her daughters that they should finish school and go into teaching or nursing so that they would not have to depend on a man for everything. She had seen her sister in Okinawa in an unhappy marriage because she had no way of supporting herself. Education was a way out of the plantations. Many Nisei went on to excel in the fields of medicine, law, engineering, nursing, education, and finance, among others.

Group identity and mutual dependence was valued and fostered by the forming of *sonjin kai*—clubs that were originally based on the location in Okinawa from which the members came. Annual picnics, New Year's parties, and other get-togethers helped people keep in touch. They provided help for people in crisis with sickness or deaths in the family.[23] During World War II, these clubs were disbanded. After the war, various types of clubs emerged: those with ties to locations in Okinawa, such as *sonjin kai* and *doshi kai;* those with ties to localities in Hawai'i, such as Maui Okinawa Kenjin Kai and Wahiawa Kyoyu Kai; and others with special interests, such as Hui O Laulima Women's Club and the Young Okinawans of Hawai'i. The United Okinawan Association served as the umbrella organization for these clubs. In 1995, the by-laws and the name of the organization were changed in order to allow people of other ethnicities to participate and even become officers in the association. The new name is Hawai'i United Okinawa Association (HUOA), and it has fifty member clubs statewide.

A New Ethnocultural Identity

Okinawan-Americans in Hawai'i have actively sought a distinct ethnic identity. Beginning in the 1980s, the more frequent use of the term "Uchinanchu" rather than Okinawan to identify themselves, individually and collectively, has served as a powerful symbol of their independent identity and expression of their ethnic pride. Using a word for their ethnic identity from their own language rather than Japanese or English strongly proclaims their structural distinction from Japanese-Americans.[24] As noted by Kaneshiro, "The main component of Uchinanchu identity has always been the deeply rooted need to separate and distinguish itself from Japanese (American) identity."[25] The Uchinanchu Spirit encompasses an open, giving, sharing, supportive, helping, and encouraging heart; fellowship and cooperation; hard work; Okinawan cultural awareness; and emphasis on family.[26] Humility is also an important value to the Okinawans.[27] Many refer to this Uchinanchu Spirit as "the spirit of *yuimaru*" (gladly working together in mutual dependence). These are cultural values that are unchanging and have been passed down through the generations. Other values have been shifted as a result of the need for new group adaptive strategies and life goals over time.

The Uchinanchu immigrated to Hawai'i with their cultural values of nonviolence and practice of not bearing arms. With World War II, however, there was a shift in the Uchinanchu intragroup adaptive strategy of avoiding violence that had been reinforced by the Satsuma rule in which the Okinawans were disarmed in the 1600s. Many Okinawans from Hawai'i enlisted and plunged into violent battle. They returned home with medals and commendations for their bravery and accomplishment in war as part of the 442nd Regimental Combat Team and the 100th Infantry Battalion. Each unit from Hawai'i was highly decorated and praised. Once they got home, the adaptive strategy again shifted as they turned their energy to obtaining college and trade school degrees, using the federal GI Bill assistance. By the early 1950s, many veterans completed schooling and returned to Hawai'i as architects, engineers, lawyers, accountants, teachers, and doctors.

The Okinawans' strong desire for social equality dates back centuries, because of years of domination by outside rule. Thus it is not surprising that the Uchinanchu who had witnessed the suffering of their parents on the plantations were attracted to labor union movements and politics to address social issues. The Nisei had learned the value of helping each other in the spirit of *yuimaru* and applied it to labor and political advancements. Japanese, Okinawans, and Filipinos joined hands to strike against plantations to demand just treatment and fair pay. The prominent Okinawan labor union leaders of the postwar era include Thomas Yagi of Maui, Yasuke Arakaki and Yoshito Takamine of Hawai'i Island, and Goro Hokama of Lāna'i.

The Democratic Party of Hawai'i embraced Japanese- and Oki-nawan-Americans and encouraged them to run for political office. Some became state senators and representatives, while others were elected to county seats. Okinawans such as Robert Oshiro, a prominent lawyer and political strategist, worked behind the scenes to elect Governors John Burns, George Ariyoshi, and John Waihee to establish public policies that benefited everyone in Hawai'i.

Much of the bigotry and discrimination by Japanese-Americans toward the Okinawans in Hawai'i declined after World War II. Relations between the two ethnic groups improved because they grew up together in the same plantation camps or urban neighborhoods and served together in the U.S. Army's "Go for Broke" 100th and 442nd Battalions. They also shared a common status as "second-class citizens" under the haole oligarchy.[28] Following the war, intermarriages between Uchinanchu and Japanese-Americans as well as with other ethnic groups became common. As the second-generation Uchinanchu matured into adulthood, they began to assume leadership roles in their communities and in larger society. This resulted in a cultural assimilation and loss of traditional culture. The cultural distinctiveness of the Okinawan-American ethnic identity became less apparent.

As a result of intermarriage, many third- and fourth-generation Okinawan-Americans are of mixed Japanese-Okinawan ancestry or are a mixture of other ethnic groups. Those who were Japanese-Okinawan were often informed by their parents that they were different from Japanese-Americans, but they were not necessarily told what the differences were. As a result of the second-generation's American assimilation, many third- and fourth-generation Uchinanchu were not exposed to their Okinawan culture unless they were raised in multigenerational households. Unfortunately, these subsequent generations of Okinawans no longer lived the traditional culture of their grandparents. With the assimilation of Hawai'i-born Uchinanchus into the greater Island community, the language and religion of Okinawa lost their importance in the family.

In the 1970s, with the release of Alex Haley's *Roots*, an ethnic revival became a part of America's popular culture. This revival was important to the numerous cultural groups in Hawai'i, including the Okinawan community. For many, knowing one's cultural roots became a positive value, and the Uchinanchus in Hawai'i began to form a new relationship with their ancestral homeland. During the 1980s and 1990s, a unique bond developed between the Hawai'i Uchinanchu community and the people of Okinawa. This grew upon the relationship established with the relief effort organized by the Uchinanchu in Hawai'i in World War II. The battle of Okinawa had completely devastated the island of Okinawa, and the survivors were in desperate need of aid. At first, the Hawai'i Uchinanchu community was hesitant to organize a relief effort because of the prevailing anti-Japanese sentiment. In response, after much discussion, the United Okinawan Association (UOA) was organized. It was made up of village club associations rather than individuals. The UOA played an important role in Okinawa's postwar recovery by sending clothing, livestock, and other essentials to help the people get back on their feet after the devastation of battle.[29]

In 1980, the UOA commemorated the eightieth anniversary of the Okinawan immigration to Hawai'i with a yearlong celebration underwritten by the Hawai'i State Legislature. As part of the celebration, the Okinawan Prefecture Government—in remembering the post–World War II help they had received from the Hawai'i Uchinanchu when it was most needed—sponsored a study tour to Okinawa for thirty-five young Nisei and Sansei between the ages of eighteen and thirty-five. The participants attended lectures and visited numerous historical sites. The highlight of the tour was when the participants visited their ancestral village or town and met their relatives. Many reported a sense of belonging and a connection to their ancestral roots. Okinawa was not simply their ancestral homeland; it was now a tangible part of them. The overwhelming hospitality and generosity of the people and the government of Okinawa reflected their deep appreciation for the invaluable relief aid that the Uchinanchu in Hawai'i gave after World War II. The people of Okinawa had not forgotten what the grandparents and the parents of the young Sansei had done to help them survive in the aftermath of the Battle of Okinawa.[30]

The 1980 tour to Okinawa was a turning point for the third-generation Sansei. It awakened them to their heritage and instilled a pride in being Uchinanchu. A decade later, the Hawai'i Uchinanchu community saw a need to nurture new leaders from among the fourth and fifth generations and used the same process of visiting the homeland.

HUOA is a vibrant group that sponsors the annual Okinawan Festival, a two-day event attracting over 50,000 people that provides an opportunity to get an up-close look at Okinawan culture. There is a genealogy booth where Uchinanchu can trace their roots to the old country. The festival features Okinawan food, music, dance, and cultural activities. Popular foods include the *andagi,* an Okinawan donut;

traditional pig's feet soup; and the *andadog*, a local favorite, which is a hotdog dipped in *andagi* batter and fried to a golden brown. Entertainers from Okinawa and Hawai'i feature classical and contemporary music and dance, *taiko* drumming, and as karate demonstrations. Cultural performances play a significant role in preserving the interest in things Okinawan. Many of the local performers are third-, fourth-, and fifth-generation Okinawans.[31]

To further promote the interest and value of Okinawan culture, the HUOA nominates young Uchinanchu students from Hawai'i for two scholarships offered by the Okinawa Prefectural Government to study in Okinawa for one year. HUOA also publishes a membership newsletter called *Uchinanchu*, maintains a Web site, and produces a television program called *Hawai'i Okinawa Today*. This program focuses on HUOA activities and promotes tours to Okinawa to provide the Hawai'i Uchinanchu an ancestral homeland experience.[32]

The HUOA participates in non-Okinawan activities such as the annual food drive and sponsors a community outreach program to share Okinawan culture with people who are less fortunate and who are working diligently to rebuild their lives. The focus of this annual event is to share the traditional Okinawan culture and heritage through summer picnic foods, games, music, and dance.

THE OKINAWAN-HAWAIIAN CONNECTIONS

There are many parallels between the personality traits and social values that characterize the Okinawans and the Hawaiians. The *'ohana* concept overlaps the Okinawan concepts of *ichariba chode* and *yuimaru*. Today, for the Sansei and Yonsei Uchinanchu, the traditional values of mutual cooperation and hard work and keeping the family first have converged with Hawai'i's local values. Just as the Hawaiian renaissance began in the late 1960s with a resurgence of interest in culture and historic events, the Uchinanchus of the late twentieth and early twenty-first centuries are going through a cultural renaissance. The Uchinanchu Spirit and the Aloha Spirit are intertwined in the emergence of a new ethnocultural identity of the Okinawan-American.

According to Ueunten, "The Okinawan ethnic community in Hawai'i represents an interesting case as its membership consists largely of people who voluntarily assert their Okinawan identity. That is, membership in Okinawan community is not determined merely by one's Okinawan ancestry but also one's actions in affirming his/her Okinawan heritage. A person thus becomes part of the Okinawan ethnic community by getting involved in its activities."[33] Okinawan identity appears to be strongest among the younger generation who have more in common culturally and socially with other local people in Hawai'i and Americans in general than did their Uchinanchu predecessors. With the blending of culture and ethnicity in Hawai'i, one does not have to have Okinawan blood to participate in the resurgence of Okinawan pride. The Hawai'i United Okinawa Association was specifically renamed to replace the word "Okinawan" in 1995, in order to be inclusive of people of all races who are interested in Okinawan culture.

Biopsychosocial Factors

With the emergence of a new ethnocultural identity among the Uchinanchu, adaptive group strategies have led to some evolution of intragroup values (such as taking up arms in World War II against Japan and the Okinawa Prefecture) and shared intergroup values *(yuimaru* and *laulima; makutu* and *pono)* that helped them integrate into the Hawaiian milieu. But the question arises as to whether there are hardwired biologic and sociocultural characteristics, traits, or behaviors that have been retained versus others that were not protected and were more malleable. Longevity is a trait that is thought to be both hardwired and built into the genes as well as malleable and dependent on environmental factors.

The Okinawans are known for their good health and longevity. According to 2001 health statistics, coronary heart disease occurs in Okinawa at a rate of one-fifth that in the United States. Cancers of the breast, ovary, and prostate in Okinawa occur at one-fourth the rate in America.[34] Uchinanchu men in Hawai'i had fewer cancers than men from other prefectures in Japan.[35] Okinawans live the longest, disability-free life, with six times more centenarians per 100,000 than the United States.[36] Now how much of this healthy longevity is hardwired—innate to the people of Okinawa via genetics—versus how much is modifiable by environmental factors?

Recently, B. J. Willcox and his team have identified what appear to be human "longevity genes" that may contribute to a long life and good health into old age. Studying men of Japanese and Okinawan ancestry, it was found that men who had certain genetic variations within the FOXo3A gene led extra long, healthy lives.[37] However, other factors besides genetics are known to have an impact on longevity. In Okinawa, stressful jobs and westernized diets are some of the risk factors for poorer health resulting in the steady decrease of life spans, especially of

Okinawan males, over the last few decades. Only those currently older than age sixty-five retain their advantage for longer lives.[38]

The Okinawan Centenarian Study, a twenty-five-year longitudinal study that began in 1976, identified four factors that contribute to healthy aging and longevity: a low caloric density diet, exercise, a stress-reducing psychospiritual outlook, and the utilization of both Eastern and Western health care practices.[39] The traditional Okinawan diet was rich in vegetables and fruit, low in fat and high in fiber and complex carbohydrates, and had half the caloric density (calories/gram of food) of the American diet.[40] Studying the diet, health and longevity of Okinawans, Japanese, and Americans, there is evidence that caloric restriction (typical in the traditional Okinawan diet) leads to longer life spans and less age-related illness such as cardiovascular disease and certain forms of cancer.[41] Okinawans live about five or six years longer than Americans (to age 82 or 83). The old Okinawan practice of *hara hachi bu*, eating until one is 80 percent full, helps reinforce caloric restriction.

The Okinawans attribute their longevity to the food they consume and believe that food is life's medicine. This follows the Chinese saying, "Food and medicine are of one source."[42] Hiroko Sho studied the nutritional practices of the Okinawans, who believe that everything that one eats becomes transformed into flesh and blood; in effect, you are what you eat.[43] Before and after a meal, they would thank the food for giving them nourishment and providing medicinal value. Leafy green vegetables, tofu, kombu, bittermelon, beans, sweet potatoes, rice, fish, and pork are lightly seasoned with salt and miso. Turmeric and mugwort are other spices used in Okinwan cuisine. Greg Plotnikoff, M.D., a world expert on Japan's traditional herbal medicine, states that bittermelon is high in antioxidants and may have blood sugar–lowering effects.[44] Okinawan mugwort has been found to have an antimalarial effect and has been used to treat fever, and tumeric has anti-inflammatory and antioxidant effects.[45]

Exercise in Okinawa was traditionally valued and practiced by all. Martial arts, dance, gardening, and walking were favorite forms of exercise thought to increase one's ki, or life energy. The Okinawan's psychospiritual outlook helped reduce their stress levels. Nature and ancestor veneration were keystones in this outlook, and prayers were most often for health.[46] The Okinawans' spirituality is based on the idea that the gods and the ancestors watch over and take care of them. They believe that through meditation, they could develop the spiritual qualities of love, compassion, and wisdom that increase one's longevity.

Ikigai, or "the reason for waking up in the morning," is also thought to be a contributing factor to a long, healthy, and happy life.[47] A person who is able to continue on in their traditional role in their family and community, feeling needed and of use into their old age, may survive longer than a person who loses that role. Kamada Nakazato, the 102-year-old *noro* of her village, stated, "Sometimes you can best take care of yourself by taking care of others."[48]

Finally, the Okinawans' acceptance and use of both Eastern and Western modalities for healing leads to healthy aging and long life. Many go to regular medical doctors and still consult with the shaman. Herbal remedies and massage are used, along with medication they receive from the doctor.

These factors all promote healthy aging in the Okinawans but are not hardwired and protected in a person's makeup. One can choose not to eat healthily or to exercise. One can choose not to take medication or herbal remedies. So are there any characteristics of the Okinawan that may be hardwired? Herbert Benson, founder of the Mind Body Medical Institute at Harvard, wondered if we are "wired for God."[49] He believes that our beliefs and spiritual practices may be encoded into our physiology. Willcox gives a possible example of this in a group of aged women in a nursing home. Many were nonresponsive and seemingly unaware of time or their surroundings as they neared the end of life. On every first and fifteenth days of the month, these women would spontaneously start praying and singing religious songs. These days of the month have a certain religious significance in Okinawan spirituality. After practicing these rituals for fifty years or more, could this have become encoded into their minds, bodies, and spirits?

Summary and Conclusions

The experience of the Okinawans immigrating to Hawai'i was influenced by the values, goals, and inborn characteristics with which they came. The Okinawans who then stayed in Hawai'i were influenced and changed by the experience of immigration and the integration into a new society. Passed down through the generations are the enduring qualities of mind, body, and spirit that have helped these people weather adversity and thrive in Hawai'i. A new ethnocultural identity evolved as adaptive strategies and life goals changed over time and again were passed down through the generations in the Islands. As the Okinawans set down roots in the Territory of Hawai'i, a sense of pride and belonging allowed them to send their sons to war in 1941 and stirred social and political activism in the 1950s and 1960s. Education and intermarriage further broadened the horizons of the Uchinanchu, but the interest in and love of things Okinawan has persisted until today due to the stewardship of organizations such as the Hawai'i United Okinawa Association.

THE FUTURE OF UCHINANCHU IN HAWAI'I

Over a century ago, twenty-six adventurous Okinawan young men set foot on O'ahu. They were followed by thousands of Okinawans who settled in Hawai'i. According to HUOA, in 1979 over 70 percent of the Uchinanchu who married had spouses of Japanese descent, 20 percent married people of other ethnicities, and only 10 percent had Okinawan spouses. From the fourth generation onward, there will probably be only few people of solely Okinawan ethnicity. These part-Okinawans will likely find their other roots in different parts of the world. Currently there are few Issei (first-generation immigrants) alive. What will keep the future generations connected to their Okinawan ancestors and culture? The answer lies in the Uchinanchu Spirit and the concept that being Okinawan is a mind-set and way of living. Beyond the cultural context lies a core value system. Being Okinawan is not measured by blood quantum. Okinawan values such as *yuimaru, makutu,* and *ichariba chode* are enduring and guide one in "living Okinawan."

The way one connects with the Okinawan culture varies according to one's interest. For some, the Okinawan performing arts, language, food, and martial arts may appeal. For others, the economic opportunities between Okinawa and the world will peak interest. Political policies of Okinawa may intrigue some. In 2006, Punahou School students started an Okinawan/Japanese Cultural Club for those interested in Okinawan culture. In 2008, the University of Hawai'i at Mānoa opened the Center for Okinawan Studies, the first of its kind outside of Japan. The continuing interest in things Okinawan is a testament to the fortitude and adaptability of the Uchinanchu in Hawai'i, which led to their successful integration into the Hawaiian Islands.

Further Reading

Buettner, D. *The Blue Zones: Lessons for Living Longer from the People Who've Lived the Longest.* Washington, D.C.: National Geographic Society, 2008.

Ethnic Studies Oral History Project. *Uchinanchu: A History of Okinawans in Hawai'i*. Honolulu: University of Hawai'i Press, 1981.

Hokama, S. *The History of Okinawan Language.* Tokyo: Hosei University Press, 1982.

Kerr, G. H. *Okinawa: The History of an Island People.* Rutland, VT: Charles E. Tuttle, 1958.

Lebra, W. P. *Okinawan Religion.* Honolulu: University of Hawai'i Press, 1966.

Willcox, B. J., D. C. Willcox, and M. Suzuki. *The Okinawa Program: How the World's Longest-Lived People Achieve Everlasting Health and How You Can Too.* New York: Clarkson Potter, 2001.

Notes

1. A. W. Sharp, *The Pacific Islands,* San Diego: Lucent Books, 2003.

2. G. H. Kerr, *Okinawa: The History of an Island People,* Rutland, VT: Charles E. Tuttle, 1958.

3. B. J. Willcox, D. C. Willcox, and M. Suzuki, *The Okinawa Program: How the World's Longest-Lived People Achieve Everlasting Health and How You Can Too,* New York: Clarkson Potter, 2001.

4. Kerr 1958.

5. Ibid.

6. Ethnic Studies Oral History Project, *Uchinanchu: A History of Okinawans in Hawai'i,* Honolulu: University of Hawai'i Press, 1981.

7. Ibid.

8. Y. S. Matsumoto, "Okinawa migrants to Hawai'i," *Hawaiian Journal of History* 16 (1982): 125–137.

9. A. Kikumura, *Issei Pioneers: Hawai'i and the Mainland, 1885–1924,* Los Angeles: Japanese American National Museum, 1992.

10. Matsumoto 1982.

11. R. Adaniya, A. Njus, and M. Yamate, eds., *Of Andagi and Sanshin: Okinawan Culture in Hawai'i,* Honolulu: Hui O Laulima, 1988.

12. Ibid.

13. Ibid.

14. D. Buettner, *The Blue Zones: Lessons for Living Longer from the People Who've Lived the Longest,* Washington, D.C.: National Geographic Society, 2008.

15. Ibid.

16. Matsumoto 1982.

17. Ethnic Studies Oral History Project 1981.

18. Willcox et al. 2001.

19. Matsumoto 1982.

20. Willcox et al. 2001.

21. Ibid.

22. Buettner 2008.

23. Adaniya et al. 1988.

24. J. Y. Okamura, *Ethnicity and Inequality in Hawai'i,* Philadelphia: Temple University Press, 2008.

25. N. Kaneshiro, "Uchinanchu Identity in Hawai'i," in *The Japanese American Contemporary Experience in Hawai'i,* ed. J. Y. Okamura, Honolulu: Social Process in Hawai'i, 2002: 75–94.

26. Town and Village Association of Okinawa Prefecture and Okinawa City Mayors' Association, compilers, "The Nisei/Sansei Hawai'i-Okinawa Study Tour," unpublished reports and essays available through the Hawai'i Okinawa Center, Waipahu, and the International Exchange Division of the Okinawa Prefectural Government Office, Naha, Okinawa (1981).

27. M. Arakaki, "Hawai'i Uchinanchu and Okinawa: Uchinanchu Spirit and the Formation of a Trans-National Identity," in *Okinawa Diaspora,* ed. Ronald Y. Nakasone, Honolulu: University of Hawai'i Press, 2002: 130–141.

28. W. Ueunten, "The Maintenance of the Okinawan Community in Hawai'i," master's thesis in sociology, University of Hawai'i, 1989.

29. Arakaki 2002.

30. Ibid.

31. *Uchinanchu: The Voice of the Hawai'i United Okinawa Association* 110 (August/September 2007).

32. Ibid.

33. Ueunten 1989.

34. Willcox et al. 2001.

35. G. N. Stemmermann, A. M. Y. Nomura, P. H. Chyou, I. Kato, and T. Kuroishi. "Cancer incidence in Hawaiian Japanese: Migrants from Okinawa compared with those from other prefectures," *Japan Journal of Cancer Research* 82 (1991): 1366–1370.

36. Willcox et al. 2001.

37. B. J. Willcox, T. A. Donlon, Q. He, R. Chan, J. S. Grove, K. Yano, K. H. Masaki, D. C. Willcox, B. Rodriguez, and J. D. Curb, "FOXo3A genotype is strongly associated with human longevity," *Proceedings of the National Academy of Sciences* 105(37) (2008): 13,987–13,992.

38. B. J. Willcox, D. C. Willcox, H. Todoriki, A. Fujiyoshi, K. Yanok, Q. He, J. D. Curb, and M. Suzuki, "Caloric restriction, the traditional Okinawan diet and healthy aging: The diet of the world's longest-lived people and its potential impact on morbidity and life span," *Annals of the New York Academy of Science* 1114 (2007): 434–455.

39. Willcox et al. 2001.

40. Ibid.

41. Willcox et al. 2007.

42. M. Yamazato, ed., *Ryukyuan Cuisine,* Naha City: Okinawa Tourism and Cultural Affairs Bureau, 1995.

43. H. Sho, *Minami no Shima no Gaku Eiyo,* Urasoe City, Okinawa Prefecture: Yugen Kaisha Okinawa Shupan, 1988.

44. Buettner 2008.

45. Ibid.

46. Willcox et al. 2001.

47. Buettner 2008.

48. Ibid.

49. Willcox et al. 2001.

CHAPTER 7

The Hispanics

Lisa Sánchez-Johnsen

Overview and Demographics

The terms "Hispanic" and "Latino" are used to describe those whose ethnic origins can be traced to Latin America: Mexico, Puerto Rico, Cuba, Central or South America, or other Spanish, Hispanic, or Latino countries/regions. The terms do not include Brazilians, since their background can be traced to Portuguese origin. Although there are regional differences in the use of these terms, in Hawai'i there does not seem to be any clear preference. Therefore, in this chapter, both terms will be used interchangeably.

In the United States, over 45 million people (about 16 percent of the population) are Hispanic, making them the largest ethnic minority group in the country.[1] Latinos come from over twenty different countries and may be of any racial background. Despite this heterogeneity, what all Latino groups have in common is their native Spanish language and cultural values. According to the most recent 2008 data, Latinos comprise approximately 9 percent of Hawai'i's 1.2 million population.[2] The American Community Survey three-year estimates indicate that the two largest Latino ethnic groups in Hawai'i are Puerto Ricans (about 38,000) and Mexicans (about 29,000), but Latinos from every Latin American country are represented in Hawai'i.[3]

This chapter focuses on the ethnocultural identity of Hispanics/Latinos and the contributions Hispanics have made in Hawai'i, the new multicultural identity of Latinos in Hawai'i, and future directions regarding their ethnocultural needs.

A Brief Review

EARLY SPANISH INFLUENCE: LATE 1700S TO EARLY 1800S

It is often reported that the first person of Hispanic decent who settled in Hawai'i was a sailor from Spain named Don Francisco de Paula Marin, who arrived in Honolulu in either 1793 or 1794. Marin was known for being a confidant, business advisor, bookkeeper, physician, and interpreter to King Kamehameha I. The king also gave Marin permission to marry certain members of the Hawaiian royal court. It is often cited that Marin was at the bedside of King Kamehameha I when he died.[4]

As a native of Spain's Andalucian agricultural region, Marin developed knowledge and skills in cultivating plants and herbs and their medicinal uses. He introduced many plants (and foods) to Hawai'i and has been called the first "gentleman farmer" in Hawai'i. Although he did not introduce the pineapple to Hawai'i, he was the first person to successfully cultivate a pineapple crop in 1813. Marin also planted the first grapevines, established the first vineyard in Honolulu, and made wine. In the early nineteenth century Marin was one of the most influential Europeans in Hawai'i.[5]

EARLY MEXICAN IMMIGRATION TO HAWAI'I: LATE 1700S TO 1800S

The early Mexican influence in Hawai'i began when King Kamehameha I received heads of longhorn cattle as a gift in 1793 from British explorer Captain George Vancouver. The cattle were allowed to roam freely and multiply on Hawai'i Island. In the early 1830s, after the cattle began to create problems due to their increasing numbers, King Kamehameha III brought in Mexican cowboys (called vaqueros in Spanish) from California to Waimea, Hawai'i, to teach the Hawaiians how to manage cattle. The Mexican vaqueros were experts in horsemanship *(charrería)*, roping, and cattle-handling practices, and they taught these skills to the Hawaiian cowboys, called *paniolo*. The *paniolo* era brought another culture to Hawai'i, and this culture significantly shaped the ranching industry, which is still prevalent today. With the arrival of the vaqueros, new techniques such as roping (which was particularly useful when the *paniolo* hunted wild cattle) and using the braided lariat (to teach the roping of cattle) were introduced to the *paniolo*. The vaqueros also brought different types of horse gear to Hawai'i. This included things such as new types of saddles, spurs, and curb-type bits. It is also thought that the special neck rope used by *paniolo* is possibly a remnant from the vaquero tack. Finally, the vaqueros brought many distinct types of clothing that were introduced to the *paniolo*, including new types of hats, jackets, shawls, and bandanas, which eventually were used as neckerchiefs.[6] The materials, techniques, and clothing introduced by the vaqueros essentially developed a cattle culture and industry that created a lasting legacy of *paniolo*. The home of the *paniolo* is Waimea on Hawai'i Island on Parker Ranch, which was once the largest ranch in the United States. Of note, along with teaching Hawaiians how to tend cattle, the Mexican vaqueros also introduced Hawaiians to the guitar, which will be discussed later. It is believed that some vaqueros stayed in Hawai'i, while others returned to California.

LATER MEXICAN IMMIGRATION TO HAWAI'I: 1900S TO PRESENT

The next migration of Mexicans occurred in the 1930s, when Mexicans moved to Hawai'i to work in the pineapple industry. Later, in the 1960s and 1970s, Mexicans came to the new state to work in the construction industry during the era when there was an increase in tourism in Hawai'i. In the late 1980s and early 1990s, larger numbers of laborers were hired from Arizona and California to work again in the pineapple industries on Maui and Moloka'i. From agricultural business, Latinos have moved on to other opportunities and now work in various occupations.

PUERTO RICAN IMMIGRATION TO HAWAI'I: 1900S TO PRESENT

The first arrival of Puerto Ricans in Hawai'i coincided with two events in Puerto Rico and Hawai'i. In 1899, the San Ciriaco hurricane killed more than three thousand people in Puerto Rico and severely destroyed crops and the economy. At the time of the hurricane, Puerto Ricans had a history of working in coffee and pineapple plantations. At the same time, the Hawai'i Sugar Planters Association (HSPA) was seeking workers to assist in the sugarcane industry, and they recruited Puerto Ricans to work in Hawai'i.

The first group of Puerto Rican plantation workers arrived on Maui on December 23, 1900. The three-year labor agreement between the HSPA and the Puerto Ricans permitted them to be transported from Puerto Rico to Hawai'i and obtain an agricultural job, housing, and medical care. However, they ultimately found themselves in less desirable conditions than they were promised by the HSPA. By 1902, there were approximately five thousand Puerto Ricans who settled across four islands. A second group of 683 Puerto Ricans arrived in 1921. At the end of their contract, most Puerto Ricans stayed in Hawai'i, but some moved to California or elsewhere in the United States. Finally, after World War II, additional migrant Puerto Ricans came to Hawai'i.[7] In the year 2000, Puerto Ricans celebrated one hundred years of their arrival through a year-long commemoration. The descendents of the early Puerto Ricans are now called "Local Ricans," "Boricua Hawaiiana," or "Boricua Hawayano."

HISPANICS TODAY

In 1994, a large group of Hispanics of various ethnicities attended the bicentennial celebration of Hispanics in Hawai'i. A highlight of that event was the dedication of the "Marin Tower" in Honolulu to commemorate two hundred years of Hispanic presence in Hawai'i. Today, over 215 years later, Hispanics are found across the state and have made important contributions to the culture and lifestyles of Hawai'i.

Ethnocultural Identity

A number of *internal characteristics* and *external behavior patterns* are commonly seen in Latinos. Below, these are defined in three areas: individual, family, and sociocultural.

INDIVIDUAL

Cultural values and worldviews are critical to understanding Latino identity. *Personalismo* refers to emphasizing interpersonal relationships. In describing Latino values, Santiago and colleagues note that *cariño* is a description of the type of caring and affection that is shown in interpersonal relationships.[8] It is demonstrated in verbal (e.g., adding the suffix *-ito* or *-ita* to words as a term of endearment) and nonverbal (e.g., hugs) communication. They further note that *dignidad* (dignity) refers to a person being worthy and respected and includes actions that enhance a sense of pride; *simpatía* describes a style of interpersonal relationships that promotes pleasant social interactions; and *confianza* refers to trust and familiarity in interpersonal relationships. Together, these values enhance personal relationships.

FAMILY

Family. One of the most significant Latino values is *familismo,* which relates to the importance placed on the immediate and extended family and also includes nonfamily members. Family closeness and cooperation are highly valued, and the family provides physical, emotional, financial, and social support. If a person is Catholic, as part of their baptism it is also customary for them to have a *compadre* (godfather) or *comadre* (godmother) to provide support to the child and their family and promote a sense of family and community.[9]

Family structure, gender roles, and generational status are also important among Latinos. Overall, according to the 2007 Population Estimates, the Latino population in Hawai'i is relatively young (approximate median age is twenty-six years), the majority were born in the United States (93,987), and 42 percent of those who are ages fifteen and over are married.[10] In terms of family structure, in traditional Latino families the father is the head of the household, but most of the child-rearing tends to be matriarchal in nature. Many Hispanic women in Hawai'i also work outside of the home. In addition, *abuelos* (grandparents) and *compadres* have a significant role in childrearing and providing other types of support. Finally, the Latino gender roles of *machismo* and *marianismo* are helpful in understanding Latino worldviews. *Machismo* is a culturally prescribed way for a man to behave. It conveys a man's responsibility to protect and care for his family. *Marianismo* is a culturally prescribed way for a woman to behave. The concept of *marianismo* comes from the Christian name of "Mary" or the "Virgin Mary," and it connotes that a female should honor the model of the Virgin Mary. *Marianismo* also conveys the notion that a woman should be virtuous, self-sacrificing, humble, and nurturing.[11] Finally, an important part of Latino family structure and identity is related to generational status. First-generation Latinos tend to be more traditional, be less acculturated to mainstream American society, and predominately speak Spanish. Second-generation Latinos tend to be in a transitional state, and they may speak Spanish or English. Third-generation Latinos may be bicultural, and often they experience a loss of the Spanish language.

Family Values and Goals. In general, Latino culture tends to be collectivistic in nature. Collectivism emphasizes the needs, objectives, and points of view of the group, versus individualistic cultures that focus on personal needs. Collectivism is also related to the Latino value of *comunidad* (community). In addition to the Latino values cited above, an important value is *respeto,* or respect. *Respeto* implies deference and obedience to those who are older than oneself or to those in a higher position, such as authorities. The Latino value of respect can be seen in traditional families where those who are younger ask for blessings, particularly when greeting elders, and through the use of formal communication styles in certain situations.[12]

Educational and Occupational Patterns. Education is an important value in Latino communities. About 23 percent of the Hispanic population in Hawai'i is currently enrolled in college or graduate school. In addition, among the Hispanic population ages twenty-five and over, one-third have some college or associate degrees, nearly 11 percent have a bachelor's degree, and 5 percent have a graduate or professional degree.[13] Across the United States, Hispanics tend to prefer to go to college in a location that is close to where they live, in concert with the Latino value of *familismo*. However, the fall 2007 enrollment of Hispanics across the University of Hawai'i (UH) system was only 2–3 percent (1,204), with the highest enrollment at the university's Hawai'i Island Hilo campus.[14] Together, this data indicates that Latinos who have some college or higher may either be attending other universities in Hawai'i or elsewhere or that they have moved to Hawai'i after attending college.

In terms of occupations, Latinos today are found in every segment of the workforce, and approximately 71 percent of Latinos ages sixteen and older are in the labor force, a number slightly higher than the population in general (65 percent).[15] Moreover, 27 percent of Latinos are in management, professional, and related occupations. Latinos in Hawai'i are also more likely to be in service occupations (24 percent); construction, extraction, maintenance, and repair occupations (13 percent); and production, transportation, and material-moving occupations (12 percent) than the population in general in Hawai'i. Over the past three to five years, there also appears to be an increase in the number of Latino professionals who have moved to Hawai'i and possess a higher educational degree. As the Hispanic community grows, there will also be a parallel increase in the number of Hispanic professionals who will make substantial contributions to Hawai'i.

How the Family Has Been Influenced over Time. Latino families have been influenced over time through the effects of intermarriage. For the most part, intermarriages have strengthened Latino cultural values, particularly as they relate to *familismo*. One reason that this has occurred may be because the Hispanic emphasis on the family is similar to the value that other groups place on the 'ohana (family). Therefore, this value is strengthened. The extended family, grandmothers, and *compadres* also continue to play an important role in the family.

SOCIOCULTURAL

Sociocultural factors affecting Latino identity are described below.

Language Issues. The majority of Hawai'i's Hispanic community speaks English. However, there are differences in English proficiency based on length of residence in the United States, age, generation, acculturation, and ethnicity. Data from the 2007 Population Estimates indicates that 28 percent of Hispanics in Hawai'i who are over age five speak a language other than English at home.[16] In 2006, Governor Lingle signed a language access bill into law that required the state and state-funded programs to develop plans to provide interpretation services and translated documents. Many services and publications, however, are not yet available in Spanish.

Dress or Clothing. Hispanic clothing styles are as diverse as their countries of origin. The typical Latino clothing style that is conjured in one's mind includes items that are colorful and bold; have ruffles, flowers, and embroidery; skirts and dresses for women; and cowboy-style clothing for men. Traditional Mexican clothing includes items such as the *huipil* (sleeveless tunic), *quechquemitl* (a capelike poncho), *rebozo* (shawl or scarf), Mexican folkloric dresses for women, and sombreros and boots for men. Although Latinos brought their native clothing to Hawai'i, today there is no distinctive clothing style that is characteristic of Latinos, and Latino clothing is virtually indistinguishable from other styles in Hawai'i.

There does seem to be a resurgence in some spectrums of Latino clothing as it relates to the traditional guayabera or Camisa Yucatan, often called the "Mexican Wedding Shirt." Although more traditional Latinos may wear this shirt, it is also gaining popularity among younger and more acculturated Latinos, as well as non-Latinos. There are a few distinct differences between the various ethnic versions of these shirts (e.g., the Filipino Barong Tagalog and the Samoan "Safari Shirt"), but overall they are very similar, and this is an additional reason why Latinos may blend easily into the culture of Hawai'i.

MUSIC AND DANCE

It is nearly impossible to discuss Latino culture without mentioning this significant facet of their culture.

Early Influence of Mexican Music. When the Mexican vaqueros returned to their homeland after teaching the Hawaiian cowboys how to tend cattle, some of the Mexicans gave them their guitars. The Hawaiians integrated elements of Mexican and Spanish music into their traditional music, which influenced the development of Hawaiian slack key guitar music. The fact that the first three winners of the

Grammy Award for the Best Hawaiian Album were slack key collections is a testament to the enduring effect of Mexican influences on Hawaiian music.

Early Influence of Puerto Rican Music and Dance. In the early 1900s, Puerto Rican dance and music were an important part of plantation life. For Puerto Ricans, this included their traditional music, called *musica tipica* or *musica jibaro,* or what later became known as *kachi-kachi* music. On the plantation, Puerto Ricans played the guitar, *cuatro,* accordion, mandolin, *guiro,* claves, and drums.[17] There were frequent dances on Saturday nights, where lively music and dances were enjoyed by both Puerto Ricans and non-Puerto Ricans. Today Puerto Ricans still play *kachi-kachi* music. In fact, Puerto Ricans in the homeland have commented that the style of music played in Hawai'i is nearly identical to the music that is traditionally played in Puerto Rico, illustrating how well local Puerto Ricans have preserved this tradition.

Latino Music and Dance in General. Latino music and dance are as diverse as the communities that they represent. Latino music radio shows play a significant role in the Latino community, both in terms of connecting the community to its cultural roots and in providing advertisements and programming specific to Latinos. These radio stations play traditional Puerto Rican music, Mexican music, Cuban music, salsa, merengue, reggaeton, and other Hispanic music. Equally important to the Hawai'i Latino music scene is the growing number of musicians, promoters, and disk jockeys who help to market Hispanic music and culture across numerous venues. Latino music is enjoyed by people of all ethnic groups, and music and dance celebrations attract a diverse local and national crowd. Finally, Latinos and non-Latinos are being exposed to dance styles such as salsa, merengue, *cumbia,* and ballet *forklórico* (traditional dances that include folk culture and costumes) at nightclubs and/or through dance performances, with dancers who are equally likely to be Latino as non-Latino.

FOOD

Hispanic foods are as heterogeneous and diverse as their native countries.

Puerto Rican Food. Puerto Rican food is influenced by Spanish, African, and indigenous Taino Indian food. Some of the more popular Puerto Rican foods in Hawai'i include *pasteles* (a meat filling wrapped in grated and seasoned green bananas and steamed in banana or ti leaves), *arroz con pollo* (rice with chicken), *arroz con gandules* (rice with pigeon peas, called *gandude rice* in Hawai'i), *bacalao* (salted and dried cod), *empanadillas* (turnovers with meat, seafood, cheese, or fruit), and *mofongo* (fried green plantains or yuca with pork rinds and garlic). There are a few places where Puerto Rican food can be bought, including at Hispanic festivals and specialty grocery stores and from Latino catering companies and select roadside vendors.

Mexican Food. Mexican restaurants have existed in Hawai'i since at least the late 1960s. However, until approximately the late 1990s there were almost no traditional taquerias (or taco stands) that are typical in communities across the United States with large populations of Latinos. Since the year 2000, there has been a notable increase in the number of Mexican restaurants in Hawai'i. The reason for this change may be related to Mexicans and other Latinos moving from agricultural industries and into food service and restaurant industries. Although there has been an increase in Mexican restaurants, a number of classic restaurants have also closed down. Some of the more popular Mexican foods that can be found in Hawai'i include traditional favorites such as *tamales, menudo, carnitas, chili rellenos, tacos al pastor, carne asada, burritos,* and *ceviche.*

Hispanic/Latino Food in General. Small Hispanic grocery stores (called *mercardos* or *supermercardos*) serve a significant function in terms of a location where imported Latino foods, drinks, spices, goods, and fresh foods can be bought, and several stores exist in Hawai'i. Finally, foods from other Latin American countries such as El Salvador are often served in venues such as church gatherings and Latino festivals, and Cuban food in particular is gaining popularity in Honolulu. In general, Hispanic/Latino foods and restaurants attract Latino and non-Latino patrons. Most often, though, these foods are eaten in the kitchens of Latino families as a way of celebrating their culture and nourishing their bodies, minds, and souls.

TRADITIONS AND CUSTOMS

Several Hispanic traditions and customs are celebrated in Hawai'i and are a way of strengthening ethnocultural identity. These traditions tend to be celebrated on a pan–Hispanic/Latino basis, which allows various ethnic groups to participate together.

Five traditions have their basis in religious customs. The Feast Day of Our Lady of Guadalupe is one of the most important days of the year for Hispanic Catholics, who celebrate a famous Marian apparition. In fact, the image of Our Lady of Guadalupe is likely the most popular cultural and religious image of Mexico. During this feast day in Hawai'i, in addition to religious ceremonies, certain Mexican communities invite mariachi bands from the continental United States to perform for them. Las Posadas is a nine-day celebration that recreates the trials that Mary and Joseph may have encountered before arriving in Bethlehem, where Jesus was born. It culminates in a celebration for the entire family, with live music, dancing, food, and games. There is typically a Las Posadas celebration on O'ahu. El Dia de Los Tres Reyes (Feast of the Three Kings, or Epiphany) is celebrated by Hispanics of various ethnic groups in Hawai'i. Other traditions such as El Dia de los Muertos (The Day of the Dead) are celebrated less frequently but can still be found in some Latino families in Hawai'i. More commonly, All Souls Day, which is a day of honoring the deceased in the Catholic tradition, is celebrated by Latinos and non-Latinos. Finally, Quince Años, a celebration honoring a girl's fifteenth birthday that signifies a girl's transition to a young woman, is a tradition among some Latinos (mostly Mexicans). It includes a religious ceremony and a party with family, friends, food, and dancing.

Festivals and sports are also popular among Latinos in Hawai'i. Somos Amigos (We Are Friends) is a yearly festival celebrating Hispanic and Portuguese culture that has been held on Maui since 2000. In addition, the Hawai'i Hispanic Heritage Festival (celebrating National Hispanic Heritage Month), various salsa dance festivals, and Cinco de Mayo are celebrations attended by Latinos and non-Latinos. In Mexico, Cinco de Mayo is a regional festival commemorating the Battle of Puebla that is *only* celebrated in the Mexican state of Puebla. However, in Hawai'i, like much of the United States, many restaurants and bars have Cinco de Mayo events, but these generally have more to do with restaurant marketing than with the Battle of Puebla. Finally, various sports traditions must be highlighted. Baseball, softball, and boxing are popular among Puerto Ricans, while soccer is popular among Mexicans and other Latinos. These traditions promote a sense of cohesion and strengthen community, family, and social relationships.

SPIRITUALITY AND RELIGION

Espiritualidad (spirituality) and religion are integral to understanding Hispanic identity. Religion and spirituality help to provide meaning and direction to daily life, and a belief in God or a higher being is important for Latinos. The use of the phrase *Si Dios quiere* (If it is God's will) implies a belief that individuals cannot control the will of God.[18]

Religion is incorporated into the lives of Hispanics by praying and attending religious services, several of which are conducted in Spanish. Catholicism has traditionally been the primary religion for Hispanics. However, there are also growing Protestant, Christian, and Seventh-Day Adventist communities in Hawai'i, and Hispanics may be of any religious denomination. *Santeria*—a belief system among some Latinos of Caribbean decent that blends Catholic and African traditions—tends to be less prevalent among Hawai'i's Latinos.[19]

Spirituality and religion may also be integrated in the homes of Latinos and seen specifically in the display of religious items and altars. These altars contain religious objects such as statues, pictures of saints, candles, crucifixes, holy water, or pictures of the deceased.[20] During El Dia de los Muertos celebrations, mummies or skeletons may be displayed. Overall, it is the belief in a higher power that appears to be retained through the acculturation process.

SOCIOECONOMIC AND POLITICAL PATTERNS

Hispanics can be found across the socioeconomic strata. According to the U.S. Census, the median family income in 2007 inflation-adjusted dollars was almost $54,000, which was slightly below the total population median family income of almost $64,000.[21] Moreover, the poverty rate was nearly 8 percent for all Hispanic families and people for whom poverty status is determined, which is slightly higher than the population in general of about 5.5 percent. Furthermore, over 41 percent of Hispanics (vs. nearly 60 percent of the population in general) live in owner-occupied housing units, with an average of 3.23 people (vs. 2.99 people) living in the house. For Latinos in Hawai'i, increases in social status appear to be through business ownership or ventures and/or by obtaining a higher educational degree.

Political Patterns. Overall, few Hispanics/Latinos have held political positions. Recently, however, the first person of part-Hispanic descent was confirmed as a circuit court judge in Hawai'i. As a group, the political viewpoints of Hispanics/Latinos might be described as moderate—neither conservative nor liberal. This moderate or centrist viewpoint allows Latinos to avoid the extreme left or right and instead hold a middle-of-the-road political position. The political patterns of Latinos in Hawai'i also appear to differ according to the issue being addressed, as there are certain topics (e.g., immigration) that may be more important for Latinos. In addition, while less acculturated Latinos may also be less involved in politics and slightly more conservative, as they receive information about different political viewpoints, their political positions may change.

HEALTH, MENTAL HEALTH, AND ALTERNATIVE/FOLK HEALTH
PRACTICES

Hispanics tend to view health from a holistic point of view in which the body, mind, and spirit are connected, as opposed to the Western perspective, in which the mind and body are separate. Spirituality and religion may also influence health beliefs. This can be seen when a person does not obtain a certain health screening due to a belief that all events (including illnesses) are predetermined by God or another powerful force. For some more traditional Latinos, health beliefs and practices are sometimes guided by supernatural beliefs in health or behavior or a belief that the natural environment, individual qualities, spirits, or witches cause illness or disease.[22] Belief in supernatural forces causing illness can be seen in what is called *mal de ojo* (the evil eye), which is caused by a person who is jealous staring at someone and that person becoming ill.

In Hawai'i, the majority of Hispanics use Western medicine for their health. However, traditional medicine may also be used, particularly among those who are less acculturated. According to Santiago-Rivera and colleagues, Latinos may seek help from folk healers such as *curanderos* (among Mexicans), *espiritistas* (among Puerto Ricans), *santeros* (among Cubans), or herbalists, who may assist with various health, mental health, spiritual, and personal issues.[23] Latinos may also seek help from Native Hawaiian or Asian healers versus *curanderos* because the former are more accessible in Hawai'i. However, Native Hawaiian or Asian healers may not be familiar with traditional folk illnesses such as *ataque de nervios* (similar to a panic attack), *empacho* (upset stomach), and *susto* (fright) that may exist among Latinos. Finally, *botánicas* are shops that sell Hispanic/Latino folk medicine, herbs, oils, candles, statues, medicinal plants, and other health and religious items used in traditional or alternative healing practices. However, *botánicas* are not prevalent in Hawai'i. Interestingly, other ethnic shops that cater to Hawaiian or Asian healing practices are more widely available, and some Latinos may go to these shops instead of the few places that sell Latino-focused folk medicine.

In general, the health needs of Hispanics/Latinos in Hawai'i are greatly underserved, since there are few providers that can assist with their physical and mental health needs due to language and/or cultural barriers. Recently, there has been a slight increase in the number of Spanish-speaking health care providers in the regional military hospital, and they are now able to serve the military and their dependents. To address some of the health needs of Hispanics in Hawai'i, the Hawai'i Hispanic/Latino Health Community Advisory Board was developed in 2003. It provides feedback to enhance the cultural appropriateness of health research programs focusing on Latinos in Hawai'i in the areas of obesity, physical activity, and tobacco use, since these health issues are associated with the four major causes of diseases and deaths in Latinos.[24] It is hoped that results from these research studies will provide information about how to develop programs that aid in the goal of having healthy Hispanic/Latino communities, families, and individuals in Hawai'i.

A New Ethnocultural Identity

As the result of sociocultural interactions that have transpired between Latinos and other ethnic groups since their first arrival in Hawai'i, changes have occurred in the ethnic identity of Hispanics/Latinos from their native country to their current ethnocultural identity. The new identity of Hispanics/Latinos has been influenced by a number of factors such as sociocultural interactions with the Native Hawaiian host culture; intragroup relationships and intragroup structures; and intergroup relationships, which will be described below. As a result of these relationships and interactions, a new multicultural and multiethnic cultural identity has emerged.

INFLUENCE OF THE NATIVE HAWAIIAN HOST CULTURE

One way that the Hawaiian host culture has influenced and affected the cultural identity of Latinos has been through the common values shared by Native Hawaiians and Latinos in areas such as the importance of the family, interpersonal relationships, respect, religion/spirituality, community, food, and music. In terms of a strong family value, the Hawaiian value of the *'ohana* emphasizes taking care of family members and multiple generations living in the same house, which are similar values for Latinos. The Hawaiian concept of "calabash families" is also similar to the concept of compadres, or coparenting of children. In some Hawai'i Latino families, calabash families and compadres simultaneously exist. In Hawaiian culture, interpersonal relationships are strongly valued and interpersonal space and distance while communicating to others is similar in both cultures. In fact, the warm and welcoming Spanish phrase, *"Mi casa es su casa"* ("My house is your house"), is similar to the Hawaiian phrase, *"E komo mai"* ("Welcome," or literally, "Enter [toward the speaker]"), and illustrates the parallel warmth and hospitality that exists in both cultures. Finally, respect for elders *(kūpuna)* and deference to authority, spirituality, and a strong emphasis on the community, food, and music are similar values in both cultures.

An additional way of exploring the influence of Hawaiian culture on Latino identity is to examine the aspects of the word "aloha" and to illustrate the way that it parallels Latino values. "Aloha" means "to give or share the breath of life," and each letter reflects a Hawaiian value.[25] The Hawaiian value of *akahi* (kindness) is similar to the Latino value of *personalismo;* the value of *lōkahi* (unity) is similar to Latino values of community and collectivism; the value of *'olu'olu* (agreeable) is similar to *simpatia;* the value of *ha'aha'a* (humility) is similar to *respeto* (respect); and *ahonui* (patience) relates to the Latino value of perseverance and working hard.

Finally, the influence of the Hawaiian culture can be seen in Latino cultural traditions. For example, while Quince Años may still be celebrated in Hawai'i, the Quinceañera may now wear a Hawaiian dress, muumuu, and a lei, and also dance hula. Moreover, although Latinos may wear guayaberas, there is also a recent development of the "Hawaiian guayabera" or the "shakabere," which is a guayabera with a Hawaiian print. Together, the common cultural values and integration of Hawaiian customs have allowed Hispanics to strengthen their values and customs, since they are supported by the Hawaiian culture.

INTRAGROUP RELATIONSHIPS AND THE EVOLVING INTRAGROUP SOCIAL STRUCTURE

Hispanic/Latino identity has also been influenced by intragroup relationships and an evolving intragroup social structure. Intragroup relationships are strengthened by the fact that events and services in Hawai'i tend to be conducted on what has been called a pan-Hispanic basis, with people uniting based on their common Hispanic/Latino identity versus their individual ethnicity. There are at least three reasons for this. First, unlike other larger communities across the continental United States, there are no Hispanic ethnic enclaves or neighborhoods (barrios) in Hawai'i that have the potential to segregate individual Latino groups. Second, Hispanics are often mistakenly considered to be a small ethnic community in Hawai'i, which makes it important to join together as a group. Third, Hispanics are often physically unidentifiable, due to their similarities with other ethnic groups in Hawai'i such as Portuguese or mixed-race Hawaiian and Asian ethnicities. Together, this has resulted in Latinos being drawn together by their common identity as Hispanics/Latinos. In addition, organizations and events generally cater to all Hispanics, which has helped to foster an identity that is pan-Hispanic. This pan-Hispanic identity is similar to the Aloha Spirit in terms of living and sharing with each other.

Evidence of the pan–Hispanic/Latino ethnic identity can be found in the various prominent Hispanic organizations that have emerged since the late 1990s. These organizations have strengthened Hispanic culture through social and business events by focusing on all Latino ethnic groups. They typically provide services, education, and advocacy for Latinos. By bringing people together on a pan-Hispanic basis, a sense of *comunidad* (community), a key value for Hispanics, is strengthened. As early as 1931, there have been organizations that serve specific Latino ethnic groups, such as Puerto Ricans. However, events are often co-celebrated with other Latinos (e.g., El Dia de los Tres Reyes).

At the same time, the intragroup social structure of Latinos has also been affected by within-group differences in citizenship, English language proficiency, occupational and educational attainment, income, acculturation level, and ethnicity. For example, Puerto Ricans are U.S. citizens by birthright, and this sets them apart from other Latino groups whose members are not automatically U.S. citizens if they were born outside of the country. Moreover, for those who do not speak English, the ability to access English programs may exacerbate within-group differences. The social structure of Latinos has also been affected by the migration of new Hispanics to Hawai'i over the past ten years. The influx of new Latinos, often with a higher education degree, has created a broader social class structure of middle- and professional-class Latinos in various segments of the workforce. The result of this appears to be a Latino cultural renaissance, which has served as an impetus for Latinos to join together in various endeavors to support each other.

Finally, intragroup conflict may exist due to negative stereotypes about Hispanics that have been recently highlighted in the media. These stereotypes tend to focus on Hispanics being undocumented, dealing drugs, or only working in the agricultural industry. These stereotypes are overgeneralizations that undermine the significant contributions that Hispanics have made in Hawai'i. Conflict may result because individuals do not want to be associated with the small segment of the Hispanic community from whom these stereotypes are derived.

INTERGROUP RELATIONSHIPS: THE NEW MULTICULTURAL/ MULTIETHNIC IDENTITY

The ethnocultural identity of Hispanics/Latinos is also affected by relationships that they have with other ethnic groups. Overall, there is significant interest from non-Hispanics to engage in what would be considered traditional Hispanic activities, as evidenced by multiethnic salsa classes and competitions, large groups of multiethnic people attending Latino business and social events, and large groups of non-Hispanics who eat Latino food.

The positive relationships that Latinos have with other ethnic groups were evident even in the early plantation era, when Puerto Ricans welcomed other ethnic groups to their Saturday night dances. Today, the relationships that Hispanics/Latinos have with Portuguese and Brazilians in Hawai'i are particularly noteworthy. Specifically, Hispanic and Portuguese communities on Maui celebrate both of their cultures during an annual festival on Maui. In addition, the Brazilian martial arts and dance called *copeira* is frequently performed at Hispanic festivals in Hawai'i. One reason for the positive relationship between these communities may be their common cultural values, despite not sharing the Spanish language.

The ethnocultural identity of Hispanics has also been influenced by intermarriages between Hispanics and other ethnic groups. In the early 1900s plantation era, intermarriages between Latinos and non-Latinos may have been related to their skin color. For example, in the early plantation days, Puerto Ricans with light skin tended to marry those who were also light skinned, such as Portuguese or Spanish, and those with darker skin tended to marry others with dark skin, such as Hawaiians and Filipinos.[26] However, marrying based on skin color may be less likely in contemporary Hawai'i. Instead, Latinos are more likely to marry based on common value systems and worldviews, with their legacy of multiple heritages possibly leading them to be more open to having relationships with non-Latinos. Similar to Latinos across the United States, Hawai'i's Latinos have high rates of interracial marriages and relationships. Intermarriages may also differ according to generational status and Hispanic ethnicity, with some groups (e.g., Puerto Ricans or second-generation Latinos) being more likely to marry or have relationships with those outside of their ethnic group than others (e.g., first-generation Latinos). Evidence of a history of interracial or interethnic relationships can be seen in the high proportion of Hispanics who report that they are multiracial compared to the general Hawai'i population.[27] For example, a greater proportion of Latinos report having two races (nearly 21 percent vs. 15 percent), three races (17 percent vs. 7 percent), and four or more races (a little over 3 percent vs. less than 1 percent) compared to the population in general. Finally, across the United States, terms such as *mestizo* (those of Spanish and American Indian or indigenous descent) and *mulatto* or *criollo* (those of European, American Indian, and African heritage) are used to describe Latinos with multiple heritages, but these terms are less common in Hawai'i. Perhaps this is because Hawai'i has such a high proportion of people who have multiple heritages, and people are typically referred to as "hapa" if they have mixed ethnic or racial backgrounds.

In many ways, it appears that a Hispanic/Latino cultural renaissance is emerging in Hawai'i, resulting in a new Hispanic/Latino ethnic pride *(orgullo)* and identity. This cultural renaissance appears to be occurring from both within and outside of the Hispanic community in Hawai'i. Support from within the Hispanic community has been highlighted due to the recent reemergence of a Hispanic newspaper and numerous Latino businesses. This revitalization has strengthened intragroup and intergroup relationships and the ethnic pride of Hispanics in Hawai'i. For some single or mixed-race Latinos who did not previously identify as Latino, the reemergence of these outlets may have allowed them to increase their cultural awareness and embrace their Latino identity, which may not have been previously supported to the same degree due to a lack of a critical mass of Latinos actively advocating on their behalf vis-à-vis the mainstream culture in Hawai'i. Business ownership and activities, music, and dance appear to be a key manner in which Latinos are perpetuating their culture and sharing their culture and values with non-Latinos. The Hispanic cultural renaissance from outside of Hawai'i has also strengthened their ethnocultural identity. Specifically, there has been an increase in media attention about Hawai'i's Hispanics through local newspapers and national television shows (e.g., *¡Despierta America!, Hispanics Today,* and *¡Caliente!*). These all serve to foster ethnic pride and knowledge about the Hispanic community.

Not all intergroup relationships have been positive, however. Recently there have been several social and political situations that have affected intergroup relationships. In one of these events, undocumented

Mexicans were arrested on Maui and O'ahu. In another event, a councilman used a racial slur to describe Hispanics in Hawai'i. This event led to political activism and education about the significant influence of Hispanics in Hawai'i. It also illustrated the diverse support of Latinos in Hawai'i, since people from various ethnicities and races attended a rally protesting the use of the offensive word. These events also appear to have ignited some negative feelings and discrimination directed toward Latinos. However, this sentiment does not appear to be widespread, as it sometimes is in cities across the United States. Finally, when monoracial or multiracial Latinos move away from Hawai'i, they may experience prejudice or discrimination or be subjected to "authenticity testing" or questioning regarding their ethnic background. This may occur because of their multiracial background, because they may not speak Spanish, or because the influence of Hawaiian culture on Latino identity or behavior differs from that of the mainstream U.S. society.

As intergroup relationships between Hispanics and other ethnic groups in Hawai'i have grown, a new multicultural or multiethnic Latino identity has emerged. Even for monoracial or monoethnic Latinos, the process by which they acculturate to the local culture of Hawai'i creates an opportunity for a new Hawai'i Latino identity to develop. A bicultural individual is someone who has the capacity to operate in two cultures. For Latinos, this process involves learning about and integrating the local culture of Hawai'i along with American cultural values. This may include acquiring aspects of the Hawai'i lifestyle and integrating local practices (e.g., speaking Pidgin, having the Aloha Spirit), customs (e.g., burning fireworks on Independence Day), and food (e.g., plate lunches and Spam musubi). The new Hawai'i multicultural Latino identity is characterized by having ethnic pride and celebrating their culture, simultaneously adopting the values and traditions of other ethnic groups, and sharing the common local culture.

Biopsychosocial Factors

Despite the cultural shifts that have occurred through the generations for Hispanics/Latinos in Hawai'i, there are a number of characteristics, traits, and/or behaviors that have been retained in what are presumed to be protective behaviors. There are also sociocultural characteristics, traits, and/or behaviors that appear to be malleable or modifiable. In this section, biopsychosocial factors that have affected Latino ethnocultural identity are reviewed.[28]

In terms of the characteristics, traits, and/or behaviors that have been retained, there are a number of what are presumed to be protective behaviors that have changed very little over time. In describing these characteristics, stereotypes about Latinos must be avoided, as there is a vast amount of diversity within Hawai'i's Latinos due to their countries of origin, acculturation, generational status, ethnic identity, urban/rural residency, and island of residency. In terms of physical characteristics, there are no features that can be considered uniquely Hispanic/Latino, as they are diverse in their physical stature and color of their skin, hair, and eyes. One reason for their physical diversity may be that many Latinos have a multiracial background due to the historical influences in their countries of origin. Although some Latinos may not acknowledge their multiple heritages, this is often displayed in their diverse physical characteristics.

Additional characteristics and behaviors that have been retained among Latinos include cultural values related to the family, collectivism, community, spirituality, and respect. The importance of Latino music, dance, and food is also retained. A sense of pride in one's ethnic group is also a growing trend among some Latinos, as evidenced by the increasing number of organizations that promote Latino culture in Hawai'i. Finally, health beliefs and practices are sometimes thought to be biological in nature. On a national basis, the leading causes of death among Latinos are heart disease, cancer, cerebrovascular disease, and diabetes. Several Hawai'i community leaders have noted that the most pressing health issues for Latinos include obesity, diabetes, heart disease, cancer, dementia, depression, domestic violence, and HIV/AIDS.

Several sociocultural characteristics, traits, and/or behaviors seem to be malleable or modifiable over time for Latinos. Over time, individuals who are more acculturated may adhere less to certain traditional Hispanic values and traditions. Through the process of acculturation, sometimes cultural values or traditions are lost, weakened, or changed due to competing cultural norms from the host society. For example, with increasing generations and acculturation levels, Latino gender roles have become more flexible in contemporary Hawai'i. An additional characteristic that appears to change over time is the ability to speak Spanish. Specifically, generational status and acculturation level may affect the ability to speak Spanish, with many second- or third-generation Latinos, as well as those with greater acculturation, losing the ability to speak Spanish. This phenomenon also occurs throughout the United States. For some in Hawai'i, speaking Spanish has been replaced by the ability to speak Pidgin English. For example, the word *pasteles* has become "pateles" and *abuela* is now "aguelita." There is also a tendency for later generations to speak Spanglish, which is a mixture of Spanish and English. One of the reasons for the loss of the Spanish language through the generations or through the process of acculturation is because parents either do not teach Spanish to their children or because children may speak Spanish less due to pressures from others to speak English. Speaking English is also valued and influences the rate at which Hispanics acculturate, since certain opportunities (e.g., educational) may arise due to the ability to speak English.

Additional characteristics that appear to change over time relate to specific religious affiliations, political patterns, and Hispanic traditions. Although a strong emphasis on spirituality remains for Latinos, there seems to be a tendency for the specific religious affiliations to change slightly from being primarily Catholic to having greater religious diversity. An increase in Protestantism in particular has been a notable change over time in Hawai'i, as well as across the United States and in various Hispanic countries. Political patterns also appear to change through the process of acculturation, with Hispanics becoming slightly more moderate in their political opinions. Finally, certain customs, such as Quince Años, Dia de los Muertos, and Feast of the Three Kings may also be celebrated less frequently as Latinos become more acculturated, as they lose knowledge about Hispanic traditions and customs, and/or as they begin to adopt new traditions. In summary, exposure to the Hawaiian culture as well as other cultures has strengthened certain Latino values since they are reinforced by the Hawaiian culture. These values appear to be important regardless of acculturation level or Latino ethnicity. However, Spanish language skills, religion, political patterns, and some Latino traditions have changed over time.

Summary and Conclusions

Hispanics/Latinos are the largest and fastest growing ethnic minority group in the United States, and they represent nearly 10 percent of the population in Hawai'i. Hispanics of various ethnic groups have played a significant role in shaping Hawai'i's cultural landscape: (1) from the early contributions of Spaniard Don Francisco de Paula Marin, in terms of his influence on the horticultural industry, and as an advisor to King Kamehameha I; (2) from the contributions of the early Mexicans in the ranching industry and shaping slack key guitar music;

(3) from the later influence of the Puerto Ricans in the agricultural industries; (4) to the current Hispanics/Latinos in Hawai'i. There is a dearth of information about the physical, mental, and cultural needs of Latinos in Hawai'i.

There are several important and unmet needs in Hawai'i's Hispanic community. First, there is an urgent need for health, education, social service, and legal programs for Hispanics. Second, there is a need for Spanish language radio and television stations, as there are no full-time Hispanic programs available for the mainstream public. Media is critical in disseminating information and services available in the community, while creating a source of cultural cohesion and decreasing the isolation experienced by Latinos living so far from their native countries. Third, there is a critical unmet need for additional spiritual and religious services and Hispanic/Latino grocery stores and *botánicas*. Such services are crucial in preserving Latino cultural values and traditions. Fourth, there is a need to have resources available for Hispanics so they do not lose their ability to speak Spanish and so that they can also learn English. The key seems to be retaining the Spanish language through the acculturation process. Fifth, there is a need to increase the political involvement of Latinos in the Hawai'i judicial, legislative, and executive branches so that various Hispanic/Latino needs in Hawai'i are met.

Finally, fostering Latino ethnic pride and identity is also critical, since this may assist in developing a positive self-image and preserving Latino culture. The fact that Latinos look physically similar to other ethnic groups, as well as the fact that they share similar surnames with Portuguese and Filipinos, may have also led to a nonrecognition of Latinos in Hawai'i. As a result, Latinos have had to work hard to establish themselves as a distinct group as well as to preserve their cultural values and traditions. This is especially true for Puerto Ricans, who have had to preserve their culture for over 110 years, with few increases in their population. With an increase in Latino restaurants, dance, music, media, and travel agencies, this will help to bring ethnic pride and awareness to Latinos and to the mainstream public. In addition, as accomplishments of Latinos are highlighted, they will also be recognized as a community with a key constituency.

As descendents of the early Hispanics/Latinos in Hawai'i continue to populate the Islands, as Latinos intermarry, and as newer groups of Latinos move to Hawai'i, there is the potential for the identity of Latinos to be strengthened, and the identity of Hawai'i may in turn be influenced by Latinos. It is clear that the cultural values of family, community, spirituality, music, dance, and food will continue to be a part of the legacy of Latinos in Hawai'i. Over time, there may also be more Latino ethnic-specific organizations catering to the needs of Latino groups such as Mexicans. At the same time, it is likely that pan-Hispanic organizations that serve an increasing multicultural Latino community will continue to exist. In the same way that Latinos are changing the cultural landscape across the United States, we can expect that Latinos will continue to contribute to Hawai'i. This will likely result in the revitalization of Hispanic/Latino culture and what may be called the Hispanization or Latinization of Hawai'i.

In conclusion, the Hispanic/Latino ethnocultural identity appears to be in a transitional state, with a Latino cultural renaissance emerging. So, what is the twenty-first-century Hispanic/Latino in Hawai'i? Today's Hispanics/Latinos are individuals who have become a part of a society that allows them to retain and celebrate their culture while creating a new culture together—the local culture of what is uniquely Hawai'i. By having pride in their ethnic group and celebrating their culture, simultaneously adopting the values and traditions of other ethnic groups, and sharing the common local culture of Hawai'i, a new Hawai'i multicultural Latino identity has been created. Hawai'i's Hispanic/Latino community will continue to contribute to and learn from the great multicultural society that is Hawai'i—in the same way that their ancestors did in early Hawai'i.

Further Reading

Bergin, B. *Loyal to the Land: The Legendary Parker Ranch, 750–1950.* Honolulu: University of Hawai'i Press, 2003.

Gast, R. H., and A. C. Conrad, eds. *Don Francisco De Paula Marin: The Letters and Journals of Francisco de Paula Marin,* from the Hawaiian Historical Society. Honolulu: University of Hawai'i Press, 2002.

Marin, G. "Issues in the measurement of acculturation among Hispanics." In *Psychological Testing of Hispanics,* ed. K. F. Geisinger. Washington, D.C.: American Psychological Association, 1992: 235–251.

Phinney, J. S. "Ethnic identity and acculturation: Advances in theory, measurement, and applied research." In *Acculturation: Advances in Theory, Measurement, and Applied Research,* ed. K. M. Chun, P. B. Organista, and G. Marin. Washington, D.C.: American Psychological Association, 2003: 63–82.

Sánchez-Johnsen, L. "Health disparities research with Hispanics/Latinos." *Hawai'i Medical Journal* 65(3) (2006): 89–90.

Santiago-Rivera, A. L., P. Arredondo, and M. Gallardo-Cooper. *Counseling Latinos and La Familia: A Guide for Practitioners.* Thousand Oaks, CA: Sage Publications, 2002.

Notes

1. U.S. Census Bureau, "U.S. Hispanic population surpasses 45 million, now 15 percent of total," accessed May 22, 2009: http://www.census .gov/Press-Release/www/releases/archives/population/011910.html , p. 1.

2. State of Hawai'i Department of Business, Economic Development and Tourism, "Table 1: Annual Estimates of the Population by Sex, Race, and Hispanic or Latino Origin for State of Hawaii: April 1, 2000 to July 1, 2008," accessed May 22, 2009: http://hawaii.gov/dbedt/info/census/popestimate/2008_county_char_hi_file/08_hi_countchar_tab1.pdf.

3. U.S. Census Bureau, "2005–2007 American Community Survey 3-year estimates," generated by Lisa Sanchez-Johnsen using American Fact Finder, accessed February 22, 2009: http://factfinder.census.gov.

4. R. H. Gast and A. C. Conrad, eds., *Don Francisco de Paula Marin: The Letters and Journals of Francisco de Paula Marin,* from the Hawaiian Historical Society, Honolulu: University of Hawai'i Press, 2002.

5. Ibid.

6. B. Bergin, *Loyal to the Land: The Legendary Parker Ranch, 1750–1950,* Honolulu: University of Hawai'i Press, 2003: 97.

7. B. C. Souza, "The Puerto Rican house: La casita," in *The Puerto Rican House: La Casita,* ed. Hawaii Plantation Village, Waipahu, HI: The Friends of Waipahu Cultural Garden Park, 2001: 11.

8. A. L. Santiago-Rivera, P. Arredondo, and M. Gallardo-Cooper, *Counseling Latinos and la Familia: A Guide for Practitioners,* Thousand Oaks, CA: Sage Publications, 2002.

9. Ibid.

10. U.S. Census Bureau, "2007 American Community Survey 1-year estimates," generated by Lisa Sánchez-Johnsen using American Fact Finder, accessed September 23, 2008: http://factfinder.census.gov.

11. Santiago-Rivera et al. 2002: 49–51.

12. Ibid.: 113, 159.

13. U.S. Census Bureau 2007.

14. University of Hawai'i Institutional Research Office, "Fall enrollment report," accessed May 6, 2009: http://www.hawaii.edu/iro/maps .php?category=Enrollment.

15. U.S. Census Bureau 2007.

16. Ibid.

17. Souza 2001: 15.

18. Santiago-Rivera et al. 2002: 44–46.

19. Ibid.: 45.

20. Ibid.: 46.

21. U.S. Census Bureau 2007.

22. Santiago-Rivera et al. 2002.

23. Ibid.

24. L. Sánchez-Johnsen, "Health disparities research with Hispanics/ Latinos," *Hawai'i Medical Journal* 65(3) (2006): 89–90.

25. State of Hawai'i, "The Aloha Spirit Law," *Hawai'i Revised Statutes,* 1986, Chap. 5, Sec. 7.5.

26. Souza 2001: 14.

27. U.S. Census Bureau 2007.

28. G. Marin, "Issues in the measurement of acculturation among Hispanics," in *Psychological Testing of Hispanics,* ed. K. F. Geisinger, Washington, D.C.: American Psychological Association, 1992: 235–251; J. S. Phinney, "Ethnic identity and acculturation: Advances in theory, measurement, and applied research," in *Acculturation: Advances In Theory, Measurement, and Applied Research,* ed. K. M. Chun, P. B. Organista, and G. Marin, Washington, D.C.: American Psychological Association, 2003: 63–82.

CHAPTER 8

The Koreans

Jane Chung-Do, John Huh, and Mark Kang

In order to best understand Koreans and Korean culture in Hawai'i, one has to first understand the historical context of the nation. Korea is among the oldest civilizations in the world, tracing their heritage to 2333 B.C. It is a small country in size and population compared to its surrounding neighbors, Japan, China, and Russia. Consequently, Korea has been repeatedly invaded and under the control of Mongols, Chinese, and Japanese.[1] This repeated occupation has had a tremendous influence on the culture and character of Koreans. They pride themselves on their resiliency, persistence, and fighting spirit. According to the 2000 U.S. Census, over 41,000 Koreans reside in the State of Hawai'i. Despite being a relatively small ethnic community when compared to other Asian groups such as the Japanese, Chinese, and Filipinos, Koreans have played an important role in the immigration history of Hawai'i and the evolution of local culture.

History

THE FIRST WAVE OF KOREANS

Although a few came to Hawai'i before the twentieth century, 1903 marks the first organized arrival of Koreans to Hawai'i. The plantations were in need of field laborers to offset the dominance of Japanese laborers and viewed Koreans as a new, inexpensive labor group. In late 1902, 54 males, 21 females, and 22 children departed Korea for Hawai'i. They arrived in Honolulu on January 13, 1903, and were assigned to work on the Waialua sugar plantations on O'ahu. Thereafter, Koreans continued to immigrate to Hawaiʻi in small numbers. By 1905, some 7,900 Korean immigrants were living and working in Hawaiʻi. About 90 percent of these immigrants were males, 6 percent children, and 4 percent women.[2]

These early Koreans immigrated to Hawaiʻi looking for new opportunities to enhance their quality of life. Although many were initially hesitant about leaving their homeland, the involvement of American missionaries helped reinforce early recruitment efforts. Reverend George Jones, a Methodist missionary who was residing in Korea at the time, was instrumental in recruiting members of his congregation to immigrate to Hawaiʻi, with nearly half of the first Korean immigrants being from his church.[3] The Korean church community in Hawaiʻi was prepared for their arrival, and to this day it continues to play a major role in providing social networking opportunities, emotional support, and cultural connections for Korean immigrants in Hawaiʻi. For early Korean immigrants, the church was much more than a place to practice their religious beliefs. It was a place where they could speak their own language, share their own food, and be themselves.[4] The growing Japanese control of Korea also contributed to the decision for many to leave the political instability brewing in their country. Despite leaving their homeland, many shared strong patriotic sentiments for Korea and planned to return in the future. When Japan forcibly annexed Korea in 1910, many Koreans living in Hawaiʻi mourned, as they felt they had lost their homeland and their nation.[5]

Stories of Japanese oppression and struggles of Koreans in the homeland fueled a simmering nationalistic movement along with anti-Japanese sentiments among Koreans living in Hawaiʻi. Many worked toward raising money for the Korean independence movements in Hawaiʻi and the continental United States. Meanwhile, the Japanese government severely restricted Korean immigration to Hawaiʻi due to concerns that they would adversely affect the existing Japanese immigrant population.[6] In addition, the Immigration Exclusion Act of 1924 further restricted Koreans and other Asians from immigrating to the United States, thus keeping the population of Koreans in Hawaiʻi relatively small for many years.[7]

Because of the lack of Korean women in Hawaiʻi, many bachelors found solace in drinking, gambling, prostitutes, and fights over women.[8] To address this, the Hawaiʻi government and the sugar plantations adopted a picture bride system. When the picture brides arrived in Hawaiʻi, however, many found that the men they had agreed to marry were much older than they appeared in the pictures they sent.

Although some of these marriages resulted in an unhappy family life, many helped maintain Korean family values and traditions. The majority of the brides also significantly contributed to their families' finances by working soon after their arrival. Their efforts also extended beyond their families by tirelessly raising funds to support Korea's sovereignty efforts and helped the assimilation of Koreans in Hawai'i. Moreover, these women established numerous educational, religious, and political organizations in Hawai'i.[9] This was a remarkable achievement considering that there was only one women's association established in Korea during this time, compared to the many that were flourishing in Hawai'i. For example, they established the Korean YWCA, where they learned English and shared Korean culture through dance and music with the rest of the Hawai'i community. At the same time, the number of Koreans working on plantations dwindled, as many ventured into Honolulu for entrepreneurial pursuits. Koreans came to be regarded as one of the most mobile groups, perhaps partly influenced by the loss of their homeland.[10]

THE SECOND WAVE OF KOREANS, POST-1960S

When the limitations of the Immigration Act of 1924 were lifted in the 1960s, the United States reopened its doors to the next and largest wave of Korean immigrants. Compared to the first wave of immigrants, many of those in the second wave were more educated and included families. In fact, about 32 percent of Koreans immigrating to the United States between 1970 and 1980 were college educated, compared to the average of 6.8 percent of Korean adults living in Korea and 16.2 percent of Americans.[11] Despite their education or professional training, the lack of English proficiency among Korean adults limited their job opportunities. Many could find jobs only in the service industry or became entrepreneurs of small businesses that primarily serviced Korean clientele. This negatively affected the socioeconomic mobility of many Korean immigrants, especially for males who had attained high educational or professional status in their home country but were forced to take jobs that were of lower status and less prestige in their new homes.[12]

Ethnocultural Identity

THE EFFECT OF WAR ON KOREAN IDENTITY

Korea suffered through multiple wars in the past century. Although there were extended periods of stability prior to 1890, the Sino-Japanese

War in 1894 reignited the fighting to gain control over Korea. Japan's victory led to its influence and military presence in Korea. Ten years later, when Russia sought greater port access during the Russo-Japanese War, Japan occupied Korea and annexed the country in 1910. During this occupation, Japan attempted to ban Hangul, the Korean language, from schools and publications and forced Koreans to abandon their Korean names.[13] Korean history texts were destroyed or altered, and much of Korea remained in poverty and fear under Japanese rule. During World War II, almost 3 million Koreans were forced into labor, with thousands of Korean women forced to become "comfort women" for Japanese soldiers. Others worked in factories in Hiroshima and Nagasaki and suffered through the atomic bombings. When the comfort women and bombing victims eventually returned home to Korea, they found themselves shunned or feared by other Koreans. At the end of World War II, Korea was liberated from Japan, but much of the country was left impoverished, its resources exploited, and the country's infrastructure undeveloped.[14]

Soon after, Korea was politically divided into the North and South by the Soviet Union and the United States respectively. This political division led to an invasion by the North Korean Communist forces into South Korea in 1950, triggering the start of the Korean War.[15] The Korean War has been referred to as a proxy war for the Cold War between the United States and the Soviet Union, and although it ended in 1953, an official peace treaty was never signed and tensions between the two Koreas exist to this day. The Korean War further ravaged the country and its people. It is estimated that 2 million Korean civilians were killed or wounded during the war.

This pattern of repeated trauma by occupation and wars on Korean soil continues to remain a strong part of the Korean identity. Even since the armistice of the Korean War, there continue to be flashes of conflict between the North and the South, which reinforces a sense of instability. Nevertheless, many come to the United States with a great sense of Korean national pride and recognize the fragility of their cultural identity.[16] Given the repeated invasion and occupation of Korea, there is an ingrained sense of mistrust of outsiders and non-Koreans among some older Koreans, especially those of Japanese descent.[17] Having lived through and survived these wars, many first-generation Korean immigrants may seek out the comfort and security of other Koreans. This may explain the significant numbers of Koreans involved in the Korean Christian community, where they are able to maintain the Korean culture and their Korean relationships. However, the close-knit nature of Korean organizations may create a sense of exclusiveness to the larger society.[18]

As for the younger generations of Korean-Americans in Hawai'i, the Korean War connected second- and third-generation Korean-American soldiers with their ancestral homeland as they served in intelligence units by providing translation services for the U.S. military.[19] U.S. servicemen, including many non-Koreans, were stationed in Korea and married Korean women. The War Brides Act of 1946 allowed these brides to immigrate with their new husbands to the United States.[20] In addition, the U.S. Congress passed the McCarran-Walter Act in 1952, which allowed Korean-born immigrants to become American citizens, giving preference to students and professional workers.[21] As a result of these two laws, over 14,000 Korean War orphans, brides, workers, and students immigrated to the United States during this time period.

Many of these war brides saw marriage as a survival strategy to escape the harsh life in Korea.[22] While some happily integrated into the local society, others struggled with adjusting to life in the United States. Some members of the Korean community shunned them, often referring to these women as "western sluts."[23] Without job skills and social support, some sought employment in bars and cocktail lounges as waitresses and hostesses.[24] These establishments soon became known as "Korean bars" by the wider local community and the media. Although the Korean community pressured the media to stop using this term in their reports, stereotypes of Koreans running bars and working as hostesses remain in Hawai'i today.[25]

MARRIAGE AND IDENTITY

The relatively small Korean population in Hawai'i, in combination with the influx of war brides, contributed to the trend of high interracial marriages. The large number of war brides and the subsequent sponsoring of family reunification were instrumental in the maturation of the Korean immigration pattern.[26] This was already a common pattern found among other ethnic groups in Hawai'i.

The interracial marriage rate in Hawai'i was about 12 percent in 1916 and rising.[27] Between 1955 and 1983, during which the largest number of Koreans immigrated to the United States, the interracial marriage rate among Koreans was one of the highest among Asian groups in Hawai'i, with Korean women intermarrying at rates ranging from 73 to 88 percent and men ranging from 51 to 80 percent.[28] In

other parts of the country, particularly Los Angeles County, the interracial marriage rate for Korean Americans was much lower.[29] This may
be in part due to the lingering effects of California's antimiscegenation
laws, which were finally repealed in 1948. In contrast, intermarriages
were generally accepted in Hawai'i's communities. However, a substantial drop in interracial marriages among Asian-Americans—from 25 to
15 percent—occurred nationally between 1980 and 1990. The decline
in interracial marriages was particularly striking among Koreans,
as they fell from nearly 30 percent in 1980 to just 7 percent in 1990.
The growth of the Korean population and increased acceptance of the
Korean culture may be partly responsible for this decrease.

Between 1952 and 1954, Koreans had one of the highest divorce
rates compared to other ethnic groups at 44 percent. The average
divorce rate for interracial marriages was 20.4 percent among the general population, 10 percent for Japanese, and 13 percent for Chinese
couples.[30] In comparing Koreans in Hawai'i versus Koreans in their
homeland, the divorce rate among Korean immigrant men was three
times higher than for men in Korea, and for Korean immigrant women
it was was five times higher than in Korea.[31] Although a large portion of
this high rate of divorce may be attributed to marriages between Korean
women and non-Korean U.S. servicemen, the overall Korean immigrant population also experienced higher rates of divorce compared to
the population in Korea. While divorce is traditionally frowned upon in
Korean culture, it has become more accepted to those who have acculturated to Western norms. Upon immigration, Korean women experience increased economic roles in the financial status of their families,
thereby modifying their traditional gender roles as homemakers. Also,
the weakened socioeconomic mobility of Korean men due to their difficulty in obtaining jobs may have further weakened the traditional
patriarchal structures of Korean society and may have contributed to
conflicts in marital relations and higher rates of divorce.[32]

THE NEXT GENERATION OF KOREANS

Although Koreans had one of the highest rates of public dependency and juvenile delinquency in the 1930s, education is a deep-rooted
tradition in Korea that has continued in Hawai'i.[33] Koreans have historically placed great emphasis on education, which serves as an important
indicator for social status in Korea.[34] Many Korean immigrant parents
make tremendous sacrifices for the advancement of their children's
education. Their children's successes are a direct reflection of the family

and bring pride and honor to their parents, as evidenced by the efforts of early Korean immigrants who quickly placed their children in school. Between 1910 and 1930, the number of Korean children between the ages of six and thirteen attending school progressively grew to surpass the number of Japanese and Chinese children.[35] By 1930, the rate of Korean children attending school was the highest among all ethnic groups after Caucasians. This strong emphasis on education allowed the next generation of Koreans to make their way into professional occupations. However, as the younger generations of Koreans became educated in Western schools, many lost their Korean proficiency.

The younger generations of Koreans integrated into the evolving local culture and had many more opportunities to interact with people of other ethnicities than the first generation. Because Koreans were considered Japanese nationals during World War II, some were forced to register as enemy aliens and placed in internment camps with Japanese families.[36] While this angered many older Koreans in Hawai'i, it pushed the younger generation of Koreans to identify and prove themselves as being American to the rest of the community. They found themselves feeling internally conflicted. They recognized the sacrifices and hard work of their parents, yet found it difficult to identify with their parents' values. They also found it difficult to relate to the same anti-Japanese sentiment and instead developed close relationships with their Japanese peers, along with people of other ethnicities. Moreover, political struggles among Korean organizations led by first-generation Koreans prevented the younger generations from identifying with the Korean culture.[37]

ROLE OF RELIGION AND CHRISTIANITY

Since its introduction in 1794, nearly 30 percent of South Koreans identify themselves as Christians today.[38] Some of the earliest Christians in South Korea were Roman Catholic missionaries, but persecution by the ruling Korean dynasty limited the growth and proselytization of the faith. Only after the treaty with France in 1886 were Protestant missionaries free to openly expand their churches. However, this quickly ended under Japanese colonialism, which started a new wave of persecution by the Japanese government. After the Korean War, multitudes of Koreans joined Christian churches, and this explosion has not ceased. Protestant missionaries accentuated the Christian message that was easily acceptable and desired by Koreans who were looking for hope during a time of political instability. Korean churches emphasized

God's ability to improve living conditions and grant one's wishes for health and material blessings.[39] During the postwar era, at a time of economic and cultural revitalization, Christianity took firm hold and was quickly incorporated into the new Korean identity.

Although Christianity has taken hold of South Korea, it has had an even greater influence on Korean immigrants, with nearly 70–80 percent of Korean-Americans identifying themselves as Christians.[40] This is not surprising, given the Church's influence and impact on early immigrant recruitment and support. About 53 percent of the Korean-American community in Chicago identified themselves as Christians prior to leaving Korea. However, nearly half of those who did not affiliate themselves with Christian churches prior to their arrival subsequently joined a church once they immigrated to the United States. Interestingly, other Asian immigrants have not followed these patterns. For example, 71 percent of Koreans surveyed in Chicago were affiliated with Christian churches, compared to only 32 percent of Chinese and 28 percent of Japanese surveyed.[41]

Koreans in Hawai'i are believed to follow a similar pattern as in Chicago. One of the oldest and largest Christian churches outside of South Korea is located in Hawai'i. The Christ United Methodist Church is in Honolulu and plays a pivotal role for the Korean community of Hawai'i.[42] The church not only teaches Christian values but also helps perpetuate Korean culture. Members of the congregation regularly gather and share traditional Korean meals at the church hall. The church is the hub of social services, where medical professionals offer screening exams and referrals and children attend classes to learn Hangul. Korean churches in the United States have become a place not only for spiritual fellowship but also for social support and cultural connection.

CURRENT STATUS OF KOREANS IN HAWAI'I

Immigration from Korea has declined from an annual average of more than a thousand in the 1980s to less than three hundred in recent years, largely attributed to the economic development of South Korea.[43] As a result, the number of professional immigrants has decreased as the number of immigrants of lower socioeconomic status has increased in recent years.[44] Many Korean men often come alone to find jobs and establish themselves before bringing their families to join them later.[45]

As already noted, about 41,000 Koreans currently live in Hawai'i, including part-Koreans, who account for a sizable portion (43 percent) of the population. Hawai'i has one of the highest number of Korea-born

Koreans among all states.[46] About 17,000 Koreans living in Hawai'i were born in Korea, which comprises 42 percent of the Korean population in the state.

Most Koreans continue to prefer urban living, with 87 percent living on Oʻahu.[47] The median income for a Korean household was estimated to be $38,000 in 1999, just below the state average, with 13 percent of Koreans falling below the poverty line.[48] The types of jobs that Koreans tend to have are similar to their Japanese and Chinese counterparts, although fewer Koreans occupy professional positions. Korean women are largely employed in service-oriented occupations.[49] Many Koreans own their own businesses such as grocery stores, restaurants, and beauty salons.[50] This may be due to the fact that many new immigrants are ineligible for public employment until they establish residency. In addition, self-employment has helped Korean immigrants achieve economic mobility. Studies have found that self-employed Koreans enjoy higher levels of income and home and car ownership compared to those who are not self-employed, despite having similar education levels, English skills, and length of residence in the United States.[51]

HEALTH STATUS AND PRACTICES

Many traditional Koreans believe that illness comes from an imbalance of harmony, whether the imbalance is in their bodies or interpersonal relationships.[52] It may also be seen as the result of failing to properly pay tribute to their ancestors. In health care matters, family members are traditionally informed first.[53] The family will then inform the patient of the diagnosis. First-generation Koreans tend to rely on family and friends for referrals before they turn to public institutions. Koreans may psychosomatize their pains and complain of vague aches, which are well-known disorders in Korea.[54] *Shin-byung* and *hwa-byung* are two examples of culture-bound syndromes in the behavioral health literature. *Shin-byung* is a syndrome that initially presents with anxiety and vague somatic complaints, followed by dissociation and possession by ancestral spirits. *Hwa-byung* is another syndrome that translates as anger syndrome.[55] It is thought to be attributed to the suppression of anger. Symptoms include insomnia, fatigue, panic, fear of impending death, indigestion, loss of appetite, difficulty breathing, palpitations, generalized aches and pains, and a feeling of fullness in the abdominal region.[56]

Koreans of older generations tend to underutilize social and health services. This may be due to lack of knowledge about these services, limited English proficiency, or feelings of shame and discomfort. Working with existing Korean resources that provide health education and services may be helpful in reaching first-generation Koreans, especially the elderly. Korean churches are beginning to respond by offering health education classes that consider the effect of immigration. For example, nutrition classes are provided that encourage the elderly to decrease their sodium intake and increase their calcium intake by giving concrete examples with Korean dishes.[57] Because elderly Koreans may have limited English proficiency, health professionals who are Korean or are familiar with the culture and/or the language are needed to improve the health status of Koreans in Hawai'i.

Acculturation has been found to impact the health of Korean immigrants. For example, acculturated Korean women are more likely to smoke than women in Korea. This may be explained by the differences in gender norms that allow females to smoke in America but make it frowned upon in Korean society. However, acculturation has an opposite effect on Korean men. Because it is acceptable for Korean males to smoke in Korea, males who identify highly with Korean culture are more likely to smoke, while acculturated men are less likely to smoke. Acculturation also affects the level of physical activity and diet of Korean immigrants.[58] Acculturated men and women tend to engage in light physical activity more than bicultural and traditional Koreans; however, acculturated men were more likely to consume more fat in their diets and have higher body mass index (BMI).

A New Ethnocultural Identity

The literature on early Koreans lacks any mention of the influence of the Native Hawaiian culture on the first wave of Koreans. This may be largely due to the suppression of the Native Hawaiian culture in the first half of the twentieth century. In addition, the early Koreans were focused on regaining political independence for their home country, which may have prevented them from fully interacting and integrating with other cultures. Although Korean nationalistic pursuit parallels the political and cultural struggles of Native Hawaiians in some ways, interaction between the two ethnic groups appears to have been limited in the early half of the century.[59]

But as first-generation Koreans raised and gave birth to their children in Hawai'i, the Korean community grew much more diverse, as seen by the large portion of part-Koreans in Hawai'i. Many second- and third-generation Koreans married other ethnicities, creating hybrid ethnic identities. Considered hybrid because these generations grew up without an official homeland and lacked resources for cultural connections, the Korean identity was often displaced by more dominant and established ethnicities.

The indigenous Hawaiian cultural renaissance of the 1970s, along with the influx of the post-1960s Korean immigrants to Hawai'i, helped Koreans in Hawai'i regain a sense of cultural pride in their heritage. As indigenous Hawaiians rediscovered their traditions and language, Koreans of all generations also began establishing resources to reclaim their cultural identity. For example, the Center for Korean Studies was established at the University of Hawai'i at Mānoa in 1972 to broaden the teaching of Korean history and culture. It is the oldest and largest center for Korean studies in the United States and supports the largest concentration of Korean scholars and resources outside of Korea. The Center for Korean Studies has created a gathering place for all generations of Koreans by providing a scholarly foundation of Korean history and culture.[60]

KOREAN YOUTHS' STRUGGLES WITH ETHNIC IDENTITY

The younger generations of Koreans who were born and/or raised in America report feeling caught between their parents' traditional Korean values and the individualistic Western values taught in their schools and practiced by their peers.[61] Western ideals espouse that children have the right to disagree with their parents and express their emotions freely, while their traditional Korean parents may see this as being disobedient and disrespectful. Traditional Korean family values are based on Confucianism, which calls for obedience from the child to the parents, filial piety, and respect for elders. In addition, Korean parents may not show physical and verbal affection as openly as American parents, which may confuse and frustrate some Korean youths.[62] At the same time, Korean parents may push their children to be academically successful and put much emphasis on their grades and school performance. As a result, many Korean youths do well in school. Some are not as successful, however, which may intensify parent-child conflicts. This conflict may be further exacerbated when both parents work long hours, leaving their children unsupervised for most of the day. Because immigrant children also tend to learn English more quickly than their parents, the children may need to act as translators for their parents, decreasing parental confidence and unintentionally subjecting these children to an undue burden.[63]

As Korean families adjust and acculturate, traditional family expectations and duties may change and evolve to adapt to the dominant social norms.[64] For example, younger generation Koreans may move away from home in pursuit of their educational and career goals and eventually live far away from their parents. This impacts expectations of filial piety, as Korean children may no longer live at home to take care of the family.[65] Many children of Korean immigrant parents recognize the sacrifices of their parents and express the desire to take care of their families, even from a distance. For example, young Korean adults may regularly send money to their families as a sign of appreciation and filial piety.

Although Koreans have roots in plantation history that began over a hundred years ago, negative stereotypes and misrepresentations exist among the local community and broader society. Because of the large influx of Koreans after the 1960s, the primary image of the Korean community in Hawai'i is of first-generation Koreans in churches, restaurants, bars, and retail stores. These stereotypes are largely shaped by the images that the wider community has of the post-1960s wave of first-generation Koreans. Koreans are often stereotyped as aggressive and hot-tempered business owners. In addition, the proliferation of bars run by Koreans has had a devastating effect on the image of Korean women in Hawai'i by implying that Korean women are money-hungry and promiscuous.[66] Although the ethnic composition of these bars has changed over the years, the industry has created a lasting image of Korean women as being "bar girls." As Korean youths attend schools and interact with the wider community, they become exposed to these stereotypes through jokes, comments, and media portrayals. Along with youths' natural desire to belong, these negative stereotypes may drive them to distance themselves from their Korean identity. Some youths may learn to overcome these stereotypes and integrate their Korean identity into their self-perceptions, while others may internalize these stereotypes, leading them to disconnect from their Korean identity.

The younger generation of Koreans is not only comprised of second- and third-generation Koreans but also includes an intermediary called the 1.5 generation. The 1.5 generation Koreans, or *ilchom ose*, represent a concept created by the Korean community to describe the diverse group of immigrant children who were born in Korea but immigrated with their parents to America at a young age.[67] Consequently, they were raised and educated in America for most of their lives. Technically they are of the first generation like their parents, but their experiences often vastly differ from the experiences of their parents. This generation tends to be bilingual or able to understand some Korean. Although the 1.5 generation is foreign-born, they can often pass as being American-born and native English speakers. They may have some early memories of being teased and alienated for not being able to speak English. An immigrant of this generation soon learns that he or she is an "outsider" or an "FOB" in the broader community. Being identified as an FOB, which stands for "Fresh off the Boat," is a negative identity that sets immigrants apart from the wider local community.[68] Because language acquisition is generally easier at a younger age, youths who may have immigrated to America at an older age may retain a Korean accent. Because having an accent is an audible marker of an immigrant, youths who immigrated at an older age may have more difficulties being accepted and integrating into the broader culture.[69]

On the other hand, lacking Korean proficiency can constrain these youths' ability to be fully accepted as a Korean by the first-generation Korean community. Although many 1.5 or second generations of youth can speak Korean at a conversation level, they may not be able to engage in formal conversations, using proper honorifics indicating respect of social status in the community. Failing to use honorifics appropriately is heavily frowned upon in Korean culture. Because the Korean community is primarily led by the first-generation Koreans, Koreans of younger generations may feel marginalized in their own ethnic community, thereby preventing them from embracing their Korean identity.[70] To maintain their Korean proficiency, some parents may enroll their children in Korean language schools, which are operated mostly by religious groups in Hawai'i. Some Korean youths find themselves wanting to better communicate with their families and further their understanding of their heritage, and they choose to enroll in Korean language classes themselves when they reach adulthood.[71]

There are, however, multiple aspects of the Korean culture that can be maintained aside from language proficiency. Being exposed to Korean people, traditions, values, food, and media can help with shaping youths' identities. The level of exposure to Korean culture largely depends on the youths' surroundings and support system.[72] For example, the level of Korean spoken in the home, the number of Korean peers they associate with, the number of Korean relatives living in Hawai'i, and their level of participation in the Korean church may all have strong influences on shaping their ethnic identity.

Despite the challenges that younger generations of Koreans face, many are able to negotiate and move between their two cultures. Also, immigrants in Hawai'i may have a third cultural identity available to them.[73] A strong sense of localness that permeates Hawai'i provides an ethnic identity option for Asians that is not generally available in the continental United States. Being seen as a local in Hawai'i can imply acceptance and belongingness to the wider community. Therefore, there is a distinct difference between "local Koreans" and "FOB Koreans."

Despite the arrival of Koreans during the plantation era of Hawai'i over one hundred years ago, Koreans are often marginalized from the local identity for three primary reasons.[74] First, Korea's political history led early Koreans to resist an association with the local identity, which was largely dominated by the Japanese. Second, the high rate of marriages to other ethnicities has diminished the Korean identity. Last, the large and recent influx of post-1965 Korean immigrants created the perception that Koreans in Hawai'i are foreigners and not part of the local community.

Interestingly, Koreans are recognized as a distinct group in Hawai'i, unlike in the continental United States where Asians are generally lumped into one group by the mainstream culture.[75] Although California has the largest number of Korean-American residents in the country, Koreans comprise less than 1 percent of the state's overall population. In contrast, Koreans make up over 4 percent of Hawai'i's population. Most people in Hawai'i can distinguish among Korean, Japanese, and Chinese surnames and are generally aware of the cultural practices of these different ethnic groups. Notably, Korean food—such as kimchi, *bibimbap,* and *kalbi*—has grown in popularity and is commonly found in many local restaurants. Some Korean dishes have evolved to become original Hawaiian-Korean local dishes—such as *meat-jun*—and can only be found in Hawai'i.

KOREAN FAMILY DYNAMICS

While in many traditional Korean families the husband was the primary source of income, this has shifted since the plantation era. Picture brides were often much younger than their husbands, which often put them in working roles to assist with the family income.[76] As their husbands aged, they became the primary source of income.

Since then, Korean wives in Hawai'i have played a significant role in earning income for their family. More recently, Korean women have adapted and have found themselves working in the larger community more than their male counterparts. For example, in a family business, the wife may have the role of interacting with clients and employees, whereas the husband may work more behind the scenes. While the Korean family structure is considered to be patriarchal, it has evolved to be matriarchal in many ways. The mother is often responsible for many of the domestic decisions and functions of daily life in the home.

In working-class families, parents tend to be more dependent on their children. Language and cultural barriers keep the parents more marginalized from the larger society. Their children may act as interpreters and be expected to interface with the non-Korean community. Parents often work and socialize in places where Korean is spoken, which is often the primary language at home. Korean culture and values tend to be maintained more strongly in these families. In middle-class families, the children help their parents in many of the same ways. However, the parents are less dependent on them because at least one parent is usually fluent in English. The children of these families may have more freedom to follow their own goals and aspirations.[77]

INTRAGROUP RELATIONSHIPS

Traditional Korean values are reflected in the Korean flag. A white background represents purity of the people. The center yin and yang represent conflict in harmonious balance. The four trigrams have various interpretations that are reflective of traditional Korean values: harmony, symmetry, balance, and circulation; humanity, courtesy, knowledge, and righteousness; father, son, daughter, and mother. These values are pervasive in family, social, and occupational relationships. The needs of the family or community outweigh the individual desires in Korean culture. This can often be in conflict with more Western values of independence, individual rights, and happiness. This conflict commonly appears in the different generations in families.

Since the 1970s, large numbers of first-generation Koreans have dominated Korean community organizations. Many of these organizations have emphasized the maintenance of Korean culture and ancestry and assisted the Korean-speaking community and its people. Until recently, the younger generations of Koreans, as well as Koreans with plantation roots, were underrepresented in these prominent Korean community organizations.[78] One primary explanation for this divide may be related to the issue of language. Much of the Korean identity and culture is centered on language. Many Korean organizations with significant first-generation membership operate in Hangul, thereby excluding those who do not speak the native language. If they are not able to speak Korean, they may not be seen as a true Koreans by the older first generation.

Another explanation of this intergenerational divide may be attributed to cultural differences. First-generation Koreans are firmly shaped by Confucian values and place great emphasis on the hierarchy of interpersonal relationships and obedience to superiors. The young are expected to be submissive and respectful to elders, and men have authority over women. These values are in direct opposition to the more Western values of personal freedom, independence, and gender equality. First-generation leaders interpret the more assertive, critical, or informal mannerisms of younger generation Koreans toward older immigrants as ignorance of their cultural roots and values.[79] In contrast, younger Koreans may generally value democratic rule and equal opportunity and may reject hierarchical structures. Despite these intracultural differences, the Korean community is beginning to recognize that the language and cultural barriers of the first generation limit them from political representation, mainstream resources, and outside institutional support, and second-generation leaders recognize that they have limited ability to mobilize the abundant resource networks within the Korean community. In more recent years, the leadership of these organizations has evolved to include a more diverse representation of Koreans.

Despite comprising a relatively small portion of Hawai'i's total population, Koreans have established a Korean radio station, a TV channel, and several newspapers. In addition to publicizing community events and local news, these sources serve as a link between Korea and Hawai'i by keeping Koreans living in Hawai'i aware of the political and social situations in Korea. Although most of these newspapers cater to first-generation Koreans, as almost all articles are written in Hangul, accessibility for nonproficient Koreans has recently improved. For example, the *JoongAng Daily* and the *Korea Times* have articles written in English that are now available on their Web sites.

KOREAN ADOPTEES

Over 110,000 Korean adoptees currently live in the United States, comprising 5–10 percent of the Korean-American population. Korean adoption began in the 1950s with the first wave of biracial GI children.[80] As Korea faced poverty and economic instability, an upsurge of full-Korean children were placed into orphanages. In addition, the stigma given to unwed or single mothers coupled with the lack of social services drove Korea to allow almost unrestricted adoption of orphaned Korean children overseas. Today some two thousand Korean children are adopted into American families every year, making Korea the third-highest country in transnational adoption rates behind Russia and China. Over half of the adoptees in the United States are now adults and have begun collectively asserting their unique identity as Korean-Americans. A nonprofit organization called the Korean Adoptees of Hawai'i (KAHI) was created in 2006 by a Korean adoptee who was raised in Hawai'i.[81] KAHI is comprised of about sixty members who were raised in Hawai'i and the continental United States. It has hosted numerous cultural and political events, including a minigathering in October 2008 that attracted over a hundred Korean adoptees from ninety countries. This minigathering was a smaller version of "The Gathering," an annual event that began in 1999 in Washington, D.C., where over four thousand Korean adoptees from the United States and Europe gather to celebrate the growth and diversity of the Korean adoptee community and to continue to share and publicize their concerns, ideas, and experiences.

Korean adoptees may face an identity crisis earlier than most adolescents, especially if they are adopted into non-Asian families where they may not look like other members of their family.[82] Koreans adoptees who grew up in Hawai'i, however, may have an easier time adjusting and accepting these differences, given the large presence of Asians in Hawai'i. But Korean adoptees who grew up in communities without a large presence of other Asians and other Koreans may have more difficulty integrating their Korean identity.

Although the South Korean government has made policy reforms to publicly recognize and welcome Korean adoptees in South Korea, adoptees often struggle with their ethnic identities, especially in the context of Korean values. Because of the strong emphasis that Koreans place on blood and family ties, many Korean adoptees feel that the Korean community has not openly accepted them and struggle with not feeling "Korean enough." To accommodate the increasing voicing of Korean adoptees' needs, more resources are emerging, such as Web sites, cultural camps, and support organizations for Korean adoptees and their families. However, older generations of Korean adoptees may not have had these resources while they were growing up.[83] Because the focus of immigrants during those times was on assimilation, it was not until the 1970s that adoption agencies began encouraging adoptive parents to openly address and embrace ethnic differences among their family members and to actively encourage their children to explore their cultural identity.

INTERGROUP RELATIONSHIPS

In 1976, the Voice of Korea, a commercial radio and broadcasting station, was established in Honolulu for the purpose of commercial and radio broadcasting, with one hour per week being devoted to Korean programming on KIKU-TV (a Japanese channel). In ten years, Korean television broadcasts grew in Hawai'i until a Federal Communications Commission license was granted in 1985 to operate KBFD-TV, which is fully devoted to Korean broadcasts.[84] Although local cable companies in Hawai'i first refused to carry KBFD-TV in their basic cable package, the Korean community successfully rallied against their initial decision. This allowed more Koreans and non-Koreans to become exposed to Korean culture through television shows. With non-Korean speakers and non-Korean viewership increasing, KBFD began providing English subtitles for many Korean dramas, otherwise known as K-Drama. Since then, the popularity of Korean dramas among non-Koreans has dramatically increased.

In response to this popularity, major online retailers such as Amazon.com and Walmart have started selling DVDs of K-Drama series. There are two main genres of Korean dramas, with the first genre typically involving conflicts in marital and family relationships and often complicated by love triangles. The other genre depicts dramatizations of Korean history and often involves complex storylines with elaborate costumes, martial arts, and swordsmanship.[85] Those who are fans of K-Drama state that the main appeal is their compelling and wholesome storylines that focus on relationships and families.[86] They also believe that K-Dramas are less violent and provocative than American soap operas. K-Dramas often portray family values that the older Asian generation can relate to. In addition, K-Drama series last anywhere from sixteen to over a hundred episodes, but they always have a conclusion. In contrast, American soap operas have never-ending plots that may frustrate or bore viewers.

A study conducted in Hawai'i found that a majority of the 270 people who were randomly sampled have watched Korean drama before.[87] The study also found that being exposed to Korean dramas affects viewers' perception of the country and increases their desire to visit Korea and purchase Korean products. In response to the increased interest, travel agents now offer tours that visit filming locations in Korea. Chat rooms, blogs, and fan clubs devoted to the latest K-Drama series have sprung up online and across the country. For example, the Hawai'i K-Drama Fan Club was founded in 2002 by two local Japanese women with twenty members.[88] Since then, membership has grown exponentially, with the majority of the membership being comprised of non-Koreans. Club members volunteer at the annual Korean Festival in Honolulu and help with various fundraising efforts that often benefit Korean associations. More recently, Korean pop music, film, and celebrities have been receiving international attention, which has expanded to Hawai'i's communities. This phenomenon of the growing popularity of Korean pop culture has been coined as the Korean Wave, or *hallyu*.[89] In addition, international attention and curiosity were enhanced by the 1988 Olympics taking place in Seoul, Korea, renewing Koreans' sense of ethnic pride.

Biopsychosocial Factors

In order to survive colonization, a civil war, and immigration, Koreans have had to adapt to their environment, be industrious, and make sacrifices for their children. These hardships have created a culture of people who are resilient, resourceful, and persistent. Others may perceive these traits as being emotionally passionate, highly expressive, or even confrontational.[90] These types of impressions developed early in the history of Korean immigration as Koreans became known for their fiery protests. Protesting is part of the cultural norm in Korea, with about 11,000 protests occurring yearly. This cultural norm was transferred to Hawai'i early in the immigration history of Koreans. The early Koreans in Hawai'i organized to protest the annexation of Korea by Japan by burning all their possessions that were made in Japan and boycotting Japanese products. During World War II, Koreans in Hawai'i vehemently protested against being identified as Japanese by wearing "I am Korean" buttons. Shortly after the large immigration wave of the 1970s, Korean vendors in the International Marketplace in Waikīkī protested by carrying signs written in red to symbolize the blood, sweat, and tears of their hard work and wailing on the side of the streets. Although these actions were culturally appropriate in Korea, it was unusually graphic and disturbing for the rest of Hawai'i's community.[91] In addition, the current political turmoil and the danger posed by the North Korean government also have reinforced these stereotypes of Koreans being "aggressive" and having "fiery tempers."

Koreans emphasize the importance of education as an instrument in elevating social status—not only of the individual but also of the family and the nation. This is evidenced by Korea having the highest number of doctorates per capita in the world.[92] Koreans recognize the important role played by education in the economic and political rise of Korea. This emphasis has been maintained in Hawai'i and the continental United States. Korean preschools in the continental United States emphasize education and knowledge at an early age. Korean parents in Hawai'i often make enormous sacrifices to enroll their children in private schools and hire tutors.[93] The perception is that one could lose one's wealth, stature, business, home, and family, but not one's education. Education gives rise to opportunity.

Summary and Conclusions

As psychotherapists look to their Korean clients' past to better understand them, Korea's history needs to be examined to understand Korean culture in Hawai'i. It is equally important to keep in mind that culture is fluid and Koreans in Hawai'i are a heterogeneous group. The Koreans that arrived in 1903 came from a very different Korea than those that came after the 1960s. Prior to the 1960s, the Koreans in Hawai'i were predominately comprised of the plantation workers, picture brides, and war brides. Their numbers were relatively small and they created a unique Korean culture in Hawai'i that was shaped by high rates of interracial marriage. The large influx of Koreans in the 1970s and 1980s eclipsed this Korean culture that developed during the plantation era. Consequently, the perception of Koreans and the Korean culture is heavily influenced by these recent immigrants, whose life experiences are vastly different from those who were longtime residents of Hawai'i. Immigrants tend to maintain the culture of their homeland at the time of their migration. Thus, the culture in 1903 Korea was quite different from the culture of the post-1960s Korea, which is also very different from the culture of Korea today. The war-torn Korea has had a significant impact on the older generations of Koreans, although effects varied depending on whether the events were experienced from a distance in Hawai'i or experienced firsthand in Korea. The second and third generations of Korean plantation workers have had different experiences of Korean culture than the 1.5 and second generations of the post-1960s immigrants. Koreans employed in the service industry have had different experiences than those in more professional occupations. Koreans who have a religious affiliation may have a different cultural experience than those who do not. This diversity within the Korean culture in Hawai'i can create complexities in defining the Korean identity, even within its own community. As Korea continues to grow economically and politically, the country will also receive more international attention. Hawai'i has been particularly welcoming of these Korean influences, which continue to shape the Korean identity among Koreans and the wider community of Hawai'i.

Further Reading

Chang, R., and W. Patterson. *The Koreans in Hawai'i: A Pictorial History, 1903–2003*. Honolulu: University of Hawai'i Press, 2003.

Ch'oe, Y. *From the Land of Hibiscus: Koreans in Hawai'i, 1903–1950*. Honolulu: University of Hawai'i Press, 2007.

Danico, M. Y. 2004. *The 1.5 Generation: Becoming Korean American in Hawai'i*. Honolulu and Los Angeles: University of Hawai'i Press and UCLA Asian American Studies Center.

Foster, J. R., H. I. Fenkl, and F. Stewart. *Century of the Tiger: One Hundred Years of Korean Culture in America, 1903–2003*. Honolulu: *Manoa Journal*, Centennial Committee of Korean Immigration to the United States, and University of Hawai'i Press, 2003.

Jeon, M. "Avoiding FOBS: An account of a journey." *Working Papers in Educational Linguistics* 17(122) (2001); 82–106.

Kim, E. "Korean adoptees' role in the United States." In I. J. Kim, ed., *Korean-Americans: Past, Present, and Future*. Elizabeth, NJ: Hollym International Corp., 2004:108–202.

Kwon, B. *Beyond Ke'eaumoku: Koreans, Nationalism, and Local Culture in Hawai'i*. New York: Garland Publishing, 1999.

Okamura, J. *Ethnicity and Inequality in Hawai'i*. Philadelphia: Temple University Press, 2008.

———. "Why there are no Asian Americans in Hawai'i: The continuing significance of local identity." *Social Process in Hawai'i* 35 (1994): 161–178.

Patterson, W. *The Ilse: First-Generation Korean Immigrants in Hawai'i, 1903–1973*. Center for Korean Studies, University of Hawai'i. Honolulu: University of Hawai'i Press, 2000.

———. *The Korean Frontier in America: Immigration to Hawai'i, 1896–1910*. Honolulu: University of Hawai'i Press, 1988.

Purnell, L. D., and S. Kim. 2003. "People of Korean heritage." In L. D. Purnell and B.J.Paulanka, eds., *Transcultural Health Care: A Culturally Competent Approach.* Philadelphia: F.A.Davis Co.: 249–278.

Notes

1. L.D.Purnell and S.Kim, "People of Korean heritage," in *Transcultural Health Care: A Culturally Competent Approach,* ed. L.D.Purnell and B.J.Paulanka, Philadelphia: F.A.Davis Co., 2003: 249–278.

2. M.Haas, M., *Multicultural Hawai'i: The Fabric of a Multiethnic Society,* New York: Garland Press, 1998.

3. H.Sunoo and S.Shinn, "The heritage of the first Korean women immigrants in the United States: 1903–1924," *Korean Christian Scholars Journal* 2 (1977):142–171.

4. Y.Ch'oe, *From the Land of Hibiscus: Koreans in Hawai'i, 1903–1950,* Honolulu: University of Hawai'i Press, 2007; W.Patterson, *The Korean Frontier in America: Immigration to Hawai'i, 1896–1910,* Honolulu: University of Hawai'i Press, 1988.

5. Ch'oe 2007.

6. Patterson 1988.

7. E.Kim, "Korean adoptees' role in the United States," in I.J.Kim, ed., *Korean-Americans: Past, Present, and Future,* Elizabeth, NJ: Hollym International Corp., 2004: 180–202.

8. Ch'oe 2007.

9. D.L.Murabayashi, "Korean women's activities in Hawai'i: 1903–1950," paper presented at the Conference of the 80th Commemoration of Chongsan-ri Battle, Yanbien, People's Republic of China, 2000.

10. Patterson 1988.

11. P.G.Min, "Korean immigrants in Los Angeles," in *Immigration and Entrepreneurship: Culture, Capital, and Ethnic Networks,* ed. I.H.Light and P.Bhachu, Piscataway, NJ: Transaction Publishers, 2004: 185–204.

12. W.M.Hurh and K.C.Kim, "Correlates of Korean immigrants' mental health," *Journal of Nervous and Mental Disease* 178(11) (1990): 703–711.

13. Purnell and Kim 2003.

14. J.Yuh, "Moved by war: Migration, diaspora and the Korean War," *Journal of Asian American Studies* 8(3) (2005): 277–291.

15. Purnell and Kim 2003.

16. Y.K.Harvey and S.Chung, "The Koreans," in J.F.McDermott, W.Tseng, and T.W.Maretzki, eds., *Peoples and Cultures of Hawai'i: A Psychocultural Profile,* Honolulu: University of Hawai'i Press, 1980: 135–154.

17. Ch'oe 2007.

18. M.Y.Danico, *The 1.5 Generation: Becoming Korean American in Hawai'i,* Honolulu and Los Angeles: University of Hawai'i Press and UCLA Asian American Studies Center, 2004.

19. R. Chang and W. Patterson, *The Koreans in Hawai'i: A Pictorial History, 1903–2003*, Honolulu: University of Hawai'i Press, 2003.

20. P. G. Min, *Asian Americans: Contemporary Trends and Issues*, Thousand Oaks, CA: Sage, 1995.

21. M. K. Quinlan, "Review: Beyond the shadow of camptown: Korean military brides in America," *Oral History Review* 31 (2004): 97–99.

22. Ibid.

23. G. E. Jang, "Not so happily ever after," *KoreAm Journal* (2005) accessed in 2009 from http://www.koreamjournal.com/Magazine/index. php/kj/2005/september/artist_s_trax/not_so_happily_ever_after; R. M. Lee, "The coming of age of Korean adoptees: Ethnic identity development and psychological adjustment," in I. J. Kim, ed., *Korean-Americans: Past, Present, and Future*, Elizabeth, NJ: Hollym International Corp., 2004: 203–224.

24. Harvey and Chung 1980.

25. Danico 2004.

26. Yuh 2005.

27. R. Schmitt, "Demographic correlates of interracial marriage in Hawai'i," *Demography* 2 (1965): 463–473.

28. T. Labov and J. Jacobs, "Intermarriage in Hawai'i, 1950–1983," *Journal of Marriage and the Family* 48(1) (1986): 79–88.

29. H. H. L. Kitano, W. T. Yeung, L. Chai, and H. Hatanaka, "Asian-American Interracial Marriage," *Journal of Marriage and the Family* 46(1) (1984): 179–190.

30. C. Cheng and D. Yamamura, "Interracial marriage and divorce in Hawai'i," *Social Forces* 36 (1957): 77–84.

31. H. Im, "Strengthening families in the Korean/Asian immigrant community," white paper submitted to the U.S. Department of Labor by the Korean Churches for Community Development, 2003.

32. P. G. Min, "Changes in Korean immigrants' gender role and social status, and their marital conflicts," *Sociological Forum* 16(2) (2001): 301–320.

33. Ch'oe 2007.

34. Purnell and Kim 2003.

35. Ch'oe 2007.

36. Patterson 1988.

37. Danico 2004.

38. Hurh and Kim 1990.

39. A. Kim, "Korean religious culture and its affinity to Christianity: The rise of Protestant Christianity in South Korea," *Sociology of Religion* 61(2) (2000): 117–133.

40. Hurh and Kim 1990; C. T. Chang, "Korean ethnic church growth phenomenon in the United States," paper presented at the American Academy of Religion in Claremont, CA, 2006.

41. Kim 2000.

42. "Christ United Methodist Church," (n.d.), Retrieved March 22, 2010, from http://www.cumchawaii.com/.

43. J. Okamura, "Why there are no Asian Americans in Hawai'i: The continuing significance of local identity," *Social Process in Hawai'i* 35 (1994): 161–178.

44. Min 1995.

45. Chang and Patterson 2003.

46. J. Yau, "The foreign born Koreans in the United States," Migration Information Source, 2004, retrieved May 2009: http://www.migrationinformation.org/usfocus/display.cfm?ID=273.

47. Okamura 1994.

48. Department of Business, Economic Development and Tourism, "Table 1.33: Ranking of races," in *State of Hawai'i Data Book 2002*, retrieved February 2009 from http://hawaii.gov/dbedt/info/economic/databook/db2002/section01.pdf.

49. Ibid.

50. Okamura 1994.

51. P. G. Min, "Korean immigrants in Los Angeles," in I. H Light and P. Bhachu, eds., *Immigration and Entrepreneurship: Culture, Capital, and Ethnic Networks*, Piscataway, NJ: Transaction Publishers, 2004: 185–204.

52. Purnell and Kim 2003.

53. J. G. Lipson, S. L. Dibble, and P. A. Minarik, *Culture and Nursing Care: A Pocket Guide*, San Francisco: University of California San Francisco Nursing Press, 1996.

54. N. Palafox and A. Warren, eds., *Cross-Cultural Caring: A Handbook for Health Care Professionals in Hawai'i*, Honolulu: Transcultural Health Forum, 1980.

55. Purnell and Kim 2003.

56. B. J. Sadock, V. A. Sadock, P. Ruiz, and H. I. Kaplan, *Kaplan and Sadock's Comprehensive Textbook of Psychiatry*, 9th ed., Philadelphia: Wolters Kluwer/Lippincott Williams & Wilkins, 2009.

57. Dr. Soo Kyung Lee, personal communication, March 5, 2009.

58. S. Lee, J. Sobal, and E. A. Frongillo, "Acculturation and health in Korean Americans," *Social Science and Medicine* 51 (2000): 159–173.

59. J. Van Dyke, "Reconciliation between Korean and Japan," *Chinese Journal of International Law* 5 (2006): 215–239.

60. Esther Kwon Arinaga, personal communication, June 2009.

61. C. Yeh, "Age, acculturation, cultural adjustment and mental health symptoms of Chinese, Korean, and Japanese immigrant youths," *Cultural Diversity and Ethnic Minority Psychology* 9 (2003): 34–48.

62. Danico 2004.

63. R. G. Chung, "Gender, ethnicity, and acculturation in intergenera-

tional conflict of Asian American college students," *Cultural Diversity and Ethnic Minority Psychology* 7(4) (2001): 376–386.

64. Danico 2004.

65. Im 2003.

66. Danico 2004.

67. Ibid.

68. M. Jeon, "Avoiding FOBS: An account of a journey," *Working Papers in Educational Linguistics* 17(1–2) (2001): 82–106.

69. Danico 2004.

70. Ibid.

71. Jeon 2001.

72. Danico 2004.

73. Ibid.

74. B. Kwon, *Beyond Ke'eaumoku: Koreans, Nationalism, and Local Culture in Hawai'i,* New York: Garland Publishing, 1999.

75. Okamura 1994.

76. Sunoo and Shinn 1977.

77. Danico 2004.

78. Ibid.

79. Ibid.

80. Katie Putes, personal communication, March 13, 2009.

81. Ibid.

82. Lee 2004.

83. E. Kim, "Korean adoptees' role in the United States," in I. J. Kim, ed., *Korean-Americans: Past, Present, and Future,* Elizabeth, NJ: Hollym International Corp., 2004: 180–202.

84. KBFD-TV, "History of KBFD-TV," (2009), retrieved May 2009 from http://www.kbfd.com/eng/history.html.

85. Wikipedia, "Korean drama" (2009), retrieved May 2009 from http://en.wikipedia.org/wiki/Korean_drama.

86. J. Song, "Korean drama craze reaches United States," *Rocky Mountain Collegian* (2006), retrieved May 2009 from http://www.collegian.com/media/storage/paper864/news/2006/03/23/National/Korean.Drama.Craze.Reaches.United.States-1713951-page3.shtml.

87. Y. C. Cho and J. Agrusa, "How the media is a significant promotional tool to deliver marketing messages to audiences?" *Internatioanl Business & Economics Research Journal* 6(10) (2007): 61–74.

88. Nora Muramoto, personal communication, May 2009.

89. Song 2006.

90. Harvey and Chung 1980.

91. Danico 2004.

92. Purnell and Kim 2003.

93. Haas 1998.

CHAPTER 9

The Filipinos

Anthony P. S. Guerrero, Ricardo Bayola, and Celia Ona

The Filipinos in Hawai'i are originally from the Philippines, an archipelago of over seven thousand islands in the western Pacific Ocean, south of Taiwan and north of Indonesia and eastern Malaysia. While proto-Australoid peoples inhabited parts of the Philippines as remotely as 50,000 B.C., current Filipinos are mostly descended from seafarers who left their putative Austronesian homeland in Taiwan around 4000 B.C. Filipinos therefore share a common ancestry—remarkably reflected in biological markers, culture, and language—with other Austronesian peoples, who are spread widely throughout the Indian and Pacific Oceans: from Madagascar in the far west to Polynesia (including New Zealand [Aotearoa], Hawai'i, and Easter Island [Rapa Nui]) in the east.

While Filipinos maintain strong roots in their aboriginal and Austronesian heritage, they have been influenced throughout history by many other peoples that have either visited or attempted to colonize the Philippines, most notably Chinese, Indian, Arabic, Spanish, and American. The degrees of influence vary by geography. For instance, while most Filipinos in the northern and central Philippines are Roman Catholic (deriving from Spanish colonization), most Filipinos in the southern Philippines are Muslim (deriving from Indian and Arabic influences).

Given the significant ethnic and cultural diversity that exists among Filipinos, one should therefore be mindful of the inherent challenge in any attempt to describe a singular Filipino culture. *Ethnologue: Languages of the World* lists no fewer than 171 separate languages (of

201

which many are not mutually intelligible dialects of one another) in existence in the Philippines.[1] It is also interesting to note that what we now know as the Philippines became a single nation mostly by virtue of unification under the Spanish government (which named the islands after King Philip II of Spain). The country includes within its borders ethnic groups that also live in other Austronesian nations, including Indonesia (formerly colonized by the Dutch), Malaysia (formerly colonized by the British), and Taiwan (now populated predominantly by Han Chinese). It is likely that the demarcations of any of these nations might be different if not for outside influence and colonization.

An exhaustive review of the emigration history of Filipinos to Hawai'i is beyond the scope of this chapter and is well reviewed in other references (see Suggested Reading List, particularly the Philippine History Site at http://opmanong.ssc.hawaii.edu/filipino/filmig.html and Ponce and Forman's chapter in *Peoples and Cultures of Hawai'i: A Psychocultural Profile*).[2] However, it is vitally important to be familiar with the background of Filipino migration to Hawai'i in order to understand the current socioeconomic and cultural situation of Filipinos in Hawai'i. The following is provided as a brief summary of the context and history of Filipino migration to Hawai'i.

As an outcome of the 1898 Spanish-American War, Spain ceded the Philippines to the United States. However, in the first decade of the 1900s the Philippines fought for its own independence against the United States. In this bloody war, known as the Philippine-American War, hundreds of thousands of Filipinos died. The Philippines subsequently became an American colony.

Around the same time, Hawai'i had also come under the control of the United States, following the deposition of Queen Lili'uokalani in 1893 and the subsequent annexation of Hawai'i as a territory. The economy of Hawai'i at the time was largely dependent on agricultural products exported to the United States. The Hawaiian Sugar Planter's Association continued to seek new sources for inexpensive foreign labor. The first documented migration of Filipinos to Hawai'i occurred in 1906 in the context of these recruitment efforts.

The original Filipinos to work in Hawai'i's sugar plantations were from the Tagalog region of the Philippines, where the capital city of Manila is located. These *sakadas* joined the other ethnic groups from Asia and elsewhere who had already been working in Hawai'i sugar plantations for several decades. Subsequently, most of the *sakadas* were from the relatively rural and agricultural (though not sugar-farming)

Ilocos region of the Philippines. Of interest, Ilocanos had been known for their industriousness and for having already migrated to other parts of the Philippines in order to seek better opportunities and fortunes.

The number of Filipinos that immigrated to Hawai'i grew exponentially, to the point that they eventually represented the largest ethnic group among the plantation workers. According to modern accounts, plantation owners preferred Filipino laborers for several reasons, including (1) the fact that Filipinos worked for the lowest wages (in a system in which the different ethnic groups were purposefully segregated from each other); (2) the fact that Filipinos were viable alternatives to other groups who had gained experience in organizing strikes to advocate for better working conditions; (3) the Filipinos' status as U.S. subjects and therefore exempt from U.S. laws barring importation of labor elsewhere; and (4) their industriousness, in spite of the grueling conditions that were imposed upon plantation workers. It will be noted, however, that Filipino labor leaders subsequently emerged in historically important strikes.

The last major importation of Filipino labor occurred in 1946, just prior to the granting of Philippine independence in an effort to replenish the supply of plantation workers after many had been diverted to the defense industry during World War II. Following that, significant emigration from the Philippines continued to occur in the context of the original immigrants' petitioning of their families and the Immigration and Nationality Act of 1965, which further allowed Filipino medical professionals (mostly physicians and nurses) to immigrate to the United States. In fact, the significant emigration of Filipino nurses has led to the Philippines currently being the leading supplier of nurses to the United States, including Hawai'i. Catherine Ceniza Choy argues that the origins of this migration lie in the creation of an Americanized hospital system during the U.S. colonization of the Philippines.[3] Objectively speaking, it is likely that the modern health care system of the United States would not be what it is today without the immigration of Filipino health care workers.

Filipinos in Hawai'i are therefore the product of these waves of immigration and the social and historical contexts that surrounded them. Filipinos are the fourth-largest ethnocultural group in Hawai'i (after the Japanese, Hawaiians, and Caucasians). Approximately 56 percent of the Filipinos in Hawai'i are immigrants. The majority of Filipinos in Hawai'i continue to be of Ilocano ancestry and represent the full spectrum of proximity of immigration, ranging from recent immigrants to the great-great-grandchildren of immigrant plantation workers. Filipinos are distributed throughout all of the main Hawaiian Islands, but they are in higher concentration in geographic locales that approximate (though not exactly) the original plantations. Census tracts with high proportions of Filipinos in Hawaiʻi include the Waipahu and Kalihi areas of the island of Oʻahu and the entire island of Lānaʻi.

While there is also tremendous variety in the educational and occupational backgrounds of Hawaiʻi's Filipinos as a result of the more recent waves of migration and upward social mobility, as a group they are on the lower rungs of the socioeconomic ladder in Hawaiʻi, not unlike the situation during the plantation era. As reviewed in Cunanan et al., the average per capita income for Filipinos is $16,000, compared to $29,000 for Japanese, $27,000 for Chinese, and $21,000 for the state population as a whole.[4] While the figure is higher for Filipinos than it is for Native Hawaiians (with an average per capita income of $14,000), it is noteworthy that many Filipino families send significant portions of their income back to relatives in the Philippines (again, similar to the practice of the earlier plantation workers). In Hawaiʻi, only 11 percent of Filipinos hold bachelor's degrees, compared to 18 percent for the whole state. As reviewed in Infante Nii and Creamer, Filipinos are underrepresented in higher paying managerial and professional jobs and overrepresented in lower paying farming, cleaning, and service jobs.[5] All of these socioeconomic facts are significant to consider in the overall emotional adjustment of Filipinos in Hawaiʻi, who may also face discrimination (dating from the plantation era) and acculturative stress related to more recent immigration.[6]

A recent study that involved focus groups on Filipino adolescents, parents, young adult professionals, and community leaders revealed several interesting findings: (1) that for the most part, Filipinos in Hawaiʻi did not seem to match the Asian "model minority" stereotype; (2) that risk factors for Filipino youth in Hawaiʻi include negative stereotypes, low ethnic pride and lack of role models, lack of adult supervision (that may be related to the need to work several jobs), acculturative pressures and breakdown of traditional values, and lack of available youth programs; and (3) that protective factors for Filipino youth in Hawaiʻi include connections to Filipino family and culture and religion.[7] Indeed, a follow-up study that surveyed Filipino youth in Hawaiʻi and their parents suggested that low Filipino cultural identification is a risk factor for delinquent behavior and that a potential mechanism by which this trait predisposes to delinquent behavior is via suboptimal relationships with adult caregivers and adverse peer influences.[8] Because of the potential importance of Filipino cultural identification in the emotional well-being of Filipinos (especially Filipino youth) in Hawai'i, we believe that it is important to further describe and understand "traditional" Filipino ethnocultural identity and the modern ethnocultural identity of Filipinos in Hawai'i. The following sections of this chapter will elaborate on these concepts.

Ethnocultural Identity

As noted in the previous section, Filipinos are a unique blend of many diverse cultures and influences. For the purposes of this chapter, and as a preface for the remainder of the discussion on ethnocultural identity, it is important to appreciate the significance of regional differences and regional pride among Filipinos. First, among the Filipino ethnic groups, controversies abound as to what language (national or regional) should best be used to describe Filipino traits. Some may feel that a description of common traits in the official Pilipino language is a slight to their regional dialect and culture. Indeed, the supposed primacy of Pilipino (based on standardized Tagalog spoken in the Manila region) as the nation's official language (and language used in several psychological studies on Filipinos to date) is put to a test when talking to Ilocano Filipinos in Hawai'i who may understand a bit of Pilipino but functionally communicate in Ilocano. Second, different Filipino subgroups may proudly recognize their differences from each other and feel that any attempt to describe a "Filipino culture" is akin to lumping Asians or Orientals together as a group without sensitivity to significant ethnic differences, and/or that it is a potentially emotionally laden reminder of the foreign colonization that unified the Philippines as a single country. It is posited that the developmental trajectory of the indigenous Filipino culture was interrupted by Spanish and American colonization, and hence Filipinos may grieve (consciously or unconsciously) about what we may have lost in terms of our identity and potential contributions to the world.

Mindful of these important issues, we will nevertheless attempt to describe (with the use of Pilipino terminology where appropriate) what we believe are the salient features of the Filipino ethnocultural identity.

Based on cross-cultural comparisons, we propose that, among Filipinos, the spirit of kinship and camaraderie *(bayanihan)* is likely derived from Austronesian origins, the close family ties and family hierarchy are likely derived from Chinese origins, and the Roman Catholic faith and festive and passionate temperament are likely derived from Spanish origins.

To understand the Filipinos is to accept the family as the strongest unit of the Philippine society, where traditional family core values of loyalty, respect, and a sense of gratitude and devotion to parents for life are inculcated. For Filipinos, the family is the source of identity and emotional and material support. Within the family there is a hierarchical system from the oldest to the youngest. The importance of family is impressed from childhood; children never attain equal footing with their parents, who are treated with respect and a debt of a lifetime. Children are expected to serve them to their death. There is no need for nursing homes; putting one's parents in a nursing home will incur shame (*hiyâ*, described further in this section). Loyalty to the family is expected and absolute. The good of the members must take precedence over the individual. Filipinos believe that they must live up to acceptable norms of behaviors that bring collective pride; failure to do so brings shame not only to themselves but to the family.

There are specific cultural norms, role definition, and ego ideals that have transformed the traditional image of Filipino women through each succeeding generation, from the so-called Maria Clara (referring to the noble and virtuous heroine in the novel *Noli Me Tangere,* written by the national Filipino hero and author Dr. José Rizal), who is shy, demure, modest, self-effacing, and dependent, to the more modern, assertive, self-sufficient, and autonomous person, as a result of a combination of factors such as westernization, education, and profession. The transformation has been more evident with the changing economic times, with more women out in the workforce becoming the breadwinners for the family and occupying roles that traditionally belonged to men. This role reversal may be a source of marital conflict, regardless of economic necessity, for psychological reasons: It may erode the Filipino man's "macho" image and the societal role expectation that men "bring home the bacon."

Borrowing from Erik Erickson's concept of epigenesis—that all development processes unfold in a succession of stages from birth to adulthood—it is proposed that the personality and psychological makeup of Filipino men is shaped and determined by various roles and responsibilities.[9] It is said that a "good Filipino son is more important than a good husband." The Filipino son, particularly the oldest son, carries enormous responsibilities, including continuing the family name in perpetuity (the most important one), serving as a role model for younger siblings, and devoting oneself unconditionally to one's parents for life. Oftentimes the oldest son sacrifices his own happiness for family obligations. Interdependence is encouraged and autonomy is discouraged, for "the good of the many must take precedence over the individual," and it is not uncommon that the whole family as a clan lives under one roof or in one compound.

Indeed, with a strong family and community orientation, the *self-construct* of Filipinos has been described as being more *interdependent/collectivist* (with a strong emphasis on group goals and achievement, nurturance, and closeness) and less *independent/individualistic* (with a strong emphasis on personal goals and achievement, self-reliance, and creativity) compared to westerners (see Triandis for a further discussion on the individualism-collectivism spectrum).[10]

The Filipinos are fun-loving people. They always have reason to celebrate and get together in such events as fiestas. The Filipinos are known for their hospitality and would go to extremes, such as selling their prized possessions to provide for guests. Filipinos are also known to draw upon humor as a means of coping with the burdens of everyday life—not to trivialize difficult situations, but to facilitate acceptance of events over which they have no control.

Being from one of only two Asian countries with a significant Roman Catholic majority (the other is East Timor), most Filipinos have faith in God as a source of hope and resilience during tough times. Innate religiosity and faith leave matters in God's hands: *bahalà na* (described further below) implies an absolute trust, which others may view as defeatist resignation, but among Filipinos it is a source of strength to endure insurmountable circumstances and suffering.

Along these lines, in examining the social behavior of Filipinos, four terms are often highlighted in the literature: *bahalà na* (literally translated as letting God [Bathalà] decide, conventionally interpreted to mean "fatalism," and more appropriately interpreted as "determination"); *hiyâ* (conventionally translated as "shame," but probably more appropriately translated as "propriety"); *utang na loob* (conventionally translated as "debt of gratitude," but probably more appropriately translated as "gratitude and solidarity"); and *pakikisama* (conventionally translated as "smooth interpersonal relations," but probably more appropriately translated as "companionship and esteem.").[11] Dr. Virgilio Enriquez, founder of Sikilohiyang Pilipino (indigenous Filipino psychology), and colleagues have pointed out that these terms were highlighted in early studies by nonindigenous observers who, at best, did not fully appreciate the subtleties of the indigenous languages (with complex affixation systems that can dramatically alter the meanings of root terms, such as *hiyâ*) and did not consider either related opposing or complementary values (such as *lakas ng loob* [guts/determination] and *pakikibaka* [resistance]) or the core indigenous values (such as *kapwà*, or shared identity) underlying the surface behaviors, and at worst, they perpetuated the oppression of Filipinos by highlighting what likely are colonial and accommodative behaviors.

Several of the aforementioned cultural traits may influence Filipinos' approach to self-care, conceptualization of illness and other problems, and help-seeking. Even in Hawai'i, it is not uncommon for Filipinos, with their strong spiritual orientation, to attribute both psychological and general medical conditions to supernatural causes and hence seek help from traditional healers (e.g., *herbolarios*). They may also attribute psychological problems to spirit possession, which is widespread enough in the Philippines that it may or may not indicate a pathological condition.[12] For example, depending upon the identity of the possessing spirit, the condition could be welcomed, disliked, or feared.

As a group, Asians in general and Filipinos in particular may attach stigma to seeking and receiving counseling and therapy. In Hawai'i, Filipinos—along with Chinese, Hawaiians, and Japanese—seem to underutilize mental health services in comparison to Caucasians.[13] For example, in the Filipino American Community Epidemiological Survey (of almost 2,300 adults) conducted in San Francisco and Honolulu, Gong et al. found that Filipino-Americans frequently utilize lay practitioners as opposed to the professional system as a source of care for mental health problems.[14] They further found that concern with "face" and being a monolingual Filipino-language speaker decreased the likelihood of utilizing mental health specialty care. As part of this same study, Abe-Kim et al. found that high religiosity correlated with more help-seeking from clergy but not necessarily less from mental health professionals, while high spirituality correlated with less help-seeking from mental health professionals.[15]

Not infrequently, Filipinos in Hawai'i have sought mental health services only as a last resort, with a notable delay in treatment and support services. It is felt that feelings of *hiyâ* may pose a barrier in sharing problems. Substance abuse, domestic violence, and physical abuse may therefore go underreported because of fear of shaming the family and losing them in the process of getting help; shame to the family may be seen as more hurtful than any other individually experienced distress.

A New Ethnocultural Identity

In this section, we propose that the Filipinos of Hawai'i currently represent a diverse group, with a unique ethnocultural identity that maintains significant threads of continuity with traditional Filipino ethnocultural identity and that also reflects molding by the various social and historical forces that Filipino immigrants faced in the past 104 years, including the upward social mobility that likely drove much of the immigration. This reflects an adaptive integration of the culture of Hawaiians (who are fellow Austronesians with the Filipinos) and other peoples in Hawai'i in what likely is a mostly multicultural society. (This is in contrast to the *melting pot*—with low preservation of heritage cultures and identity, or a segregated or exclusionary society.) It is worth noting that as early as between 1948 and 1953, the percentage of Filipino intermarriages had risen to 35 percent (almost twice what it had been twenty years earlier), the majority occurring to Hawaiians, Caucasians, and Japanese.[16] These statistics would indicate that today's Filipinos in Hawai'i are likely significantly intermingled with other ethnic groups and cultural influences.

When asked about traditional Filipino culture, second-generation Filipino-Americans cite a variety of characteristics, including cultural celebrations, use of Philippine languages, matriarchal families, respect for the elderly as a source of wisdom, and education as an opportunity to achieve upward mobility. They may also recall examples of how Filipino cultural characteristics have changed in Hawai'i—for example, the replacement of conservative dress with "urban hip-hop" attire, the migration from the traditional Roman Catholic Church to contemporary Christian churches (with multimedia presentations), and the incorporation of various elements of local culture (ranging from food to language).

It is commonly believed that Hawai'i's multicultural society is very harmonious with the inclusive and welcoming nature of Filipino culture. If Berry's different modes of acculturation are applied—namely, *integration, assimilation, separation,* and *marginalization*—the authors propose that Filipinos most likely fall on the integration corner of the spectrum (i.e., high maintenance of heritage culture and high seeking of relationship with larger society).[17]

When asked to describe Filipino characteristics that seem to be prominent, notwithstanding years of outside influence, second-generation Filipino-Americans cite the strong family ties, strong personal relationships, and musical/artistic abilities that they observe in Filipinos, whether they be first, second, or later generations.

In reviewing the characteristics of Hawai'i's Filipinos throughout the life cycle, there are several examples that illustrate the interface between traditional culture, social environmental pressures, and integration of other cultures in Hawai'i. During pregnancy and childbirth, there are various superstitions that Filipinos living in Hawai'i appear to subscribe to.[18] For example, these include prohibitions on certain activities during pregnancy and ways to determine the sex of the baby. In Hawai'i, Filipino baby names often reflect current trends among Filipinos elsewhere, including adopting the mother's maiden name as one of the given middle names (similar to Spanish tradition), combining elements of both parents' names to produce a hybrid first name, creating new spellings of a common name, such as by inserting the letter "h" into the name, creating a nickname out of the initials of the first and middle names, or applying other "cute" nicknames (common ones being "Boy," "Baby," or "Pinky," which are carried even through adulthood). Another is nicknames that involve reduplication of a part of the original name (such as "Jun-Jun" for a boy who is a junior or "Ton-Ton").

Filipinos appear to have the lowest rates of breastfeeding at six months of age among the various ethnic groups in Hawai'i.[19] As physicians, the authors of this chapter do indeed observe breastfeeding cessation attributed to a *perceived* incompatibility between continued breastfeeding and a successful return to work, typically in the context of a family striving for both upward social mobility and financial survival in the United States.

Similar to other cultures in Hawai'i, Filipinos tend to have lavish celebrations for their offspring at their one-year birthday, often in conjunction with the child's baptism, and again at high school graduation. If not concurrent with the high school graduation, a traditional "coming of age" celebration may also occur on the eighteenth birthday (also called a debut for females). But the "coming of age" celebration in Hawai'i generally does not have as high a priority for families as the high school graduation, depending on the degree of local acculturation. It is not uncommon for Filipino children to live with their parents until either completion of education (including higher education) or marriage.

Filipino weddings in Hawai'i may highlight traditional Filipino wedding rituals derived mainly from Spanish Roman Catholic rituals, including the coin ceremony, in which coins are passed from the groom to the bride and then back to the groom. This custom symbolizes prosperity and the sharing of resources for the future family's benefit. Furthermore, the veil ceremony symbolizes unity and the pledge of protection from the groom, to whom the bride's veil is also pinned. Finally, other wedding customs are the cord ceremony, which symbolizes unity and infinite love between the bride and groom when they are joined with a figure-eight cord; and the candle ceremony, which symbolizes God's presence in the joined lives and spirits of the bride and groom, who together light a unity candle from their individual candles, which are then extinguished. Filipino weddings often include a multitude of sponsors or godparents. Filipino wedding receptions in Hawai'i may include a traditional money dance, in which guests present cash to the dancing bride and groom, who may in turn pass the money to each other. These customs are commonly structured according to local Hawai'i traditions, including humorous commentary by an emcee, a professionally produced slide show, and local music.

Adulthood for Filipinos in Hawai'i is often a balance between raising children, earning enough money to survive in the socioeconomic climate of Hawai'i (and in many cases providomg for family back in the Philippines), and tending to the needs of older relatives, who often live in the same extended family household. Grandparents are often very involved in child care and may view this as a normative role.[20] Grandparents and other extended family may play an important role in addressing health disparities among Filipino youth in Hawai'i, including possible nutritional deficiencies and high rates of dental caries.[21]

Filipino customs around death have strong Roman Catholic influences (e.g., particularly the nine-day Novena) and reflect an overall belief in life after death and the eminent presence of the spirit of the deceased. Braun and Nichols have described how traditional customs and beliefs have been modified by other cultures (including modern American culture) in Hawai'i, for example, a shorter duration of mourning (less than a year) when family members must wear black and greater acceptability of cremation.[22]

In the following table, we summarize how Filipino values, beliefs, and customs molded by historical and local influences appear to be manifest in the practices and behaviors of modern Filipinos in Hawai'i.

Table 9.1. Filipino values, beliefs, and customs manifested in the practices and behaviors of modern Filipinos in Hawai'i

TRADITIONAL AND LIKELY ENDURING VALUE, BELIEF, OR CUSTOM	HISTORICAL OR IMMIGRATION-RELATED INFLUENCE	"LOCAL" SOCIO-CULTURAL INFLU-ENCES IN HAWAI'I	PRACTICE, BEHAVIOR, OR OTHER OUTWARD MANIFESTATION
Spirituality	Immigration from northern (mostly Roman Catholic) regions of the Philippines	"Liberaliza-tion" of religion; multiculturalism	Variable to regular attendance at Roman Catholic or other Christian church services
Family orientation	Adaptation to hard-ship and need to share resources	Congruence with "local" family values	Extended family homes
			Frequent family gatherings
			Cooperation around child care
Upward social mobility and seek-ing of a better life	"Natural selec-tion" for this value among those choosing to immi-grate to Hawai'i	Local standards for what constitutes higher or lower social status	Adoption of lat-est fads reflecting social status; risk for materialism
		Challenging local economy	Potential over-employment
			Emphasis on school achievement
	Sending of money and other resources back to the Philippines	Availability of jobs that may or may not pay well in U.S. dollars but that enable higher earn-ings than jobs in the Philippines	Regular sending of money (often, sub-stantial portions of the paycheck) back to the Philippines (e.g., via Western Union, Xoom, and other companies)
	Current immigra-tion laws		Strategic plans to enable immigration of relatives
Culture of caring	Allowances for immigration of nurses and certain other profession-als in the face of shortages	Market for care homes and ongo-ing shortage of registered nurses	Desirability of careers in the health professions
			Majority of care homes in Hawai'i operated by Filipinos

Table 9.1. *(continued)*

TRADITIONAL AND LIKELY ENDURING VALUE, BELIEF, OR CUSTOM	HISTORICAL OR IMMIGRATION-RELATED INFLUENCE	"LOCAL" SOCIO-CULTURAL INFLU-ENCES IN HAWAIʻI	PRACTICE, BEHAVIOR, OR OTHER OUTWARD MANIFESTATION
Connection to the mother country	Maintained by original immigrants	Multiculturalism, overall ethnic pride	Cell phones and calling cards
			Trips to the Philippines (usually, via one of the two airlines—Philippine Airlines and Hawaiian Airlines—that currently offer direct flights)
			Popularity of the Filipino Channel (TFC)
			Specialty stores and groceries in Hawaiʻi, notably in the Kalihi and Waipahu areas of Oʻahu
Filipino arts		Multiculturalism, local modifications	Local and Western-influenced music and other arts
			Popularity of karaoke
			Success of certain Filipino-American artists/musicians
Filipino food			Filipino food items as part of local "comfort food" (e.g., chicken adobo with white rice and macaroni salad, as part of a local "plate lunch")
Filipino life celebrations			Lavish baptisms, first birthdays, high school graduations, weddings that integrate components of "local" culture and customs

Biopsychosocial Factors

This section attempts to summarize what is known about Filipino ethnicity and culture in Hawai'i from biological, psychological, and social perspectives and to expand on the notion of malleability and evolution of cultural identity. As noted in the previous section, we believe that the Filipinos who immigrated to Hawai'i were likely selected for adaptability and ability to harmoniously integrate other cultural influences—notwithstanding potential hardwired or enduring adaptive characteristics, as well as the probability that Filipinos, as a result of conscious or subconscious resentment toward colonization, may also have important anchors that resist change and maintain an indigenous identity.

To discuss potential hardwired characteristics among Filipinos as a group lends itself to potentially negative stereotyping: the thick accent, the slaughtering and eating of "black dog," or the eating of strong-smelling foods such as dried salted fish and salted shrimp paste, or *bagoong*. For there is more to Filipinos than stereotypes. The concept of hardwiring may incorrectly imply a static rather than dynamic phenomenon, modifiable by both the individual and the environment. We have gleaned from self-reflection, observations, and interviews with Filipino consultants in Hawai'i appropriate examples of biological, psychological, and social characteristics that are relatively enduring and prominently manifested (albeit in a modified, adaptive form) even with years of living in Hawai'i.

Some enduring traits have biological origins. For example, Filipinos have been found to have higher rates of conditions that may reflect natural selection by the environments in which they evolved. They include thalassemia, a type of anemia, usually mild, that may have been protective against malaria; glucose-6-phosphate dehydrogenase deficiency, an enzyme deficiency that poses some limitations on food choices and medications and that, again, may have been protective against malaria; relative intolerance of milk products and alcohol; and thyroid dysfunctions, including thyroid cancer.[23] Certain physical characteristics are also typical of Filipinos, such as smaller stature, darker complexion, and smaller nasal bridges relative to the "average American" or "average European." While these physical characteristics are neither inherently good nor bad, they may have a negative or positive impact on body image or even the perceived ability to succeed in a Western-centric world. One study found that Filipino male youths living in Hawai'i may be at particular risk for body and self-image dissatisfaction.[24]

Moving into the social and psychological area, certain traits are likely to have been enduring because of the Filipino language. The respectfulness and familial orientation observed among Filipinos is also reflected in various terms for which there is no English translation: for example, the grammatical inclusion of *po'* in sentences to indicate respect toward the one being spoken to; and specific terms for older brother/male relative/male peer (*kuya* in Tagalog, *manong* in Ilocano), older sister/female relative/female peer (*ate* in Tagalog, *manang* in Ilocano), and even younger people (*nonoy/nene* for a younger male/female sibling in Bicolano, *ading* for a younger person in Ilocano). Another enduring physical expression is the *mano po'* greeting, involving placing one's forehead on the hand of the person being respected (e.g., an older relative, priest, or other). The *relative* (though by no means absolute) gender equality in Filipino families is reflected in the finding that— other than words for "mother," "father," "female," and "male"—there are few gender-specific terms (for example, to say "sister" in Tagalog, one would need to say "sibling who is female") and no gender-specific pronouns (often exposing Filipinos to teasing when males are referred to as "she" and females are referred to "he") in the indigenous Filipino languages. It may also be hypothesized that the observed affiliativeness of Filipinos and attentiveness to personal relations is reflected in the distinction (among pronouns) between "we" (first-person plural, inclusive of the person being spoken to) and "we" (first-person plural, *not* inclusive of the person being spoken to). This characteristic exists in other Austronesian languages as well, including the Hawaiian language ('Ōlelo Hawai'i). Other terms (such as *utang na loob*) introduced in the section on ethnocultural identity, by virtue of their existence without an exact English translation, may reflect relatively enduring cultural characteristics.

As gleaned through self-reflection, observation, and consultation with informants, there are several psychological and social traits that seem very enduring among Filipinos, even among second-generation Filipinos (and beyond) who have lived for most of their lives in Hawai'i. These include a fun-loving nature (whether manifested in the fiestas in honor of the hometown patron saint or the block party with impressive spreads of ethnic and local food in the garage), musicality (including an apparent ability to effortlessly mimic celebrity singers and musicians), and spirituality/religiosity (whether practiced in a traditional Roman Catholic church, in a contemporary nondenominational Christian service, or via traditional animistic beliefs).

In the following table, we summarize the biological, psychological, and social/cultural characteristics that we feel are important to consider in meaningfully understanding Filipinos in Hawai'i.

Table 9.2. Summary of biological, psychological, and social/cultural characteristics important to consider in working with and meaningfully understanding Filipinos in Hawai'i

Biological
Body image; relevant facial and body characteristics
Physical health and illnesses (e.g., thyroid disorders) in self and family

Psychological
Self-esteem and how one achieves it
Education and career aspirations
Talents (e.g., music) and recreational activities

Social
Family jobs and income
Amount of money sent back to the Philippines
Number of people in the household
Adult supervision and time spent with youth
Peer influences (positive or negative)
Expected versus desired roles in the family and in other relationships
Closeness with the community and neighborhood
What part of the Philippines originally from

Cultural
What part of the Philippines originally from
Generation in Hawai'i
Wave of immigration (e.g., plantation worker, health professional)
Cultural identification and practices (with examples, including language) of self, adult caregivers, and peers
Degree of perceived conflict or integration of culture
Ethnic/cultural pride
Community of residence in Hawai'i
Religious/spiritual practices
Explanations of health conditions and preferred sources of help

Summary and Conclusions

We began this chapter with the intention of further describing ethnocultural identity of modern Filipinos in Hawai'i. We have described how Filipinos, with a culture deeply rooted in family and spirituality, have survived numerous adversities throughout history and have resiliently adapted to other cultural influences in Hawai'i and other realities of their current social environment.

We hope that readers in Hawai'i and elsewhere in the world can appreciate how from a scholarly perspective, the story of the Filipino experience in Hawai'i can play a role in helping immigrant groups who have shared similar experiences. We especially hope that Filipino readers of this chapter have experienced a validation of their cultural experience in Hawai'i and will benefit from an awareness of the challenges that they continue to face as an ethnocultural group removed from the mother country. Finally, we hope that readers of other ethnic groups in Hawai'i—particularly the Hawaiians—can sense the gratitude of these Filipino authors (and likely many other Filipino immigrants) for welcoming us to Hawai'i and allowing a synergistic sharing of cultures to take place.

Further Reading

Enriquez, V., ed. *Indigenous Psychology: A Book of Readings*. Diliman, Quezon City, Philippines: Philippine Psychology Research and Training House, 1990.

Infante Nii, E., and B. Creamer. "Silent struggle yields first fruits of labor." *Honolulu Advertiser*, October 10, 1999: A1, A8.

Pe-Pua, R., and E. Protacio-Marcelino. "Sikolohiyang Pilipino (Filipino psychology): A legacy of Virgilio G. Enriquez." *Asian Journal of Social Psychology* 3 (2000): 49–71.

"The Philippine History Site." http://opmanong.ssc.hawaii.edu/filipino/filmig.html. Accessed March 19, 2009.

Ponce, D. E., and S. Forman. "The Filipinos." In *People and Cultures of Hawai'i: A Psychocultural Profile*, ed. J. F. McDermott, W. S. Tseng, and T. W. Maretzki. Honolulu: University of Hawai'i Press, 1980: 155–183.

Notes

Authors' note: We would like to thank our consultants and informants for their useful input, synthesized into the content of this chapter.

1. R. G. Gordon Jr., ed., *Ethnologue: Languages of the World*, 15th ed., Dallas: SIL International, 2005, online version: http://www.ethnologue.com/, accessed March 19, 2009.

2. D. E. Ponce and S. Forman, "The Filipinos," in *People and Cultures of Hawai'i: A Psychocultural Profile*, ed. J. F. McDermott, W. S. Tseng, and T. W. Maretzki, Honolulu: University of Hawai'i Press, 1980: 155–183.

3. Choy, Catherine Ceniza. *Empire of Care: Nursing and Migration in Filipino American History*. Durham, NC: Duke University Press, 2003.

4. V. L. Cunanan, A. P. S. Guerrero, and L. Minamoto, "Filipinos and the myth of the model minority," *Journal of Ethnic and Cultural Diversity in Social Work* 15(1–2) (2006): 167–192.

5. E. Infante Nii and B. Creamer, "Silent struggle yields first fruits of labor," *Honolulu Advertiser*, October 10, 1999: A1, A8

6. A. P. S. Guerrero, E. S. Hishinuma, N. N. Andrade, S. T. Nishimura, and V. L. Cunanan, "Correlations among socioeconomic and family factors and academic, behavioral, and emotional difficulties in Filipino adolescents in Hawai'i," *International Journal of Social Psychiatry* 52(4) (2006): 343–359.

7. Cunanan et al. 2006.

8. A. P. S. Guerrero, S. T. Nishimura, J. Y. Chang, C. Ona, V. L. Cunanan, and E. S. Hishinuma, "Low cultural identification, low parental involvement, and adverse peer influences as risk factors for delinquent behaviour among Filipino youth in Hawai'i," *International Journal of Social Psychiatry* 56(4) (2010): 371–387.

9. D. S. Newton, "Erik H. Erikson," in *Kaplan & Sadock's Comprehensive Textbook of Psychiatry*, 8th ed., ed. B. J. Sadock and V. A. Sadock, Philadelphia: Lippincott Williams & Wilkins, 2004: 749.

10. H. C. Triandis, "The self and social behavior in differing cultural contexts," *Psychological Review* 96(3) (1989): 506–520.

11. R. Pe-Pua and E. Protacio-Marcelino, "Sikolohiyang Pilipino (Filipino psychology): A legacy of Virgilio G. Enriquez," *Asian Journal of Social Psychology* 3 (2000): 49–71.

12. J. C. Bulatao, *Phenomena and Their Interpretation: Landmark Essays, 1957–1989*, Manila: Ateneo de Manila University Press, 1992.

13. J. L. Chin, "Mental health services and treatment," in *Handbook of Asian American Psychology*, ed. L. C. Lee and N. W. S. Zane, Thousand Oaks, CA: Sage, 1998: 485–504.

14. F. Gong, S. L. Gage, and L. A. Tacata Jr., "Helpseeking behavior among Filipino Americans: A cultural analysis of face and language," *Journal of Community Psychology* 31(5) (2003): 469–488.

15. J. Abe-Kim, F. Gong, and D. Takeuchi, "Religiosity, spirituality, and help-seeking among Filipino Americans: Religious clergy or mental health professionals," *Journal of Community Psychology* 32(6) (2004): 675–689.

16. T. Labov and J. A. Jacobs, "Intermarriage in Hawaii 1950–1983," *Journal of Marriage and the Family* 48(1) (1986): 79–88.

17. J. W. Berry, "Globalisation and acculturation," *International Journal of Intercultural Relations* 32 (2008): 328–336.

18. Hawaii Community College Division of Nursing and Allied Health, "Traditional health beliefs student pages," 2007, http://www.hawcc.hawaii .edu/nursing/transcultural.html, accessed May 19, 2009.

19. S. R. Pager, J. Davis, and R. Harrigan, "Prevalence of breastfeeding among a multiethnic population in Hawaiʻi," *Ethnicity & Disease* 18(2 suppl. 2) (2008): S2-215–218.

20. M. R. Kataoka-Yahiro, C. Ceria, and M. Yoder. "Grandparent caregiving role in Filipino American families," *Journal of Cultural Diversity* 11(3) (2004): 110–117.

21. J. R. Javier, L. C. Huffman, and F. S. Mendoza, "Filipino child health in the United States: Do health and health care disparities exist?" *Preventing Chronic Disease* 4(2) (serial online) (2007), accessed May 19, 2009, available from http://www.cdc.gov/pcd/issues/2007/apr/06_0069.htm.

22. K. L. Braun and R. Nichols, "Death and dying in four Asian American cultures: A descriptive study," *Death Studies* 21 (1997): 327–359.

23. J. R. Clark, S. J. Eski, and J. L. Freeman, "Risk of malignancy in Filipinos with thyroid nodules: A matched pair analysis," *Head & Neck* 28(5) (2006): 427–431.

24. A. Yates, J. Edman, and M. Aruguete, "Ethnic differences in BMI and body/self dissatisfaction among whites, Asian sub-groups, Pacific Islanders, and African-Americans," *Journal of Adolescent Health* 34(4) (2004): 300–307.

CHAPTER 10

The Blacks

John W. Hawkins and Emily A. Hawkins

The history of blacks[1] in Hawai'i is primarily a story of independent arrivals, not the story of migrant laborers or missionaries who came in groups. For that reason, their story is very unlike the other groups in Hawai'i. Until World War II, these arrivals came from the U.S. mainland to settle in a place where they could work and live without the fear of slavery and its aftermath. Each one tells an individual tale, and those who stayed became part of Hawaiian society in their own way. After the war, those who stayed once again blended into Hawaiian society, often with a spouse of another race. Each of them lived life as a citizen of Hawai'i, proud of being black, but not often asked to identify him or herself by race.

The major sources describing the historical and ethnocultural perspective of blacks in Hawai'i used in this chapter are the following: (1) the journal *Social Process in Hawai'i*, Dr. Miles Jackson as guest editor; (2) data in the State Archives containing information contributed by Darlene E. Kelley; (3) two consultants for this chapter, Dr. James Horton and Dr. Winifred Simmons;[2] and (4) information obtained from our interviewees.

The earliest known settlers of African ancestry came to Hawai'i in 1810. Most of the early arrivals were crew aboard merchant or whaling ships. Kelley cites an individual called "Black Jack," or Mr. Keaka'ele'ele, living on O'ahu when Kamehameha conquered the island in 1796.[3] Keaka'ele'ele became a sail master for King Kamehameha II and made his living in the maritime industry. Many in the crews of the merchant and whaling ships were descendants of black Portuguese men from the Cape Verde Islands (see chapter 4, "The Portuguese").[4]

Another early settler was a Mr. Anthony Allen, an ex-slave, who had arrived in Hawai'i in 1810 and married a Hawaiian woman. Marc Scruggs quotes Maria S. Loomis, a missionary wife, in writing about Allen:

> Among the residents of this Island is a Black man native of Sche-nectady named Allen. He has been our constant friend, has daily furnished us with milk and once or twice a week with fresh meat and vegetables. He has also made us a number of other valuable presents.... He lives on a beautiful plain called Wyteta [Waikīkī] about two miles from this village.... He stood at his gate to wel-come us into a neat little room treated us to wine, sat down with us a short time and left us to prepare for dinner. His wihena [wahine] kept in her little bedroom seated on the mat with her babe about 8 months old. His little daughter Peggy a bright child of six years was very attentive. Dinner being ready we were in invited to the eating house.... After dinner we walked out to view his territories. He has a large enclosure with 8 or 10 house[s], which are an eating, cooking, and sleeping house. The rest are occupied by boarders and tenants.[5]

Mr. Allen became a very successful resident of Hawai'i. He pros-pered in a number of enterprises. He opened a farm, ran a boarding house for seamen, built the first school in the Islands, and the first road to Mānoa Valley. The monarchy gave Mr. Allen land, which he could pass on to his descendants. This land is the current site of Washington Intermediate School. Mr. Allen died in 1835 a well-respected member of the Hawaiian society.

Betsy Stockton was an ex-slave of the president of Princeton University who had used the library of her ex-master and attended evening classes at Princeton Theological Seminary.[6] She arrived in Hawai'i accompanying the Charles Stewart family with a group of missionaries in 1822. She quickly learned the Hawaiian language, and responding to requests from Hawaiians she established the first school for common-ers. This school for *maka'āinana* is the site upon which Lahainaluna School presently stands. Although she was in Hawai'i for only two years, her school served as a model for the Hilo Boarding School.[7] One of the missionaries in the group, C. S. Stewart, had this to say regarding Bessie Stockton:

Within three days, two other infants have been brought to our yard, in most distressing situations; one, with a shocking wound on its arm, from a cut by a broken bottle, and the other almost expiring with the croup. Both are already in a state of safety; and probably have been rescued from death by the prompt exertion of [Bessie], who took them immediately under her care. (July 4, 1823, journal entry)[8]

A precursor to the Royal Hawaiian Band, a royal brass band, was commissioned in 1834 by King Kamehameha III. This band consisted of four blacks, with George Washington Hyatt as the first master. These men were part of a group of maritime individuals who stayed in Hawai'i to become cooks, barbers, tailors, and/or members of musical groups.[9]

Although a diminishing labor force precipitated a discussion about importing African-American workers for the plantations, there was resistance on the part of the power brokers of Hawai'i. Nordyke notes that in 1881, U.S. Secretary of State James G. Blaine urged the importation of blacks for the cultivation of rice and sugar in Hawai'i, with the reasoning that "The Hawaiian Islands cannot be joined to the Asiatic system. If they drift from their independent station it must be toward an assimilation and identification with the American system, to which they belong by the operation of natural laws and must belong by the operation of political necessity."[10]

But John E. Bush, a hapa Hawaiian and president of the Kingdom of Hawai'i's Board of Immigration, reported that the Legislature was decidedly averse to Negro immigrants.[11] With the continuing need for labor, however, the Hawaiian Sugar Planters' Association recruited a number of black families to work on Maui in 1907. Nordyke makes an interesting observation that does have an impact on the African-American community presently: "Many of these people merged with the residents through intermarriage and association with local groups but others returned to the U.S. They did not establish a separate homogeneous community and their identity as Blacks [was] diffused with that of other Island ethnic groups."[12]

Immigration

African-Americans in Hawai'i were not part of a large immigration movement similar to the Euro-Americans (e.g., sailors, merchants, missionaries, and bankers) or the Chinese, Portuguese, Japanese, Okinawan, or Filipino ethnic groups that worked as plantation workers. Many African-Americans who came and stayed in Hawai'i pursued careers in the professional, business, athletic, and entertainment fields. Four phases of immigration patterns can be identified: during the nineteenth century, the twentieth century up to World War II, World War II (1941–1945), and post–World War II.

During the nineteenth century, black immigrants came as runaway or freed slaves from America and as sailors from the Caribbean islands, the Portuguese colonies, and Africa. They arrived on trading, whaling, and merchant ships from various parts of the world. Many had skills as sailmakers, musicians, barbers, cooks, navigators, and educators.

From 1900 to World War II, the blacks who settled in Hawai'i were professionals in education, law, and entrepreneurial areas. One of these professionals included Carlotta Stewart Lai, who arrived in Hawai'i with her father in 1898 and became the first black principal in Hawai'i. After graduating from O'ahu College (Punahou School) and then completing the requirements for a Normal School teaching certificate in 1902, she taught at Punahou. In 1909 she was promoted to principal of the Ko'olau Elementary School and served as a principal and teacher for the next seventeen years, retiring in 1945.[13] In 1901, William Crockett arrived in Maui as a legal representative for a small group of African-Americans recruited to work for plantations on Maui. Even after most of the group left, Crockett and his wife stayed. Their son, Judge Wendell Crockett, married a part-Hawaiian woman and followed in his father's footsteps, becoming a lawyer. He would later become the first black judge on Maui. From 1913 to 1918, the U.S. Army's all-black 25th Infantry Regiment was assigned to Hawai'i. This regiment, known as the "Buffalo Soldiers," had a record of distinguished military service. One of their significant contributions to Hawai'i during their assignment period here was the construction of a building and a trail leading up to the summit of Mauna Loa that served as an access to a research station that would become part of the Volcano National Observatory.

World War II is noted for the arrival of entire military units. Historically, this was a time when minorities would increasingly demand and receive equal status and respect in military and civilian life. Bailey and Farber discuss the changing relationship of racial identities and cultural influences in chronicling the 1942 assignment of the all-black 369th Coastal Artillery Regiment to Hawai'i: "The men of the 369th would use their training, their character, and the opportunities of wartime Hawai'i to change the racial boundaries of white and black.... These men saw themselves as outstanding soldiers who wanted to be treated as such."[14]

Along with Bailey and Farber, Broussard describes race relations in Hawai'i during World War II:

> The relatively tolerant and tranquil racial atmosphere that African Americans such as T. McCants Steward and his daughter Carlotta had encountered in Hawai'i during the early decades of the twentieth century changed dramatically with the importation of American service personnel. White servicemen and their commanding officers attempted to recreate the segregated policies and practices that had existed on the mainland for nearly a century, and, to a large extent, they succeeded. White servicemen, for instance, spread vicious rumors about black people in general and black soldiers in particular, portraying them as thieves, rapists, murderers, criminals, and carrying a multitude of diseases. Blacks could not be trusted under any circumstance, and were a particular menace to the islands' female population.[15]

According to Bailey and Farber these military men left after World War II and took their Hawai'i experiences back to the continental U.S.: "Some were bitter.... Others never forgot the new friends of all races they made. Most saw their experiences in Hawai'i as mixed—and complicated."[16]

The post–World War II period saw an increased movement of blacks to Hawai'i, not as a large group but as individuals seeking educational, professional, and business opportunities. Many blacks are part of contemporary Hawai'i's large military presence, but most of these individuals and their families return to the U.S. mainland after serving their tour of duty. There is also an older, often retired group that moved to Hawai'i either part or full time. Among this older group of black professionals was journalist and poet Frank Marshall Davis, who remained until his death forty years later in 1986. Davis received much attention after being referred to as "Frank" in President Barack Obama's *Dreams from My Father.* He contributed to the young Obama's developing identity. Davis had also been instrumental in the labor movement when Hawai'i was changing from a plantation economy to the present economy.[17]

In the 2000 census, there were 33,000 individuals who listed black or African-American as one of their ethnicities, or about 3 percent of Hawai'i's total population of 1.2 million. Seventy-three percent (22,000) of these ethnic blacks identified only one race and most (about 21,000) were on the island of O'ahu, home to Hawai'i's U.S. military units. According to the Redistricting Data, P.L. 94–171, Hawai'i's black or African-American population is projected to grow to approximately 42,000 by 2025.

Ethnocultural Identity

Question: "Do you consider yourself to be part of an African-American community?" Answer: "A black community, yes, but not an African-American community." This answer is indicative of the challenge in naming this chapter.[18] To use "African-American" as a heading for this chapter would have been a bit of a misnomer or at least a misleading catchall. A considerable number of the people covered in this chapter were not born here but have come as immigrants from other places. "Immigrant" means anyone not born in Hawai'i; therefore, North Americans of all groups who move here are considered immigrants. In the conversation between Marsha Joyner and Pōkā Laenui, Laenui clarifies the use of "immigrant" by saying, "However they arrive, as slaves, free people, military, all who come in are, nonetheless, immigrants in the eyes of the indigenous community.... When they stay, they become settlers."[19]

The persons of African descent who reside in Hawai'i are a mix of many peoples. Some have come directly from Africa, primarily as students; others have come directly from the Caribbean or are of Caribbean descent but have come via North America. And finally, there are those who were born and raised in North America. Some of our African-American interviewees would have limited the scope of the group included here. The authors, however, have decided to include all persons of African descent in order to look at the broadest possible group, and consequently we have labeled this chapter "The Blacks." This title best represents the diversity within the subgroups in Hawai'i. The census data does not separate blacks and African-Americans.

To complicate the picture even more, black immigrants have often married and had children with nonblacks, resulting in a significant number of mixed race or hapa individuals. In the 2000 U.S. Census, a third of resident blacks in Hawai'i listed more than a single heritage. While the "one-drop" rule would define them as African-American or at least black in the continental United States, the multicultural milieu of Hawai'i results in a variety of community-accepted identities. According to Root, the racial mixes about which there has been the most concern are those boundaries between groups that are very socially distant— that is, blacks and whites and Japanese and whites.[20] Tatum presents an interesting discussion on the "one-drop" rule:

> Physical appearance was an unreliable criterion for maintaining this boundary (between races) because the light-skinned children of White slave masters and enslaved Black women sometimes resembled their fathers more than their mothers. Ancestry rather than appearance became the important criterion. In both legal and social practice, anyone with any known African ancestry was considered Black.... Known as the "one-drop rule" this practice solidified the boundary between Black and White.[21]

For most citizens of the United States, this "one-drop" rule is still applicable and only applies to blacks in America. The best current example of this is the forty-fourth president of the United States, Barack Obama. For most of us in Hawai'i, Mr. Obama is hapa: He is as much white as he is black. Yet he is referred to as the "first black American president." African-American scholar Professor James Horton posits that the term "race" was primarily a social construct:

> And here is where it really gets interesting. You got some places, for example, Virginia—Virginia law defined a black person as a person with one sixteenth African ancestry. Now Florida defined a black person as a person with one eighth African ancestry. And Alabama said, "You are black if you got any black ancestry, or any African ancestry at all." But you know what this means? You can walk across a state line and literally, legally, change race. Now what does race mean under those circumstances? You give me the power, I can make you any race I want you to be, because it is a social, political construction. It is not a matter of biology.[22]

The authors suggest that for this chapter, the use of the terms "race" and "ethnicity" represent two separate entities. As Dr. Horton describes above, the use of "race" has become a social and political construct. "Ethnicity" relates to the ancestral background that incorporates one's cultural traditions, values, and beliefs.

Racism has greatly affected how blacks have been accounted for in the history of Hawai'i and how blacks in Hawai'i have identified themselves. Historians have largely omitted mention of early black settlers and their accomplishments. Carrying forward to today, this diminishes the contribution of blacks, making them nearly invisible. Two notable examples involve Hawai'i bandmasters and the work toward a cure for leprosy.

In a recent biography of a nonblack musician, his great-great-grandfather is given as the first bandmaster of the Royal Hawaiian Band. However, the Royal Hawaiian Band had grown out of King Kamehameha III's band, which was composed of black musicians with black bandmasters Oliver in 1836 and George Washington Hyatt from 1845 to 1848.[23] In the quest to find a cure for leprosy, credit was not appropriately attributed to Alice Ball, the first African-American to teach at the University of Hawai'i in the early 1900s. Ball was a chemistry instructor who extracted chaulmoogra oil and found that when injected, it relieved some of the symptoms of Hansen's disease.[24] Historical omissions such as these have resulted in blacks being marginalized and erased in the popular history of Hawai'i, even though there are several individuals whose contributions are equal to or greater than the recorded historical figures.

When touring the United States in 1849, two of Hawai'i's future kings were identified as "Coloreds" and treated so badly that they returned to Hawai'i with a strong desire not to be in a close alliance with the United States and be mistaken for black. Prince Alexander Liholiho gave this account of his trip from Washington, D.C., to New York City in June 1850:

> The next morning while at the Station waiting for the baggage to be checked, Mr. Judd told me to get in and secure seats. While I was sitting looking out of the window, a man came to me and told me to get out of the carriage rather unceremoniously saying that I was in the wrong carriage. I immediately asked him what he meant. He continued his request, finally he came around to the door and I went out to meet him. Just as he was coming in, somebody whispered a word into his ears—by this time I came up to him, and asked him his reasons for telling me to get out of that carriage. He then told me to keep my seat. . . . I found out he was the conductor, and probably had taken me for somebody's servant, just because I had a darker skin than he had. Confounded fool. . . . Here I must state that I am disappointed at the Americans.[25]

Is it any wonder that descendents of black fathers and Hawaiian mothers chose to identify as Hawaiian from the earliest times? Many blacks live in Hawai'i without being aware of this history and the individuals who have come before. Due to the lack of segregated housing, their small percentage in the total population, and the variety of black occupations in Hawai'i, daily life does not even include a physical sense of being in a community with other African-Americans. We may acknowledge each other on a very basic level with a nod or the raising of an eyebrow, but closer association is reserved for the organizations or subgroups to which one may belong. Within the black community, there are strong feelings about the different subgroups. Some African-Americans are quick to point out that Africans and mixed-race people (hapa) are not part of their group. Among hapa blacks, some may not identify themselves as African-Americans but rather as "other" or local. Since the larger community in Hawai'i does not force them to choose, they have a freedom that those in North America do not. The one subgroup that may be clustered as being monolithic is the military service personnel, especially those who live on base.

THE FAMILY

For African-American families, the presence and availability of the extended family is extremely important. Families tend to be hierarchical and are likely to be strict, to hold demanding behavioral standards, and to use physical discipline. This is a shared feature with many of Hawai'i's ethnicities. According to Nicholson and Barbarin, grandmothers generally play a major role in the maintenance of the African-American family.[26] The African-American family is more likely to care for aging or dying family members. And the key cultural features for African-American families are (1) spirituality, (2) mutual support, (3) ethnic identity, (4) adaptive extended family structures, and (5) church as offering both ideological and instrumental support.

For the traditional black family, where family is a safe place, education is extremely important. What is also important for many blacks is the perseverance in working toward racial equality and working harder and smarter to overcome challenges of perceptions about blacks. Elders are never called by their first name, and they would demand that younger generations be consistent in their actions and exhibit good behavior.

Scott described the nature of the African-American culture in the following manner:

African-Americans are drawn from a diverse range of cultures and countries in Africa, later from the Caribbean and from Central and South America. They share a history of enslavement, acculturation, and racial oppression which give relevance to the initial bond of African heritage. Culture serves certain vital psychological and social functions; it is the material and source of group's identity. Culture includes the basic conditions of the existence of a people—their behaviors, style of life, values, preferences, and creative expressions.[27]

According to Scott, African-American culture was a synthesis of African and Euro-American cultures. There are aspects of Euro-American culture that African-Americans subscribe to and have incorporated into their communities; however, there are parts of the African-American life that set them apart.

BLACK VALUES AND CREATIVITY

Values of the black community as celebrated in the holiday of Kwanzaa include unity, self-determination, collective responsibility, entrepreneurship, drive, creativity, and faith. These values were and are practiced by blacks in historical and contemporary Hawai'i. For example, the entrepreneurial spirit is embodied by Wally Amos and many other accomplished business leaders in Hawai'i. Amos learned to bake cookies from his aunt's recipe, then improved and developed from it his own Famous Amos chocolate chip cookie business nationwide. He had a passion for literacy, became the national spokesperson for Literacy Volunteers of America (1979 to 2002), and helped thousands of adults learn how to read. In 1987, he also hosted a television series designed to teach others how to read through a 1987 educational television series entitled *Learn to Read,* produced by Kentucky's Educational Television and Detroit's WXYZ-TV.[28]

Creativity and faith flourish in black churches and the performing arts in Hawai'i. Fraternal organizations provide mentoring and scholarships in recognition of their responsibility to the younger generation. The joy that sustained African slaves in America and continues to nourish the African diaspora in Hawai'i can be found in celebrations of Juneteenth, Martin Luther King Jr. Day, and Black History Month and in the African drumming and dancing groups throughout the Islands.

BLACK EDUCATION IN HAWAI'I

Discussing educational achievement is made difficult by the flu-idity of the blacks in Hawai'i. Adults arriving in Hawai'i are often col-lege bound or college graduates. The statistics on college success for Hawai'i athletes reflect the same difference from nonathletes as seen in other NCAA schools.

Primary and secondary education in Hawai'i is a difficult experi-ence for many African-American youth. Newcomers of all races find that their style of communication may be abrasive to their local classmates, resulting in teasing or ostracism. In addition, the more collective ori-entation of participation, which is part of many of Hawai'i's immigrant cultures and very strong in the host culture, values cooperation over competition. To succeed in the continental U.S., assertiveness is a desir-able trait. Consequently, successful students from the mainland may find that both their teachers and fellow students fault them for being pushy or loud. For African-American students, this is in addition to rac-ist name-calling and teasing. Hairston documents the experiences of African-American military students.[29] Even though the African-Amer-ican students took the name-calling very seriously, teachers may have advised the students to not take it so seriously. One teacher said that "if people take race seriously in Hawai'i, they will have an unpleasant experience," revealing an attitude shared by other local teachers.[30] Hair-ston summarizes: "It is evident in Hawai'i that African-Americans are considered socially inferior due to historical implications of racism and colonialism. Local students use racial slurs and epithets as well and colo-nialized perceptions to objectify African-American students in school."[31]

One of the students in Hairston's study grew up in Hawai'i in a retired military family. Her experience was different from the others, as she had a lot of local friends at school that she socialized with, while the others only socialized with African-American friends at school. This girl had taken on a dual identity—one as a local and one as an African-American.[32] That dual identity is a feature that members from all ethnic communities in Hawai'i embrace. Professor Harry Ball once described how each family in a neighborhood had their ethnic culture, but out on the street where the kids were growing up with their peers a new culture was being formed that they would pass on to their children.[33] This mirrors the historical development of Hawaiian Creole English or Pidgin.

Other African-American students who shared many of the same

experiences with the girl in Hairston's study were primarily in a group of lighter-skinned black youth.[34] The authors and those interviewed have observed that skin color is a factor in discrimination among all groups in Hawai'i. Even within families, darker skinned children feel the difference. Young people growing up in Hawai'i can tell you that if a restaurant has a Waikīkī site as well as one in a neighborhood, the darker skinned workers would not be placed at the Waikīkī site. With tourism being the bread and butter for Hawai'i's economy, businesses try to meet the perceived expectations of tourists who expect their "Hawaiians" to have a fair, part-Asian face.

New Ethnocultural Identity

The "Smith" family (a fictitious name) has three generations in Hawai'i, with a fourth on the way. While the grandparents are first-generation immigrants who came and settled in Hawai'i as adults, their second-generation children (now parents) were raised in Hawai'i. Among the third-generation siblings, two chose to go to the U.S. mainland for college, one attended college in Hawai'i, and one went to work after marrying young. In this third generation, two have lived on the U.S. mainland for long periods. Between the four siblings, two have African-American spouses and two do not. The fourth generation (or grandchildren) is comprised of only two "pure" African-Americans and nine hapa children. Within this family, only the grandmother and the parents are involved in black organizations, but one of the grandchildren is organizing a display for the Martin Luther King Jr. Day celebration. Three other grandchildren are in a reggae group performing mostly Jawaiian music (a genre blending Jamaican Reggae and Hawaiian music) and occasionally classic Motown. Like other families in Hawai'i, one of the third generation and two of her children have moved to Las Vegas, where they are identified as part-Hawaiian. For the grandparents' sixtieth wedding anniversary, the entire multigenerational family comes together to celebrate at the local golf course with 250 of their closest friends. Their local minister blesses the event and the food, which has dishes from every Hawai'i ethnic group.

In reality, there are very few, if any, family members who have married exclusively blacks from the second generation onward. Thus it is difficult to address the question of how the group and its ethnocultural identity has evolved. Upon arrival, African-Americans carry with them the values of both the Euro-American and black cultures; that is, they have no truly separate homogenous culture, except those who come from African nations such as Kenya.

As people who became bicultural over the past two hundred years, adapting and adding compatible values from the new culture of Hawai'i is not difficult. For those from the Caribbean, there is an immediate resonance and identification with those aspects of Hawai'i that derive from island culture.

Setting aside the substantial military community, which accounts for perhaps as many as two-thirds of the blacks in Hawai'i, their small number coupled with interracial marriage results in a highly permeable, loosely cohesive group that openly invites nonblacks into its activities. Is this also attributable to the Hawaiian openness that blacks have benefited from? Probably this is true. This openness is noticeable to Caucasians who have been excluded from black activities on the U.S. mainland.

In trying to look at the effect that local cultures have had on blacks in Hawai'i, it is important to remember the various black subgroups.

African-American military families in Hawai'i quite often live on base, shop at the exchange, and function socially on base without much need to become part of the larger community. For some, there is a feeling similar to being in other, non–U.S. or overseas assignments. For others, Hawai'i is noted as the place where there are more racist epithets than in other U.S. places.[35] For this group, the superficial culture of Hawai'i may be absorbed, including the giving and receiving of leis, removal of shoes in the house, and using the _shaka_ hand sign. Some of the foods of Hawai'i are similar to those in African-American culture, including luau (steamed taro leaves), which is similar to collard greens, and _na'au_ (pig intestines or tripe). If those foods were eaten before coming to Hawai'i, the Hawaiian version will become a favorite.

The focus on food as an indispensable part of any social function is shared between both the local and the black culture. Another shared value is the importance of family, including respect for elders and the wisdom of ancestors. Among those interviewed, most felt that addressing elders formally (such as "Mr." or "Mrs.") was an outward sign of this. Use of a unique way of communicating other than English—that is, one's own language, whether it be Pidgin, black English, Laotian, Korean, or Hawaiian—is also both a unifying and identifying feature shared among Hawai'i's communities.

Related to the language issue but more obscured is the bond between groups that have been or continue to be oppressed minorities, especially between African-Americans and Hawaiians. It was the civil rights movement of African-Americans that fired up and instructed the fight for sovereignty among Hawaiians. There is also a special bond between some African-Americans and Euro-Americans given their shared culture and common longing for aspects of life on the U.S. mainland.

THE MILITARY AND OTHER SUBGROUPS

Just as the African-American community is not homogenous, neither is the military. A diversity of experience begins with a separation between commissioned and enlisted personnel. Off base, the officers are part of a professional community and can be more easily included in the discussion of African-American individuals in the wider community, unlike their enlisted counterparts, who may have short terms of service in Hawai'i existing primarily on base.

Single men and women in the military have the additional experience of looking for relationships and dating while here. The young people who were interviewed agree that when it comes to dating, there is no limitation to the possible mixes with people of other ethnicities. An individual may prefer to date within his or her own group, but the ratio of military men to women allows females more choice of staying within the African-American group. Male African-Americans are more likely to need to date in the broader military community or the scene off base. One of the local nightclubs is reported to be an African-American scene on Friday nights. If dating results in the subsequent union with a member of a local family, this becomes a factor in many of the decisions for military personnel to remain in Hawai'i.

One group that bridges the African-American military community with African-American civilians comprises those who have retired from the military in Hawai'i or have come back after having served in the military. The community for these people depends on their family situation, their occupation, and their interests. For those who have a local spouse, the family of the spouse becomes the extended family and perhaps social group. For those returning to work near or on base, particularly those with base privileges, remaining close to the African-American military community is more likely.

Individuals may have come as singles or as a nuclear family for a specific purpose. For the athletic teams of the University of Hawai'i, Chaminade University, and Hawai'i Pacific University, particularly the football and basketball teams, many African-American individuals are recruited from the U.S. mainland. Once these student athletes arrive, they become part of an amalgamated Hawai'i group that crosses ethnic lines. Professionals who arrive to take up positions in medical practices, law firms, churches, or other areas become part of the multicultural middle class both at work and in their community.

THE ABSENCE OF A FORMAL BLACK COMMUNITY

One of the factors in dissuading African-Americans from staying in Hawai'i after moving here is the lack of a visible presence of an African-American community. Some find that they truly miss the comfort of their culture.[36] It is rare for a social or community gathering to have a majority of African-American individuals. Indeed, in looking at the NAACP as an African-American organization, some interviewees would not include it because it has a majority of non–African-American active members. The authors hosted a party that featured their daughter's African dance and drumming group, a group consisting of Africans, African-Americans, mixed-race locals, and Caucasians. One of the attendees, an African-American, commented that this was the largest number of blacks that he and his children had seen in one place since arriving in Hawai'i.

Those who stay live a multicultural life, often blending into the general local population. Diverse neighborhoods often become the primary community group. Survival—specifically, making a living in Hawai'i—leads to separateness, which by extension also creates what may appear to be indifference in place of an expected African-American unity. Interviewees noted that the nod shared universally between African-Americans rarely results in closer ties. Outside of Hawai'i, blacks often create a group, but in Hawai'i that doesn't seem to happen. Indigenous Hawaiian activist and attorney Pōkā Laenui offered his insight by reflecting that families who have become generational in Hawai'i do not feel the "need to find glorification for identity" that recent arrivals might feel, adding that the children raised here have very different needs.[37] It is only when the children from interracial families leave Hawai'i that they are faced with the need to make choices. But in contrast to Hawai'i, on the U.S. mainland others often define them and then act on those judgments.

President Obama wrote,

And yet, when I look back on my years in Hawai'i, I realize how truly lucky I was to have been raised there. Hawai'i's spirit of tolerance might not have been perfect or complete, but it was—and

is—real. The opportunity that Hawai'i offered—to experience a
variety of cultures in a climate of mutual respect—became an
integral part of my world view, and a basis for the values that I
hold most dear.[38]

This tolerance allows blacks in Hawai'i to relax their guard against
racist acts. Those who continue to hold back or take seriously everything around them are very uncomfortable with Hawai'i's home-grown
way of joking. Researchers and others have noted that in Hawai'i, teasing has its own unique place.[39] One of the tests that newcomers to local
groups get is the ability to respond good-naturedly to teasing, including
stereotyped teasing. Everyone belongs to a group that will be fodder for
these jokes. In the entertainment industry, comedians use a lot of ethnic jokes for Hawai'i audiences, but when they take their act to the continental U.S., those jokes don't work as well.[40] As a part of the United
States, laws are in place that dissuade the use of this type of humor, and
this type of joking is becoming much less robust, but residents who
claim a Hawai'i or local culture and who do not want to fully adopt the
American culture resist the suppression of ethnic humor. For adults,
the consequences of this type of humor may be nil, but when carried
into the educational setting, it can affect performance and expectation,
which has a negative effect.[41] If the stereotyping is a seed planted in
the fertile mind of an insecure child, he or she may never realize full
potential. A truism here is the quote: "Perception trumps reality, and a
heartfelt belief actualizes itself."

PRESIDENT BARACK OBAMA

President Barack Obama was born and spent most of his youth
in Hawai'i before making his mark at Harvard, in Chicago, and on the
history of the United States. His wife Michelle has said, "To understand
Barack, you need to understand Hawai'i." His exposure to the many
cultures of Hawai'i, as well as his life abroad, have contributed to his
ability to relate to people and leaders from both developed and nonde-
veloped countries. The need to be able to operate in appropriate ways
in a multicultural society that marks success in Hawai'i contributed to
his ability to speak to voters from Iowa's farmlands and to the urban
communities of all races. Although multicultural, Hawai'i continues to
be infected with racism, and Obama was subjected to it while growing
up. However, as with other blacks born and raised in Hawai'i, he did
not have an African-American identity typical of the U.S. mainland. He

turned to ex-Chicago mentor Frank Davis in high school, who helped guide his search. His subsequent residence and work in Chicago have done much to fill that lack, but until he had shown his strength among voters, black leaders were questioning his identity.

Summary and Conclusions

In this chapter, we have seen how blacks in Hawai'i are first and foremost individualists who have chosen a path that took them out of one community into another, which may be principally their own family, perhaps interracial. Blacks can be said to form minicommunities, with only one of substantial numbers: the African-American military community. Unlike other ethnic groups, most longtime Hawai'i residents with black ancestry are mixed and living in multicultural families and communities. Although blacks have been in Hawai'i from the arrival of the earliest explorers, their presence has been missed in most historical reports of the Islands. When the need for association with other blacks arises, there are various organizations and activities, including church, educational, and fraternal, that provide venues for gatherings. As newcomers become longtime residents, their participation in these groups wanes.

Further Reading

Broussard, A. S. "Carlotta Stewart Lai: An African American teacher in the Territory of Hawai'i." *Social Process in Hawaii* 43 (2004): 70–88.
———. "The Honolulu NAACP and race relations in Hawai'i." *Hawaiian Journal of History* 39 (2005): 115–133.
Davis, F. M. *Living the Blues: Memoir of a Black Journalist and Poet.* Madison: University of Wisconsin Press, 1992.
Farber, D., and B. Bailey. *The First Strange Place: The Alchemy of Race and Sex in World War II.* New York: Free Press, 1992.
Jackson, M. M., ed. *They Followed the Trade Winds: African Americans in Hawai'i.* Special ed. of *Social Process in Hawai'i* 43, Honolulu: Department of Sociology, University of Hawai'i at Mānoa, 2004.
Miles, A. "Racism in Hawaii: Myths and Realities." *Honolulu Magazine* 30 (July 1995): 44–47, 67.
Nordyke, E. "Blacks in Hawai'i: A demographic and historical perspective." *Hawaiian Journal of History* 22 (1988): 241–255.
Takara, K. W. "The African diaspora in nineteenth-century Hawai'i." *Social Process in Hawaii* 43 (2004): 13.

Tatum, B. D. *Why Are All the Black Kids Sitting Together in the Cafeteria?* New York: Basic Books, 1997.

Notes

1. The reason this title was chosen rather than "The African-Americans" is discussed later in the chapter.

2. James Horton, Ph.D., is professor emeritus, George Washington University, and a frequent lecturer at the University of Hawai'i. Winifred Simmons, M.D., is a retired psychiatrist who practiced and raised her family in Hawai'i.

3. D. E. Kelley, "Keepers of the culture: A study in time of the Hawaiian Islands, Part 1: African-Americans of the Hawaiian Islands," retrieved May 29, 2008, from http://files.usgwarchives.net/hi/statewide/newspapers/africana5nw.txt.

4. E. Knowlton Jr., "Cape Verde, West Africa, and Hawai'i," *Social Process in Hawai'i* 43 (2004): 89.

5. M. Scruggs, "There is one black man, Anthony D. Allen," *Social Process in Hawai'i* 43 (2004): 24.

6. K. W. Takara, "The African diaspora in nineteenth-century Hawai'i," *Social Process in Hawaii* 43 (2004): 13.

7. Ibid.: 15.

8. C. S. Stewart, *Journal of Residence in the Sandwich Islands during the Years 1823, 1824, and 1825*, 2nd ed., New York: John P. Haven, 1828: 147.

9. Kelley 2008.

10. E. Nordyke, "Blacks in Hawai'i: A demographic and historical perspective," *Hawaiian Journal of History* 22 (1988): 241–255; R. Kuykendall, *The Hawaiian Kingdom, 1874–1893: The Kalakaua Dynasty*, vol. 3. Honolulu: University of Hawai'i Press, 1967, p. 141.

11. Nordyke 1988: 241.

12. Ibid.: 245.

13. A. S. Broussard, "Carlotta Stewart Lai: An African American teacher in the Territory of Hawai'i," *Social Process in Hawaii* 43 (2004): 70.

14. B. Bailey and D. Farber, *The First Strange Place: Race and Sex in World War II*, Baltimore: Johns Hopkins University Press, 1992: 142.

15. A. S. Broussard, "The Honolulu NAACP and race relations in Hawai'i," *Hawaiian Journal of History* 39 (2005): 115–133.

16. Bailey and Farber 1992: 165.

17. K. W. Takara, *Fire and the Phoenix: Frank Marshall Davis*, Ph.D. diss., University of Hawai'i, 1993: 9.

18. The interviewees for this chapter ranged in age from the late twenties to seniors and were evenly split between males and females who have lived in Hawai'i from two to forty-seven years, including four Hawai'i-born.

Among them, the predominant occupation was education; other occupations included medicine, religion, community organizing, and the arts.

19. M. M. Jackson, ed., *They Followed the Trade Winds: African Americans in Hawai'i*, special ed. of *Social Process in Hawai'i* 43, Honolulu: Department of Sociology, University of Hawai'i at Mānoa, 2004: 247.

20. M. P. P. Root, ed., *Racially Mixed People in America*, Newbury Park, CA: Sage Publications, 1992: 3–11.

21. B. D. Tatum, *Why Are All the Black Kids Sitting Together in the Cafeteria?* New York: Basic Books, 1997: 169.

22. Public Broadcasting System (PBS) Series, "James Horton interview on Race: The power of illusion: Episode 3, 'The house we live in,'" retrieved from: http://www.pbs.org/race/000_About/002_04-about-03.htm, 2003.

23. City and County of Honolulu, "Bandmasters of the Royal Hawaiian Band," March 28, 2008, Retrieved on June 14, 2010, from http://www.co .honolulu.hi.us/rhb/bandmasters.htm; Nordyke 1988: 243.

24. D. Guttman and H. R. Miller (aka Hugeaux), "The history of African Americans in Hawai'i," prepared for the African American Cultural Diversity Center, 2010 (Web site: www.aadcch.org), retrieved on June 14, 2010, from http://www.hugeaux.com/historyhawaiiafroamer.htm.

25. J. Adler, ed., *The Journal of Prince Alexander Liholiho*, Hawaiian Historical Society, Honolulu: University of Hawai'i Press, 1967: 108–109.

26. J. Nicholson, "Characteristics of African American families: Based on the work of Oscar Barbarin, PhD," University of North Carolina, School of Social Work, Powerpoint, 2002, Retrieved from http://ssw.unc.edu/RTI/presentation/PDFs/aa_families.pdf.

27. H. J. Scott, "The African American culture," *View Point: Commentaries on the Quest to Improve the Life Chances and the Educational Lot of African Americans*, Pace University, June 2005, retrieved from http://www.pace.edu/emplibrary/VP-THEAFRICANAMERICANCULTURE_ Hugh_J_Scott.pdf.

28. W. Amos, "About Wally Amos: Biography," retrieved June 14, 2010, from www.wallyamos.com; "Learn to Read," description of literacy program hosted by Wally Amos (1987), retrieved from http://www.tv.com/learn-to-read/show/25402/summary.html#.

29. K. Hairston, "Somewhere under the rainbow, race and gender: African-American military students in Hawai'i public schools," Ph.D. diss., University of Hawai'i, 2004: 169–170.

30. Ibid.: 176.

31. Ibid.: 178.

32. Ibid.: 190–191.

33. Personal communication with Dr. Harry Ball, professor of sociology, University of Hawai'i, 1983.

34. Hairston 2004: 191.

35. Ibid.: 174.

36. Ibid.: 237.

37. Jackson 2004: 244–245.

38. B. Obama, "A life's calling to public service," *Punahou Bulletin*, fall 1999: 29.

39. A. Awaya, "Hawai'i military impacted schools and programs to assist with student transitions," paper presented at the Hawai'i Education Research Association conference, University of Hawai'i Mānoa Campus, Honolulu, March 10, 2003; C. Blair, *Money, Color and Sex in Hawai'i Politics*, Honolulu: Mutual Publishing, 1998: vii, 200; A. Miles, "Racism in Hawaii: Myths and realities," *Honolulu Magazine* 30 (July 1995): 44–47, 67.

40. Miles 1995: 45.

41. Ibid.: 46.

CHAPTER 11

The Samoans

John R. Bond and Faapisa M. Soli

The Samoan archipelago is comprised of nine main volcanic islands located in the central Pacific about 10 degrees south of the equator. It is situated almost precisely in the center of a vast equilateral triangle that spans much of the South Pacific and stretches across the equator into the north-central Pacific. This Polynesian Triangle is anchored on the southwest corner by New Zealand; its base stretches five thousand miles eastward to Easter Island, and its apex is found approximately an equal distance to the north in Hawaiʻi. The first recorded European contact with the Samoan archipelago occurred in 1722, a half century prior to James Cook's arrival in the Sandwich (Hawaiian) Islands. Jacob Roggeveen, captain of a Dutch West India ship, first sighted the easternmost island of Taʻū while on a westerly course in the South Pacific.[1]

During the last several years of the nineteenth century, a decades-long contest between England, Germany, and America for control of Samoa intensified. In the spring of 1889, there were no less than seven warships of these three powers riding at anchor in Āpia Harbour and prepared to support the efforts of their respective governments. However, on the sixteenth of March, just prior to the commencement of open conflict, a severe hurricane destroyed six of the seven ships. This apparently served to cool the pending hostilities and the conflict was moved to Berlin, where the three Western powers agreed upon a treaty.[2] In December of 1899, following decades of vying for control of Samoa, a tripartite convention resulted in a political bifurcation of the Samoan islands. England's primary acquisitions at the Berlin parley were Tonga and the Solomon Islands. Savaiʻi and ʻUpolu, the two major islands at the western end, came under German control. In the early 1900s, the five smaller islands to the east became an unincorporated trust territory of the United States, and they continue in that status as American Samoa or Amerika Samoa.

Of the American group, the westernmost is also the largest island, Tutuila, and contains the capital, Pago Pago, with one of the largest and safest harbors in the entire South Pacific. Under American trusteeship, American Samoa's governor was appointed by the U.S. Department of the Navy from 1900 to 1951. In 1956, the secretary of interior appointed the first native Samoan governor, who later became the first elected governor in 1977. In 1979, they also began electing their nonvoting representative to the U.S. Congress. Citizens of American Samoa are called U.S. nationals and are treated as any other American regarding travel. They also receive most of the benefits available to U.S. citizens, except the privilege of voting in national elections.

In 1914, at the start of World War I, New Zealand occupied German Samoa, which became Western Samoa, a New Zealand mandate. At the conclusion of the Second World War in 1945, Western Samoa's status changed to that of a New Zealand–United Nations trusteeship. In 1962, Western Samoa gained its independence and was also known as the Independent State of Samoa. Finally, in 1997 the "Western" was dropped and its name is now simply Samoa. It has a parliamentary, democratic form of government that consists of a head of state, prime minister, premier, and cabinet members. Citizens of Samoa require a visa to enter the United States.

Although Samoa and American Samoa have been separated politically for over a century, the kinship ties that have bound them together for a millennium continue the cultural congruity of all Samoans to the present date. The Samoan language is the same among the islands; however, the residents of Samoa notably exhibit a British accent when speaking English as opposed to the American accent possessed by residents of American Samoa. While they are well aware of the differences in their political status, both Samoan entities are more importantly aware of and influenced by their lineage and traditions, irrespective of international borders.

Samoa is roughly five times the size of American Samoa and has a population three times larger. Neither Samoa has had a truly self-sufficient economy during the past century. The early 1950s saw the beginning of large-scale movements of American Samoans to both Hawai'i and the continental United States, as well as Western Samoans, who traveled to New Zealand. Samoa had largely depended upon New Zealand for both financial aid and as a place where its young adults went to seek education and employment. American Samoa, likewise, has been heavily dependent upon the United States for financial support, and many of its youth have come to either Hawaiʻi or the U. S. mainland for both schooling and economic opportunities.

The population of American Samoa is currently estimated at 66,000, and Samoa's at 220,000.³ According to the 2000 U.S. Census, some 130,000 Samoans (full-Samoans and part-Samoans) live in the United States, with Samoans residing in each of the fifty states and the District of Columbia. Samoans are the second-largest Pacific Island group in the United States after Hawaiians. California, Hawaiʻi, and Washington report the largest Samoan populations.

In 1925, there were 33 Samoans living in Lāʻie on Oʻahu. In 1951, about 117 Samoan naval personnel were in Pearl Harbor, and by 1970 there were some 5,733 Samoans in Hawaiʻi. The 2000 census indicates that the Samoan population in Hawaiʻi is estimated at approximately 16,000, or 28,000 including part-Samoans.⁴ This number represents less than 3 percent of Hawaiʻi's 1.2 million population total.

Support for American Samoa from the United States has been substantial, to the extent that its per capita income has been approximately three times that in Samoa. In recent years, this disparity has served to create an eastward population movement between the two Samoan island groups and also to increase the number of Samoans from the western islands continuing on to either Hawaiʻi or the continental United States. Still, the majority of Samoans in Hawaiʻi remain those from American Samoa.

Traditional Samoan Culture: *Faʻa Samoa:* The Samoan Way

The Samoan people are Western Polynesians, similar to the natives of Tonga and Tokelau. Although several intriguing theories exist connecting Polynesians to American Indians or Basques, it is generally held that individuals from Southeast Asia are the ancient ancestors of Polynesians. Tonga and Samoa were likely settled first, in about 1300 to 1000 B.C., after which the migration continued. Centuries later and thousands of miles to the east, Easter Island was probably reached by about A.D. 500, and two thousand miles to the north, the Polynesian voyagers likely arrived in Hawaiʻi between A.D. 300 and 1000.

Samoans, like all Polynesians, are typically quite tall, with brown skin; thick, wavy, black hair; and a scarcity of body hair. The Samoan language is described by Peter Bellwood as one of variations of the Austronesian linguistic family, which spans the Pacific, halfway around the globe.[5] It is composed of the five vowels used in English and only twelve consonants—both greatly augmented by a variety of pronunciational devices. Howells comments that the most unique feature of the Samoan language is its use of a special set of what he calls "honorific terms."[6] These comprise a collection of deferential words that are used in place of ordinary ones to show respect to anyone, but they apply especially when one is addressing chiefs, elders, and clergy.

The single most important element in Samoan social organization is the *aiga*, which is essentially a very broad extrapolation of the Western concept of the extended family. From the moment of birth, every Samoan has roots in the extended families of both father and mother. Each is special and important in determining how an individual relates to all others throughout his or her lifetime.

Historically, the primary geopolitical unit of Samoan society is the village. Each village is comprised of different *aiga*. Within and parallel to the *aiga* matrix is the organized designation of the various chiefly ranks and titles—the *matai* system. Each *aiga* has its own number of titles, which tradition maintains have all come from God. The village is governed by the *fono* (village council), comprised of the *matai* of each *aiga*. In the *fono*, most matters are decided by consensus, but important decisions require unanimity. In this and many other ways, the very nature of the social organization hierarchy in Samoa differs significantly from those of a number of other Polynesian groups.

In general, eligibility to a *matai* or chiefly title is through both service and kinship connections and is conferred by deliberation and consensus within the *aiga*. The *matai* who make up the *fono* vary in status, and the *matai* with the highest status represents the village in the district *fono*. The result is a complex, interwoven relationship among the various titles, with their origins often lost in antiquity. Although most of the titles are held by men, females can also hold *matai* titles.

Within the elaborate *matai* system, a high chiefly title still carries with it considerable prestige and authority. However, it also bears a host of carefully enumerated duties and responsibilities. The hereditary basis regarding titles is not rigidly adhered to and allows elective progression to occur. The relationship among titles is historically based. There are Samoan chiefs who now call Hawai'i home but who readily travel back to the Samoan islands when needed. Although there are no "villages" in

Hawai'i, its Samoan community continues to respect the *matai* system, for it is Fa'a Samoa—the Samoan Way. Typically, the titled members of the village are more mature, reinforcing another important aspect of the Samoan value system—respect for elders. Blessings bestowed by elders are significant and honorable in the *aiga*. Being respectful is a moral principle that is not only shown toward elders but also to anyone older, which includes an older sibling or acquaintance.

Because of the familiarity, dominance, and sense of belongingness of the *aiga* in village life, there is a tendency felt by some Samoans to view individuals outside of one's *aiga* with caution. But strangers and guests are always welcomed in the home with hospitality. All Samoans have traditionally grown up as an integral part of their *aiga*, but there have sometimes been conflicts between different families. The relationships between individuals of different *aiga* are usually influenced, if not directed by, the relationships between their respective *aiga*. Typically, however, the relationships between various families, particularly those in the same village, are close and amicable, as are those of the individual members of each family. This relationship is important, as it is the foundation of another important component in the Samoan culture—*fa'alavelave*.

When there is a funeral, a wedding, or the bestowing of an important title to a certain individual, it means that immediate and extended families are expected to help, either voluntarily or involuntarily. The assistance may be in the form of giving one's time to help with chores or contributing *ie toga* (fine mats), food, and especially money. Although this custom is respected, too many *fa'alavelave* can also cause severe financial hardship and become a burden to many families, especially when one is the benefactor and not the recipient. Even in Hawai'i, Samoan families continue with this obligation to their *aiga* either willingly or unwillingly, not only locally but also in the Samoan islands.

Another important element within the *aiga* is status, a matter of primary concern in the Samoan social and political systems. One's status tends to indicate his specific place within the intricate *aiga-matai* hierarchy, which is critical not only for Samoans living in Samoa but also for those residing in foreign communities. Knowing where one fits into the system provides a sense of identity and comfort, as well as providing guidelines for appropriate interaction with other Samoans. In most cases, paramount chiefs and pastors possess high status. Government officials and those with prominent professional and successful careers are also highly esteemed.

In addition to the *aiga* and *matai,* virtually all aspects of Samoan culture emphasize the importance of togetherness, group orientation, and deference. While this has undoubtedly been encroached upon by several centuries of contact with the competitiveness and individualism of Western culture, it remains an important value for Samoans. Today, whenever opportunity allows, Samoans living in other lands seem to inherently congregate tightly together, not only because it is economically convenient, but perhaps reflecting their past experiences in Samoa. Samoan hospitality simply does not allow refusing a relative food or shelter. This, however, may run afoul of customs or laws in countries where eight or ten persons living in a single two-bedroom house is not acceptable. In addition to sharing domiciles, Samoans overseas also tend to congregate with their brethren geographically by country, state, or a specific locale within a city. The strong and pervasive influence of the combined *aiga-matai* system has likely been the reason why, perhaps more than any other cultural group in Hawai'i, Samoans have maintained very strong kinship ties over a lifetime and across thousands of miles.

Individual Life Cycle

The evolution of the Samoan adult is predicated upon a two-decade-long indoctrination that focuses upon relatively few traditional core values. It is group oriented and directed and produces citizens who are closely tied to both their primary groups and to the Samoan culture. The most significant aspect of the early phases of Samoan childrearing is the paramount importance of the group relative to that of the individual. In this context, the group incorporates the *aiga,* the village, the *matai,* and the entirety of the Samoan people and culture. In addition to the emphasis upon deference for the Samoan culture in its entirety, the cultural education of Samoan children has traditionally had three basic goals. One is a comprehension of and respect for the complex *aiga* social structure. Another is a grasp of the family titles and the *matai* system in general. The third is a thorough understanding of correct social behavior to avoid bringing any disharmony or shame to the *aiga,* the *matai,* or the village. All children learn these basic axioms in order to live their lives Fa'a Samoa.

Small children are typically placed in the care of older siblings to keep them from harm, to provide for their basic needs, and most importantly, to make sure they do not intrude unduly in adult matters.

The eldest child is expected to be a role model and provide support for the younger children. Boys are to protect their sisters and assist in laborious tasks. Girls help out with household tasks and caring for the younger siblings. Children are taught to be on their best behavior, for they are a reflection of their parents and the whole *aiga*. All adolescents growing up in the village have been thoroughly immersed in the traditions and folklore of the culture.

In the village, it is not only the siblings and biological parents but virtually all the adults within the *aiga* who serve as parental figures with regard to discipline and learning. In contrast to their counterparts in America and Europe, where the first two decades of learning have been largely conducted by two parents and a relatively small coterie of teachers, the overall education of a Samoan child literally "takes a village." This is still largely the case, even though the past two centuries of increasing contact with the outside world have created the opportunity for church and public schooling and the introduction of a broader Western perspective. These new educational settings afford Samoan youngsters a glimpse of a wider world, but they have not eliminated the still-important triad of educational goals.

Growing up in Hawai'i, where one is away from the village and no longer surrounded by the extended family, the education of the child is broadly influenced by the American way of life. The clothing fashion styles, language, food, and the media pop culture soon begin to shape a new lifestyle. Although most of the children who move to Hawai'i at a young age or are born and raised in Hawai'i do not speak the Samoan language fluently, most of them would understand it. Parents or grandparents typically speak Samoan, and the child responds in English.

As an adult, one is expected not only to take an active part in providing for one's family but to also assume responsibilities regarding the extended family. The placement of an elderly member of the *aiga* in a nursing home is unheard of in Samoan families. This sense of duty is in response to the love and care received from both parents and grandparents. In Hawai'i, Samoan families continue to hold steadfastly to these traditions.

There is little reason to believe that the psyche of individual Samoans, like those of people elsewhere in the world, is devoid of avarice, jealousy, or any of the other negative emotions that can readily lead to anger and hostility. It may be puzzling for the Western observer, aware of the high value placed upon domestic tranquility, to witness the speed with which a Samoan parent or parent surrogate responds to the misbehavior of a child with what appears to be harsh physical punishment. While some Samoans, cognizant of Western child abuse laws, may tend to deny or at least minimize this common disciplinary tactic, others are inclined to defend the behavior.

The defense is typically based upon one of two different justifications. Neither varies significantly from the reasons frequently put forth by many Western parents accused of being excessively harsh with their children. The first is that the dramatic castigation in response to inappropriate behavior of a child is necessary to discourage future behavior that may disrupt the serenity of the family or village. A great many Samoans have adopted Christianity, both avidly and literally, and the second justification for corporal punishment is that the physical punishment of a misbehaving child is biblically prescribed. Many Samoans are quick to point out that the disrespect they perceive non-Samoan children showing their parents, teachers, and elders is clearly indicative of the timidity and ineffectiveness of permissive Western parenting techniques. And again, discipline is not only the prerogative of the biological parents in Samoa but of the various surrogate parents as well.

In spite of the harsh punishment of children, it is also true that most of the Samoan cultural values are antithetical to aggression. Fa'a Samoa stresses that any behavior is unacceptable that is discourteous to elders, brings shame to the *aiga* or village, disrespects the *matai,* or dishonors the culture as a whole. Such behavior is rarely perceived as simply an act by one individual against another but rather as a collective transgression involving the families of both parties. It is not that the misbehaving individual fails to be denigrated; he or she is. But it is traditionally the responsibility of both the offender and his or her *aiga* to make amends and right the wrongs that have been done. Often it is the village *matai* who will determine what the appropriate atonement will be and will decide when the offense has been appropriately rectified. This tradition continues in Hawai'i, as leaders of each family or church attempt to resolve any major conflicts that resulted in physical harm or property damage. As the Samoan people become more knowledgeable about the judiciary system and their rights, some are opting to settle disputes in court. However, customarily an apology is rarely rejected, and it is sometimes accompanied by gifts and monetary donations as a token of humility or profound regret of the conflict, depending on the situation.

Compare the typical American childrearing by one or two parents with the traditional Samoan child reared by his entire village. The physical discipline is likely to be both swifter and harsher. Generally, Samoans tend to be considerably less verbal with their children than American parents. At the age when the American child is beginning to move into the verbal phase of the process, the Samoan child is still likely embroiled in an extension of the physical. There is little concern about the advantage of being able to control the child from a distance since the number of surrogate parents virtually blankets the child. Even when the child is older, the constant presence of parental figures willing to instruct, direct, or punish obviates or significantly reduces the necessity for the child to internalize the lessons learned.

As the Samoan child matures, an important difference has occurred between the development of his conscience and that of his American contemporary. The American child has developed an internalized, working conscience that is useful in many different circumstances. In contrast, in Samoa, the Samoan child's reliance upon others for guidance has led to a dependency upon a pragmatic, working conscience. He or she is quite able to function appropriately as a member of his or her *aiga,* village, and culture, and he or she behaves Fa'a Samoa. Even later, family elders are not only present in the village during an individual's formative years, but they are still there to encourage appropriate behavior during one's adult years.

The distinction between the two developmental models, however, is not readily apparent as long as both the Samoan and American remain in their respective cultures. It is when the two individuals move to a different social environment that the difference is often evident. The portability of an internalized conscience makes it invaluable when the American leaves his family or even his culture. This is not the case with the Samoan, for whom the indicators of desirable or undesirable behavior have always come from the environment itself. In a different culture, the new behavioral indicators he perceives may be confusing at best and misleading at worst. The result is that the ease and speed of his successful acculturation may be seriously impaired.

The Role of Religion

European and American missionaries of various denominations were prominent among the early Western settlers of the various Polynesian islands. In the past two centuries since their arrival, they have had a profound impact upon virtually all of these lands. The missionaries have often been characterized as harsh and smothering in their criticism and alteration of the heretofore natural, unfettered, and idyllic lifestyle, which the French philosopher Rousseau had idealized in his concept of the "noble savage." With their often narrow concepts regarding sin and decorum, many of the early missionaries launched sincere efforts to convert the heathen natives into Christians with little thought regarding the centuries of culture they were attempting to change.

Notwithstanding this fact, it is also true that they provided great benefits for the Polynesian people, as Bellwood has observed.[7] They constructed written languages where none had existed. They informed the natives of these isolated islands about the world around them and taught entire populations to read both religious and secular works. Samoans shared a belief with other Polynesians that a single paramount god—Tagaloa—was the creator of the earth, multiple heavens, and more specifically for Samoans, the islands of Samoa and its inhabitants. Culbertson et al. suggest that in Samoa the acceptance of Christianity was likely facilitated by an ancient Samoan legend in which the goddess of war, Nafanua, predicted the coming of a new God with far greater powers than all the existing Samoan gods.[8] Although the Wesleyans arrived in Samoa from Tonga in 1828, the great impact of Christianity upon Samoa really occurred two years later when the London Missionary Society (LMS) arrived. The new religion was accepted by the Samoan people in place of the traditional religion. This relatively rapid displacement appears to have been facilitated by a kind of rationalization in which the Christian God was perceived as an affirmation of the existing Samoan belief in a single Supreme Being. Aiding the missionary cause was the propitious decision by both the LMS and later the Mormon Church to support Fa'a Samoa by letting church government be handled within the village structure. As a consequence, the Christian faith remains very strong and is widely practiced by Samoans both at home and abroad.

According to Holmes, the Sabbath in a Samoan village offers many insights into secular life in the community.[9] After the predawn ringing of the church bell, there is hurried cooking activity, as it must be done prior to sunrise. Sunday clothing, typically white, is donned and the females take special care with their hair. Before eight, families leave their *fale* (houses) and proceed to the church, where they are seated— women on the left, men on the right. The choir is at the front and there is special seating for important *matai* and their wives. At the rear are the children's pews, monitored by one or more village elders with canes used to minimize any disruption by occasional raps on the youngsters' heads. Religious services occur almost continually the entire day, and the exuberance, repetitive rhythm, and robust voices of the faithful are clearly heard everywhere. This is in sharp contrast to the earlier, pre-Christian worship of Tagaloa, which always occurred in silence. The ringing of the bell at four o'clock signals the more casual afternoon service, which is devoid of children; they will attend their own service later.

An interesting contrast with Euro-American services is the formality and very public manner in which offerings are conducted relative to the private, almost surreptitious procedure in Euro-American churches. The difference underlines the importance of both the communality of the village members and also of the emphasis upon giving as a means to achieve or retain status in Samoan society. After the last hymn, the church deacons stand in front of the Communion rail and read the names of all the church families. As each name is read, a member of the family comes forward and places its offering on the table. The amount of the offering is announced aloud by a deacon, who also records it in the record book. As Holmes observes, it is not surprising that the contributions are usually substantial.

Even today, villages enforce the importance of making time to worship God daily by implementing the *sa*, or curfew. Usually around six or seven in the evening, the *aumaga* (village police), comprised of selected village men, announces the *sa* using a shell horn. Everyone is required to go inside their home and use this time to conduct a family prayer, or *lotu*. In a sense, this time is an enforced "mandatory family time." During this quiet and peaceful time, one can hear the different hymns sung by each family and witness the earnest prayers offered as everyone sits on the floor in the form of a circle. An hour later the horn is sounded again, which signals the end of the *sa*. The villagers are allowed to freely roam around, continue with their yardwork, or simply socialize. Finally, around nine or ten at night, another *sa* is carried out and this is specifically for all the children and youth. They are required to be at home sleeping or doing schoolwork and are not allowed to wander around the village. This measure not only helps the families but also serves as a preventive measure for any possible problematic youth activities.

Traditional Samoan families in Hawai'i continue to have family *lotu* in their homes in the evenings. This family *lotu* time is considered an important element of the Fa'a Samoa. However, more and more Samoan families no longer make time for this custom, as parents are busy with work and children with extracurricular activities or other such matters. Traditional and religious leaders often refer to the absence of this ritual as one of the main reasons why the *aiga* structure weakens, because families are not spending time in prayer and with each other.

Religion continues to play an important part in the lives of almost all Samoans at home and abroad. It would be difficult today to find a Samoan who identifies himself as either an atheist or an agnostic. Churches are and are likely to remain the hub of Samoan life, both in the home islands and in Samoan communities abroad.

A number of Samoan churches can be seen around Hawai'i. Their members can be observed wearing the traditional formal wear—the women their *puletasi* (a two-piece dress) and the men with their buttoned-up shirt including a tie and *ie faitaga* (wraparound skirt). Those who are part of the choir are usually required to dress in all white. It is important to know that Samoan churches are formed not because they choose to worship separately from other ethnic groups but because they understand the Samoan language best. All worship services are conducted in Samoan, including singing and the sermon, which is preached using the Samoan-translated Bible.

The Samoan churches in Hawai'i also play a significant role in bringing Samoans together and helping to preserve the Fa'a Samoa. Different Samoan churches, often of different denominations, get together annually and showcase various talents such as singing, traditional *siva* (dance), skits, and the opportunity for fellowship with each other. Samoan families in Hawai'i continue the tradition of having a big *toana'i* (feast) after church services. This is usually the favorite time for many and provides another opportunity for the *aiga* to spend time together.

Samoans in the Western World

In both Samoas, the economy has historically been subsistence agriculture and village based. Work was traditionally delineated along several dimensions: gender, age, and skill level. The growing male child was expected to gradually assume most of the heavy physical work, including fishing, harvesting the fields, preparing food using the *umu* (underground oven), and for those with the requisite skills, house and canoe building. Young females were trained to make mats and baskets, tend the family garden, and help with a variety of tasks around the *fale*. As it has in many other parts of the world, the past half century has brought about a clouding of gender roles in Samoan life, with young men and women both seeking higher levels of education and leaving the villages in search of paid employment.

Light industry and tourism have gradually begun to find a place in both Samoas. However, copra, fish, bananas, and other foodstuffs generated in the villages scattered around the various islands remain important not only for sustenance but also for the continuation of the Samoan lifestyle. Because of its value as an important food source, the coconut remains an important crop, and almost all parts of the palm tree are employed in a great many ways for food, handicrafts, and construction.

During most of the last century, neither the village life nor the economy of the western islands of Samoa was significantly altered. This was not the case with American Samoa. During and after World War II, the presence of the military, followed by increased funding by America, resulted in a large increase in the U.S. commercial and sociopolitical presence.

Early Europeans visiting the islands frequently commented upon the Samoans' skill in both sailing and fishing. As a result, they were frequently referred to as the "Navigators of the Pacific." Perhaps with this in mind, in the mid-1900s the United States attempted to improve the American Samoa economy by building a fish cannery in Pago Pago. The plan was for Samoans to process Samoan-caught tuna. This effort has been only moderately successful.[10] With access to other sources of government largess and the ready availability of canned seafood in the stores, many Samoans apparently declined to either work in the cannery or go to sea to provide the fish for it. As a result, vacant jobs both ashore and afloat were filled by Asians, whose presence contributed to varying degrees of racial discord on the main island of Tutuila.

The Second World War also brought about another change to American Samoa, which has probably had the greatest impact of all. A growing number of young Samoan males had a glimpse of the "American Dream" and wished to pursue it. They discovered that although they lacked the sufficient skills to enter the U.S. marketplace directly, there was a way to do it tangentially through the American military. So many American Samoans enlisted in the U.S. armed services during the 1950s and 1960s that within a short time it appeared there were as many Samoans living overseas as there were in American Samoa. Even today, Samoans have a strong military tradition as they willingly and loyally continue to serve the United States. American Samoa has one of the highest military recruitment per capita rates of all the states and territories. The opportunities and benefits offered by the military are enticing, especially in contrast to the few employment options in

American Samoa. The economy at home benefited from the receipt of allotment checks, and it was not very long before a generation of more affluent and worldly Samoan veterans began to leave the military and settle down in places such as Long Beach in Southern California and Honolulu. In recent years, these Samoan communities often come together to bid farewell to the sons and daughters preparing for deployment to the Middle East. Unfortunately, they have also come together all too frequently to mourn the death of their fellow Samoans killed in battle. American Samoa regrettably has the highest per capita fatalities in the Iraq war.[11]

The shift from the Samoan lifestyle to a westernized one has apparently produced negative health effects in the Samoan community. Samoans are generally felt to be among the most obese ethnic groups in the world. A greater percentage of Samoans living in Hawai'i are statistically overweight relative to Samoans living in either American Samoa or Samoa. This problem leads to an increased number of Samoans with high blood pressure and cardiovascular disease. In a recent study that compared the mortality age of the different ethnic groups in Hawai'i, it was found that Samoans had the shortest life expectancy.[12] This can be attributed to a variety of factors, including lifestyle, socioeconomic status, perception of Western medicine, and lack of health care coverage.

New Ethnocultural Identity

An important element to be considered in the migration process of Samoans is the concern that the longer and farther away they move, the higher the possibility of letting go and losing some important aspects of their culture. The acculturative stress experienced by Samoans has not been fully studied, nor how much it impacts their settlement in Hawai'i. Some of the difficulties experienced by Samoans in Hawai'i include a language barrier, lack of adequate training, lack of resources or awareness thereof, and responsibilities to the *aiga*. The lifestyle back in the Samoan islands in terms of employment, technology, and education does not completely prepare Samoans for life in Hawai'i or the United States in terms of the necessary skills and adequate experience required. Although most Samoans are bilingual, English is a second language and the older generation is usually not fluent in it. This creates the problem of the younger generation having difficulties coping with both the Samoan traditional way of things and the local culture in Hawai'i.

In an effort to complement and update the data available for this chapter, twenty-one interviews were conducted, either individually or in small focus groups. All of the interviewees were Samoan and were born in Samoa, American Samoa, or Hawai'i. Males and females were almost equally represented, and their ages ranged from late teens to the late fifties. All are currently residents of Hawai'i and have been here for periods of time varying from a few to over forty years, some since birth. All volunteered to both respond to questions and share their own thoughts and impressions.

They were asked about their prior lives in the Samoan islands, their move to Hawai'i, and their lives in their new home. The group was virtually unanimous in acknowledging the value of their continuing ties with their *aiga,* their church, and to a lesser degree, their *matai.* In a variety of ways, they also were very clear regarding the importance to them of their generalized Samoan traditions. Only the younger ones in their teens or twenties, whose residence in Hawai'i has been relatively brief, appeared to be comfortable regarding the possibility that a gradual acculturation into the core culture of Hawai'i could result in an erosion of some of their Samoan heritage. Almost all of the older respondents in their thirties to fifties, along with one in her late twenties, made it clear that, although there was much they liked about their lives in Hawai'i, they had no real intention of becoming a permanent part of the polyglot group they perceived as the core of Hawaiian culture.

An interesting constant in the responses of young and old alike was their dislike of the absence or laxity of authority in all phases of life in Hawai'i. They offered numerous examples to support their feelings, including childrearing, school behavior, religion, sexuality, and the attitude and behavior toward elders.

Almost all of the respondents reported being aware that in Hawai'i there exists a generally negative attitude regarding Samoans, although none of them felt they had suffered personally from it. They knew that Samoans have a reputation in the state of being tough, aggressive, and larcenous and members of organized crime. One also remarked that even vocationally, Samoans were stereotyped as always being in positions such as security guards and nightclub bouncers. This brought about a lively discussion, as some group members said that this wasn't just stereotyping—it was factual. The issue was ameliorated when all agreed that in years past, most Samoans new to Hawai'i had gravitated to either menial labor jobs or ones that were security related, but that now, many more were seeking higher education and the social, economic, and class privileges that result from it.

The respondents were almost evenly split regarding the appropriateness of the local anti-Samoan prejudice. Slightly more than half of one group indicated that they believed the negative bias was the result of the "bad" non-Samoan conduct of a very small minority of Samoan males. This subgroup felt that most of these antisocial Samoans had unfortunately distanced themselves from their family, their church, their leaders, and their cultural ties and had subsequently lost their moral compass. They implied that had these delinquents been encompassed by the "village," they would not have acted criminally or aggressively.

The remainder of the group responding to this issue tended to be defensive. Although they acknowledged personally knowing some Samoans who have behaved badly, they intimated that Samoans were probably no more deserving of this sobriquet than any other racial or cultural group. When asked why they felt Samoans in particular had garnered this unwanted reputation, some attributed it to the intimidating size of many Samoan males or once again to the lure of the unfettered and morally lax lifestyle in Hawai'i, without recognizing that the same enticements would be present for all acculturating groups.

Overall, it seems fair to say that growing up in a traditional village in Samoa is probably not a very effective preparation for life in urban Hawai'i. It is certainly not uncommon for any new group of immigrants to acquire negative or less than savory stereotypes. The discussants suggested indirectly that at least part of the reason may be because a significant number of Samoans living in Hawai'i are essentially lukewarm at best regarding their desire to "blend in" with Hawai'i's core culture. This impression did not stem from direct statements on the topic by the Samoan respondents but rather from their personal answers to several related questions. Even those who have lived here for a decade or two and who felt generally positive about their lives in Hawai'i appeared reticent about becoming part of the Hawaiian mix. As noted earlier, this feeling seems to reflect the concern that identifying with the core Hawai'i culture would require relinquishing some of their Samoan identity. In their answers to a multiple-choice question, all of those interviewed, including three who had moved to Hawai'i thirty or more years ago, perceived themselves as "Samoans in Hawai'i"—not "Hawaiians" or even "Samoan Hawaiians." Even those who have lived in Hawai'i for three or four decades reported a continuing strong affiliation with their *aiga*, their Samoan identity, and to a lesser extent, their *matai*.

The interviewees were also asked about intermarriage. Three of them had non-Samoan spouses and responded that in Hawaiʻi, there is a lot of intermarriage of Samoans with Hawaiians or part-Hawaiians. They commented that this is not surprising since the cultures and traditions are similar in so many ways. Others also noted that a majority of Samoans, even in Hawaiʻi, do not intermarry but wed other Samoans. However, the marriage of a Samoan to someone of a different ethnicity is not uncommon, and it is not dishonorable to the Faʻa Samoa.

There was a general consensus that the problems of Samoan youth in Hawaiʻi today are because they are out of touch with traditional cultural values. In an effort to help increase Samoan cultural awareness and to preserve their culture, various Samoan organizations, with help from the City and County of Honolulu, instigated a weeklong celebration of the Samoan Flag Day in Hawaiʻi. This observance reflects the celebration held annually in American Samoa to commemorate its becoming a U.S. territory. A large number of participants travel from both Samoas to join Samoans from the mainland during this celebration. Throughout the week, there are performances of cultural songs and dances, and traditional food and apparel is sold to the public. The event is celebrated each year to uphold the spirit of unity among the Samoan people and promote cultural awareness.

There are also a number of other positive aspects relating to Samoan immigration to Hawaiʻi. One is the broad base of countrymen already present who can provide support and guidance for the newcomers. For Samoan children, improvements in the educational system in Samoa have served to lessen the stress of entering Hawaiʻi's school system. The continuing shift in Samoa from the agricultural, communal life of the village to a cash economy has also helped adults enter the Hawaiʻi job market. In addition, more than a half century of TV and other media exposure to Euro-American ways has minimized the shock of the transition, which to some extent should also be reduced by the fact that, imbedded within the trappings of life in modern Hawaiʻi, evidence of its common Polynesian origins is ubiquitous.

Finally, there are the individual Samoan successes in Hawaiʻi. These have been prominent in a number of endeavors, including sports and the successes of local Samoans in high school, college, and professional football; the entertainment world; academia, with an increasing number of Samoans receiving advanced degrees in a variety of fields; and in the attainment of professional status, where Samoans have succeeded in the fields of medicine and law. More recently, Samoans have had good cause to be elated and inspired by the election of a part-Samoan as the mayor of Honolulu.

Summary and Conclusions

In retrospect, if there is any single aspect regarding Samoan culture that sets it apart from other Pacific Island groups, it is likely the manner in which Samoans have dealt with the aftermath of European contact. The Samoans dealt with Western discovery and intrusion in a different manner. Although they were not immune to internecine conflict, the strong family ties that stretched across the various islands of the archipelago had created a relatively peaceful atmosphere prior to the arrival of the first Europeans. The extensive *aiga* network was tightly interwoven. The *matai* filigree that permeated all the islands of the archipelago also served to unify Samoans to a degree that was relatively unique among the island realms of nineteenth-century Polynesia.

The resulting cohesiveness allowed the Samoan people, exposed to unfamiliar Euro-American customs, language, values, and religions, to accommodate to them without losing or doing irreparable damage to their own hereditary customs, language, values, and religion. They accomplished this largely by absorbing selected portions of the foreign inputs in a way that resulted in their being amalgamated into the traditional Samoan way of life. Fa'a Samoa was modified but without doing it irreparable harm, and this actually served to strengthen its value as a critical part of the cultural cement.

The result was the avoidance of a dramatic internal schism and strong internal conflicts of the kind that occurred elsewhere in Polynesia. In Samoa, the new ways were sometimes ignored, while in other instances they were adopted intact; more often, however, they were subtly woven into the traditional Samoan customs or language. A quaint example of the latter came about because pea soup was apparently one of the early and more common imports of canned goods shipped to Samoa. Over the years a linguistic displacement has somehow occurred, so that today in Pago Pago, if you wish to purchase a can of corned beef, you simply ask for *pisupo*—a preferred choice of food for Samoans even in Hawai'i and abroad.

Because of the strength, depth, and tenacity of Fa'a Samoa, the Samoan people have managed to retain much of what existed in precontact days. The consequences of this cohesive, group-focused, cultural durability for Samoans who emigrate to other lands such as Hawai'i seems to be severalfold. By its very nature, Fa'a Samoa serves to encourage cultural cohesiveness, wariness of outsiders, and the insulation of Samoans living abroad. These all likely serve to retard acculturation into a host culture. In addition, Samoans have traditionally been raised in an extended family environment in which literally dozens of parental surrogates are always nearby to quash or punish asocial behavior. This reduces the need for an individual sense of right and wrong. As a result, when they emigrate, some Samoans may have more than the normal degree of difficulty adapting to the rules and laws in a society that presumes that its citizens have evolved some form of personal, internalized conscience.

It has been almost sixty years since the major migration of Samoans to Hawai'i occurred. This Pacific population may be understudied in some areas because much of the research lumps Samoans in a "Pacific Islanders" or "Asian-Americans and Pacific Islanders" category. Disaggregated research shows that the Samoan adolescents in Hawai'i have high rates of actual arrests, incarceration, and gang involvement and are at increased risk for self-reported youth violence.[13] The Samoan community and its leaders are concerned and are taking action by coming together to help its youth. It is generally believed that an important part of the solution involves reminding Samoan juveniles of their cultural values and the Fa'a Samoa. This illustrates an important point regarding the education of Samoans. In most instances, the prioritization of the Fa'a Samoa and responsibilities to the *aiga* can actually become a challenge to a youth. For example, a child with a lot of homework would most likely have to help out with household chores upon arriving home by cleaning up or preparing dinner or both, help watch the younger siblings and care for any elderly family members, attend church youth practice, and then finally have time to study and do schoolwork. Many community leaders conclude that noninvolvement in the Samoan culture is one of the primary reasons why Samoan youths encounter problems. However, as one interviewee pointed out, Samoan juveniles know very well about their culture, but the problem is rather the lack of a good education or stressing the importance of obtaining a higher education as a means of improving the quality of life and an opportunity to better provide for oneself, one's family, and one's community.

Any acculturational reticence noted earlier does not appear to be due to a pervasive dislike of Hawaiian or Western culture. It is more likely because as a people, Samoans differ in several important ways from most of the other groups who have emigrated to Hawai'i. As a relatively small, homogeneous, and isolated group, Samoans have been able to sustain a more unified sense of their own history, identity, spiritual beliefs, and culture. This has continued to unify the entire Samoan archipelago even after over a century of political bifurcation. Until now this has allowed Samoans to essentially cherry-pick those aspects of the Western world that they choose to incorporate into their own culture rather than the converse. Samoans have modified their dress, their eating habits, their economics, and even their religion as a result of Western contact. They have been far more resistant, however, in allowing any significant changes to the pillars of their traditional Samoan society.

It is important to note that any family, community, or government-related decisions made in the Samoan islands often inadvertently have an effect on a large number of Samoans overseas. Fa'a Samoa provides Samoans with an ancient unifying code and a solid sense of kinship both at home and abroad. Even in a foreign land, no Samoan is alone if another Samoan is nearby. As their world is becoming increasingly westernized, Samoans too will likely relinquish some of the cultural identity they have so steadfastly maintained for centuries.

As this process takes place, like other groups before them, they may finally begin to think of themselves not as "Samoans in Hawai'i" or "Samoans in California" but rather as "Samoan Hawaiians" or simply "Hawaiians"—but they will very likely be among the last to do so.

Further Reading

"American Samoa Government." Official Web site: http://americansamoa.gov/, 2009.

Bellwood, P. *The Polynesians: Prehistory of an Island People.* London: Thames and Hudson, 1978.

Culbertson, P., M. N. Agee, and C. O. Makasiale. *Penina Uliuli: Contemporary Challenges in Mental Health for Pacific Peoples.* Honolulu: University of Hawai'i Press, 2007.

Gao, G., and P. Perrone. *Crime in Hawai'i 2005: A Review of Uniform Crime Reports.* Honolulu: Office of the Attorney General, State of Hawai'i, 2007.

"Government of Samoa." Official Web site: http://www.govt.ws/, 2009.

Gray, J. A. C. *Amerika Samoa: A History of American Samoa and Its United States Naval Administration.* Annapolis, MD: United States Naval Institute, 1960.

Holmes, L. D. *Samoan Village.* New York: Holt, Rinehart and Winston, 1974.

Howells, W. W. *The Pacific Islanders.* London: Weidenfeld and Nicolson, 1973.

MacDonald, J. M. "The effect of ethnicity on juvenile court decision making in Hawai'i." *Youth Society* 35(2) (2003): 243–263.

Mayeda, D. T., E. S. Hishinuma, S. T. Nishimura, O. Garcia-Santiago, and G. Y. Mark. "Asian/Pacific Islander Youth Violence Prevention Center: Interpersonal violence and deviant behaviors among youth in Hawai'i." *Journal of Adolescent Health* 39 (2006): 276.e1–276.e11.

Mayeda, D. T., L. Pasko, and M. Chesney-Lind. "You got to do so much to actually make it: Gender, ethnicity, and Samoan youth in Hawai'i." *AAPI Nexus* 4(2) (2006): 69–93.

Ngan-Woo, F. E. *Fa'asamoa: The World of Samoans.* New Zealand: Office of the Race Relations Conciliator, 1985.

Notes

1. J. A. C. Gray, *Amerika Samoa: A History of American Samoa and Its United States Naval Administration*, Annapolis, MD: United States Naval Institute, 1960: 3–4.

2. Ibid.: 80–102.

3. *CIA World Fact Book,* "American Samoa," retrieved May 29, 2009, from https://www.cia.gov/library/publications/the-world-factbook/geos/aq.html.

4. P. M. Harris and N. A. Jones, "We the people: Pacific Islanders in the United States," *United States Census 2000 Special Reports,* 2005, retrieved from http://www.census.gov/prod/2005pubs/censr-26.pdf.

5. P. Bellwood, *The Polynesians: Prehistory of an Island People,* London: Thames and Hudson, 1978.

6. W. W. Howells, *The Pacific Islanders,* London: Weidenfeld and Nicolson, 1973.

7. Bellwood 1978.

8. P. Culbertson, M. N. Agee, and C. O. Makasiale, *Penina Uliuli: Contemporary Challenges in Mental Health for Pacific Peoples,* Honolulu: University of Hawai'i Press, 2007.

9. L. D. Holmes, *Samoan Village,* New York: Holt, Rinehart and Winston, 1974.

10. Gray 1960.

11. E. Faleomavaega, "American Samoa death rate in Iraq War is highest among all states and U.S. territories," U.S. Congress [Press Release, March 23, 2009] retrieved from http://www.house.gov/list/press/as00_faleomavaega/asdeathratehighestamongstates.html.

12. C. B. Park, K. L. Braun, B. Y. Horiuchi, C. Tottori, and A. T. Onaka, "Longevity disparities in multiethnic Hawai'i: An analysis of 2000 life tables," *Public Health Reports* 124(4) (2009): 579–584.

13. G. Gao and P. Perrone, *Crime in Hawai'i 2005: A Review of Uniform*

Crime Reports, Honolulu: Office of the Attorney General, State of Hawai'i, 2007; J. M. MacDonald, "The effect of ethnicity on juvenile court decision making in Hawai'i, *Youth Society* 35(2) (2003): 243–263; K. Umemoto and V. Verwudh, *Preliminary Analysis of Juvenile Arrestees in Waipahu Using 2001 Juvenile Justice Information Systems (JJIS) Data,* Honolulu: University of Hawai'i Department or Urban and Regional Planning, 2003; D. T. Mayeda, E. S. Hishinuma, S. T. Nishimura, O. Garcia-Santiago, and G. Y. Mark, "Asian/Pacific Islander Youth Violence Prevention Center: Interpersonal violence and deviant behaviors among youth in Hawai'i," *Journal of Adolescent Health* 39 (2006): 276.e1–276.e11.

CHAPTER 12

The Thais

Michael Fukuda and Anongnart "Mickie" Carriker

The Southeast Asians

"Southeast Asia" has been used for decades by Western historians to represent the geographic region east of India and south of China, and as such, the term covers a vast land area, numerous political states, and a multitude of peoples. Countries within the Southeast Asia categorization include Brunei, Cambodia, East Timor, Indonesia, Laos, Malaysia, Myanmar, the Philippines, Singapore, Thailand, and Vietnam. The term and classification continues to be used, perhaps simply to differentiate countries in the region from those in East Asia (e.g., China, Korea, and Japan). Whereas the distinctions among East Asian countries and cultures have long been acknowledged by Western scholars, Southeast Asia is often viewed as a more or less monolithic entity and Southeast Asians as part of a somehow connected, interrelated society. On the contrary: The extraordinary diversity of cultures and customs within the region cannot be overstated.

Still, because of Hawai'i's unique history of interactions with those who came from other places and its resultant multiracial, multicultural society, the experiences of those from the countries of Southeast Asia in the Hawaiian Islands are important to explore here. Within the confines of this volume, only a fraction of the Southeast Asians in Hawai'i can be explored and discussed. The editors have chosen to explore three significant groups in Hawai'i—the Thais, the Vietnamese, and the Cambodians—each with its own chapter, beginning with this chapter on the Thais. Notably, geographic linkage does not necessarily mean there are corresponding political or cultural linkages among the groups. As the reader will discover, however, while there are many differences among the three groups, they are indeed linked by their common experience of developing a unique ethnocultural identity as part of the multicultural Stew Pot that is Hawai'i.

Overview and Demographics

Thailand, also known as the Land of Smiles, is well known for its hospitality and generosity. Seen as the gateway to Southeast Asia, it is an independent country bordered by Laos, Cambodia, Myanmar, and Malaysia. The government is a constitutional monarchy, with King Bhumibol Adulyadej as head of state. The king has guided the country for sixty-three years and has the distinction of being the longest-reigning monarch in the world. Thai people have great respect and admiration for King Adulyadej, relying on his wisdom and generous nature to lead the kingdom to prosperity.

Thailand has a surface area of 198,000 square miles (similar to California) and a population of approximately 65 million. Ethnic Thais make up 75 percent of the population, with 14 percent Chinese, 3 percent Malay, and the rest belonging to various hill tribes. Theravada Buddhism is the national religion, with 94 percent of the population belonging to this group.[1] Buddhist teaching praises the "middle path and detachment"; avoidance of extremes in emotion and anger is seen as desirable behavior. This theme impacts all aspects of Thai life and is seen throughout the life span.

Emigration from Thailand is relatively recent, beginning in the 1960s with a small number of professionals (physicians, nurses, and engineers) moving to the United States for occupational opportunities. During the 1980s, semiskilled and unskilled workers moved to the Middle East, taking advantage of the oil-rich region's expanding economy. During the 1990s, East and Southeast Asian economies experienced tremendous growth, drawing workers away from the Middle East, the United States, and Europe.[2]

The 2000 census for Hawai'i reported 1,200 individuals listing Thai ethnicity only, and almost twice that many claiming a combination of Thai and other Asian ethnicities. Thais immigrate to Hawai'i for educational and employment opportunities, along with family obligations. The first two categories tend to be transient, obtaining their educational or economic goals and returning to Thailand. The family group represents those who plan to permanently reside in the state, with Hawai'i-based spouses or family that have established Thai-themed businesses.[3]

Unlike other Southeast Asian peoples, Thais do not emigrate because of political or economic instability. Thailand was never colonized; subsequently most leave the country permanently to join family or to follow a spouse to their home country. Those following a spouse are usually in the U.S. military, making the population transient (moving to a new duty station every three to four years).

While only a small Thai community exists in Hawai'i, it is an ideal location for Thai immigration. Hawai'i has a warm climate, proximity to other Southeast Asian ethnicities, and food/produce availability similar to home, making it an ideal area to resettle.

Ethnocultural Identity

Understanding Thai culture requires knowledge of *chaat, sasaana,* and *phra maha kasat,* or the nation, religion, and the monarch. This forms the foundation of the Thai house: Respect for country, religion, and the royal family sets the tone and behavior over the life span.

Thais have great respect for their country and take pride in its accomplishments. As previously mentioned, Thailand is the only Southeast Asian country not colonized by Europe. Criticizing elements of the nation is tolerated amongst Thais; however, criticism from outside Thailand is never tolerated.

Buddhism in Thailand differs from religious practices in the West. Thais do not pray to a supreme being; rather they pray for themselves or others, recalling the teachings of Lord Buddha (serenity, enlightenment, purity of mind, tongue, and action).[4] Thais believe in Karma—good and bad actions create energy that lasts beyond one's lifetime. Providing *tham boon* (merit) is accomplished by visiting the local *wat* (temple). Performing religious acts at the *wat* and giving to the poor during one's life increase the chances of a better life when reborn, or they ultimately may lead to stopping the rebirth cycle and entering a state of Nirvana viewed as Buddhist paradise.

The king and royal family are highly respected for their works on behalf of the country and people. The king has championed projects that help rural and remote villages improve agricultural productivity, decreasing poverty and bringing hope to the people. Thais love their king and queen; travel to any home in Thailand and you will find several portraits of the king and royal family. Thais will not tolerate any criticism of the king or royal family.

Thailand is a vertical society, with its history going back to fifteenth-century rule under King Trailok of Ayuthaya (the old capital of Thailand). A system was developed ranking citizens under the *sakdi na,* a point system based on occupation. A peasant rated 25 in the system, a craftsman 50; the ultimate was a top official in government, rating 10,000 points. The system also allowed access to land grants and social and economic benefits commensurate with rank.[5] *Sakdi na* was abolished by King Chulalongkorn, although vestiges of this system remain in the Thai psyche.[6]

Modern Thais still believe in a hierarchical system, and when meeting someone for the first time they will try to determine their status. While upward mobility exists in Thai society, Buddhists belief in rebirth, and one's current status based on past acts is strongly instilled. This accounts for the modern-day adherence of those in lower status, hoping to improve their status in the next life through good deeds and acts.

Family is most important to Thais, with family cohesion and cooperation being crucial to surviving a challenging environment. Parents sacrifice for their children, and children in return practice *katanyu.* In this tradition learned early in life, children understand that if someone does good for you, you are expected to return the favor. *Katanyu* applies especially to the bond between child and parent staying strong throughout the life span, and it accounts for the many extended families seen in Thai households. An adult Thai child, no matter how far from home, will always support his or her parents.

Discovering one's place in society is taught early on; children learn (through language) their place and when to show respect. Their parents are referred to as Mae and Poh (Mother and Father), with the prefix Khun (Mrs. Mother and Mr. Father). Older siblings also have a place in respect: They are addressed as Pee Chai or Pee Sau (older brother or sister or a close older friend). Younger siblings are referred to as Nong.

While it may seem that children in Thailand lead strict lives, in actuality they are pampered. The main learning objective is that children become polite and respectful of their elders. Some Thai adolescents moving out of the country must modify their behaviors yet still respect their elders. Anecdotally, one Thai teenager told a story about buying a car. He felt the salesman was very respectful, even though he was older. The adolescent bought the car and brought an older Thai friend to pick up the car. When the friend discovered what the adolescent had paid, he immediately renegotiated a fair price for the car. The adolescent was stunned that his Pee Chai, who was younger than the salesman, actually raised his voice to get a better deal (more on this later).

As the child transitions to adolescence, school and peer group become important. Those that show aptitude and have financial resources enter college and obtain careers in business or civil service. During their time in school, respect for teachers and older students is reinforced as it was in childhood.

In Hawai'i, adolescents represent separation from parents and developing one's own identity. A Thai adolescent in Hawai'i may experience this through the peer group; however, ties to the family remain strong. The family identity and respect for parents protect the teenager from rebellious acts. A Thai teenager who attends college and works part time gives all of her salary to her mother. The family does not need the money; however, the teenager willingly parts with her salary to help support the family.

When an adolescent enters adulthood, marriage is considered a good way to maintain family stability and continuation of the family line. Traditional Thai courtship is conservative, not allowing the potential couple to date without an escort (usually the woman's older sister or friend). After courtship, the bride and groom's family must agree and approve before the couple is allowed to marry. Some families require *sin sot* (a dowry) for the wife. This goes back to the theme that all children practice *katanyu*, the bride price thanking the parents for raising a wonderful wife. This also replaces the work the daughter would have done for the family. This practice is changing, however, some families no longer participating or giving the money back to the groom. The act of *sin sot* becomes more one of face (a pride issue) than a monetary contribution.

Adult men are usually the major wage earners, with the wife running the household. Both move into comfortable lives and in times of turmoil fall back on teachings they learned as children. Thais believe in calm and dignity (the middle path) and feel that outbursts of emotion are distasteful. Keeping a *jai yen* (cool heart) is better than having a *jai ron* (hot heart). *Mai pen rai* (no problems or worries) is a good way of saving face when becoming angry. Instead of giving in to *jai ron* and having an outburst, the Thai coolly says, *"mai pen rai,"* and the problem is de-escalated. As previously mentioned, however, criticizing the government or the king will likely result in extreme hostility, and it is something a non-Thai should never do. *Mai pen rai* or *jai yen* will not solve this problem once spoken.

Religion

The *wat* is the center point of religion for Thai life. Two exist in Hawai'i on the island of O'ahu. Both allow laypeople to practice *tam boom*—making merit through supporting monks (who take a vow of poverty) with gifts and food, to the ultimate: a male ordaining as a monk for a short period of time. A male entering the monkhood provides much merit to his parents, allowing them to enter a better life in rebirth.

Death also takes part at the *wat*, with important rituals such as washing the body and providing joss sticks and flowers for the casket. A seven-to-ten-day waiting period before final cremation allows the family to grieve and prepare for the final ceremony. During this time, one will see few tears and more of a stoic appearance, helping the person to move onto the next birth. Tears and sobbing would hold back the person's journey to the next life.

A New Ethnocultural Identity

As mentioned previously, *jai yen* and *mai pen rai* could be face-saving acts that allow Thais struggling in rural areas to form together and work as a collective group to survive times of adversity.

Farming in the northeast of Thailand requires great cooperation; families rely on relatives and neighbors to help with planting and harvesting of rice. Villages that did not have this cooperation suffered and eventually stopped working the land. Thus over a period of years, *jai yen* and *mai pen rai* may have become a phenotype expressed through language as a survival mechanism. Saving face becomes an issue for all: Losing the cooperation of one person, their family, or a neighbor could lead to catastrophe, as the harmonious community work ethic would be lost.

Thais in Hawai'i

As previously mentioned, the Thai teenager who bought an over-priced car was shocked when his Pee Chai (older brother or friend) raised his voice at the salesman. Instead of getting into a fight, the salesman smiled and lowered the price of the car. The teenager's friend had adapted to the negotiation tactics required for the situation. Two things surprised and taught the Thai teenager a cross-cultural lesson: First, in America (even in multicultural Hawai'i), age is not as important as the principle of getting a fair bargain; and second, in certain situations, negotiating a fair price, even with an older Euro-American male, will result in respect and deference to a younger man who asserts himself. This is a cultural lesson in adjusting to living in Hawai'i (and America).

Thais in Hawai'i have preserved their lifestyle and follow cultural practices established in Thailand generations ago. Because they are a small, tight-knit group, change has not come to their culture; however, they have learned to adapt and appreciate the many cultures of Hawai'i.

Thais share their culture through yearly events such as Songran (Thai New Year) and the King and Queen's Birthday. Both are open to the public and also include other Southeast Asian countries. The events are seen as opportunities to share their culture with their new host culture.

Adaptation

Thailand is a complex country, with a language that focuses on being polite and respectful. Often a simple "yes" or "no" is not simple at all. "Yes" may be said not to offend the person, yet no action will be taken on the request. Raising one's voice or becoming angry results in a "loss of face," thus demeaning oneself in front of the person from whom help is required.

The Hawai'i Thai community practices its own culture; however, Thais have learned to adapt to Hawai'i and its Western traditions. In Thailand there are many shades of gray, whereas in Hawai'i issues can be polarized or black and white. Our Thai teenager who tried to buy a car did not know that Hawai'i decisions were black and white and assumed he was getting the best deal, as the salespeople were polite (when, in fact, they were getting the highest price for the car). His friend, having been in Hawai'i longer, had adapted to the Western ways and was able to negotiate and lower the price of the vehicle.

Summary and Conclusions

Despite having a small population, Thai people in Hawai'i have preserved their home culture, providing a protective factor when adapting to the diverse cultures of Hawai'i. Generosity and friendliness are key Thai approaches when seeking harmony in a Hawai'i community that focuses on outcomes, not process.

It is unique that most have adapted to the black-and-white, out-come-oriented Western approach, while maintaining the best of

Hawai'i culture. Aloha and *'ohana* are important processes familiar to Thai culture, demonstrated through the sharing of music, dance, and food at various festivals in the Islands.

Those encountering a Thai for the first time will be better prepared if they can determine if the person has adapted to Hawai'i. Cultural barriers will become less if both parties understand the straightforward approach of the West, keeping in mind that the Thai person will respond in a way that will preserve the relationship and not let anyone lose face if possible.

Further Reading

Cooper, R. *Culture Shock! Thailand: A Survival Guide to Customs and Etiquette.* Singapore: Marshall Cavendish Editions, 2007.
Jones, R. *Thailand: A Quick Guide to Culture and Etiquette.* Portland, OR: Graphic Arts Publishing Co., 2006.

Notes

1. *CIA World Fact Book: Thailand,* retrieved February 6, 2009, from https://www.cia.gov/library/publications/the-world-factbook/geos/th.html.
2. C. Supang, "Thailand's responses to transnational migration during economic growth and economic downturn," *Sojourn* 14 (1999): 162–165.
3. The Honorary Royal Thai Consulate provides language translation and social services to Thai nationals living in Hawai'i. The consulate maintains contact with Thais in Hawai'i, providing a rich source of information on the Thai community.
4. M. Keller, *Living Thai Ways,* Bangkok Book House: Bangkok, 2004: 49. According to Keller, Buddhism is a way of life, and it is not theistic; one can become enlightened by freeing oneself from pain and suffering. Life is impermanent, and the desire for self-ambition (to become "someone" in pursuit of fame and fortune) or clinging to pleasure leads to suffering. Freedom from self and desire liberates the heart from greed, jealousy, and hatred (the cause of pain and suffering). Once this state is obtained, it opens the heart to kindness and the mind to wisdom.
5. R. Jones, *Thailand: A Quick Guide to Culture and Etiquette,* Portland, OR: Graphic Arts Publishing Co., 2006: 32.
6. Thais new to Hawai'i will assess status when interacting with others, although they recognize the hierarchical system is not static and can change based on social and economic variables. The hierarchical system in Thailand is also undergoing change, as evidenced by the current political situation in the country.

CHAPTER 13

The Vietnamese

Christine Su and Paul Tran

While many Vietnamese who now live in Hawai'i also came to the
United States by boat, they set out from their homeland neither because
they were curious about foreign lands, fueled by religious conviction,
nor anticipating employment. Rather, they left because they had to: War
in mainland Southeast Asia in the 1960s and 1970s, particularly in
Vietnam, led thousands to flee and seek refuge elsewhere. Beginning in
1975, a mass exodus of refugees landed initially in Thailand, Malaysia,
the Philippines, and even Indonesia. Because many escaped on rick-
ety fishing boats or wooden rafts, as news of their attempts to escape
emerged they became known as "boat people," particularly by the American media. Throughout the late 1970s and early 1980s, thousands were
relocated from refugee camps in Asia or the Pacific Islands (particularly
Wake Island and Guam) to France, Canada, Australia, and the United
States. Most of those who came to the United States originally settled
in California, Florida, and Texas, although there were refugees who had
relatives or sponsors in Hawai'i. The majority of the Vietnamese refugees currently in Hawai'i, however, are tertiary migrants—that is, their
journeys took them to the mainland United States (or other countries)
before they came to Hawai'i. Much has already been written about the
history and journey of Vietnamese refugees to the United States. This
chapter focuses on the Vietnamese in Hawai'i and the ways in which
life in Hawai'i has enabled the Vietnamese to become successful.

The 2000 U.S. Census reported that there were 7,900 Vietnamese
in the state of Hawai'i, with an additional 2,100 who identified as Vietnamese in combination with other races or ethnicities. The Vietnamese

are the largest Southeast Asian group in Hawai'i.[1] Many of these are second and even third generation, and they arrived at different times or waves (see Table 13.1 below). More than 90 percent of the 10,000-plus Vietnamese live in the City and County of Honolulu, where for the most part they have thrived and succeeded, especially in business and education, and they have adapted well to life in the Islands.

Ethnocultural Identity

Vietnamese ethnocultural identity is incredibly complex. However, there are two major patterns that have been significantly influential in shaping a collective Vietnamese identity: Vietnam's history of domination and colonization and its traditional village life. Certainly one could argue that of the many other characteristics, any one is the major influence on Vietnamese identity. The authors have chosen to focus on these two areas because they seem to have been most influential in shaping Vietnamese identity in Hawai'i today.

HISTORY OF DOMINATION AND COLONIZATION

Intragroup Relations: China. As discussed at length by Nguyen and Kehmeier, the Vietnamese have continuously struggled against domination by other nations and empires.[2] "Almost from its birth," they write, "this race of people was threatened by absorption into other civilizations."[3] China repeatedly invaded Vietnam for nearly a thousand years. The sheer size and power of Chinese legions could have overwhelmed the Vietnamese, yet they resisted assimilation and eventually regained political independence from the Chinese in A.D. 939. Notably, however, during their long history of interaction with Vietnam, the Chinese instilled many of their beliefs and traditions in Vietnamese society, including Confucianism, a code of social behavior stressing that man should live in harmony with others and seek to improve himself as an individual for the good of the family/community. Confucianism asserts that one's role and duty in life comes from one's situation in relation to others—in other words, one should know his or her place in society and act accordingly and appropriately. Similarities between Vietnamese and Chinese culture, customs, and ideology remain and continue to influence Vietnamese life both in Vietnam and in Vietnamese diaspora; these are evident in Vietnamese language, demeanor, filial devotion, religion (particularly Buddhism and Taoism), and social support structure. Andrew Forbes comments that "the relationship between the two countries is in many ways a family affair, with all the closeness of shared values and bitterness of close rivalries."[4]

Intragroup Relations: France. In the nineteenth century, France sought to expand its overseas empire, much of which it had lost to Great Britain and the United States. Motives for this expansion included desire for raw materials, trade, and cheap labor, as well as glory and prestige. France also wished to convert nations and peoples to Roman Catholicism and to promote French culture abroad. In Southeast Asia, France conquered part of Vietnam that was then known as Cochin China, and by the end of the nineteenth century it had added Annam and Tonkin (also part of present-day Vietnam), Cambodia, and Laos to its empire. By 1914, France had amassed an empire of more than 4 million square miles and 60 million people.

As with the Chinese, the Vietnamese relationship with the French is complex, and clarifying it is beyond the scope of this chapter. Still, French influence on the Vietnamese, particularly those who lived in urban areas, must be mentioned. Perhaps more so than with the Chinese, from whom they wished to remain distinct, the Vietnamese did to a certain extent become part of French society and politics. While not considered equals by the French, some Vietnamese—especially those who had converted to Catholicism—were able to serve in lower levels of French government and make decent wages. In addition to the political or bureaucratic framework that France instilled into Vietnamese society, French clothing styles, mannerisms, language, foods, and ideologies made their way into Vietnamese life and practice. Furthermore, there was considerable intermarriage (or if not marriage, interethnic sexual relations) that resulted in mixed French-Vietnamese offspring. Vietnamese students were able to study at universities in France and became exposed to various ideologies and involved in political movements. One of these students, Ho Chi Minh, joined the Communist Party, returned to Vietnam, and joined the Communist Viet Minh in northern Vietnam.

During World War II, Japan occupied Vietnam, loosening French control. After the war ended, France attempted to regain control but failed. In 1954, the Geneva Accords ended France's colonial presence in Vietnam and temporarily partitioned the increasingly hostile northern and southern parts of the country into two states at the 17th parallel. Ngo Dinh Diem was appointed prime minister of southern Vietnam, and soon thereafter Ho Chi Minh became the leader of northern Vietnam.

In the aftermath of World War II, North Vietnam came to be supported by the People's Republic of China and the former USSR, while South Vietnam was supported by the United States. Tensions between North and South and the other parties involved quickly escalated into the Vietnam War.

Intragroup Relations: The United States. American intentions in Vietnam in the latter part of the twentieth century cannot be accurately categorized as either attempts to dominate or colonize; however, the United States did wish to persuade the Vietnamese of the iniquity of Communism and the authority of democracy and meritocracy. The ideological and military struggles that ensued would forever change the destinies of both countries and their people. Vietnamese identity—traditionally defined by family, village, and nation—to many became family, village, and North or South. The North/South addition had a significant effect on the Vietnamese identity as individuals and how they interacted with family. Anecdotally, Vietnamese in Hawai'i reported the need to make sudden adjustments to long-established gender and family roles, with significant disruption to psychosocial functioning described later in this chapter.

VILLAGE LIFE

The cradle of Vietnamese society was the village. Enclosed behind a tall hedge of bamboo, each village was a separate entity, complete with its own population, customs, even its own deity enshrined in the communal house—a tiny world within the world of Vietnam.[5]

As delineated above, the Vietnamese village is a microcosm of Vietnamese society itself. In the village, one has a "place"—that is, based upon one's position in the family and in the village, he or she knows how to act and what to do.

Intergroup Relations: Family, Village, Nation. The family—and in particular, one's immediate family—is the basic unit of Vietnamese society. In the village, Vietnamese families function via a largely Confucian, hierarchical system with specific roles based upon age, elders being the most highly respected. Special reverence is given to one's ancestors, "elders" whom they believe continue to influence the lives of the living. Family members practice rituals venerating their forbears and find comfort knowing that through these rituals their ancestors receive proper spiritual nourishment. Traditional roles place the father as the economic provider, responsible for the well-being of the family.

It is not unusual for fathers to give up everything for their children, especially their sons, nor for eldest male children to take on responsibility for parents, grandparents, siblings, and other family members. The mother's role is to take care of the household, including her husband, children, and in-laws. Parents are expected to arrange for suitable partners for both their male and female children and generally to ensure happy futures for them. Finally, older children, particularly females, are expected to care for and rear younger children.

Beyond the immediate family and other relatives, village life requires that families work together, assisting each other with planting and harvesting of crops, for example. Like other countries in Southeast Asia, Vietnamese village life is based upon water-rice agriculture, and thus many customs and rituals celebrate the harvest or ask for the success of the harvest. Cultural practices, including festivals or ceremonies, are attached to the village community; marriages, for example, are arranged very carefully so as to benefit both families and the village.

Vietnamese value self-improvement, particularly through study and scholarship; however, those who succeed have an automatic obligation to take care of both family and village.

As discussed above, the Vietnamese have faced centuries of domination, colonization, and other attempts to change their culture. After World War II, the country itself was divided in two. Vietnamese themselves have been forced to move repeatedly and rapidly, whether within Vietnam or beyond its physical borders. Thus "nation" here arguably refers more to identity—knowledge of and loyalty to history, culture, and tradition that defines one as Vietnamese—than to the physical place, although given the duration of and sentiment about the Vietnam War, one's origin as "northern" or "southern" Vietnamese is also of consequence.

ADJUSTMENT TO LIFE IN THE UNITED STATES

Most historians agree that the categorization of Vietnamese migration to the United States is best explained in terms of "waves."[6] The exact breakdown of waves, in terms of years, however, differs from historian to historian. Here we use broad, approximate time periods simply to provide the reader with a sense of the makeup and characteristics of each the various refugee/migrant groups from Vietnam so that they may be analyzed comparatively (Table 13.1).

The traumatic psychological and physical affects of the refugee

Table 13.1. Vietnamese immigration waves

WAVE	DATES OF ARRIVAL	SOCIOECONOMIC BACKGROUND	REASONS FOR MIGRATION	NUMBERS
FIRST	The weeks leading up to the fall of Saigon in April 1975 and continuing until 1977	Largely urban, educated professionals, doctors, lawyers, teachers, businesspersons; spoke some English	Affiliated with southern Vietnamese government; in some cases had worked for American military or companies; many airlifted out of Vietnam	90,000– 100,000
SECOND	Late 1970s to mid-1980s	Mostly rural farmers, less educated than first wave; sometimes referred to as "boat people" because they fled by the thousands by boat[1]	Sought to escape oppression and major social, economic, and political reforms instituted by northern Vietnamese government	200,000– 400,000 (thousands died at sea)
THIRD	Late 1980s	More similarities to second wave than first; limited skills, mostly agrarian backgrounds	Former prisoners of reeducation camps, including former U.S. military and govt. employees who did not escape during the first wave;[2] Amerasian children	100,000
FOURTH	1990s to present day	Known as "new" migrants; less affected by former political upheaval than predecessors; both urban and rural	Many have relatives in the United States who sponsor them; others come for economic and educational opportunities	300,000[3]

1. Some of the "boat people" who escaped Vietnam during the second wave were ethnic Chinese, who had been driven out by the Vietnamese government.

2. In 1988, the U.S. Department of State finally reached an agreement with the Vietnamese government to allow many of them to leave through the Orderly Departure Program. An estimated 100,000 were released to join family members overseas.

3. This number was derived from an extrapolation of the U.S. Census data for Vietnamese in 2000 and the American Community Survey for 2007.

experience may never fully be understood nor resolved. Prior to the first wave coming to the United States, it is estimated that a million or more North Vietnamese resettled to the South. The majority of those who migrated were landowners or Catholics fearing political persecution.[7] This added complexity increased stress on the refugees, who through generations had fought foreign colonization and now found themselves at war with their own nation and fellow countrymen. However, Hawai'i presented a unique opportunity for Vietnamese migrants to rebuild their lives. Hawai'i provided an opportunity to reestablish the loss of economic and social status, with social support systems in place through well-established Asian and Southeast Asian communities.

HISTORY OF DOMINATION AND COLONIZATION—AND SURVIVAL

The previous section mentions the many attempts made by the Chinese, French, and others (including clashing factions within Vietnam itself) to dominate and control the Vietnamese. The Vietnamese have resisted these attempts and to a great extent retained their uniqueness; interestingly, however, they have also learned to do so while seeming to surrender some of their identity—at least outwardly—in order to survive. Nguyen and Kehmeier comment that for the Vietnamese, "passive resistance has been developed to a fine art, leading to flexibility and adaptability in the face of many years of occupation and political domination."[8] This outward flexibility is apparent among the Vietnamese who have settled in Hawai'i.

Intragroup Relations: The Chinese. Most of the refugees from Vietnam in the first and second waves arrived in California, Florida, Texas, and the Washington, D.C., area. While adjustment was extremely difficult, the large numbers of refugees relied upon and assisted each other, forming mutual assistance associations, community organizations, and businesses. In Hawai'i, the initial numbers of Vietnamese who arrived were much smaller (approximately 3,500 in 1979). Some of the second wave had family members to sponsor them, and they were supported by kin economically, socially, and psychologically. They too formed mutual assistance associations, although due to their small numbers they usually did so in collaboration with other Southeast Asian groups. However, a peculiar yet not unfamiliar relationship developed between the Vietnamese in Hawai'i and the Chinese, who had been established in the state for more than a century.

In an article about the changing face of Honolulu's Chinatown, *Honolulu Weekly* author Margaret Seeto writes,

While long ghettoized and orientalized with an inscrutable mystique, American Chinatowns have stood as havens for Chinese immigrants unfamiliar with laws and languages of their new lands.... Established settlers could help newcomers from their home territories find jobs and places to live. Societies formed based around commonalities ranging from last names to districts to cities to provinces, and became signature resources in Honolulu's Chinatown and others around the world.[9]

Indeed, Chinatowns developed across the United States as support systems for Chinese immigrants. In Hawai'i, the Chinese store was a cultural institution, where one could go not only to purchase supplies but to mail letters, get medical attention, and ask for translations. In Honolulu, Chinatown sprang up in the downtown area early on, and though twice devastated by fire it was rebuilt by the community.

In recent years, however, the Chinese community's need for Chinatown has become less urgent. It is still used and considered a valuable resource, but as the Chinese have assimilated into local culture, with generations of Chinese now born in Hawai'i and/or intermixed with other races, members of the community can now choose to be involved with Chinatown, accept its assistance, and celebrate its offerings—or not.

As larger numbers of Vietnamese began to arrive in Honolulu, however, particularly in the 1990s, Chinatown offered a practical, functional framework for their own adjustment.[10] As discussed in previous sections, the Vietnamese, while perhaps not enthralled by the Chinese, understand much of their culture and customs and could follow in their footsteps—particularly in terms of forming businesses and striving for education.[11]

Walking down the streets of Chinatown, one passes noodle shops and French-Vietnamese bistros (some with lines around the block) and stores selling Vietnamese movie DVDs. Calendars with photos of Vietnamese models or celebrities line the walls of many grocery markets and cafés, and in some areas there are as many signs in Vietnamese as there are in Chinese. One hears Vietnamese being spoken in lei shops, where family members sit around tables and string them by the dozen.

"VILLAGE LIFE" IN HAWAI'I

In the Vietnamese village, all inhabitants worked to ensure the success of one's family, one's village, and therefore one's nation. While a traditional village structure does not exist in Hawai'i, the Vietnamese community has created modified villages that function to support the family and the group. The first wave of Vietnamese in Hawai'i, for example, included members of the educated class. These migrants formed associations and businesses, and when subsequent waves arrived they assisted their kinsmen to acclimate as well. Haines suggests that while the refugee experience certainly disrupted Vietnamese family structure, the concept of kinship and its obligations retained "not only its predictable importance, but also much of its shape."[12] Actual or blood kin remained the most important; however, those "elders" who had arrived in Hawai'i first sought to help those who had newly arrived, working toward harmony within this new Vietnamese "village." They provided newer immigrants with jobs and provided social and cultural support, introducing them to others in their networks and holding cultural festivals and so forth. The result has been astonishing economic success. Notably, Vietnamese businesses have branched beyond Chinatown and can be found throughout the City and County of Honolulu. A well-known French-Vietnamese sandwich shop and bakery that opened in Chinatown in 1984 now has more than twenty stores throughout O'ahu and the continental United States.

In Hawai'i, Vietnamese fishermen have pooled their resources to support their business endeavors, particularly when traditional financial institutions would not provide them with loans. Each member of the group makes an investment that will assist in building one member's business; he has a vested interest in the success of that business, as he will eventually call upon those resources himself.

A second "village" analogy can be made with the religious institutions frequented by Vietnamese in Hawai'i. As already noted, a significant number of Vietnamese converted to Catholicism during the French colonial period. As refugees, they readily accepted the sponsorships offered by the Catholic Church. They also accepted services offered by other churches; voluntary agencies (known as "volags") such as the U.S. Catholic Conference, the International Rescue Committee, and Church World Service welcomed and helped to take care of their initial needs upon arriving in the United States. These refugees continued to attend church services and became involved in related community groups, and as they became more self-sufficient, they helped new arrivals to adjust.

A New Ethnocultural Identity

While Hawai'i is not without its interethnic tensions, Vietnamese in Hawai'i have faced less discrimination in the Islands than in other areas. Many in the continental United States conflated the Vietnamese refugees with Communism and viewed them as "the enemy" responsible for America's only wartime defeat. Tensions between Vietnamese and other ethnic groups in Hawai'i seem to stem from the perception that the Vietnamese are "clannish" and even haughty. One Chinatown resident commented about Vietnamese shopkeepers, "They don't talk-story with you, like others. I feel like they are arrogant and only like other Vietnamese." The Vietnamese proclivity to put family first, village second, and others last may lead others to perceive that they are not only outside of the Vietnamese social paradigm but that they are treated condescendingly or disrespectfully.

Most tensions tend to happen within the Vietnamese community itself, rather than between the Vietnamese and other ethnic groups. There are exceptions, such as the Vietnamese gang activity that has emerged among some adolescents; however, the growing pains of adjusting to life in Hawai'i have been more intergroup than intragroup based. The most noticeable of these are generational and gender differences between the traditional and the new ethnocultural identities.

GENERATIONAL DIFFERENCES

Generational differences are not exclusive to Vietnamese-Americans specifically nor to immigrant groups generally. Thus the claims of an elderly Vietnamese woman that she can tell the difference between American- or Vietnamese-born youth because the American-born Vietnamese does not show respect to his or her elders will resonate across ethnic groups. Rather than taking care of elders, she asserted, youths expect to be served and do not clean up after themselves, whereas in Vietnam children would feed their elders first and then clean up without being asked.

Anecdotal information also suggests that American-born Vietnamese are less likely to participate in cultural events and rituals.

Vietnamese parents tend to place enormous pressure on their children to succeed academically. Such success reflects well upon their family and upon the Vietnamese community. Yet the parents want their children to keep their focus on family and village, while also blending into American society. Furthermore, since many of the second- and third-wave migrants are from lower-income rural backgrounds, their children's academic success contributes to their social standing.

Because of their lower-income backgrounds, however, the children may not have the resources to succeed in education (particularly higher education) in the United States. In Hawai'i, those from lower-income households usually cannot attend private schools—mostly college preparatory schools. Yet stable blue-collar jobs that used to pay enough to support a family are becoming increasingly rare, so higher education is pursued intensely. Continuously rising tuitions also make college a lofty goal.

The children, moreover, face both rising aspirations—pushed by their parents, driven by culture and social expectations and by themselves, as American consumer culture drives them to want to earn and buy more—and shrinking opportunities.

GENDER DIFFERENCES

The Confucian and village life paradigms within which the traditional Vietnamese family operated made men the household providers and women the child rearers, the latter being subservient to the former. In the United States, however, economic circumstances—particularly those for refugees (and for those who live in Hawai'i)—often warrant that women work outside the home. The independence created for women by this situation may be perceived as disrupting the social order, and men can perceive a loss of their power and status. Fear about this loss has led to men's violence against their wives and other female family members.

A relatively recent yet highly lucrative phenomenon in the Vietnamese-American community is the plethora of Vietnamese-owned or -run nail salons. The Vietnamese seem particularly adept at running the salons, so much so that one Vietnamese-American on the U.S. mainland was able to contract with Walmart to open salons in more than nine hundred of their superstores across the country. At the time of this writing, there were numerous Vietnamese nail salons in Honolulu, with additional shops throughout the state.

Summary and Conclusions

In August 2008, the first Freedom Boat exhibition came to Hawai'i. Now colorfully painted yellow and red, the Freedom Boat is one of the actual boats used by Vietnamese refugees to flee from Vietnam to the Philippines in the 1970s. Those who attended the exhibition were saddened by the past, yet they were inspired by the steadfastness and dignity of those who had come to the United States in much the same way and not only survived, but thrived.

Further Reading

Do, H. D. *The Vietnamese Americans.* Westport, CT: Greenwood Press, 1999.

Freeman, J. M. *Changing Identities: Vietnamese Americans, 1975–1995.* Boston: Allyn and Bacon, 1995.

———. *Hearts of Sorrow: Vietnamese-American Lives.* Stanford, CA: Stanford University Press, 1989.

Edelman, B., ed. *Dear America: Letters Home from Vietnam.* (For the New York Vietnam Veterans Memorial Commission.) New York: Norton, 1985.

Isaacs, A. *Without Honor: Defeat in Vietnam and Cambodia.* Baltimore: Johns Hopkins University Press, 1983.

Vo, L. T. "The Vietnamese American experience: From dispersion to the development of post-refugee communities." In *Asian American Studies: A Reader,* ed. J. Y. S. Wu and M. Song, New Brunswick, NJ: Rutgers University Press, 2000: 290–305.

Notes

1. The approximate numbers of other Southeast Asians in Hawai'i are as follows (the numbers of those who identify with more than one group are indicated in parentheses): Laotian: 1,800 (2,400); Thai: 1,000 (2,000); Cambodian: 200 (300); Hmong: 20 (22). Source: U.S. Census Bureau, Summary File 1 Hawaii (July 25, 2001); compiled by the Hawaii State Department of Business, Economic Development and Tourism, Hawaii State Data Center.

2. D. L. Nguyen and D. F. Kehmeier, "The people of Indochina: The Vietnamese," in *Peoples and Cultures of Hawai'i,* ed. J. F. McDermott, W. S. Tseng, and T. W. Maretzki, Honolulu: University of Hawai'i Press, 1980: 200–217.

3. Ibid.: 202.

4. A. Forbes, "Southeast Asia: Why Vietnam loves and hates China," *Asia Times Online,* April 26, 2007, retrieved July 2, 2009, from http://www.atimes.com/atimes/Southeast_Asia/ID26Ae01.html.

5. Nguyen and Kehmeier 1980: 202.

6. S. Karnow, *Vietnam: A History,* New York: Viking Press, 1983; M. Niedzwiecki and T. C. Duong, "Refugee arrivals to the U.S. from Southeast Asia, fiscal years 1975–2002," in *Southeast Asian American Statistical Profile,* Washington, D.C.: Southeast Asia Resource Action Center, 2004: 10.

7. S. Chan, *Vietnamese Americans 1.5 Generation: Stories of War, Revolution, Flight and New Beginnings,* Philadelphia: Temple University Press, 2006.

8. Nguyen and Kehmeier 1980: 205

9. M. Seeto, "A legacy's changing face: Cultural organizations struggle to chart a course in a new Chinatown," *Honolulu Weekly* (cover story), October 15, 2008.

10. The phenomenon of Chinatowns becoming "Vietnam-towns" or "Little Saigons" has been noted in many U.S. cities, including New York, Boston, Chicago, Oakland, Los Angeles, and others. A similar phenomenon has been noticed in Canada (e.g., in Vancouver and Toronto).

11. In speaking with business and restaurant owners in Chinatown, one receives mixed responses as to whether the Vietnamese in Hawai'i—and in particular, in Chinatown—are ethnic Vietnamese or ethnic Chinese from Vietnam. Some are quick to point out that they are either ethnically Vietnamese or ethnically Chinese, while others seem more indifferent about the distinction.

12. D. Haines, "Kinship in Vietnamese refugee resettlement: A review of the U.S. experience," *Journal of Comparative Family Studies* 19(1) (1988): 1–16.

CHAPTER 14

The Cambodians

Christine Su

Navigate a river by following its bends; negotiate a culture by following
its customs.

—Khmer proverb

During the second or third weekend of the month of April, surrounded by the beauty of the Wai'anae Range, Khmer families and
friends gather early in the morning to pray, chant, and make offerings
to monks dressed in saffron robes.[1] In the afternoon, adorned in beautiful silks or other traditional clothing, they begin to dance, sing, perform
dramas and comedic skits, play traditional games, and eat delicious
Khmer food well into the night. For many, this celebration is much
like those they experienced back in Cambodia, out in the countryside,
sounds of Khmer music filling the air, sharing simple good food and
conversation. The annual festival, Chenam Tmey (Khmer New Year),
celebrates the end of the harvest season and is appreciated by Cambodians in Hawai'i either because they lived the custom or have listened to
countless stories about it recounted by their elders.

These stories, however, tell of times before war and political repression in Cambodia, for which the small Southeast Asian nation has
become infamous. These were times that preceded the brutal Khmer
Rouge, the Communist regime that overtook Cambodia from 1975 to
1979, during which their beloved traditions were banned and their stories had to be hidden deep within their hearts.

The story of Cambodians in Hawai'i is indeed in large part the
story of war and of refugees, uprooted and displaced from their home-

land. However, it is also the story of tremendous resilience, courage, hope, and renewal.

Cambodians in the United States: Fractured Lives

More than 200,000 individuals in the United States identify as Cambodian-Americans, and like refugees from other countries, they have lived fractured lives characterized by persecution, escape, displacement, relocation, and adjustment. It is important to acknowledge, however, that while refugees from other Southeast Asian countries such as Vietnam or Laos share similar status in the United States, the circumstances in their home countries that led them to become refugees are different, and these differences inform their respective cultural identities. More specifically, while Khmer, Lao, and Vietnamese were all displaced due to war and invasions by outsiders, the Cambodians also suffered greatly at the hands of their own leaders and supposed protectors. As a result, much of what they understood to be Khmer was damaged or destabilized.[2]

HISTORICAL BACKGROUND

Throughout the 1970s, Cambodia was embroiled in civil struggles between numerous political factions—particularly between those loyal to King Sihanouk and those loyal to the U.S.–backed military general, Lon Nol. Cambodians were not unfamiliar with war and its consequences. Thus when the Khmer Rouge—which until then was known primarily as a rogue guerilla faction that kept to itself in the Cambodian jungle—entered the capital of Phnom Penh on April 15, 1975, and announced it was taking control of the country, Cambodians lined the streets in celebration. Decades later, a Khmer interviewee here in Hawai'i recalled, "You know, I can still remember how happy I was, waving a flag and smiling. I thought, 'Now we will have peace.'"

The Khmer Rouge, however, brought chaos, not peace. Soon after their arrival, Khmer Rouge soldiers began emptying Phnom Penh, forcing its inhabitants into the countryside.[3] Even those who were already living in rural areas were often relocated to different zones, and urbanites and villagers alike were forced to work on collective farms.[4] Believing that transforming Cambodia into a nation of agricultural workers would maximize production and make Cambodia autonomous and self-sufficient, the Khmer Rouge imposed an extreme form of revolutionary Communism that essentially destroyed Cambodians' lives as they knew them.[5]

The physical and psychological horrors of life under the Khmer Rouge can never be adequately conveyed. Those who resisted the Khmer Rouge and the *angkar* (organization), as it was known, were tortured and executed. A huge number of educated Cambodians who had lived in the cities and practiced a skill or profession, such as medicine, education, music, or fine arts (identified by arbitrary criteria such as wearing eyeglasses) were also executed. The social structure of Cambodian society was uprooted: Wives were separated from husbands and parents from children. Children were instructed not to obey their elders; all loyalty was to *angkar*. Monks were disrobed or killed, temples destroyed, and the practice of Buddhism, which formed the core of Cambodian life, was forbidden. They worked seemingly endless hours building irrigation systems and planting rice, but they rarely saw the fruits of their labors. Many witnessed torture and execution of family members and watched as others died of starvation and disease. Historians estimate that up to 2 million Cambodians died during the Khmer Rouge control of 1975–1979, and thousands more perished during the subsequent instability of life both in refugee camps and in post-Khmer Rouge Cambodia.

When the Khmer Rouge fell from power in 1979, thousands attempted to escape into Thailand.[6] Not welcomed by the Thais, however, most Cambodians lingered in refugee camps for months or years along the Thai-Cambodia border before being processed for relocation to third countries, including France, Canada, Australia, and the United States. The conditions in the camps were substandard, and refugees lived with primitive sanitation, limited food, and insufficient medical care, as well as the fears and anxieties resulting from their earlier trauma. As the Khmer Rouge had kept Cambodians isolated from most of the outside world for four years, not until the early 1980s and the mass exodus of thousands of Cambodians fleeing did its terror become widely known.[7]

Between 1975 and 2002, more than 145,000 Cambodian refugees relocated to the United States, with more than two-thirds arriving between 1980 and 1985, following the passage of the Refugee Act of 1980, which opened different areas of the country to the resettlement of refugees from Cambodia, Vietnam, and Laos.[8]

CAMBODIANS IN HAWAI'I

The narrative of Cambodians in Hawai'i is unique and heretofore has been largely untold.[9] Rather than arriving as explorers or plantation workers, as did many other immigrants to Hawai'i, most Cambodians came, as one respondent put it, "either by accident or by luck, depending upon how you look at it." Indeed, of the mass exodus of refugees, few made it to Hawai'i. Early on, Cambodians settled in Long Beach, California, in Seattle, and in Philadelphia. The U.S. government also sent them to Atlanta, Boston, Chicago, Houston, Jacksonville, and other cities. Some families had American sponsors; some did not. The American people's responses to Southeast Asian refugees in general were mixed, and there was concern over having too many refugees clustered in one place. Thus policy makers attempted to scatter Cambodians throughout a dozen different cities, but none of these included Honolulu.[10] As a result, the number of Cambodians in Hawai'i is still quite small.

There are approximately seventy resident Khmer families in Hawai'i, representing a population of about 375 people. The majority live on O'ahu, with a few families on Maui, Kaua'i, and the Big Island.[11] There are also significant numbers of students from Cambodia enrolled at Hawai'i's universities—specifically the University of Hawai'i at Mānoa, Hawai'i Pacific University, and Brigham Young University–Hawai'i.

Broadly speaking, Cambodians in Hawai'i can be described in terms of three generations. The first generation of Cambodians who came to Hawai'i comprises those born before 1961 and who were at least fourteen when the Khmer Rouge took over. Their memories of the Khmer Rouge are generally adult memories, and for them adjustment has been the most difficult.[12] The second generation refers to those who were born in Cambodia after 1962 and were thus thirteen or younger during the Khmer Rouge years; they are not necessarily the offspring of the first generation, although some are. Their experiences of the Khmer Rouge, life in border camps and processing centers, and resettlement usually differ from those of their parents. As Mortland notes, "Most resettled Cambodians who experienced Pol Pot as children bore fewer scars than did their adolescent siblings and adult parents." This is not to say that their Pol Pot years were less than difficult; many witnessed the execution of family members and friends and were forced to listen to hours of "indoctrination" speeches of *angkar.* Yet they acclimated to American life more quickly than the first generation, particularly because the second generation usually attended at least a few years of school in their new homelands, where they interacted and befriended diverse children of their own age. The third generation comprises those born in 1979 (the year the Khmer Rouge were overthrown) and later,

some in the border camps, some in the United States (or other relocation countries), and thus they have little or no memory of their premi-
gration lives.

The stories of first- and second-generation refugees who came to
Hawaiʻi bear both similarities and differences to those of their counterparts who relocated to the U.S. mainland. They are similar in that they
all involved leaving their birthplace, and thus their understanding of
"Cambodianness" is influenced by life in Cambodia itself. To varying
extents, they look to the prewar past to define themselves. They are different, however, in that both the land and the people who received them
in Hawaiʻi were different.

Ethnocultural Identity

TRADITIONAL CAMBODIAN CULTURE

You know, culture can be born and it can die, and then it can be
reborn again. (Male interviewee, 50s)

To discuss Khmer culture and identity, one must acknowledge that
what Cambodians believe to be true Cambodian culture and identity is,
for the older generation, the life they knew before the Khmer Rouge.
Given the upheaval Cambodian refugees endured in Cambodia and the
feelings of helplessness, guilt, fear, loneliness, and sadness they felt as
they attempted to comprehend their changed lives in a new homeland,
it is not surprising that they look to the past—or at least to life before
war—to define "traditional" Cambodian culture. While it is important
to resist essentialist notions of Khmer culture as something static, it is
as important to acknowledge and respect what Ebihara et al. call survivors' "need to recreate an orderly universe" by returning to events, traditions, and practices that connect them to and mitigate the world around
them.[13] Accordingly, first- and some second-generation Cambodians in
Hawaiʻi describe a system that encompasses hallmarks, norms, rituals,
and rules that tell people they are Khmer, and it is these that they wish
to safeguard and to pass on to their children. These cultural signifiers
(ancestry, cultural knowledge, language, religion, and behavior) are discussed below.[14]

Ancestry: To Be Khmer Is to Be a Descendant of the Creators of Angkor.
A common theme of the responses to the question, "What is a Khmer?"
was reference to Cambodia's early history—and in particular, to the
Angkor period (the massive Angkor Wat monument was built in the

twelfth century).[15] Nearly every Cambodian household in Hawai'i displays at least one picture or painting of Angkor Wat. The walls of the Angkor monuments are covered with bas-reliefs of the stories of powerful kings and deities from Khmer mythology. For Cambodians, Angkor hearkens back to a time of greatness, a time of strong kings who consolidated disparate territories throughout the Mekong Delta region into a vast Khmer kingdom.

Children are taught to respect the magnificence of Angkor, and many Khmer families aspire to take their children to visit the Angkor complex.

Cultural Knowledge: To Be Khmer Is to Know Khmer Arts, Dance, and Music. The bas-reliefs of Angkor are also lined with dancing *apsara*—beautiful celestial nymphs who in Cambodian cosmology danced and sang to mediate between humans and gods—and stone carvings of Cambodian musical instruments and ensembles commemorating the importance of music and dance in Cambodian life. For hundreds of years, melodies and performance methods such as those chronicled at Angkor were passed on from one generation to the next, with master teachers transmitting Cambodian culture to eager pupils through movement and song. Thus, when nearly all of the artists died during the Khmer Rouge years, an integral part of being Cambodian was lost.

Language: To Be Khmer Is to Speak Khmer. All of the respondents interviewed, both male and female, asserted the following: "I know I am Khmer because I speak Khmer." While upon first reading this relationship between one's language and one's identity may seem obvious, note that Americans do not necessarily say, "I know I am American because I speak English" (i.e., native English speakers can be English, Canadian, Australian, etc.).

Piasa-khmae (Khmer language) is a source of great pride for Cambodians. Khmer language reflects Cambodia's diverse history and influences through its numerous Sanskrit and Pali words, for example. The Khmer borrowed and indigenized many French words introduced during the colonial period, as well as Chinese, Vietnamese, and English words, altered to fit Khmer pronunciation and intonation. In short, the Khmer language is a fascinating conglomerate reflective of Cambodia's colorful past.

The structure and syntax of *piasa khmae* inform social interaction. Hierarchy is evident in its terms of reference, for example, and also in the verb choices Khmer speakers make. Selection of pronouns and verbs is based primarily on age but also on familial relationship, gender, status, and wealth. Traditional Khmer do not see their ranked system of speaking as demeaning or confining; on the contrary, it enables one to know what to say and how to say it.[16]

Religion: To Be Khmer Is to Be Buddhist. Several noted scholars of Khmer history and culture have noted that "To be Khmer is to be Buddhist."[17] The significance of Buddhism in traditional Cambodian life cannot be overstated. In prewar Cambodia, the *wat* (temple) served as the center of Cambodian life, as the nucleus of education, religion and spirituality, and local politics. The *wat* was the conduit for disseminating cultural knowledge to the community through Pali chants, the *chbap* (didactic verses), the *gatiloke* (folktales), and epics such as the *Reamker* (the Khmer version of the *Ramayana* story).

When asked when or in what situations they felt "very" Khmer, the respondents mentioned going to and making offerings at the temple during different Buddhist holy days, which punctuate the Khmer calendar. One mentioned in particular is Bon Phchum Ben, a festival honoring the spirits of dead ancestors, usually held in September.

Behavior: To Be Khmer Is to Be Respectful, Polite, Patient, Modest, and Humble. Khmer believe there is something special and exemplary about their attitudes and behavior. One's deportment is extremely important in determining one's "Khmerness." Descriptions of Khmer behavior in both formal texts (e.g., the Cambodian Constitution) and informal conversation contain specific references to correct behavior. In prewar Cambodia, Khmer children were taught the *chbap*—a set of moral codes emphasizing humility, patience, honesty, modesty, and respectfulness—both by their families and in schools. Folktales passed down from generation to generation taught them accountability and responsibility, and even school curriculums included an important moral component. Moreover, according to Cambodian traditional writings, the ideal Cambodian young woman is the pinnacle of virtue: innocent, modest, well behaved (meaning reserved and quiet), obedient, and deferential to men.[18] In traditional Cambodia, young unmarried Cambodian females were not to leave the family home lest they interact inappropriately with males.

NEW ETHNOCULTURAL IDENTITY

Khmer in Hawai'i have evolved a unique, somewhat Hawai'i-specific ethnocultural identity. Perhaps the most salient characteristic of the Khmer in Hawai'i is explained by a final cultural signifier that was not directly stated by any interviewees but is implicit in their stories and their actions: *Flexibility: To be Khmer is to be flexible, to understand the impermanence of things and thus to readily adapt to change.*

While the signifiers described above call to mind an idealized pre-war Cambodia, in reality Cambodians in Hawai'i have—both of necessity and opportunity—developed a broader answer to the question, "What is a Khmer?" As one of the respondents quoted above suggests, what culture "is" changes: as he phrased it, it "dies" and is "reborn." While Cambodians in Hawai'i lament that many of their children speak little or no Khmer, for example, they understand the necessity of English as a conduit for success in American life. As noted above, they feel that to understand Khmer culture, one must understand Khmer language; likewise, in order to understand American culture, one must understand English. While "to be Khmer is to be Buddhist," in Hawai'i Khmer are also Mormon, Baptist, and Catholic as well as Buddhist. One's different religious beliefs do not negate one's identity as Cambodian; rather, the principles of Buddhism coexist with and often reinforce these beliefs. The Cambodian community has constructed a makeshift *wat* on the North Shore of O'ahu, and it is frequented by Khmer of all faiths. In fact, if a Buddhist holiday happens to fall on a Sunday, many Khmer attend church services in town and then travel to the North Shore to participate in the Buddhist ceremonies. In the Hawai'i context, Buddhism is viewed more as a philosophy for living one's life well than a sect to which one does or does not belong, and the *wat* continues to function as conduit to guide the Khmer in doing so.

Khmer definitions of "ideal" behavior have also been modified. Wartime killed a significantly high percentage of Cambodian men, and many households are headed by single (widowed) women. While in reality Cambodian women have always occupied various roles and have exercised considerable independence and authority (e.g., they typically managed family finances), the ideal female in prewar Cambodia was connected to visions and expectations of the ideal Khmer woman. Current circumstances necessitate that women behave more assertively. Family economic needs require them to obtain employment outside the home, and often this requires interacting with both males and females.

This is not to say that the Khmer have left long-standing beliefs and practices behind. On the contrary, Hawai'i has allowed Khmer to rediscover and revive those traditions they feel connect them to Cambodia and to each other. General tolerance for different cultures (particularly Asian cultures) in Hawai'i by the time of their arrival has enabled the Khmer to avoid much of the discrimination faced by their counterparts on the mainland. Perhaps also because they arrived later than other immigrant groups (who were successful in achieving rights and privileges previously unavailable to them), the Khmer have not felt compelled to wholly assimilate into the mainstream. Appreciation for various languages and fine arts has provided opportunities to pass their culture on to the third and younger generations.

For more than a decade, Cambodians in Hawai'i have pooled resources to hold Khmer language classes for youth. Dance, too, has been revived as an important signifier of Khmer culture, to the extent that the community, which did not have anyone who could perform or teach classical dance, raised funds to fly classically trained dancers in from the U.S. mainland to assist youth in preparing for Khmer New Year festivities. The community recently purchased a set of traditional Cambodian musical instruments, with the intent of offering musical instruction to community members. They have also participated in Hawai'i's multicultural festivals.

Summary and Conclusions

In the foyer, guests were welcomed by smiling Khmer ladies, dressed in beautiful silks, offering the sompeah, the traditional Khmer greeting. Bringing their hands together and nodding slightly, the ladies invited both new and familiar faces to cross the threshold, underneath an overhang of huge banana tree leaves, into the bustle of activity beyond. Once inside, the scents of plumeria and pikake flowers merged with those of savory Khmer dishes. The sounds of traditional Khmer music mingled with the hip-hop rhythms of Khmer-American youth. Glancing across the room, one observed elders in conventional Khmer dress exchanging words with young visitors in blue jeans from Waikiki. Indeed, the event was a true representation of the blend of old and new, the tradition and change that infuse Cambodian culture in Hawai'i today. For a few hours, in the cafeteria of Puuhale Elementary School in Kalihi, taxi drivers, teachers, restaurateurs, soldiers in the U.S. military, housekeepers, students and even *achaa* (lay Buddhist assistants) came together and enjoyed happy times in their new homeland, Hawai'i.[19]

Compared to other Cambodian communities on the mainland, such as those in Long Beach, California, or Lowell, Massachusetts, whose populations number in the tens of thousands, and to other ethnic groups in Hawai'i, the Cambodian community of Hawai'i is small. While the community may be small in number, they are not smaller in spirit. Cambodians in Hawai'i are resilient and represent many different professions in the Islands: They are farmers, accountants, professors, craftsmen, and entrepreneurs. They contribute to American culture in many ways. Their children attend American schools, speak English, study American history, play American sports, and strive toward achieving the American dream. Yet while Cambodians have adjusted their practices to fit their lives in the United States and in Hawai'i, they continue to celebrate their identity as Khmer.

Further Reading

Chan, S. *Survivors: Cambodian Refugees in the United States.* Urbana: University of Illinois Press, 2004.

Das, M. *Between Two Cultures: The Case of Cambodian Women in America.* New York: Peter Lang, 2007.

Mortland, C. A. "Khmer." In *Refugees in the United States in the 1990s,* ed. D. W. Haines, Santa Barbara, CA: Greenwood Press, 1996: 232–258.

———. "Legacies of genocide for Cambodians in the United States." In *Cambodia Emerges from the Past: Eight Essays,* ed. Judy Ledgerwood. DeKalb, IL: Southeast Asia Publications, Center for Southeast Asian Studies, Northern Illinois University, 2002.

Smith-Hefner, N. J. *Khmer American: Identity and Moral Education in a Diasporic Community.* Berkeley: University of California Press, 1999.

Notes

1. "Khmer" is the word that the people of Cambodia use to refer to themselves. In the native language, it is pronounced *khmae,* the "r" being silent. "Cambodian" is an anglicization of "Cambodge," the French term for Cambodia, and "Cambodien/Cambodienne" are their terms for the people of Cambodge. In this chapter, I use "Khmer" and "Cambodian" interchangeably.

2. As noted above, "Khmer" refers to the people of Cambodia, and it can be used on its own, as in *Kenyom chea khmae* (I am Cambodian), or adjectivally, as in *praecheachun khmae* (Khmer people). It is also used to refer to country, as in *sruk khmae* (Cambodia). The term "Khmer" is also used adjectivally to express identity: For example, *kaun khmae* translates literally as "Cambodian child" but is used to describe someone (ethnically

Khmer or not) who follows Khmer traditions and conducts oneself in a Khmer way.

3. By 1975, Cambodia's urban population had swollen to nearly 3 million out of a total population of some 7 to 8 million, as refugees fled fighting in rural areas.

4. The Khmer Rouge divided the country into zones that were usually controlled by a high-ranking Khmer Rouge officer.

5. The Khmer Rouge regime (1975–1979) is sometimes referred to by the name of its infamous leader, Pol Pot, as in the "Pol Pot time" or "during Pol Pot."

6. In late 1978, skirmishes between the Khmer Rouge and the neighboring Vietnamese led the Vietnamese army to invade Cambodia. By January 1979, the Vietnamese had seized control of Phnom Penh, and the Khmer Rouge fled to the west, toward Thailand, and soon thereafter the Vietnamese installed a new regime.

7. It is the story of the Khmer Rouge terror that is chronicled in the film *The Killing Fields* (1984).

8. Prior to 1975, there were few Cambodians in the United States. Those who did come were usually exchange students, primarily in California. The 1980 census listed fifty-eight Cambodians in Hawai'i.

9. T. Riddle, "Cambodians in Hawaii and their relation to employment and welfare," Research/Technical Report, Department of Anthropology, University of Hawai'i at Mānoa, May 1988. According to Riddle's study, there were 122 Cambodians in Hawai'i, including 7 non-Cambodian spouses and the children of these mixed marriages.

10. Cambodian refugees were dispersed among Atlanta, Boston, Cincinnati, Columbus, Dallas, Houston, Jacksonville, New York, Phoenix, Richmond, and Rochester (*Refugee Report 1982*, cited in C. A. Mortland, "Khmer," in *Refugees in the United States in the 1990s*, ed. D. W. Haines, Santa Barabara, CA: Greenwood Press, 1996: 244).

11. The 2000 census indicated 330 Cambodians in the state, with 292 on O'ahu, 18 on Hawai'i Island, 15 on Maui, and 5 on Kaua'i. The current figures are those cited by the Cambodian Community of Hawai'i.

12. This generational categorization system, with slight variations regarding age, is borrowed from Mortland's description of Cambodian immigrants in general: C. A. Mortland, "Legacies of genocide for Cambodians in the United States," in *Cambodia Emerges from the Past: Eight Essays*, ed. J. Ledgerwood, DeKalb, IL: Southeast Asia Publications, Center for Southeast Asian Studies, Northern Illinois University, 2002.

13. M. Ebihara, C. A. Mortland, and J. Ledgerwood, *Cambodia Since 1975: Homeland and Exile*, Ithaca, NY: Cornell University Press, 1994: 8.

14. Notably, most Cambodians in Hawai'i left Cambodia decades ago, and their signifiers of Khmer culture now differ not only from those of

their American-born children but also from Cambodians of the same age who did not leave and their children. More than one respondent noted that when he or she has visited Cambodia, it has become increasingly obvious that his or her "Khmerness"—as viewed by others or in self-reflection—is changing.

15. The general list of questions used at various points throughout the interviews is as follows: (1) Were you born in Cambodia? If so, when did you come to the United States? Did you come to Hawai'i first, or did you stop somewhere else? (2) Do you live by yourself or with family? How many people live in your household? Are all of these people Khmer? (3) Do you speak Khmer? Do you speak English? Does everyone in your household speak Khmer? (4) What does it mean to be "Cambodian"/Khmer here in Hawai'i? In other words, how do you know whether or not someone is Khmer? (5) How does the younger generation (those born in America) feel about Cambodian culture? (6) How is the Cambodian culture in Hawai'i different that in Cambodia? Explain. (7) Does religion matter here in Hawai'i? There are Cambodians who are Buddhist, Christian, and Mormon. How do you think this affects Cambodian identity, if at all? (8) Have you been back to Cambodia since you left (if born there)? How many times? How often do you return to Cambodia? (9) What do you miss most about Cambodia? What do you miss least? (10) What is the most important thing you want others to know about Cambodians in Hawaii?

16. The Khmer Rouge overturned the hierarchical language system, insisting people call each other *mit* (comrade) rather than using pronouns that reflect age, gender, and status. This caused much anxiety for Cambodians, as it also overturned their understanding of social order.

17. Ebihara et al. 1994.

18. J. Ledgerwood, "Women in Cambodian society," in *Cambodian Recent History and Contemporary Society: An Introductory Course,* Department of Anthropology and Center for Southeast Asian Studies, Northern Illinois University, 2003, retrieved December 3, 2008, from http://www.seasite.niu.edu/khmer/Ledgerwood/women.htm.

19. "Khmer connections: Building bridges at Khmer New Year 2006," Khmer festival, Cambodian Community of Hawaii, Honolulu, retrieved May 15, 2009, from http://www.hawaii.cambodiaworldwide.com/kny2006.html.

CHAPTER 15

The Micronesians

Neal Palafox, Sheldon Riklon, Sekap Esah,
Davis Rehuher, William Swain, Kristina Stege,
Dale Naholowaa, Allen Hixon, and Kino Ruben

As a part of the Hawaiian culture, a Micronesian Yapese navigator named Mau Piailug, who learned traditional navigational skill from Puluwat, an atoll in Chuuk, taught Pacific traditional navigational skills to Nainoa Thompson. Nainoa and Mau have revived the Hawaiian navigational skill and the cultural pride associated with it.

Micronesia, as drawn by cartographers, describes a geocultural area in the western and central Pacific, just north and south of the equator. Melanesia and Polynesia refer to other geocultural groups of islands in the central and eastern regions the Pacific Ocean, respectively.

The islands of Micronesia number approximately two thousand and stretch for three thousand miles across the western Pacific. The Micronesian region includes five countries and two U.S.–affiliated territories. These are, from west to east, the Republic of Palau, Guam (a U.S. territory), the Commonwealth of the Northern Mariana Islands (CNMI, a U.S. commonwealth), the Federated States of Micronesia (FSM, which includes Yap, Chuuk, Pohnpei, and Kosrae), the Republic of the Marshall Islands (RMI), the Republic of Nauru, and Kiribati. Nauru and Kiribati are former British colonies, now independent and more closely affiliated with New Zealand and Australia. There are fifteen distinct languages throughout Micronesia. These languages share Austronesian origins; however, they are as dissimilar as English and Russian.[1]

U.S. History in the Pacific

Micronesia has been under foreign colonial administration for more than four hundred years. Spain entered Micronesia in the 1500s, followed by Germany around 1860. Japan entered into the western Pacific at the end of World War I and held Micronesia as a mandated territory under the League of Nations until the end of World War II, when the United States took charge.

Following World War II, except for Kiribati and Nauru, the Micronesian islands became the Trust Territory of the Pacific Islands (TTPI) under the United Nations. The United States requested administrative oversight of several parts of Micronesia as a strategic trust, which included the islands of the Northern Marianas, Palau, Yap, Chuuk, Kosrae, Pohnpei, and the Marshall Islands. Under this agreement the United States was responsible for the economic, social, and educational welfare of the trust. In addition, the United States set up military bases and prohibited access to selected areas for security reasons.[2]

The ethnocultural template of the Micronesian peoples was greatly influenced by U.S. policy in the region for the last sixty years. A description of the relevant U.S. policy, the traditional and transitional economy of the region, and patterns of migration is crucial to understanding the ethnocultural identity of the U.S.–associated Micronesian peoples as they now live in their home islands and as they acculturate in Hawai'i. A comprehensive discussion of each of the eight U.S.–associated Micronesian subpopulations is beyond the confines of this chapter. Two of the largest groups—the Marshallese and the Chuukese—have had significant social, economic, health, and political impact on Hawai'i. Thus providing a greater understanding of these groups will be the focus of this chapter.

The Trusteeship and Compact of Free Association

The TTPI was a unique trust, unlike ten other UN trusteeships at the time. The TTPI was under the UN Security Council jurisdiction, where the United States had veto power. Under this governance, the TTPI was designated as a U.S. "strategic trust," with the United States taking administrative authority for military reasons. Before full administrative power was granted by the UN, the United States began testing its thermonuclear weapons in the Marshall Islands. There were sixty-seven nuclear weapon detonations between 1946 and 1958 in the Marshall Islands as part of the Pacific U.S. weapons testing program, which will be discussed later. Other than the intermittent influx of personnel for the nuclear testing, the TTPI remained isolated from the outside world.

In 1960 the UN issued a report that criticized the United States for neglecting the TTPI under the UN mandate and for doing little to prepare Micronesia for self-government. Following continuing criticism in the mid-1960s, the U.S. administration increased U.S. financial assistance tenfold to the region. Numerous federal and social education programs were begun and a massive contingent of Peace Corp volunteers was sent to Micronesia.

In 1965 the Congress of Micronesia (COM) was established. The COM appointed a political commission to conduct negotiations with the U.S. government beginning in 1969. The United States envisioned the strategic trust as a single federation and that the COM would negotiate as a unified political body for the federation. Early on, however, the Northern Marianas requested separate negotiations for commonwealth status. The other Micronesian entities, also rethinking their positions in the COM, began splintering and desired to negotiate separate agreements with the United States.[3]

In 1977, after a contentious break in negotiations, strategic talks were restarted. Each entity in the COM was offered one of three political states: independence, free association with the United States (independence with certain rights or powers granted to the United States), or incorporation into the United States as a territory or commonwealth. None of the political entities opted for independence. In 1986, the Northern Marianas became a commonwealth. Palau, the Federated States of Micronesia (Chuuk, Yap, Pohnpei, Kosrae), and the Marshall Islands negotiated to become Freely Associated States (FAS). The net result was that "U.S. Micronesia" was now made up of a territory (Guam), a commonwealth (Northern Marianas), and the three FAS mentioned above. The various U.S. political associations have their own rights, degrees of independence, economic relationship, and governance relationship with respect to the United States.[4]

As FAS, the three newly established Pacific Island nations conduct their own domestic and international affairs. The United States provides economic assistance in return for defense/military rights to the FAS, including the ability to have "strategic denial"—denial of access to FAS from military interests of other nations.[5]

The relationship of the FAS to the United States is described in a Compact of Free Association (COFA), and the Freely Associated States are thereby called Compact Nations, and the resulting effects of the Compact agreements are now termed the "Compact impact." It is indeed the Compact impact, the diaspora of Micronesians from the FAS, and the lives that they live that make this chapter about Chuukese and Marshallese important to the peoples of the United States and specifically Hawai'i.

The main goals of the COFA were to improve health and education and promote self-sufficiency. The U.S. Government Accountability Office (GAO) reports in 2003 and 2006 evaluated the Compact goals for FSM and RMI. The first fifteen years of the Compact in the FSM and Marshall Islands with regard to health and education have been abysmal. Furthermore, the original Compact goal of self-sustainability is not likely to be achievable according to the GAO reports.[6]

> The economic environment of the FSM and RMI have not improved significantly in recent years, and both countries show limited potential for development objectives of budgetary self-reliance and long term self-advancement....
>
> In response to remittances (emigrants and wage earners going abroad sending monies home to support families) as a means for migrants supporting their respective COFA nation: "RMI emigrants current lack of marketable skills due to inadequate education and vocational training is an obstacle to increased remittances."
>
> The FSM and RMI face notable challenges to achieving budgetary self-sufficiency and long-term self-reliance, and long-term economic advancement, given their current health and education hardship, dependence on grant assistance and need to effect reforms that are often politically, culturally, and technically difficult to implement.[7]

The impact of the U.S. policy for the sixty-five-year period between 1945 and 2010 has had profound effects on the U.S.–associated Micronesian cultures. The strategic trusteeship set the stage for (1) nuclear testing, (2) rapid economic changes, and (3) the COFA treaty. These events have significantly affected the ethnocultural identity of the Micronesian. How a massive influx of U.S. dollars and how the U.S. nuclear weapons testing program acutely changed the Micronesian way of life are discussed in the following sections.

Economy and Micronesian Culture

The Micronesian cultures as described by Francis Hezel are much deeper than the language, dances, songs, and local customs. Micronesian cultures share a common foundation from which they evolved. A common denominator of all Micronesian culture was the relationship and dependence on ancestral lands. The ancestral land was the basis of many of the Micronesian economies.[8]

The social organization, structure of family relationships, economy, shared food, and common work were related to the land. The Micronesian family was defined as the integral relationship of the household, the nuclear family, an extended family, and a lineage. Each component of the Micronesian family was equally important. Individual behavior in the family and family behavior in the community was guided by cooperative functioning to fish, farm, raise children, pass knowledge to the next generation, and to continue the traditions that allowed survival of the family lineage.

When the land-based economy changed, the relationship to the land changed, the social organization changed, and relationship and responsibilities to the family and lineage likewise changed. For the FSM and Marshall Islands, one of the defining changes to the Micronesian economy occurred because of a policy shift in the United States toward Micronesia in the 1960s (described above). While money changed hands in Micronesia before the 1960s, there was never enough wealth available that would allow an individual to act independently of the land and family.[9]

The U.S. policy in the 1960s, in response to UN criticism of neglect of the TTPI, was to aggressively develop the FSM and Marshall Islands with U.S. health and education systems, develop central government structures that would lead to employment of many central government workers, and to provide significant loans to stimulate the business sectors.

The Micronesians developed businesses, and many joined the government workforce that was heavily subsidized by the United States. These individuals then had sufficient cash to buy commodities and food. As the cash economy grew, it drove urbanization and the development of centralized government operations. Some individuals now possessed enough money to be emancipated from lineage and the land. The social organization of Micronesia was evolving through this new economy. The core culture was changing, because of Western economic development. Maintenance of the cultural norms built around family and land tenure became more difficult.[10]

This economic process determined how the Micronesian culture, the individuals, and the family were likely shaped through U.S. policy. The cultural transition has taken place in the last fifty years. Unfortunately, many of the institutions that are necessary to being successful in a moneyed economy, such as education, health, and social welfare infrastructure, were not developed simultaneously, as noted in the U.S. GAO reports on the Compacts of Free Association cited above. The economic and cultural transitions in the FSM and Marshall Islands have therefore been painful and difficult. Micronesian culture, in the face of a dynamic world economy, is challenged to develop the institutions, capacity, and necessary tools to be successful.

From a Western perspective, the evolution of the core culture has had some positive effects, including the development of a democracy and free enterprise in Micronesia. There have also been negative effects, such as dependency, loss of identity, lack of purpose, loss of community and social controls, loss of unity, and loss of lineage identification. In some of the Micronesian communities, the rapid cultural changes are thought to be reflected in the increased rates of alcohol and drug abuse, domestic violence, and adolescent suicide.[11]

Thermonuclear Weapons Testing in the Marshall Islands

The U.S. Pacific thermonuclear weapons testing program in the Marshall Islands has had a profound effect on the people and culture of the RMI. In 1946, the U.S. military began testing its nuclear weapons in the Marshall Islands. Between 1946 and 1958, sixty-seven thermonuclear devices were detonated that had an aggregate explosive power of 7,200 Hiroshima atomic bombs. This magnitude of testing was equivalent to testing one and a half Hiroshima bombs a day for the twelve-year testing period. To this day, Marshallese still suffer from the effects of nuclear testing on their homeland, which occurred more than sixty years ago.[12]

Ionizing radiation from any source, including the nuclear testing, is associated with more than twenty-one different types of cancer. A 2004 National Cancer Institute (NCI) report predicted a 9 percent above background increase in cancers in Marshallese people who lived in the RMI between 1948 and 1956. Increases in cancer rates would be highest in those areas near the test sites, although they would also occur throughout the Marshall Islands. Because of a latency period between radiation dose and the manifestation of cancer, half of the cancers (an estimated 250 cancers) will manifest themselves after 2004.[13]

From a psychosocial perspective, the impact of the U.S. nuclear weapons testing resulted in forced changes in diet, lifestyle, and culture on particular atolls of the Marshallese population. Detonation of atomic weapons was carried out on the island homes and ancestral lands where Marshallese people lived for hundreds of years. The local inhabitants were moved off their lands for the testing. Islands were vaporized and lands contaminated, thereby making return to their home atolls unsafe even now, more than sixty years after completion of the testing. The Marshall Islanders were relocated to other sites in the RMI that were not their ancestral lands. USDA canned food was provided, as the dislocated populations had no agricultural lands from which to farm. Traditional foods were replaced by processed food; active fishermen and farmers began to have sedentary lifestyles. The processed foods and lifestyle changes create greater risk for noncommunicable illnesses such as heart disease, cancer, and diabetes.[14]

Community organization and social structure, based on land and land rights, was lost. Destroying or displacing Marshallese from their ancestral lands accelerated the breakdown of the affected communities. There remains anger and distrust toward some U.S. agencies and programs because of the nuclear weapons testing. Many Marshallese still feel that the United States was experimenting on them and feel that the United States continues to handle their needs and concerns about the effects of nuclear testing in a very cavalier way.[15]

Many of the Micronesian who were exposed to nuclear radiation remain dubious about information that U.S. governmental agencies provide for them about the environmental safety of their lands. Many of the issues surrounding the weapons testing were shrouded in secrecy with classified documents, making a sense of transparency in U.S. policy difficult to achieve.[16]

Migration to the United States

One of the provisions of the COFA is that people from the Freely Associated States can enter, live, and work in the United States without a visa or green card. The peoples of the COFA nations who come to the United States and its territories or commonwealths are migrants, not immigrants or refugees, which are terms for peoples who settle in the United States from foreign countries not freely associated with the United States. Since the COFA implementation in 1986, migration from the FSM and the RMI to Guam, the CNMI, and later the United States has increased dramatically.[17] Between 1997 and 2003, RMI and FSM populations in Hawai'i increased by a little over 25 percent and 36 percent respectively. Most of the FSM growth was from the people of Chuuk.[18]

Whereas legal immigrants from other countries must by law show proof of the ability to support themselves or have work in the United States and must have appropriate health clearances, they are largely from highly educated and higher economic strata in their country of origin. Migrants from the COFA nations can freely migrate and therefore do not need to have health clearances or show an ability to support themselves. The sociodemographic composition of the COFA migrants is from all social and educational sectors. Many are not prepared for the transition. Moreover, over the last decade the economic situations in the FSM and the RMI have regressed, necessitating the need to find work elsewhere.[19] Other reasons for migration include seeking better education for children, health and medical purposes, and the need to experience progress one might not otherwise have at home.[20] Some cite the failure of the trusteeship and Compact agreements to develop the needed health and education infrastructures in these countries as an antecedent to this mass migration.[21]

Ethnocultural Identity

The last seventy-five years of colonization, westernization, and globalization in Chuuk and the Marshall Islands has had a dynamic effect on their traditional family and social structure. Many Chuukese and Marshallese who have lived through a changing family and social structure in their home islands have recently moved to Hawai'i and the U.S. continent. They are again faced with further adjustments to new family and social structures and are evolving a new ethnocultural identity.

TRADITIONAL FAMILY STRUCTURE AND TEMPERAMENT

The Marshallese and Chuukese temperament, emotional expression, and stereotypes may be best understood through an explanation of the foundations of their traditional family and social structure. Understanding the traditional Micronesian family institutions can lend some understanding into the Marshallese and Chuukese ethnocultural identity and just where their ability to acculturate into U.S. mainstream culture may be challenging.

The functional family unit of the traditional Marshallese and Chuukese society was an extended family, or the clan. Within the limited geography of the small atolls and islands of the Pacific, the clan had to be self-reliant to survive. The day-to-day functions were performed in a communal fashion. Maintaining harmony among the people within the clan was essential.

Chuuk and Marshall Islanders were raised to be an integral part of the clan and to know their place within that societal structure. Maintaining relationships and harmony was the primary concern of the clan, which meant that individualism and competitive behavior were not desired characteristics.[22]

There were clan systems of conflict resolution at every level of clan function. Larger conflicts were settled with ceremony, formal exchange of gifts, and an exhibition of remorse on the part of the offending individual(s) and entire family. Smaller conflicts were assigned to members of the extended family for intervention, individual counseling, and resolution.

There was no single word to differentiate biological father or mother from first-degree uncles and aunts in either the Chuukese or Marshallese family units where child care took place. All the first-degree aunts and uncles were expected to be responsible for the children of their brothers and sisters. In both the Marshallese and Chuukese custom, the father and mother were defined as the male and female figures responsible for the daily welfare of a child, but also all of their brothers and sisters (uncles and aunts) shared responsibility. When a marriage took place, the Micronesian parents incurred significant obligations to both sides of the family.[23]

Adoption was common. Within this structure, children could go to live in the household of the father's or mother's siblings (uncles and aunts) at the request of an older sibling. There was no formal adoption process. A request by an older sibling for a child to live in their immediate household was often expected and rarely disputed.[24]

Clan members followed a path that was largely prescribed. Individuals from a clan were chosen or were destined to hold a position of authority or to work with specialized knowledge, such as canoe building, navigation, or traditional medicine, by virtue of their lineage. Knowledge did not belong to everyone; it belonged to the lineage and to those within the lineage who were thought to be responsible.[25]

All Chuukese and Marshallese have land rights as part of a clan. In the Marshall Islands tradition, several clans were headed by an *iroij* (chief, landowner), the *alap* (clan head) managed the clan, and the *rijerbal* (worker) worked the land. The *iroij, alap,* and *rijerbal* cared for each other and had mutual respect. Resources, in general, were divided to maintain a robust community function. The *iroij* and *alap* were the decision makers and managers that resolved large disputes and handled work distribution. The Chuukese had a similar social system, except that there was no high chief.[26]

Age imparted authority within the Micronesian community. The Pacific Islander youths from these islands were taught to respect and hold their elders in high regard. Silence was the outward expression of respect for the elders in their presence. Conflict resolution within a family was accomplished through a hierarchy of elders. Older siblings were expected to take care of younger siblings and discipline them if necessary. Disciplinary decisions over serious matters belonged to the eldest paternal or maternal brother. Corporal punishment was part of the system. Grandparents were assigned the role to counsel and to guide children and had the responsibility to pass on the family tradition, as illustrated in the saying, *"Bitok pein bubu im jimma"* (Lay your head on the pillow of your grandmother's and grandfather's arm)—in other words, tradition is transmitted through close ties and communications with grandparents.[27]

Both male and female genders carried their privilege. The Chuukese and Marshallese land and chief systems were matrilineal: Land was passed from mother to eldest daughter. Chiefly titles aligned with the land rights of one's mother. Although the women transmitted land rights, men were assigned to be the spokespersons for the women. The men of the family conveyed the wishes of the eldest sister. Men were also the warriors and disciplinarians in the family.

The primary language in Chuuk and the Marshall Islands households is their native tongue. In the households of the first-generation Chuukese and Marshallese migrants in Hawai'i, the primary language remains their native tongue.

The New Ethnocultural Identity

TRANSITIONING OF FAMILY AND ETHNOCULTURAL IDENTITY

With the U.S. influence in Chuuk and the Marshall Islands, the family structure and political systems have changed. However, the role of Marshallese and Chuukese tradition remains a powerful influence in their daily lives. When democratic governments were put in place in Chuuk and the Marshall Islands by the United States, each of those countries insured that their tradition was guarded. There is a traditional court that exists as part of the court system in the RMI. Traditional issues, especially land claims, are settled in the traditional courts. In the FSM constitution, which governs Chuuk, if a traditional law conflicts with a Western law, the traditional law prevails.[28]

The centralized form of the U.S. bureaucratic government has had varying levels of success in Chuuk and the RMI. The Marshall Islands had many clans that were united through bloodlines and lineage through a high chief called the *iroij laplap*. In comparison, the clans of Chuuk were never united under a single chief by war or lineage, and thus individual clans maintained power over their own lands. This difference may account for several observations by members of the Marshallese and Chuukese communities.

Compared to the other states in the Federated States of Micronesia, Chuuk has been noted to have a less cohesive central government. Chuukese community members suggest that the existing clan system does not easily fit into a united central authority system of governance. It has been suggested that allegiance of elected officials is so strongly tied to the clan and lineage that consensus between members from different clans is difficult to achieve. It is difficult to arrive at group consensus with contentious issues in Chuukese communities involving many clans or where land issues are involved.

In contrast, the first elected president of the Marshall Islands, Amata Kabua, was also the highest traditional chief—*iroij laplap*. Hence consensus and direction of the RMI government at the time were quick and efficient. Iroij Kabua has passed away. The current high chiefs still have a powerful say in government and local decision making, if they choose to exercise that right. This blending of traditional and Western governance has at times aided Marshallese groups to arrive at consensus more quickly.

Chuukese men were typically very protective of their clan, lineage identity, and property. Frequent altercations among young males from different clans are not unusual. Carrying knives and machetes by adolescent males and young men is now commonplace in Chuuk. In the Chuukese traditional culture, a man is expected to be the ultimate defender and protector of the family. To back down from a fight for any reason is not seen as manly in the traditional Chuukese culture.[29]

People and Cultures of Hawai'i

Key informants observe that Marshallese males, though they also fight fiercely if needed, are typically more jovial and will frequently be seen joking with each other.[30] In general, there is less clan and lineage rivalry in the Marshall Islands compared to Chuuk. The Marshallese male temperament is less aggressive, and knives are not typically carried.[31]

As individual citizens, the Chuukese and Marshallese are kind and giving, and will provide help whenever requested. They care deeply for their clans and friends and will assist them, sometimes to their detriment. Providing time and money to a friend even if it infringes on one's personal financial well-being is the norm.[32]

Societal and cultural changes and the stress on individuals have resulted in high rates of male suicide, alcohol use, and domestic abuse. Adolescent and young male suicide is epidemic in Chuuk and the Marshall Islands. The common method is hanging. The immediate events surrounding the hanging are perceived by the larger local community to be minor, such as an argument with parents or an argument with a girlfriend. Alcohol is associated in only 50 percent of the cases. Several theories have been put forward as to the cause of this, including the male's loss of his role in a changing society, coupled with dissolution of the extended family structures that dealt with conflict resolution. The method of hanging is deliberate and viewed by some as a brave, manly act; therefore, the epidemic is difficult to extinguish.[33]

Domestic violence and youth violence are also more pervasive in both of these areas, also attributed to the changing extended family structure that comes with urbanization and westernization.

In responding to these societal ills, church pastors and deacons are influential in the community networks both in Chuuk and the Marshall Islands. Christianity was first introduced by missionaries in the 1700s, remains a strong influence on the Marshallese and Chuukese way of life, and continues to be a powerful institution in their homes abroad.

COFA MIGRANTS IN HAWAI'I

As Micronesians migrated from their home countries, they brought with them aspects of their clan structure, family values, and cultural attributes. A 2003 census estimated that since 1986, about 20,000 COFA migrants—11 percent of the total population of these nations—had left their island homes to live in Hawai'i, Guam, the CNMI, and the United States continent.[34] Most of the COFA migrants are Marshallese or Chuukese. The reasons they leave Chuuk and the

Marshall Islands are similar: for health care, employment, education, and better opportunities. The 2003 estimate of COFA migrants who presently reside in Hawai'i (a little over 7,200) was noted by census takers to likely be an undercount, and it was projected to actually be somewhere between 12,000 to 14,000 people. About 80 percent of the COFA migrants in Hawai'i are Chuukese or Marshallese.

The 2004 report entitled "U.S. Uninsured Project: Impacts of the Compact of Free Association on Hawai'i's Health Care System" describes the large amounts of nonreimbursable health care consumed by the migrants. These costs were disproportionately borne by U.S. hospitals and the state health systems. The U.S. federal government provides very limited support.

Although the COFA migrants comprise only about 1 percent of Hawai'i's population, there are significant proportions of COFA migrants in homeless shelters and in low-income housing compared with other peoples residing in Hawai'i.[35] In fact, 50 percent of the residents in O'ahu's homeless shelters and 80 percent of the families in large low-income housing locations of O'ahu are Chuukese or Marshallese.

Compounding these socioeconomic challenges, COFA nations' youth are noted to have a significant and increasing involvement with methamphetamine use.[36] The Honolulu Police Department and members of the adult Chuukese community observe that Chuukese youths in public housing frequently fight with Samoan youths. The fights are violent, often with involvement of knives. Serious injury frequently ensues. The Chuukese elders understand the Chuukese youth have a very strong clan identity, and that Chuukese manhood does not allow for backing down when challenged. The Chuukese community members in Hawai'i note that knives and machetes are frequently carried by young males in Chuuk, and that habit has been brought to Hawai'i. A stereotype that has now been assigned to the Chuukese by some in the Honolulu Police Department is that they are troublemakers and violent.[37] The Chuukese view is that they are brave and will defend each other and the clan at any cost and that they only fight when challenged.

Marshallese youths less commonly get involved in fights with the Samoans or with the Chuukese. They remain in their own space. It is of note that on several occasions, Samoan youths have been aggressors and clashed with Marshallese youths, mistaking them for Chuukese.

In 2008, one of the authors was instrumental in facilitating a traditional apology and peacemaking ceremony between the Chuukese community and family of a Samoan young man who was killed by a Chuukese. The traditional apology reportedly eased the anger and tension between the Chuukese community and Samoan community for a period of time. In a similar case in Chuuk, a traditional apology for the wrongful death of another clan's family member resulted in the release of the assailant from the Chuuk prison. The traditional apology is ceremonial and is presented by one clan to another. The process is not insignificant and may require days to complete. In 2008, all members of the assailant's family—including children, men, and women—crawled several hundred yards on their abdomens to demonstrate remorse to the family of the individual who had been killed. The demonstration of remorse resulted in multiple bruises and abrasions to the members of the family as they crawled. In addition, gifts to the offended family were offered. The gifts included land and rights to taro patches. As a result of this ceremonial apology, the murderer was released from a seven-year term in prison.[38] Currently, the Chuukese elders in Hawai'i are being asked to address the issue of ongoing youth violence.

A recent event speaks to the clash of cultural norms. A counselor at one of O'ahu's public schools investigated the well-being of a freshman Marshallese high school student who was not attending classes. The counselor provided a site visit to the listed address and found seventeen people—mostly extended family members, including the student's biological parents—living in a low-income two-bedroom home. The family reported that the student had moved to another location with other family members who had adopted him. The other location turned out to be a public housing location with equally crowded conditions. At both locations there were several young teens not attending school, and the student in question did not want to attend school because of a recent fight. The counselor noted that it appeared there was little concern in either household that several young teens and the student in question were not attending school. The student in question was traditionally adopted by an aunt, and the boy moved fluidly between the two households. It was difficult for the counselor to determine who was responsible for the student's actions and well-being. The counselor was concerned about crowding, students not attending school, and the fact that a student was not with his biological parents. The families did not share the urgency or priority of the counselor's concerns.

Stereotypes and perceptions of Micronesians among Hawai'i's majority populations as reported by members of the Chuukese and Marshallese community include the following: "Micronesians are dirty and like to live in crowded conditions"; "Micronesians all have *ukus* (head lice) and do not keep their children clean as the children also have *ukus*"; "Micronesian adults and children don't speak up, meaning that they don't care about learning"; and "Micronesians don't belong in Hawai'i, as they are an extreme burden to the society."[39]

Additional stereotypes garnered from members of Hawai'i's community include these: "Micronesians are poor and many live in the homeless shelters"; "Micronesians don't want to be part of the workforce and just wish to live off welfare"; and "Micronesians should be ashamed to be in the [public] housing." Health providers frequently comment how Micronesians "don't care about their personal and family health"; "they are noncompliant with medications and don't follow up when they should"; "Micronesians are always late to their appointments or don't come at all"; "they don't plan and take their time even in urgent matters."

THE CHUUKESE AND MARSHALLESE RESPOND TO STEREOTYPES

The Chuukese and Marshallese tradition is that nuclear families often slept together in a single room. The expanse of the outdoors is where they lived, where the daily activities took place, and where they celebrated. The dwellings were built with distinct functions—a building for sleeping, a building for meetings, and a building for cooking. The dwellings were simple, clean, well kept, and organized. Large houses were not ideal in that they tend to isolate family members from one another.[40]

They state that "We live in the homeless shelters because our families cannot afford Hawai'i's high housing cost." Most of the Marshallese and Chuukese adults in the homeless shelters have jobs, albeit menial service jobs, whereas "many of the other people(s) in the homeless shelters have no jobs." The transition from the homeless shelter to low-income housing is welcomed and is often the goal of Chuukese and Marshallese families. Members of the Chuukese and Marshallese community recognize that "the low-income housing units are nice" and provide housing that is "better than where I came from. The [public] housing is now my home." The public housing is similar to the close-knit communities in which they lived in their home country; many Chuukese and Marshallese families lived together in close proximity.

It is not unusual for Chuukese and Marshallese to have head lice. Head lice are thought to be a minor problem and really do not affect one's health or mean that one is dirty. The Chuukese and Marshallese community members wonder why Hawai'i people worry about such insignificant things. Manual removal of head lice by members of the family or friends, in fact, fosters socialization processes and bonding. Marshallese and Chuukese are traditionally raised to be compulsive about maintaining their hygiene.

The Chuukese and Marshallese are aware that their children frequently struggle academically in Hawai'i's schools. They note, "You [the people of Hawai'i] are so lucky that your schools have books, there are enough classroom buildings, and that your teachers are certified." There are not enough places for all the elementary school-age children in Chuuk and the Marshall Islands, and most of the teachers are not appropriately credentialed and certified.[41]

The quiet Micronesian demeanor in the classroom, the physician's office, and elsewhere is a sign of respect by first-generation Chuukese and Marshallese. Micronesians show deference to classroom teachers, physicians, and others they perceive to be authority figures. Rarely will individuals in a large group volunteer and provide an opinion, as it may not be their place to do so. Remaining silent and not maintaining a running conversation is the norm. There is no necessity to make conversation to be cordial. Long durations of silence among friends are acceptable and sometimes preferred.

They may respond, "The doctors and nurses are always rushed and they don't care about Micronesians. We feel like a burden to them."[42] The key community informants stated that explanations by the medical staff are often abrupt and rarely understandable. They explained that the priority of an individual's personal health and for the children's education follows secure housing, a secure job, and a safe environment. The key informants note that there is great difficulty navigating the health, education, and social services systems in Hawai'i. Arriving to appointments in a timely manner depends on securing transportation and deciding if the appointment takes priority over the other priorities of the day.

Summary and Conclusion

The diaspora of Micronesians, including the Chuukese and Marshallese from their homes in Micronesia to Hawai'i, was made possible through the Compact of Free Association. The quid pro quo was that the United States had strategic denial over U.S. Micronesia—that is, the ability to determine military matters in the Pacific, which included maintaining military bases in the region.

The COFA and trusteeship were intended to prepare the Micronesians for self-sufficiency and to develop their health and educational systems. As the U.S. GAO reports note, these goals were not met, and it is not likely that self-sufficiency will be achieved. The ability to freely migrate and work in the United States was a fail-safe provision. The COFA was fraught with unintended consequences, including insufficient federal support for the migration and a lack of forethought about the ramifications of the COFA migration.

Our key informants explain that many Micronesians gave of themselves and their lands for the defense of the United States. In their words, "We have many of our sons and daughters [in the U.S. military] who fight and die for the people of the U.S." "The people of the United States told us they would take care of our health and education in our home islands. They did not. When we come here seeking that care, we do not receive any kindness."[43]

As the Chuukese and Marshallese arrive in Hawai'i, U.S. territories, and the continental United States, their traditional ethnocultural identity arrives with them. It is apparent that not only was the federal government not prepared to support the migration, but the host states were not prepared to receive them. Similarly, the migrants were ill equipped for some of the challenges of their relocation.

The migrants have become major consumers of Hawai'i's health, education, and social services. With limited resources in the United States, the Micronesian community has become polarized and is targeted as a burden and different from mainstream Hawai'i.

The Micronesians from the COFA nations have faced many challenges from the confluence of U.S. geopolitics, economic transition from the sustainable land- and sea-based village life, to the introduction of Western institutions and, for many, migration. Clan and lineage ties have been stressed and in many cases broken. Culture is never static, and this is particularly true for current-day Micronesians. Micronesian youth are making their own choices about where to settle and beginning to write the next chapter for the acculturation of Pacific Islanders. Overcoming their colonial history and despite a challenging cultural transition, Micronesians are an enduring part of the fabric of Hawai'i and other regions of the United States.

Further Reading

Anderson, I., S. Crengle, M. L. Kamaka, T. C. Chen, N. Palafox, and L. Jackson-Pulver. "Indigenous health in Australia, New Zealand, and the Pacific 2006." *Lancet* 367: 1775–1785.

Hezel, F. X. *The Cultural Revolution of the 1960s in Micronesia.* 2008. Retrieved April 3, 2009, from http://www.micsem.org/pubs/articles/ famchange/cultrevolution.htm.

————. *Is That the Best You Can Do? A Tale of Two Micronesian Economies.* 2006. Retrieved April 3, 2009, from http://micsem.org/pubs/articles/ economic/taleoftwo.htm.

Palafox, N. A. "Health consequences of the Pacific U.S. nuclear weapons testing program in the Marshall Islands: Inequity in protection, health care access, policy, regulation." *Reviews of Environmental Health* 25(1) (2010): 81–85.

Palafox, N. A., L. Buenconsejo-Lum, S. Riklon, and B. Waitzfelder. "Improving health outcomes in diverse populations: Competency in cross-cultural research with indigenous Pacific Islander populations." *Ethnicity & Health* 7(4) (2002): 279–285.

Palafox, N. A., S. Riklon, A. Wilfred, and A. H. Hixon. "Health consequences and health systems response to the U.S. Pacific thermonuclear weapons testing program." *Pacific Health Dialogue* 14(1) (2007): 170–178.

Pobutsky, A. M., L. Buenconsejo-Lum, C. Chow, N. Palafox, and G. G. Maskarinec. "Micronesian migrants in U.S.: Health issues and culturally appropriate, community-based solutions." *Californian Journal of Health Promotion* 3(4) (2005): 59–72.

Riklon, S., W. Alik, A. H. Hixon, and N. A. Palafox. "The 'Compact impact' in Hawai'i: Focus on health care." *Hawai'i Medical Journal* 69(6) (2010): 7–12.

State of Hawai'i Department of the Attorney General. *Final Report of the Compacts of Free Association Task Force.* Honolulu: Department of the Attorney General, 2008.

U.S. Government Accountability Office. *Compacts of Free Association: Developmental Prospects Remain Limited for Micronesia and Marshall Islands.* Publication No. GAO-06-590, June 2006. Retrieved April 3, 2009, from Government Accountability Office Online: http://www.gao/gov/ new.items/d06590.pdf.

U.S. Uninsured Project. *Policy Brief: Impacts of the Compact of Free Association on U.S.'s Health Care System.* Honolulu: U.S. Institute for Public Affairs, 2004.

Williams, P. W., and A. Hampton. "Barriers to health services perceived by Marshallese immigrants." *Journal of Immigrant Health* 7(4) (2005): 317–326.

Notes

1. L. Albert, T. Poloi, D. Rubenstein, and G. Dever, "The Micronesians," in *Cross-Cultural Caring: A Handbook for Health Care Professionals in Hawai'i,*

ed. N. Palafox and A. Warren, Honolulu: Transcultural Health Care Forum, John A. Burns School of Medicine, University of Hawai'i, 1980: 138–158.

2. L. Poyer, S. Falgout, and L. M. Carucci, *The Typhoon of War: Micronesian Experiences of the Pacific War*, Honolulu: University of Hawai'i Press, 2001; E. Friberg, K. Schaefer, and L. Holen, "U.S. economic assistance to two Micronesian nations: Aid, impact, dependency, and migration," *Asia Pacific Review* 47(1) (2006): 123–133.

3. Albert et al. 1980.

4. W. Bodde Jr., "COMPACT negotiations," paper presented at Pacific Global Health Conference, Hawai'i Convention Center, Honolulu, June 15, 2005.

5. Poyer et al. 2001.

6. U.S. General Accounting Office, *Compact of Free Association: An Assessment of the Amended Compacts and Related Agreements*, Publication No. GAO-03-1007T, July 2003, retrieved April 3, 2009, from Government Accountability Office Online: http://www.gao/gov/new.items/d0389ot .pdf; US. Government Accountability Office, *Compacts of Free Association: Developmental Prospects Remain Limited for Micronesia and Marshall Islands*, Publication No. GAO-06-590, June 2006, retrieved April 3, 2009, from Government Accountability Office Online: http://www.gao/gov/new .items/d06590.pdf.

7. U.S. Government Accountability Office 2006.

8. Friberg et al. 2006.

9. Bodde 2005.

10. Albert et al. 1980; F. X. Hezel, *Is That the Best You Can Do? A Tale of Two Micronesian Economies*, 2006, retrieved April 3, 2009, from http:// micsem.org/pubs/articles/economic/taleoftwo.htm.

11. G. Peterson, "Lessons learned: The Micronesian quest for independence in the context of American imperial history," *Micronesian Journal of the Humanities and Social Sciences* 3(1–2) (2004): 45–63; H. Booth, "The evolution of epidemic suicide on Guam: Context and contagion," *Suicide and Life Threatening Behavior* 40(1) (2010): 1–13. http://www.micsem.org/pubs/ articles/historical/chuukcar.htm.

12. I. Anderson, S. Crengle, M. L. Kamaka, T. C. Chen, N. Palafox, and L. Jackson-Pulver, "Indigenous health in Australia, New Zealand, and the Pacific," *Lancet* 367 (2006): 1775–1785; B. R. Johnston, *Half-Lives and Half-Truths: Confronting the Radioactive Legacies of the Cold War*, Santa Fe: School for Advanced Research Press, 2007; J. Neidenthal, "A history of the people of Bikini following nuclear weapons testing in the Marshall Islands: With recollections and views of elders of Bikini Atoll," *Health Physics* 73(1) (1997): 28–36; National Cancer Institute (NCI), Division of Cancer Epidemiology and Genetics, "Estimation of the baseline number of cancers among Marshallese and the number of cancers attributable to exposure to fallout from

nuclear weapons testing conducted in the Marshall Islands," prepared for the Senate Committee on Energy and Natural Resources, September 2004.

13. National Cancer Institute 2004.

14. Government of the Republic of the Marshall Islands (RMI), "Pursuant to Article IX of the Nuclear Claims Settlement approved by Congress in Public Law 99-239: Petition presented to the Congress of the USA regarding changed circumstance," September 11, 2000; N. A. Palafox, "Health consequences of the Pacific U.S. nuclear weapons testing program in the Marshall Islands: Inequity in protection, health care access, policy, regulation," *Reviews of Environmental Health* 25(1) (2010): 81–85.

15. Anderson et al. 2006; Government of the Republic of the Marshall Islands 2000; Palafox 2010.

16. Anderson et al. 2006; Johnston 2007; Neidenthal 1997; Government of the Republic of the Marshall Islands 2000; Palafox 2010.

17. U.S. General Accounting Office 2003.

18. J. S. Omori, C. K. Kleinschmidt, E. K. Lee, C. J. Linshield, T. Kuribayashi, and D. F. Le, "Reasons for homelessness among Micronesians at a traditional shelter in Hawai'i," *Pacific Health Dialogue* 14(1) (2007): 218–223.

19. H. Heine, "Culturally responsive schools for Micronesian immigrant students," *Pacific Resources for Education and Learning* briefing paper, PB0204: 1–15, 2002, retrieved March 31, 2009, from http://www.prel.org/teams/culturally-responsive.asp.

20. Omori et al. 2007; U.S. Uninsured Project, *Policy Brief: Impacts of the Compact of Free Association on U.S.'s Health Care System,* Honolulu: U.S. Institute for Public Affairs, 2004.

21. Palafox 2010; U.S. Government Accountability Office 2006.

22. Albert et al. 1980; F. X. Hezel, *The Cultural Revolution of the 1960s in Micronesia,* 2008, retrieved April 3, 2009, from http://www.micsem.org/pubs/articles/famchange/cultrevolution.htm.

23. Hezel 2008.

24. Albert et al. 1980.

25. F. X. Hezel, *The New Shape of Old Island Cultures: A Half Century of Social Change in Micronesia,* Honolulu: University of Hawai'i Press, 2001; N. A. Palafox, L. Buenconsejo-Lum, S. Riklon, and B. Waitzfelder, "Improving health outcomes in diverse populations: Competency in cross-cultural research with indigenous Pacific Islander populations," *Ethnicity & Health* 7(4) (2002): 279–285.

26. Hezel 2001.

27. Personal communication from interviews and meeting with the Micronesians United Community Organization, March 16, 2009.

28. Hezel 2001.

29. Ibid.; personal communication 2009.

30. Key informants were members of Micronesians United, a community-based organization of Micronesian peoples who reside in Hawaiʻi. Seventeen members participated in a series of three meetings that were led by one of the chapter authors. The areas discussed included acculturation, assimilation, and cultural transition. Informants were from the following Micronesian ethnic groups: Chuukese, Marshallese, Pohnpeians, and Yapese.

31. Personal communication 2009.

32. Ibid.

33. Albert et al. 1980; Hezel 2008; Booth 2010.

34. U.S. Uninsured Project 2004; State of Hawaiʻi Department of the Attorney General, *Final Report of the Compacts of Free Association Task Force*, Honolulu: Department of the Attorney General, 2008.

35. Omori et al. 2007; U.S. Uninsured Project 2004.

36. Personal communication 2009.

37. Ibid.

38. Ibid.

39. Hezel 2001.

40. Ibid.

41. Ibid.

42. Personal communication 2009.

43. Ibid.

Conclusion

John F. McDermott and Naleen Naupaka Andrade

Do the chapters in this book tell a convincing story? It is the story of how new groups arrived successively in Hawai'i, each with a different history, and engaged with each other, leading to cultural and psychological changes. This process we have called the Hawaiian Stew Pot, in which the more enduring characteristics of each group are visibly retained, while others blend together indistinguishably into the stock or soup of the stew.

If so, then just how did it evolve?

Consider a historical overview. Over nearly two millennia, the first Polynesians and their Hawaiian descendants established a society that would tolerate, integrate, and celebrate the cultures of the immigrant groups who came to their homeland. Their ethnocultural template and its enduring qualities of aloha, *lōkahi, 'ohana, mālama, le'ale'a,* and being *pono* shaped and combined both indigenous and immigrant values, beliefs, and behaviors. As you read the chapters, you saw how some degree of assimilation occurred in the second generation for most of these immigrant groups. Thereafter, the process changed into one of interactive accommodation—that is, change—but with the individual groups retaining key elements of their own identities. By the turn of the twentieth century, Hawai'i's indigenous host culture was no longer the majority group. Asians had grown to outnumber all other ethnic groups. Yet at the same time, their ability to maintain distinct ethnic identities as Chinese, Japanese, Korean, and Filipino meant that they did not coalesce into a unified Asian majority group. Similarly, while Portuguese outnumbered Euro-American haoles, the dynamics of culture and class between these two groups prevented them from coalescing into a white majority.

At the same time, another crucial interethnic group dynamic was operating—early intermarriage. The mixed-race or hapa children of these intermarriages, many of Hawaiian *ali'i* lineage, were seen as equals, and in some cases superior, to their pure-blooded white and Asian peers.

In any case, without the presence of a clear majority group, assimilation did not occur along the lines of the contemporary U.S. melting pot. In Hawai'i, the immigrant groups could, with each passing generation, choose which aspects of their culture to retain, discard, let lie dormant, or activate. And they continue to choose—consciously and unconsciously—which aspects of other cultures they will make their own.

Similarities and Differences

Within such an evolving process, what were the similarities and differences among the ethnic groups as they successively arrived in the Islands? Overall, the most observable common values among the immigrant groups settling in Hawai'i alongside the indigenous Hawaiians were family orientation coupled with job opportunity for themselves and educational opportunity for their children. Within the framework of family first, there was a range of intensity. Strongest in family orientation, perhaps, were the Filipino, then the Portuguese, the Hispanic, Southeast Asian, and Asian. Tight hierarchies within these families were to be expected within this common value system, but they have shifted over the generations. For example, rigid gender roles and strict birth order have softened. Yet the orientation to family first remains strong in these groups even now.

Today, Hawai'i's most recent immigrants, those coming from Micronesia, organize in clans with a matrilineal tradition across the generations. Will that change, too? It probably will.

THE DIFFERENCES

So much for similarities; what about the contrasts among the groups described in this book, especially those that reach beyond the family? The most striking contrast in group values appears to be whether the group's orientation is primarily individualistic and independent or collectivistic and interdependent. In reading the chapters yourself, you have probably observed that groups with a strong family orientation also tend to value larger intragroup cooperation, or a collective approach to life, over one that is more individualistic or competitive. In these cultures, being a part of family and group achievement is more important than individual achievement. Understandably, there was a natural tension between these values as cultures interacted within the society. For example, after the haoles arrived in Hawai'i, their own individualistic values regarding property rights triumphed over traditional collective views of the indigenous population. Indeed, coupled with a shift in power, it eventually led to the overthrow of the Hawaiian government.

In the view of most of our chapter authors, the development of their immigrant group's ethnocultural identity placed more emphasis on collective achievement of the group than on that of the individual. Some, like the Japanese-Americans, are described as having developed a capacity for alternating between the goals of the group and those of the individual. Others, like the Chinese-Americans, were situation oriented; that is, they could use the two different styles as needed to adapt to whatever the situation required.

At the most collective end of this individual-to-collective spectrum, traditional home country collective values are so important to some groups that they are preserved with a special name for them in the native language. Fa'a Samoa, or the Samoan Way, represents the preservation of traditional Samoan culture in which a community composed of several *aiga* or extended families functions as a strict social structure with its own governing system. *Fa'a Samoa* is a term that maintains a protective boundary around that traditional culture, even in Hawai'i. For children growing up in this culture, the village *becomes* their family. Such a merging of individual, family, and community together can be functional or dysfunctional depending on the circumstances.

The Okinawans comprise another group living in Hawai'i that has maintained a separate traditional collective identity, at the same time integrating into the larger society. Their classical or traditional identity is called Uchinanchu, a concept containing group values of hard work and mutual dependence, embodied in a family-like fellowship developed through sharing and working together as brothers and sisters. It has served not only to preserve and protect homeland values but to separate themselves from the Japanese community in Hawai'i itself. Yet it has not kept Okinawans from succeeding individually in the larger society as entrepreneurs.

In contrast to the collectivistic orientation of most groups, the more individualistic haole or white culture erects no stigma to individual achievement beyond family or community. In fact, it is encouraged. And of special interest, perhaps, among black Americans who have chosen to settle in Hawai'i, such individual accomplishment and entrepreneurship have been a hallmark of success, such as the well-known Famous Amos. Perhaps this is a result of the unusual circumstances of black immigration history, traditionally arriving as individuals rather than in waves, and because there appears to exist no true African-American community for newcomers to join beyond the walls of the military.

Of course, cultural values are never as simple as the somewhat artificial contrast we have made between the collective and the individual. There are usually mixtures. For example, in the Hispanic-Latino culture, traditional values are specifically preserved by name and represent *both* individual and collective ways of behaving. Some of these emphasize the importance of family *(familismo)*. Others represent gender role expectations *(machismo, marianismo)*. Still others proscribe forms of interpersonal social relationships *(personalismo)*. And some even specify attitudes toward oneself and others *(dignidad, simpitica, confianza)*.

So much for the simmering ingredients of the Stew Pot; what has happened in the development of the stock or soup?

A New Ethnocultural Identity

The history of Hawai'i demonstrates how categorical racial differences have slowly changed into a dimensional society of overlapping cultures. As current population trends such as intermarriage favor an increasingly mixed or hapa population, another culturally shared pattern has emerged in place of a majority group. Euphemistically called "local," it is made up of immigrants and their descendants along with indigenous Hawaiians. It is not a well-delineated ethnocultural group; instead it is more like an ethnocultural *process* of learning to effectively navigate the boundaries of race, ethnicity, and culture—within one's self and between others with whom one establishes and maintains relationships.

Becoming local is an acculturative process that is mastered by children of most ethnic groups early on, usually by middle school. They learn how not to be *too* haole, *too* Hawaiian, *too* Japanese, and so on— the stuff of ethnic stereotyping. That is, they come to recognize the distinguishing factors of what makes them members of their ethnic group.

Then, by intuition and design, they determine which parts of their primary ethnic identity they need to set aside or let go of when establishing new friendships. They work to understand the culture and ways of their peers. Race, color, physique, and socioeconomics become secondary. They learn how to blend individual independence with group interdependence. Finally, youngsters begin to learn, practice, and gain proficiency in a common language as part of the sociocultural lifestyle that forms not only childhood but social networks for a lifetime. The result of this acculturative process is a growing number of individuals who celebrate diversity and their own primary ethnic identification *without* ethnocentric exclusivity.

Being local distinguishes a person as someone who has acculturated to Hawai'i's Island way of life and living, a place where aloha defines generosity, civility, and grace, and the *'āina* and *kai* (land and sea) are inseparable from the soul. In other words, it constitutes a genuine cultural evolution, shaped by the environment and intertwined with individual development, carrying forward a new combination of values and beliefs into personality traits that make up the future behavioral context of Hawai'i. Whether indigenous or immigrant, their ethnocultural identification is Hawaiian. Becoming more Hawaiian does not imply that they are indigenous—*kānaka maoli* will always occupy history as Hawai'i's first nations people. Instead, it is a description of an evolution toward a more encompassing ethnocultural identity, one shaped by the Islands and its people.

A caution: The term "Hawaiian" attempts a balance that moves beyond the rigidity of racial and ethnocentric discriminators. It reflects our notion, expressed in the introduction to this book, that identity is a concept influenced by where one lives, as well as by one's ancestry. In other words, we believe that culture can shape the genome. If our model of the Hawaiian Stew Pot effectively explains this development of a new ethnocultural identification, we can predict that within the next few decades the use of the term "Hawaiian" will refer not only to the indigenous Hawaiian group identified by blood or common ancestry but also to those people who have acculturated and chosen to live in Hawai'i.

Beyond the Stew Pot

A limitation of the multicultural Stew Pot model is that it may simply be seen by some as a step toward assimilation—that is, the melting pot of Euro-American culture that has dominated the continental United States for generations. If so, it may not fully explain the evolving process of ethnocultural identification that is still unfolding among indigenous and immigrant ethnic groups in twenty-first-century Hawai'i. A more appropriate metaphor today might be the *lauhala* model—the weaving together of individual, group, and family values into a useful form, like the weaving of the leaves of the pandanus tree. *Lauhala* is the material traditionally used by Hawaiians and Pacific Islanders to create essential items such as sleeping mats, baskets, hats, and bracelets.[1] The *hala* tree, from which *lauhala* comes, is one of the oldest trees on earth and was already growing in Hawai'i before the first Polynesians arrived. Individual leaves are selected for their strength, flexibility, and color—from white to tan to dark red. The weaver selects the leaves, here representing the different ethnic groups, with their differences and similarities woven together for strength, durability, flexibility, and beauty, always toward creating something new.

What will be woven into Hawai'i's evolving ethnocultural identity? We predict that the enduring factors of indigenous Hawaiian culture will continue to serve as the template around which existing and new immigrant groups will evolve. It is the weavers themselves—the leaders at the family, community, and societal levels—who determine the weaving of the behaviors and values to effectively respond to an ever-changing sociocultural environment.

As insightfully pointed out by the authors of chapter 2 in this book, the success of newcomers to Hawai'i has relied on the ability to examine their own ethnocultural identity against a canvas of contrasting cultures, each with its overt and covert ways and subtle nuances. That may present as a novel concept to Americans who have been a part of the country's traditional majority group in the past. But today America is rapidly changing its color, and the ability to examine one's own ethnocultural identity against the backdrop of others, as illustrated by the children described above, may become more and more important for all of us. As we proposed in the introduction, diversity has a corollary: It is connectedness. And that connectedness requires mutual understanding. We hope this book has contributed to that understanding.

Notes

1. C. Lo, "The life of the hala," *Hana Hou, Magazine of Hawaiian Airlines* 13(3) (June–July 2010): 66–74, http://www.hanahou.com.

Glossary

Language and Terminology Usage

Hawaiian and subsequent immigrant group native languages—i.e., words, terms, and cultural concepts other than proper nouns—are italicized throughout, followed by their definition, to call readers' attention to the indigenous or immigrant usages and meanings that are common in Hawaiʻi but are not necessarily familiar to audiences beyond these Islands.

Hawaiian word spellings and definitions that are included in the text are taken from Pukui and Elbert's *Hawaiian Dictionary*, versions 1971 and 1986.[1]

Words and Terms

Accommodation. A process by which people change their behavior to be more similar to that of the people with whom they are interacting; the process by which existing mental structures and behaviors are modified to adapt to new experiences.

Acculturation. The exchange of cultural features that results when groups of individuals having different cultures come into continuous contact. This transfer of customs is a two-way process; that is, each group of immigrants contributes some cultural traits to its new society.

Anomie. A sociological term meaning "personal feeling of a lack of norms; normlessness." It is a process that describes the breakdown of social norms and values.

Assimilation. A sociopolitical response to demographic multiethnicity that promotes the absorption of ethnic minorities into the dominant culture. Assimilation usually involves a gradual change and takes place in varying degrees; full assimilation occurs when new members of a society become indistinguishable from older members.

Bicultural. Biculturalism involves two originally distinct cultures in some form of coexistence.

Biopsychosocial. A model that posits how biological, psychological, and social factors all play a significant role in human functioning, usually in the context of health or illness. The biological component seeks to understand how the cause of the illness stems from the functioning of the individual's body. The psychological component looks for potential psychological causes, such as lack of self-control, emotional turmoil, and negative thinking. The social component investigates how different factors such as socioeconomic status, culture, poverty, technology, and religion can influence health.

Caucasian (or White). A term that usually refers to human beings characterized, at least in part, by the light pigmentation of their skin. A common definition of a white person is a person of primarily, or wholly, European ancestry.

Colonialism. The building and maintaining of colonies in one territory by people based in another. It consists of a process whereby sovereignty over the colony is claimed by the colonialists who impose a new government and often a new social structure and economy. It can also take the form of subjugation of a minority culture by a majority culture, both of whom exist in the same location. Colonialism involves unequal relationships between colonists and the indigenous population. Neocolonialism refers to a kind of unofficial colonization in which a country's government is overthrown by a larger country and replaced by a government that coincides with the larger country's interest.

Culture. The set of shared attitudes, values, goals, and behaviors that characterizes a group. Culture incorporates the patterns of human activity within a society and the symbolic structures that give such activity significance. Customs, laws, popular styles, social standards, and traditions are all examples of cultural elements. Cultural identity is the sense of self that is influenced by belonging to a particular cultural group.

Ethnic Group/Ethnicity/Ethnic Identification. An ethnic group is a group of people whose members identify with each other through a common cultural heritage. This shared heritage goes beyond race or physical characteristics and may be based upon ancestry, history, kinship, religion, language, shared territory, or nationality. Members of an ethnic group are conscious of their ethnicity; moreover, ethnic identity is further marked by the recognition from others of a group's distinctiveness.

Globalization. Globalization refers to a process by which regional economies, societies, and cultures have become integrated through a global network of communication, transportation, and trade. The term is sometimes used to refer specifically to economic globalization, though it is usually recognized as being driven by a combination of economic, technological, sociocultural, political, and biological factors. The term can also refer to the transnational circulation of ideas, languages, or popular culture through acculturation.

Haole. Early Hawaiians used this term to refer to any foreigner. It is now defined by *Merriam-Webster's Collegiate Dictionary* (2003) as "one who is not descended from the aboriginal Polynesian inhabitants of Hawaii; especially WHITE." In this book it is used to describe Euro-Americans, particularly in chapters 1 and 2 (see chapter 2 for a complete discussion of the term). For Hawai'i residents of European descent, the terms "Euro-American" or "Anglo-American" are rarely used, nor is the term "white" (although this is the preferred term used in federal reports published by the U.S. government). Rather, the term "haole" is most often used in conversation to mean "white," while the term "Caucasian" is more frequently used in written expression.

Hapa Haole. Merriam-Webster's Collegiate Dictionary (2003) offers this definition: "of part-white ancestry or origin; especially: of white and Hawaiian ancestry." It is sometimes used today to describe a person who is part-Caucasian and part-Asian or Pacific Islander.

Memes. A meme is a unit of cultural ideas, symbols, or practices that can be transmitted from one mind to another through writing, speech, gestures, rituals, or other imitable phenomena. Supporters of the concept regard memes as cultural analogues to genes, in that they self-replicate and follow evolutionary principles in explaining the spread of ideas and cultural phenomena.

Multiculturalism. The acceptance or promotion of multiple ethnic cultures applied to the demographic makeup of a specific place. As a descriptive term, multiculturalism has been taken to refer to cultural diversity. It implies a positive endorsement, even celebration, of communal diversity, typically based on either the right of different groups to respect and recognition or to the alleged benefits to the larger society of moral and cultural diversity.

Race. Race refers to the categorization of humans into populations or ancestral groups on the basis of heritable characteristics. The physical features commonly seen as indicating race are visual traits such as skin color, cranial or facial features, and hair texture. Conceptions of race and racial classifications are often controversial for scientific as well as social and political reasons. Many scientists have pointed out that traditional definitions of race are imprecise and arbitrary, and have many exceptions and many gradations, and that the numbers of races delineated vary according to the culture making the racial distinctions. The controversy ultimately revolves around whether or not the socially constructed and perpetuated beliefs regarding race are biologically warranted. Thus, those rejecting the notion of race typically do so on the grounds that such categorizations are contradicted by the results of genetic research.

Sociocultural. An umbrella term for combined theories of cultural and social evolution that aims to describe how cultures and societies have developed over time. Sociocultural theories typically provide models for understanding the relationship between technologies, social structure, the beliefs, values, and goals of a society, and how and why they change with time.

Westernization. A process whereby societies come under or adopt the Western culture in such matters as industry, technology, law, politics, economics, lifestyle, diet, language, religion, philosophy, and values. Westernization can be related to the process of acculturation—changes that occur within a society when two different groups come into direct continuous contact. It is usually a two-way process, in which Western influences and interests themselves are joined by a wish, at least by parts of the affected society, to move toward a more Westernized society in the hope of attaining Western life or some aspects of it. However, it can be a forced as well as a voluntary process, and it can also refer to the effects of Western expansion and colonialism on native societies.

Notes

1. M. K. Pukui and S. H. Elbert, *Hawaiian Dictionary*, Honolulu: University of Hawai'i Press, 1971; M. K. Pukui and S. H. Elbert, *Hawaiian Dictionary: Revised and Enlarged Edition*, Honolulu: University of Hawai'i Press, 1986.

Contributors

Naleen Naupaka Andrade, M.D., is a professor and chair of the University of Hawai'i Department of Psychiatry. Her research includes epidemiological studies of Hawaiian adolescents that determine the prevalence of psychiatric disorders and the role of culture in mental and behavioral health disorders.

Ricardo Bayola, M.D., was born and raised in the Philippines, earning his B.S. and M.D. degrees there. He was trained in psychiatry at the Medical College of Wisconsin and child adolescent psychiatry at Georgetown University. Currently he is an assistant professor in the Department of Psychiatry at the University of Hawai'i.

Cathy Kaheau'ilani Bell, M.D., holds degrees from Yale University and the University of Hawai'i Medical School's Triple Board Residency Program (pediatrics, psychiatry, child and adolescent psychiatry). Her research and training interests have included alternative medicine and Hawaiian healing practices. She has been involved at several levels in Hawaiian children's mental health with the Keiki O Ka 'Āina Family Learning Centers.

John Bond, Ph.D., was born in Shanghai, came to Hawai'i as an eight-year-old, and earned his Ph.D. in psychology from USC. During his twenty-four years as a clinical psychologist, he taught at the University of Hawai'i in the Psychology and Psychiatry Departments. Serving for several years as mental health consultant to American Samoa, he was the first acting director of Mental Health for Samoa in Pago Pago.

Kathryn L. Braun, Dr.P.H., is a professor of public health and social work and chair of the Doctor of Public Health program at the University of Hawai'i. She also serves as research director for 'Imi Hale—Native

Hawaiian Cancer Network. Her first job in Hawai'i was as an editorial assistant on *People and Cultures of Hawai'i: A Psychocultural Profile*, published in 1980.

Anongnart "Mickie" Carriker is the honorary general consul assistant for the Royal Thai Embassy in Hawai'i. She came to Hawai'i in 2003 and has been active in establishing cross-cultural experiences for Thais living in Hawai'i. Ms. Carriker is the founder of the Thai Culture Center in Hawai'i and organizer in the Hawai'i Thai Festival.

Jane Chung-Do was born in Seoul, Korea, and moved to Hawai'i when she was six years old. She is currently a doctoral candidate in public health sciences at the University of Hawai'i. She is a co-principal investigator for the Asian/Pacific Islander Youth Violence Prevention Center and implements and evaluates youth development programs. Her other research interests include cultural influences of wellness, immigrant and minority health, rural disparities, community-based participatory research, and youth empowerment programs.

Sekpa Esah is currently a pastor at the Nu'uanu Baptist Church in Hawai'i. He was born and raised in Chuuk and had his counseling and theological training at Azusa Pacific University and the Micronesian Institute of Biblical Studies (precursor to Pacific Islands Bible College). He is one of the key leaders of Micronesians United, a Micronesian community group in Hawai'i.

Michael Fukuda, M.S.W., is an academic social worker and associate chair of administration in the University of Hawai'i's Department of Psychiatry. His interests include cross-cultural issues, which led to trips to Southeast Asia and being adopted by a village in the northeast of Thailand. He uses these experiences, along with the help of the Royal Thai Embassy in Hawai'i, in his writing for this book.

Deborah A. Goebert, Dr.P.H, M.S., is an associate professor and the associate director of research in the Department of Psychiatry, University of Hawai'i. Her research interests include mental health disparities, particularly among ethnic groups in Hawai'i; violence and substance abuse prevention and early intervention; women's health; culture; and family.

Anthony P. S. Guerrero, M.D., was born in Manila but was raised since the age of two in Honolulu, Hawai'i. He is closely connected to his extended family in the Philippines and is married to a first-generation Filipino-American. He is a professor of psychiatry, clinical associate professor of pediatrics, and director of the Division of Child and Adolescent Psychiatry at the University of Hawai'i. His research interests include medical education, Filipino, Asian, and Pacific Islander mental health, and the interface between primary care and psychiatry.

Emily Hawkins, Ph.D., is a retired Hawaiian language professor at the University of Hawai'i at Mānoa. She has lived in Hawai'i for forty-five years, of which forty-two have been in an interracial family. She is currently a diversity trainer for the Episcopal Diocese of Hawai'i and chairs its Diversity Commission.

John Hawkins is a retired human resources administrator within the Hawai'i State Department of Education. He has lived in Hawai'i for forty-five years. Prior to his administrative experiences, his instructional background was in science education. He is currently serving as a member of the Standing Committee for the Episcopal Diocese of Hawai'i.

Ryokichi Higashionna, Ph.D., is a retired civil engineer, currently doing volunteer work. His previous experience includes teaching college-level civil engineering courses, heading a department in the Hawai'i State government, and performing civil engineering consulting.

Earl S. Hishinuma, Ph.D., is a professor and associate chair of research for the Department of Psychiatry, University of Hawai'i at Mānoa. He earned his Ph.D. from the Department of Psychology, University of Hawai'i at Mānoa. He is a third-generation Japanese (Sansei) in Hawai'i.

Allen Hixon, M.D., is a physician and associate professor and vice-chair of the Department of Family Medicine and Community Health, University of Hawai'i. His interests are in global health and public policy as they relate to underserved communities.

John Huh, M.D., is an assistant professor of psychiatry and the medical director of the Queen's Counseling Service at the Queen's Medical Center in Honolulu, Hawai'i. He has an interest in cultural competency education and Korean cultural mental health issues.

Gilbert Tsuneo Ikehara, MSCP, is an addiction counselor and adjunct clinical faculty in the University of Hawai'i Department of Psychiatry. Third-generation Okinawan-American, he is a grandson of the late Hyakubun and Maka Ikehara and Goze Ginoza.

Satoru Izutsu, Ph.D., is senior associate dean and professor emeritus of public health and psychiatry, University of Hawai'i. He is a Hawai'i-licensed psychologist and a Nisei born on the island of Kaua'i, Hawai'i. His academic and professional training were at the University of Hawai'i, Columbia University, and Case Western Reserve University.

Mark Kang, M.D., is a board-certified physician in psychiatry and family medicine. He was the only member of his family born in Hawai'i, while the rest immigrated from South Korea in the 1970s. His interests have focused on the boundaries surrounding medicine and psychiatry and the differences between generations of Koreans and other Asian groups.

Kwong-Yen Lum, M.D., was born in China, educated in Hawai'i, with A.B. and M.D. degrees from Colgate and Columbia Universities. He completed his psychiatry training at the Menninger Clinic. Dr. Lum is a clinical professor of psychiatry at the University of Hawai'i. He has had a long interest in ethnic studies, especially the Chinese in Hawai'i.

Courtenay R. Matsu, M.D., is an assistant professor and general psychiatry residency program director for the Department of Psychiatry, University of Hawai'i at Mānoa. She considers herself a mixture of generations of Japanese in Hawai'i as she is a Yonsei (fourth generation) by her maternal roots; however, her father emigrated from Osaka, Japan, making her a Nisei (second generation) by his roots.

Leslie Ann Matsukawa, M.D., is a clinical assistant professor of psychiatry, University of Hawai'i, and a psychiatrist in private practice whose paternal grandparents immigrated to Hawai'i from Okinawa. She has fond memories of the big family parties at her grandparent's typical traditional green plantation house in 'Ewa, O'ahu, and participation in the writing of the Okinawa chapter has helped her rediscover her roots.

John F. McDermott, M.D., is a professor emeritus of psychiatry University of Hawai'i and a fellow of Clare Hall, Cambridge University, UK. His publications include cross-cultural research on family functioning and adolescent development. National and international distinctions include a recent major award for a lifetime of work on culture and diversity.

Dale Naholowaa was born and raised in Majuro, Marshall Islands. Her father was a senior U.S. administrator in the Marshall Islands for the Trust Territory of the Pacific Islands. Currently she works at Queen's Medical Center as a medical translator for Marshallese patients.

Stephanie Nishimura, Ph.D., is an assistant professor in the Department of Psychiatry, University of Hawai'i. She has published on adolescent substance use and youth violence prevention and is focusing her attention on risk and protective factors associated with ethnically diverse adolescents. Being able to work on the Portuguese in Hawai'i chapter has been an absolute pleasure for her to gain a better understanding of her ancestral roots.

Celia Ona, M.D., is a distinguished fellow of the American Psychiatric Association. She completed her psychiatry residency at the University of Rochester School of Medicine, where she received the Teaching Award for Outstanding Performance in Undergraduate Medical Education. She has served as president of the Hawaiʻi Psychiatric Medical Association and the Philippine Medical Association of Hawaiʻi. Currently she is an assistant professor and director of the Refractory Mood Disorder Program. Dr. Ona's special interests include culture, ethics, spirituality, women's issues, health, and wellness.

Neal Palafox, M.D., is a family physician and professor and chair of the Department of Family Medicine and Community Health, University of Hawaiʻi. He lived and worked in the Marshall Islands for ten years. He currently is the principal investigator of three U.S. federally funded programs designed to develop cancer prevention, risk reduction, and screening in the U.S.–associated Pacific.

Davis Rehuher was born and raised in the Republic of Palau and has a B.A. in communication from the University of Hawaiʻi at Mānoa. He is currently an assistant program manager at the Asian/Pacific Islander Youth Violence Prevention Center. His specific area of interest is the Micronesian experience in Hawaiʻi.

Sheldon Riklon, M.D., was born and raised in the Marshall Islands. He was the lead physician located there caring for Marshall Islanders affected by the U.S. nuclear weapons testing program in the Pacific from 2000 through 2008. Presently he is working with the Department of Family Medicine and Community Health, University of Hawaiʻi.

Kino Ruben, M.O., was born and raised in the outer islands of Chuuk. He is currently a physician working at Chuuk Hospital and is the government-appointed official to the Cancer Council of the Pacific Islands for Chuuk State, FSM. He is adept in Chuukese culture and health systems.

Lisa Sánchez-Johnsen, Ph.D., was born and raised in Hawaiʻi and is currently an assistant professor and clinical psychologist in the Departments of Psychiatry and Medicine at the University of Chicago, as well as an adjunct faculty member at the University of Hawaiʻi. She has received awards and grants for her research, clinical, and teaching endeavors on Hispanics/Latinos. She is active in conducting community-based health research with Latino communities in Hawaiʻi and Illinois and has held numerous regional and national positions in Latino and ethnic minority organizations.

Faapisa M. Soli was born in American Samoa, though both her parents are from the Independent State of Samoa. She was educated in

Samoa and Hawaiʻi and is an assistant program manager for the Asian/ Pacific Islander Youth Violence Prevention Center. She is particularly interested in research regarding health concerns among Pacific Islanders, especially Samoans.

Kristina Stege was born and raised in Majuro, Marshall Islands. She completed her B.A. at Princeton University, then worked with the Marshall Islands Embassy in Washington, D.C., as an assistant to the Marshall Islands ambassador to the United States for three years. Kristina has recently completed studies in international affairs in France.

Christine Su, Ph.D., is a researcher and independent scholar living in Honolulu. The biracial daughter of a Cambodian father and a Scottish mother, her interest in ethnocultural identities is both personal and professional. She has traveled and worked throughout Southeast Asia and is an active advocate for Southeast Asians in the United States, particularly Cambodian-Americans. She received her Ph.D. from the University of Hawaiʻi in American studies with a focus on U.S.–Asia relations and currently serves as the director of research and education at an integrated communications firm.

William Swain was born and raised in the outer islands of the Marshall Islands. He worked for the RMI government for nearly twelve years. He opened up the RMI embassy in Japan, was a former RMI assistant permanent representative to the United Nations, was a former undersecretary for Asia and Far East Affairs (Majuro), and was a special assistant to the president. Currently he is translator and court interpreter and partnership assistant for the U.S. Census Bureau.

Junji Takeshita, M.D., was born in Japan and raised on the U.S. East Coast. He received his M.D. from Temple University and was trained in psychiatry at Yale University. He has lived in Hawaiʻi for the past sixteen years and is an associate professor and associate chair of clinical services for the Department of Psychiatry, University of Hawaiʻi.

Paul Tran, MSW, received his degree from San Francisco State University, where he worked with Southeast Asian youth and teenaged runaways. He is currently instructor in social work at Hawaiʻi Pacific University.

Victor Yee, Ph.D., is a clinical psychologist who has been with the faculty of the Department of Psychiatry from 1996. He is continuing to work in the area of the nexus of criminal justice and mental health in Hawaiʻi. His interest in the Chinese developed during recent research on somatization and depression among Asian groups and because of a historical interest in ancient cultures.

Index

Production Notes for McDermott / *People and Cultures of Hawai'i*
Cover design by Julie Matsuo-Chun
Interior design and composition by Wanda China with display type in
Myriad Pro and text in Scala Pro
Printing and binding by Sheridan Books, Inc.
Printed on 60# House Opaque, 500 ppi